T0202817

Communications
in Computer and Information Science

1695

More information about this series at https://link.springer.com/bookseries/7899

Arif Ahmed Sk · Turki Turki ·
Tarun Kumar Ghosh · Subhankar Joardar ·
Subhabrata Barman (Eds.)

Artificial Intelligence

First International Symposium, ISAI 2022
Haldia, India, February 17–22, 2022
Revised Selected Papers

Springer

Editors
Arif Ahmed Sk 🔟
XIM University
Bhubaneswar, India

Turki Turki
King Abdulaziz University
Jeddah, Saudi Arabia

Tarun Kumar Ghosh
Haldia Institute of Technology
Haldia, India

Subhankar Joardar
Haldia Institute of Technology
Haldia, India

Subhabrata Barman
Haldia Institute of Technology
Haldia, India

ISSN 1865-0929   ISSN 1865-0937 (electronic)
Communications in Computer and Information Science
ISBN 978-3-031-22484-3   ISBN 978-3-031-22485-0 (eBook)
https://doi.org/10.1007/978-3-031-22485-0

This Springer imprint is published by the registered company Springer Nature Switzerland AG
The registered company address is: Gewerbestrasse 11, 6330 Cham, Switzerland

Preface

On behalf of the Organizing Committee, we are pleased to present the proceedings of the International Symposium on Artificial Intelligence (ISAI 2022) held in Haldia, India, during February 17–22, 2022. This annual symposium is organized each year by the Haldia Institute of Technology in association with the Computer Society of India (CSI). We must thank this year's General Chairs, Devadatta Sinha and Xiao-Zhi Gao for the generous contribution of their time to ISAI 2022. The proceedings of ISAI 2022 were academically very rich and, in addition to paper presentations, we had six eminent professors as keynote speakers, namely, Petia Radeva, University of Barcelona, Spain; Byung-Gyu Kim, Sookmyung Women's University, South Korea; Keshav Dahal, University of The West of Scotland, UK; Shivashankar B. Nair, IIT Guwahati, India; and Nilanjan Dey, JIS University, India.

Intelligent systems developed using artificial intelligence (AI), and in particular deep learning (DL), have become game-changers in medical systems, automation, production, agriculture, decision making, etc., due to the paradigm shift in feature extraction and automated learning mechanisms, and AI is expanding into various other domains and disciplines. Therefore, ISAI 2022 aimed to synthesize the different aspects of AI, from foundations to applications. The chapters in this volume expand on the usability of AI in different application domains, such as environmental systems, sustainability, smart cities, agriculture, production, medical systems, transportation, economics, business, etc., and address different aspects of new methods that are emerging. The results of the research in the field of AI are now influencing the process of globalization, particularly in the medical, software, agriculture, manufacturing, and commercial spheres. Creating economic opportunities and contributing to monotony reduction is another thrust area for the emerging epoch of intelligent systems and AI.

ISAI 2022 covered, but was not limited to, the following topics: optimization, artificial intelligence in modeling and simulation, big data, bioinformatics, computational biology, complex modeling for decision support systems, computer vision, expert systems, fuzzy systems, natural language processing, network modeling, soft computing, pattern recognition, AI for socio-economic systems, health and medical sciences, intelligent systems for finance and business, robotics and virtual reality, and blockchain technology. This volume presents selected papers covering the recent developments in the area of intelligent systems and AI categorized into two primary tracks, Information Systems, Mathematics and Data Analyses and Applied Artificial Intelligence.

ISAI 2022 received 75 submissions from a range of researchers. All submissions were rigorously peer reviewed by at least 43 referees in a single blind process, and 30 papers were finally selected for presentation at ISAI 2022. The conference advisory committee, Technical Program Committee, and faculty members of the Haldia Institute of Technology made a significant effort to guarantee the success of the conference. We would like to thank all members of the Technical Program Committee and the referees for their commitment to helping in the review process and for circulating our call for papers. We would like to thank the CCIS editorial team at Springer for the helpful advice, guidance, and continuous support in publishing the proceedings. Moreover, we would like to thank all the authors for supporting ISAI 2022; without their high-quality submissions the conference would not have been possible.

Arif Ahmed Sk
Turki Turki
Tarun Kumar Ghosh
Subhankar Joardar
Subhabrata Barman

Organization

Chief Patron

Lakshman Chandra Seth   Haldia Institute of Technology, India

Patrons

Sayantan Seth	Haldia Institute of Technology, India
Asish Lahiri	Haldia Institute of Technology, India
M. N. Bandyopadhyay	Haldia Institute of Technology, India
A. K. Saha	Haldia Institute of Technology, India
A. B. Maity (Dean)	School of Applied Science and Humanities, Haldia Institute of Technology, India
T. K. Jana	Haldia Institute of Technology, India
Anjan Mishra	Haldia Institute of Technology, India

Advisory Committee

J. K. Mandal	University of Kalyani, India
D. P. Sinha	Kolkata, India
Aniruddha Nag	Kolkata Chapter, India
Subhabrata Roychaudhuri	Kolkata Chapter, India
Debashis Chakravorty	Kolkata Chapter, India

General Chairs

Devadatta Sinha	University of Calcutta, India
Xiao-Zhi Gao	University of Eastern Finland, Finland

Organizing Chairs

Sourav Chakraborty	Kolkata Chapter, India
Tarun Kumar Ghosh	Haldia Institute of Technology & MC Member, CSI, Kolkata Chapter, India

Program Chairs

Turki Turki	King Abdulaziz University, Saudi Arabia
Sk. Arif Ahmed	XIM University, India

Subhankar Joardar	Haldia Institute of Technology, India
Subhabrata Barman	Haldia Institute of Technology, India

Industry Chairs

Dipankar Dutta	Facebook, London, UK
Saikat Basu	Cognizant, UK
Brojeshwar Bhowmick	TCS Research, India

Finance Chairs

Rajat Kanti Chatterjee	CSI, Kolkata Chapter, India
Santanu Koley	Haldia Institute of Technology, India

Publication Chair

Sumana Kundu	Haldia Institute of Technology, India

Registration Chair

Palash Ray	Haldia Institute of Technology, India

Event Chair

Pinaki Pratim Acharya	Haldia Institute of Technology, India

Organizing Committee

Apratim Mitra	Haldia Institute of Technology, India
Bidesh Chakraborty	Haldia Institute of Technology, India
Soumitra Roy	Haldia Institute of Technology, India
Shyamali Guria	Haldia Institute of Technology, India
Mahuya Sasmal	Haldia Institute of Technology, India
Patrali Pradhan	Haldia Institute of Technology, India
Arindam Giri	Haldia Institute of Technology, India
Sabyasachi Pramanik	Haldia Institute of Technology, India
Jayeeta Majumder	Haldia Institute of Technology, India
Sanchita Saha	Haldia Institute of Technology, India
Sumanta Kuila	Haldia Institute of Technology, India
Mrinmoy Sen	Haldia Institute of Technology, India
Sunanda Jana	Haldia Institute of Technology, India
Arpita Mazumdar	Haldia Institute of Technology, India
Rajrupa Metia	Haldia Institute of Technology, India

Angana Chakraborty	Haldia Institute of Technology, India
Rajesh Mukherjee	Haldia Institute of Technology, India
Abhirup Paria	Haldia Institute of Technology, India
Biswajit Jana	Haldia Institute of Technology, India
Suryakanta Panda	Haldia Institute of Technology, India
Avijit Sarkar	Haldia Institute of Technology, India
Shaon Bandyopadhyay	Haldia Institute of Technology, India

Technical Program Committee

Abhijit Bhattacharyya	Tata Consultancy Services, India
Ajita Rattani	Wichita State University, USA
Alexander Horsch	UiT The Arctic University of Norway, Norway
Alireza Alaei	Southern Cross University, Australia
Amitava Nag	Central Institute of Technology, Kokrajhar, India
Ankit Chaudhary	University of Missouri – St. Louis, USA
Arijit Roy	University of Luxembourg, Luxembourg
Arijit Sur	Indian Institute of Technology, Guwahati, India
Asish Bera	Edge Hill University, UK
Bidesh Chakraborty	Haldia Institute of Technology, India
Bidyut Kumar Patra	National Institute of Technology, Rourkela, India
Bubu Bhuyan	North-Eastern Hill University, India
Byung-Gyu Kim	Sookmyung Women's University, South Korea
Chai Quek	Nanyang Technological University, Singapore
Dakshina Ranjan Kishku	National Institute of Technology, Durgapur, India
Daniel P. Lopresti	Lehigh University, USA
Debaprasad Das	Assam University, India
Debi Prosad Dogra	Indian Institute of Technology, Bhubaneswar, India
Deepika Koundal	University of Petroleum and Energy Studies, Dehradun, India
Dilip Kumar Gayen	College of Engineering and Management, Kolaghat, India
Dilip Prasad	UiT The Arctic University of Norway, Norway
Dinesh Dash	National Institute of Technology, Patna, India
Emanuela Marasco	George Mason University, USA
Gaurav Gupta	Wenzhou-Kean University, China
Gaurav Sharma	University of Rochester, USA
Gian Luca	Foresti University of Udine, Italy
Guoqiang Zhong	Ocean University of China, China
Haider Banka	Indian Institute of Technology (ISM), Dhanbad, India
Harish Bhaskar	The Home Depot, Canada

Heeseung Choi	Korea Institute of Science and Technology, South Korea
Jonathan Wu	University of Windsor, Canada
Josep Lladós	Universitat Autònoma de Barcelona, Spain
Juan Tapia	Universidad de Chile, Chile
Jyoti Prakash Singh	National Institute of Technology, Patna, India
Kiran Raja	Norwegian University of Science and Technology (NTNU), Norway
Krishna Gopal Dhal	Midnapore College, India
Mamata Dalui Chakraborty	National Institute of Technology, Durgapur, India
Massimo Tistarelli	University of Sassari, Italy
Milan Kumar Dholey	Hooghly Engineering and Technology College, India
Mohan S. Kankanhalli	National University of Singapore, Singapore
Monish Chatterjee	Asansol Engineering College, India
Mukta Majumder	University of North Bengal, India
Nabakumar Peyada	IIT Kharagpur, India
Naga Venkata Kartheek Medathati	Amazon, India
Oscar Castillo	Tijuana Institute of Technology, Mexico
Parikshit N. Mahalle	Smt. Kashibai Navale College of Engineering, Pune, India
Partha Pratim Roy	Indian Institute of Technology, Roorkee, India
Paula Brito	University of Porto, Portugal
Paulo Mateus	Instituto Superior Tecnico, Portugal
Piyush Kanti Bhunre	Techno India University, India
Pradyumna Kumar Tripathy	Silicon Institute of Technology, Bhubaneswar, India
Pranab K Dan	Indian Institute of Technology, Kharagpur, India
Rajkumar Saini	Luleå University of Technology, Sweden
Rifat Çolak	Firat University, Turkey
Samarjit Kar	National Institute of Technology, Durgapur, India
Sanjoy Das	Kalyani University, India
Santanu Phadikar	MAKAUT, West Bengal, India
Santanu Santra	Yuan Ze University, Taiwan
Santhosh K. K.	Nofima AS, Norway
Sasthi C. Ghosh	Indian Statistical Institute, Kolkata, India
Satyen Mandal	Kalyani Government Engineering College, India
Sebastiano Battiato	Università di Catania, Italy
Selma Tekir	Izmir Institute of Technology, Turkey
Seungho Chae	Korea Institute of Science and Technology, South Korea
Shalli Rani	Chitkara University, India

Shyamalendu Kander   Indian Institute of Engineering Science and
                          Technology, Shibpur, India
Somnath Mukherjee   Assam University, India
Soumya Prakash Rana   London South Bank University, UK
Subrata Dutta   National Institute of Technology, Jamshedpur,
                          India
Sudeep Sarkar   University of South Florida, USA
Sule Yildirim Yayilgan   Norwegian University of Science and Technology
                          (NTNU), Norway
Suman Bhunia   Miami University, USA
Svetla Petkova-Nikova   KU Leuven, Belgium
Tanmoy Maitra   KIIT University, Bhubaneswar, India
Velmani Ramasamy   Madanapalle Institute of Technology and Science,
                          India
Vilem Novak   University of Ostrava, Czechia
Veningston K.   Madanapalle Institute of Technology and Science,
                          India
Watanabe Osamu   Takushoku University, Japan
Wei-Ta Chu   National Chung Cheng University, Taiwan
Xiaoyi Jiang   University of Münster, Germany
Xingwang Li   Henan Polytechnic University, China

Contents

Applied Artificial Intelligence

Information Systems, Mathematics and Data Analyses

Anomaly Detection in IoT Using Extended Isolation Forest

Subir Panja[1,2]([✉]), Nituraj Patowary[1], Sanchita Saha[1,3], and Amitava Nag[1]

[1] Central Institute of Technology Kokrajhar, Kokrajhar, Assam, India
[2] Academy of Technology, Adisaptagram, WB, India
`panja.subir@gmail.com`
[3] Haldia Institute of Technology, Haldia, India

Abstract. The emergence of various smart services delivered by heterogeneous Internet of Things (IoT) devices has made daily human-life easy and comfortable. IoT devices have brought enormous convenience to various applications, no matter the IoT systems include homogeneous devices like in most sensor networks or heterogeneous devices like in smart homes or smart business applications. However, several known communication infrastructures of IoT systems are at risk to various security attacks and threats. The practice of discovering uncommon occurrences of conventional behaviors is known as anomaly detection. It is an essential tool for detecting fraud as well as network intrusion. In this work, we provide an anomaly-based model on the Extended Isolation Forest method. In our work, the available dataset 'UNSW_2018_IoT_Botnet_Final_10_best_Testing' has been used for the experiment. Performance indicators, including accuracy, precision, recall, and F1-Score, are used to validate the performance of our suggested system. We get an Accuracy Score of 93% and F1-Score of 96% through the experiment. In addition, the most important top 12 features have a more substantial impact on correct prediction for anomaly identification and have also been identified in this study.

Keywords: Anomaly detection · Isolation forest · Extended isolation forest · Iot security · Feature set

1 Introduction

With the lightning-fast development, the Internet is now not limited to PCs and Laptops; It has inspired a new phenomenon known as the Internet of Things (IoT). The primary purpose of this technology is to simplify people's lives by automating existing device infrastructure and entering all individuals' lives. Web services or interfaces are used to connect IoT devices to the Internet. However, some well-known IoT communication infrastructures are vulnerable to various security risks and assaults, putting IoT networks at risk. Thus, securing the IoT devices and the networks associated with the IoT system is necessary. Several security and privacy features for IoT applications have been developed and

A. A. Sk et al. (Eds.): ISAI 2022, CCIS 1695, pp. 3–14, 2022.
https://doi.org/10.1007/978-3-031-22485-0_1

implemented, but many problems remain open. Thus, the adoption of security and privacy for IoT devices is the researchers' top objective. The denial-of-service (DoS) attacks, distributed denial-of-service (DDoS) attacks, botnet, access control, identity management, governance frameworks, etc., are the serious concern in the security field of IoT [16]. Among all risks, DoS and DDoS (which are advanced versions of DoS and more difficult to prevent) cyberattacks, perhaps, are the most deadly and devastating security issues for gaining control of IoT nodes [2,9]. As a result, detection of these attacks on IoT devices has piqued the interest of experts in recent years. The three levels of an IoT architecture are the perception layer, network layer, and application layer. Malicious physical attacks on devices with sensors and unauthorized access to equipment on the Perception layer are the most common attacks, whereas, in the Network layer, the most attacks are DoS, DDoS, gateway attacks, routing attacks, information theft, information gathering, etc. Panja et al. [15] depicted different threats and attacks concerning the layers of IoT systems. However, a detection system is necessary to identify these attacks in the IoT network, known as Intrusion Detection System (IDS) [19]. IDS is classified as a Signature-based Intrusion Detection System (SIDS) and an Anomaly-based Intrusion Detection System (AIDS). In between these, SIDS, although it performs well on previously known attacks, is not dynamic because it fails on unknown attacks [1]. AIDS, on the other hand, using network parameter learning algorithms, is capable of dealing with that scenario [14]. However, Communication to IoT devices is occasionally misclassified as anomalous traffic by threshold-based anomaly detection systems, which cannot respond to different patterns of attacks. [3]. In contrast, anomaly detection methods based on machine learning performed better in reducing false positives.

The remaining part of the paper is laid out as follows: A survey of relevant work has been provided in Sect. 2. In Sect. 3, we explored our objective and motivation for doing this work. In Sect. 4, a brief description of Isolation Forest (IF) and Extended Isolation Forest (EIF) has been given. The entire methodology of our work has been described in Sect. 5. Finally, the conclusion part has been discussed in Sect. 6.

2   Related Study

Anomaly detection focuses on patterns in data that deviate from the expected pattern. Anomaly detection techniques can be used to distinguish malicious traffic from legitimate traffic. In this section, we discuss various machine learning-based anomaly detection systems in the IoT presented by different researchers. Many researchers used supervised machine learning approaches in their models to detect anomalies in IoT networks. As a result, unsupervised machine learning algorithms in IoT networks may be used to discover anomalies. Supervised learning works by training sample data from a data source that already has a categorization. The capacity to acquire and organize information using an unlabeled dataset is referred to as unsupervised learning.

Doshi et al. [6] suggested a DDoS identification for consumer IoT systems based on a machine learning algorithm. The authors proposed an unsupervised machine learning pipeline for DDoS detection in IoT traffic that includes some steps like data gathering, feature extraction, and binary classification. The pipeline has been designed to operate on network middleboxes, such as routers, network switches, or firewalls, to detect DDoS attack origins on nearby IoT devices spontaneously. It's the earliest network anomaly detection technique that emphasizes IoT-specific properties and recognizes IoT bots at the level of localized networks.

Vishwakarma et al. [21] proposed a honeypot-based malware identification strategy that uses machine learning techniques. All the data acquired by the IoT honeypot is used as a dataset asset. These datasets are for the training of functional and adaptive machine learning models. The approach is effective for starting when dealing with zero-day DDoS attacks.

Diro and Chilamkurti [5] proposed a deep learning-based IDS that depends on stateless and stateful properties to distinguish malicious traffic from regular traffic on the IoT network. The approach primarily safeguards IoT devices.

Thamilarasu and Chawla [18] developed a deep learning-based approach to identify different types of attacks in IoT, such as blackhole, opportunistic, DDoS and sinkhole, and also wormholes. The model has a 97% true positive rate and a 95% average accuracy against all types of attacks.

Hussain et al. [8] proposed a machine learning-based IDS to detect attacks like DOS, data type probing, malicious control, malicious operation, scan, etc., for the IoT devices used in a smart home.

Das et al. [4] proposed an unsupervised machine learning-based technique to develop an anomaly detection mechanism with notable performance in detecting DDoS attacks. This work aims to enhance the precision of DDoS attack detection and minimize the number of false positives. For testing, the authors utilized the NSL-KDD data set sample and 12 feature sets from earlier research to compare their composite outcomes to those of their individuals and other current models.

Nakahara et al. [13] proposed an integrated strategy that uses a white list and machine learning to remove regular communication from intrusion detection while examining additional communications using an Isolation Forest (IF) algorithm. They also compared the outcomes of anomaly detection with and without the white list to show that the recommended technique is effective.

Nakahara et al. [12] designed a method that sends statistical information from the home gateway to an analysis server to detect irregularities in IoT devices in the home network. Despite the fact that the statistical information employed in anomaly identification has been limited, they have also proven the abnormalities of numerous devices in the experiment. With Isolation Forest (IF) and K-means clustering, they proposed a method that might minimize the data quantity needed for the analysis by over 90% while still achieving high precision.

Tyagi and Kumar [20] investigated various supervised learning classifiers for anomaly and threat detection in IoT environments, including K Nearest Neighbor (KNN), Support Vector Machine (SVM), Logistic Regression (LR), Decision Tree (DT), Multilayer Perceptron (MLP), and Random Forest (RF). The authors demonstrated that both DT and RF are more accurate than the rest classifiers applied. The suggested study uses the BoT IoT dataset to derive a unique IoT-specific feature set that identifies various types of attacks. The extracted set of features is independent of attack characteristics but dependent on the IoT network. As a consequence, these features can aid in the detection of any questionable behavior in an IoT network using a machine learning model.

Seifousadati et al. [17] proposed a DDoS attack detection methodology combining machine learning and data mining approaches. To identify traffic on the network that is not real, the authors used famous machine learning methods, notably Naïve Bayes, Support Vector Machine (SVM), AdaBoost, XGBoost, K Nearest Neighbor (KNN), and Random Forest.

Hariri et al. [7] presented a method for detecting anomalies, namely the 'Extended Isolation Forest' (EIF) algorithm. EIF corrects problems with anomaly scores assigned to specific data points. The researchers explored the challenge by employing heat maps for anomaly scores, which suffer from artifacts generated by the criteria for the branching operation of a binary tree. The researchers thoroughly defined the problem and graphically displayed the method through which it happens. They recommended two techniques: randomly modifying the data before creating each tree, which results in averaging out the bias and enabling data slicing to employ hyper-plane with randomized slopes.

3   Motivation of Our Work

IoT plays a crucial part in our daily lives in the modern age. It is now used in a wide range of fields, such as home automation, smart cities, self-driving cars, smart grids, hospitals, farms, and so on. Anomaly detection in IoT is an ongoing research theme because IoT devices are prone to be attacked through different weak points. Machine Learning algorithms have become very popular and efficient in detecting anomalies, which attracted the attention of researchers. However, we have reviewed the works of many researchers where we found that some of the machine learning-based anomaly detection systems [5,11] are not suitable for IoT environments. Furthermore, anomaly Detection in IoT networks is mostly based on supervised machine learning approaches. However, in the case of unsupervised learning, the lack of guidance for the learning algorithm could sometimes be advantageous because it enables the system to search back for patterns that were not even previously examined. Thus, we planned to use unsupervised machine learning in this work. We have used the Extended Isolation Forest (EIF) algorithm, proposed by [7] for detecting an anomaly. The basic idea of Extended Isolation Forest (EIF) is similar to the Isolation Forest (IF) algorithm. In an Isolation Forest technique, data is taken from a sample of a sample and prepared in a tree structure that depends on random cuts in the values of randomly selected attributes in the data set. Data samples that extend deeply into the branches of a tree are less probable for being anomalous, whereas smaller branches are more probable for being anomalous. Extended Isolation Forest splits data using hyper-planes with random slopes (non-axis-parallel) to create binary search trees. However, as branch splits in isolation forests are frequently horizontal or vertical, it generates bias and causes abnormalities in the anomaly score map. Extended Isolation Forest, on the other hand, as choose a branch cut with a randomized slope at every branching point, eliminates the bias.

4 Isolation Forest (IF) and Extended Isolation Forest (EIF)

In this part, we provides a brief overview of the Isolation Forest (IF) and Extended Isolation Forest (EIF) algorithms, which are widely applied for anomaly detection.

Isolation Forest (IF) is an unsupervised learning method for anomaly detection which follows the process of randomly partitioning data points to isolate the anomaly from the normal instances.

- The algorithm chooses a random sample of sampled data to build a binary tree and ensemble iTree from a given dataset. The binary tree is built to isolate all the points and measure their individual path length from the root. It detects anomalies in the iTrees that are closer to the root and considers normal point that is deeper in the tree. A diagrammatic view of iTree has been given in Fig. 1.
- In order to construct an iForest, one arbitrarily sample determine a portion of the data set to generate iTrees, and it has been discovered that 256 is really a reasonable quantity of data for subsequent sub-sampling.
- iForest does not use density or distance calculations to identify anomalies; thus, this step eliminates the processing cost compared to the distance measure involving grouping, which requires linear time complexity.
- iForest need a small quantity of memory and uses the combined idea if some iTrees do not produce valid results because the integrated algorithm converts weak trees into valid trees. Because of all these benefits, iForest is proficient in detecting anomalies involving complex and large datasets.
- The Eq. 1 for calculating anomaly score for iTrees is [7]:

$$S(x, n) = 2^{\frac{(-E(h(x)))}{c(n)}} \tag{1}$$

where, $E(h(x))$ is the number of edges in a tree for a certain point (x).

$$c(n) = 2H(n-1) - \frac{2(n-1)}{n} \tag{2}$$

where, in Eq. 2, $c(n)$ is the normalization constant for a dataset of size n and $H(i)$ is a harmonic number can be evaluate by $ln(i) + 0.5772156649$ (Euler's constant) and n is the number of points used to develop of trees.

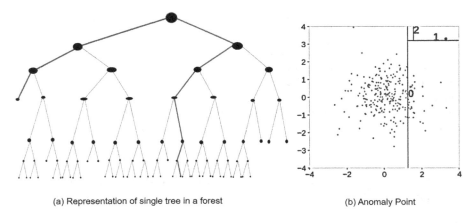

(a) Representation of single tree in a forest   (b) Anomaly Point

Fig. 1. A diagrammatic view of iTree

- In iForest, the branch cuts either vertical or horizontal; this may lead to a bias and distortions to the anomaly scoring map.

  Extended Isolation Forest (EIF) chooses a branch cut with a randomized slope at every branching point; thus, it can eliminate the bias.

- The core notion of EIF is the same as IF; however, it is dependent on the randomness of feature selection. Because specific points are 'few and unusual,' they stand out rapidly compared to random choices.
- iForest needs two pieces of records for branch cuts: a) a random characteristic or coordinate, and b) a random value for the feature from the record's variety of possible values. EIF requires two fact segments, but those are: 1) a random slope for the branch reduce and 2) a random intercept for the branch reduce, each of which can be picked from the training data's boundary of accessible values.
- Choosing a random slope for the branch reducing for an N-dimensional data set is equivalent to picking a normal vector, $\overrightarrow{n}$, evenly over the unit N - Sphere. This is simply performed by selecting a random integer from the usual normal distribution N $(0, 1)$ for each of $\overrightarrow{n}$ coordinates. As a result, the N-point spheres are evenly distributed. For the cut-off, $\overrightarrow{p}$, We simply select values from a uniformly distributed set that spans the range of values available at every intersection.
- The branching criterion for data partitioning at a specific point $\overrightarrow{x}$ will be defined after these two pieces of information are identified, as follows:
  1. If the condition is met, the data $\overrightarrow{x}$ is sent to the left-sided branch; else, it is sent to the right-sided branch.
  2. At this point, a new generalization hyper-parameter, extension-Level, is introduced. The function of extension Level is to force random items of $\overrightarrow{n}$ to be zero. The value of the extension-level hyper-parameter ranges from 0 to P-1, where P denotes the number of features. A value of 0

indicates that all gradients will be parallel in all directions, which is the behavior of an Isolation Forest. The more extension levels there are, the more parallel the divide is with the number of extension-level axes. The term "full extension" refers to a level of extension equal to P-1. This means that the branching point's slope will be randomized at all times.

EIF algorithm can fully replace the IF algorithm since it allows leveraging generalization by employing the extension-Level hyper-parameter. However, even if enough uses of EIF algorithm would exist, IF algorithm will remain in use due to its interpretability. Since the IF uses Binary Search Tree (BST), it is easy to interpret, but the interpretability of EIF is irretrievably lost with the adjustment of branching.

5   Methodology

5.1   Proposed Study

Algorithms for machine learning that are most widely used for anomaly detection were determined by reviewing related works by other researchers. In terms of effectiveness and speed, we proposed a model in our paper. The dataset titled "UNSW_2018_IoT_Botnet_Final_10_best_Testing", has been used for the experiment. After preprocessing the data, we evaluated the most common machine learning method for anomaly detection and recorded the results.

5.2   Dataset

The Cyber Range Lab at UNSW Canberra Cyber created an IoT dataset UNSW _2018_IoT_Botnet_Final_10_best_Testing", tested in a real-world testbed setting. [12], this dataset contains 5% of the original Bot-IoT dataset. Both simulated and real-world IoT attack traffic is included in the dataset. There are 733564 harmful entries and 107 normal entries in the sample. We consider binary classification in our experiment. The histogram of binary classification of the dataset is shown in Fig. 2, where the X-axis denotes the attack and normal class, and Y-axis denotes the frequency of data.

5.3   Data Prepocessing

We utilized the Google Colab environment for data preparation, which was designed by Google and allowed anybody to write instruction code and execute Python programs through the web browser. Consequently, researchers working on machine learning and data analysis will find it quite valuable. Therefore, we employed the Pandas, ScikitLearn, and Numpy packages in our preparation effort. In [10] researchers used different features and description which shows in the Table 1, are taken for our experiment:

The steps for data pre-processing is summarized as below:

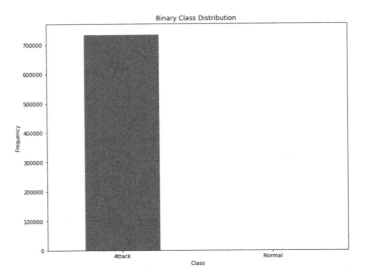

Fig. 2. Binary clasification of dataset

Table 1. Features and descriptions

Features	Description
pkSqid	Row identifier
saddr	Source IP address
Sport	Source port number
daddr	Destination IP address
dport	Destination port number
seq	Argus sequence number
stddev	Standard deviation of aggregated records
N_IN_conn_P_SrcIP	Number of inbound connection per source IP
min	Minimum duration of aggregated records
state_number	Numerical representation of feature state
Mean	Average duration of aggregated records
N_IN_conn_P_DstIP	Number of inbound connection per destination IP
drate	Destnation-to-source packets per seconds
srate	Source-to-Destination packets per seconds
max	Maximun duration of aggregated records

1. Replacing data values: There is no null values in the Dataset and contains many octal values. Therefore, we replaced octal values with a corresponding integer values.

2. Encoding categorical columns: In order to prepare the Dataset for experimental use, it is essential to convert non-numerical values into numerical values.
3. Feature Scaling: StandardScaler is used to perform Feature Scaling in Data Preprocessing. We use Standard Scalar to scale the magnitude of the feature within a certain range. Real-world data are heterogeneous and has a direct impact on performance. After scaling, data is ready to fit in the proposed model.

5.4 Evaluation Metrics

We used Accuracy Score, F1-Score, Precision, and Recall to examine the algorithm efficiency and effectiveness.

- The accuracy score is measured as the number of true predicted labels divided by the total number of labels. The formula of Accuracy Score is mentioned in Eq.(3):

$$Accuracy = \frac{(TP + TN)}{(TP + FP + TN + FN)} \tag{3}$$

- The harmonic average of precision and recall is used to get the F1-Score. Because it incorporates False Positive and False Negative, it's a good measure to use in conjunction with the accuracy score. Formulas of Precision in Eq.(4), Recall in Eq.(5), and F1-Score in Eq.(6), are mentioned in the following:

$$Precision = \frac{(TP)}{(TP + FP)} \tag{4}$$

$$Recall = \frac{(TP)}{(TP + FN)} \tag{5}$$

$$F1 - score = 2 \times \frac{Precision \times Recall}{Precision + Recall} \tag{6}$$

5.5 Confusion Matrix

A confusion matrix illustrates the classifying problem's prediction outcomes. It is an evaluation tool for machine learning classification. The genuine values of the testing data are used to assess performance. In machine learning, the Confusion Matrix aids in the detection of mistakes (FP and FN) as well as the calculation of other performance metrics values. The confusion matrix comprises four parts for binary classification (True Positives (TP), True Negatives (TN), False Positives (FP), and False Negatives (FN) as given in Table.

- True Positives (TP) occur whenever a true positive label is identified as positive by the classifier.
- Whenever the classifier identifies a genuine negative label as negative, it is called a True Negative (TN).

Table 2. Confusion matrix

Confusion matrix		Actual values	
		Positive	Negative
Precicted values	Positive	TP	FP
	Negative	FN	TN

- False Positives (FP) happen whenever a classifier misinterprets a genuine negative label as a positive.
- False Negatives (FN) happen when a true positive label is wrongly classified as negative by the classifier.

A positive event is regarded a harmful occurrence, according to cyber security research, and their right categorization is considered a real positive outcome. Because a negative event is so regular, the suitable classification is true negative. An inaccuracy in categorization can lead to the wrong classification of a regular event as a harmful one. This categorization error is considered a false positive. Similarly, classifying a harmful event as a regular occurrence is considered a false negative.

5.6   Results and Analysis

After data preprocessing, n-trees(represents no of trees)= 200, sample_size= 256 and Extension-Level=1 are fitted into EIF model. After fitting data into the model, EIF predicts the score of each data instance. We take a threshold value, and any value larger than this is considered normal because EIF returns a high score for normal instances compared to anomalous instances. We have found 681548 anomalous points and 52157 normal points through our experiment,

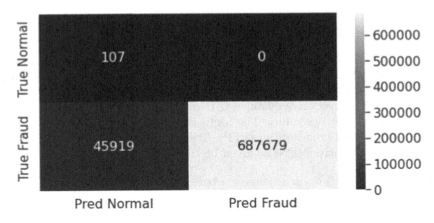

Fig. 3. Confusion matrix as per our analysis

Table 3. Anomaly detection evaluation results

EIF			
Accuracy	Precision	Recall	F1-score
93%	99%	93%	96%

which has been shown in Fig. 3. Moreover, our model accuracy is around 93% as indicated in Table 3

6   Conclusion

In this paper, we have proposed an anomaly detection model based on the machine learning algorithm 'Extended Isolation Forest (EIF)' for binary classification of 'UNSW_2018_IoT_Botnet_Final_10_best_Testing' network traffic into 'Normal' and 'Attack' classes. The proposed model's accuracy Score is 93%, and F1-Score is 96%. Our study enumerates the top 12 most crucial features for anomaly detection and has a greater influence on accurate prediction. The goal is to select the most critical features, removing any non-important features, to make the detection model more accurate and faster while preventing the overfitting of the model. We will enhance this model in the future to classify attacks according to multiple criteria (multi-level classification). In the future, we will test the performance of our approach using current and legitimate sets of data.

References

1. Alaidaros, H., Mahmuddin, M., Al Mazari, A.: An overview of flow-based and packet-based intrusion detection performance in high speed networks. In: Proceedings of the International Arab Conference on Information Technology, pp. 1–9 (2011)
2. Aljuhani, A.: Machine learning approaches for combating distributed denial of service attacks in modern networking environments. IEEE Access **9**, 42236–42264 (2021)
3. Chandola, V., Banerjee, A., Kumar, V.: Anomaly detection: a survey. ACM Comput. Surv. (CSUR) **41**(3), 1–58 (2009)
4. Das, S., Venugopal, D., Shiva, S.: A holistic approach for detecting DDoS attacks by using ensemble unsupervised machine learning. In: Arai, K., Kapoor, S., Bhatia, R. (eds.) FICC 2020. AISC, vol. 1130, pp. 721–738. Springer, Cham (2020). https://doi.org/10.1007/978-3-030-39442-4_53
5. Diro, A.A., Chilamkurti, N.: Distributed attack detection scheme using deep learning approach for internet of things. Future Gen. Comput. Syst. **82**, 761–768 (2018)
6. Doshi, R., Apthorpe, N., Feamster, N.: Machine learning DDoS detection for consumer internet of things devices. In: 2018 IEEE Security and Privacy Workshops (SPW), pp. 29–35. IEEE (2018)
7. Hariri, S., Kind, M.C., Brunner, R.J.: Extended isolation forest. IEEE Trans. Knowl. Data Eng. **33**(4), 1479–1489 (2019)

8. Hussain, F., Hussain, R., Hassan, S.A., Hossain, E.: Machine learning in IoT security: current solutions and future challenges. IEEE Commun. Surv. Tutorials **22**(3), 1686–1721 (2020)
9. Jyoti, N., Behal, S.: A meta-evaluation of machine learning techniques for detection of DDoS attacks. In: 2021 8th International Conference on Computing for Sustainable Global Development (INDIACom), pp. 522–526. IEEE (2021)
10. Koroniotis, N., Moustafa, N., Sitnikova, E., Turnbull, B.: Towards the development of realistic botnet dataset in the internet of things for network forensic analytics: Bot-IoT dataset. Future Gen. Comput. Syst. **100**, 779–796 (2019)
11. Lu, J., et al.: Integrating traffics with network device logs for anomaly detection. Secur. Commun. Netw. (2019)
12. Nakahara, M., Okui, N., Kobayashi, Y., Miyake, Y.: Machine learning based malware traffic detection on IoT devices using summarized packet data. In: IoTBDS, pp. 78–87 (2020)
13. Nakahara, M., Okui, N., Kobayashi, Y., Miyake, Y.: Malware detection for IoT devices using automatically generated white list and isolation forest. In: IoTBDS, pp. 38–47 (2021)
14. Pajouh, H.H., Javidan, R., Khayami, R., Dehghantanha, A., Choo, K.K.R.: A two-layer dimension reduction and two-tier classification model for anomaly-based intrusion detection in iot backbone networks. IEEE Trans. Emerg. Top. Comput. **7**(2), 314–323 (2016)
15. Panja, S., Chattopadhyay, A.K., Nag, A.: A review of risks and threats on IoT layers. In: Balas, V.E., Hassanien, A.E., Chakrabarti, S., Mandal, L. (eds.) Proceedings of International Conference on Computational Intelligence, Data Science and Cloud Computing. LNDECT, vol. 62, pp. 735–747. Springer, Singapore (2021). https://doi.org/10.1007/978-981-33-4968-1_57
16. Sattar, M.A., Anwaruddin, M., Ali, M.A.: A review on Internet of Things-protocols issues. Int. J. Innov. Res. Electr. Electr. Instrum. Control Eng. **5**(2), 9–17 (2017)
17. Seifousadati, A., Ghasemshirazi, S., Fathian, M.: A machine learning approach for DDOS detection on IoT devices. arXiv preprint arXiv:2110.14911 (2021)
18. Thamilarasu, G., Chawla, S.: Towards deep-learning-driven intrusion detection for the Internet of Things. Sensors **19**(9), 1977 (2019)
19. Timčenko, V., Gajin, S.: Machine learning based network anomaly detection for IoT environments. In: ICIST-2018 Conference (2018)
20. Tyagi, H., Kumar, R.: Attack and anomaly detection in IoT networks using supervised machine learning approaches. Rev. d'Intelligence Artif. **35**(1), 11–21 (2021)
21. Vishwakarma, R., Jain, A.K.: A honeypot with machine learning based detection framework for defending IoT based botnet DDOS attacks. In: 2019 3rd International Conference on Trends in Electronics and Informatics (ICOEI), pp. 1019–1024. IEEE (2019)

A Novel Dimensionality Reduction Strategy Based on Linear Regression with a Fine-Pruned Decision Tree Classifier for Detecting DDoS Attacks in Cloud Computing Environments

Swati Lipsa and Ranjan Kumar Dash$^{(\boxtimes)}$

Department of IT, Odisha University of Technology and Research, Odisha, India
`slipsait@cet.edu.in`, `rkdash@outr.ac.in`

Abstract. Cloud computing is a rapidly evolving technology that strives to minimize maintenance and management expenses by relocating high-performance computing infrastructure to the Internet. Despite its numerous advantages, it faces a myriad of security challenges. This paper addresses one of the security challenges in the cloud computing environment, namely the distributed denial-of-service(DDoS) attack. The work proposed in this paper employs linear regression method for dimensionality reduction. The linear regression method is used to find the coefficient of the determinant(R^2) among the independent attributes and the target attributes. The attributes having an R^2 value greater than a predefined threshold value are considered for the detection of the DDoS attack. A fine pruned decision tree is adopted as the classifier in terms of optimal complexity parameter and yields the least cross-validation error. The effect of the complexity parameter on the number of nodes and the depth of the tree is discussed. The fine pruned tree is trained and validated on the CIC-IDS2017 dataset. The proposed work's results are compared to the Random Forest(RF), Logistic Regression (LR) and Gradient boosting(GB) in terms of accuracy, the time required, precision, recall, F1 score, and the confusion matrix. The comparison results demonstrate that the proposed model outperforms its counterpart methods in terms of the various metrics mentioned above.

Keywords: DDoS attack · Cloud computing · Linear regression · Decision tree · Cost complexity pruning

1 Introduction

The paradigm shift in computing has lead to availability of computing and other networking resources over internet through cloud services which are offered by various cloud providers. Cloud computing provides a virtual computing environment to the users as per their hardware and software requirements. This virtual computing environment can be built and accessed using an assortment of cloud

© The Author(s), under exclusive license to Springer Nature Switzerland AG 2022
A. A. Sk et al. (Eds.): ISAI 2022, CCIS 1695, pp. 15–25, 2022.
https://doi.org/10.1007/978-3-031-22485-0_2

deployment techniques. The deployment of cloud system can be private, public or hybrid. The private cloud being an internal cloud of a company does not allow outsiders to use it without proper authentication process and is expensive owing to its high security and control features. The public cloud is freely available to the general public and is viewed as the most cost-effective deployment approach. A hybrid cloud combines the features of both private and public clouds. As the public cloud is accessible to wide range of users, it is more prone to security out-ages and failures. These security issues which are inherent in cloud computing are the major concern that needs to be carefully evaded. Among the various security concerns, a distributed denial-of-service attack must be addressed immediately since it has the potential to render the cloud system inoperable.

A distributed denial-of-service (DDoS) attack generates malicious traffic to disrupt the normal operation of the cloud system. One type of DDoS attack is state-exhaustion or protocol attacks, in which clients are denied access to services owing to the overloading of cloud system servers. This form of attack is more prevalent, and it targets the network layer. The above-mentioned prevailing situation sharply degrades the overall performance of cloud systems. Hence, it is becoming a prominent area of study, with more and more research works being contributed to it on a regular basis.

2   Related Work

DDoS attacks are gradually making inroads as the most prominent form of cyber threat. The current increase in DDoS attacks has grabbed the inter-est of researchers because they elude standard network-based detection mecha-nisms. Somani et al. [1] offer a comprehensive assessment with deep insights into the characterization, prevention, detection, and mitigation strategies of DDoS attacks available in cloud computing. The study [2] concentrates on the flooding-based attack that aims at layers 3 and 4 of the OSI 7-layer model. To detect the DDoS threat, they developed a DDoS detection mechanism based on the decision tree (C.4.5) algorithm and signature recognition approaches. In [3], the authors review the most recent development in detecting DDoS attacks utilizing artifi-cial intelligence algorithms. They suggest using a random forest(RF) tree and Naive Bayes(NB) to distinguish malicious and regular traffic for their enhanced performance. Cheng et al. [4] propose a DDoS attack detection approach based on flow correlation degree (FCD) and an improved random forest optimized by a genetic algorithm. The results of their experiment reveal that the detection model can attain higher accuracy and lower false and missing-alarm rates in a cloud computing environment while being relatively adaptable and robust. The paper [5] proposes a new detection and prevention mechanism for detecting and preventing DDoS attacks in cloud systems, where the classification is done on two levels, using fuzzy type-2 logic and support vector machines - neural net-works (SVM-NN). Amjad et al. [6] applied Naive Bayes and random forest to detect and prevent DDoS attacks and observed that Naive Bayes prediction is considerably superior to the random forest.

According to the study [7] classification algorithms specifically, the Random Forest, is adapted to detect DDoS attacks, and the detection probability is mostly driven by the fractal features of the traffic and the attack,i.e., the higher the difference in fractal attributes, the higher the detection likelihood. The work in [8] was done on the ownCloud environment. They created a new dataset with the Intrusion Detection System and employed Tor Hammer attacking tool to initiate a DDoS attack. Machine learning techniques such as Support Vector Machine, Naive Bayes, and Random Forest were used to analyze the data set, with the SVM outperforming Naive Bayes and Random Forest in terms of accuracy and precision. Tuan et al. [9] considered machine learning techniques such as SVM, Artificial Neural Network(ANN), NB, DT, and Unsupervised Learning (K-means, X-means, and so on) for Botnet DDoS attack identification. The results demonstrate that USML (unsupervised learning) is the best at distinguishing between Botnet and normal network traffic in terms of Sensitivity, Specificity, Accuracy, False Alarm Rate (FAR), False Positive Rate (FPR), MCC, and AUC. In [10] machine learning algorithms such as NB, SVM, and Decision Tree (DT), along with feature selection methods like Learning Vector Quantization (LVQ) and Principal Component Analysis (PCA), were used to classify the DDoS attacks. The result indicates that in the DT model, LVQ-based feature selection detects attacks more precisely than the other studied methods.

Four machine learning algorithms: Multi-Layer Perceptron (MLP), K-Nearest Neighbors (K-NN), SVM, and Multinomial Naive Bayes (MNB) are analyzed and compared in this paper [11] for the identification of Reduction of Quality (RoQ) attacks which is a type of DDoS attack. In addition, they proposed an approach for detecting RoQ attacks that incorporates three methods: Fuzzy Logic (FL), MLP, and Euclidean Distance (ED). On evaluating these approaches using both emulated and real traffic traces, it is found that MLP delivers the best classification results out of the four machine learning algorithms for detecting RoQ threats, while the strategy based on FL, MLP, and ED performs better than MLP at the cost of a longer execution time.

3   Proposed Model for Detection of DDoS

The dataset (D) contains m number of attributes $\{x_1, x_2, \cdots, x_m\}$ which are independent variables and the dependent class attribute y. y is a binary valued variable defined by $\{\oplus, \ominus\}$.

3.1   Dimensionality Reduction

Linear regression is implemented as a dimensionality reduction approach in this proposed work as discussed below:

The dependency of each independent variables $x_i \epsilon X$ on the target variable y can be expressed by using linear regression i.e.

$$y = \beta_0 + \beta_1 x_i \qquad (1)$$

where, β_0 and β_1 are the regression parameters (or regression coefficient or feature weights). The coefficient of determination (R^2) provides a statistical measurement on the relationship between two variables. The greater the value of this measure, the greater is the interdependence between the variables. Mathematically, it can be defined as the ratio of sum of square of explained variation to sum of square of total variation i.e.

$$R^2 = \frac{\sum_{i=1}^n (\hat{Y}_i - \bar{Y})^2}{\sum_{i=1}^n (Y_i - \bar{Y})^2} \tag{2}$$

The R^2 value of each independent variables are calculated and checked against some predefined threshold value. The variables with R^2 value less than the threshold value are discarded from the dataset.

3.2   Fine Pruned Decision Tree Classifier(FPDTC)

The pruning of decision tree(FPDTC) can be accomplished through cross validation. Let the cross validation be $V-$fold which randomly splits X into v subsets X_v such that each X_v is defined as:

$$X^{(v)} = X - X_v$$

Let, T_X be the decision tree obtained from the entire dataset X and $T_X^{(v)}$ be the trees grown on each subsets $X^{(v)}$. Let α be the complexity parameter which controls the pruning process in the decision tree. The pruned tree generated for specific value of α is $T_X^{(v)}(\alpha)$. There may be many different trees, each corresponding to a specific value of α. Thus, the problem reduces to pick the best tree in terms of its accuracy in classifying the desired classes.

The error rate of the tree $T_X^{(v)}(\alpha)$ can be estimated by using the following equation:

$$E^{CV}(T_X^{(v)}(\alpha)) = \frac{1}{V} \sum_{v=1}^V \frac{N_{miss}^V}{N^V} \tag{3}$$

While the pruned tree with the least amount of error can be determined by using the following equation:

$$E^{CV}(T_X^{(v)})_{min} = \underset{\alpha}{argmin}[E^{CV}(T_X^{(v)}(\alpha))\text{for v=1, 2, } \cdots, \text{V}] \tag{4}$$

4   Results and Discussion

4.1   Simulation Environment and Dataset

The simulation is carried out by Spyder(Python 3.7) under Anaconda environment in a MacBook Air laptop (Processor-1.6 GHz Dual-Core Intel Core i5, RAM-4 GB 1600 MHz DDR3 with MacOS Catalina).

Algorithm 1. Pruning(X,T_X, α, V)

Generate V+1 trees
for each V+1 trees **do**
    generate sequence of trees with minimum cost complexity (α)
end for
for v=1 to V **do**
    calculate error of subtree by using $E^{CV}(T_X^{(v)}(\alpha)) = \frac{1}{V}\sum_{v=1}^{V} \frac{N_{miss}^V}{N^V}$
end for
$T_X^{min} = \underset{v=1,2,\cdots V}{argmin}[E^{CV}(T_X^{(v)}(\alpha))]$
return T_X^{min}

The dataset used in this paper is CIC-IDS2017 [12]. It contains eight different (csv) files with five days of normal and intrusive traffic. However, the following two (csv) files only account for DDoS attack:

FridayWorkingHoursAfternoonDDos.pcap_ISCX.csv   and   MondayWorking Hours.pcap_ISCX.csv. The data is extracted from these (csv) files, which contain a total of 255745 instances of Bengin or DDoS attacks with 79 features.

4.2   Dimensionality Reduction

The proposed dimensionality reduction technique is used to select the features that has $R^2 \geq 0.1$. As a result, only ten features are taken into account for further processing as represented in (Fig. 1). Principal component analysis [13], a popular dimensionality reduction technique is also used to find the best features (Fig. 2).

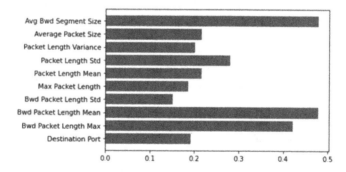

Fig. 1. Attributes with their R^2 value

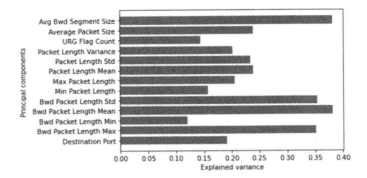

Fig. 2. Principal components with their explained variance

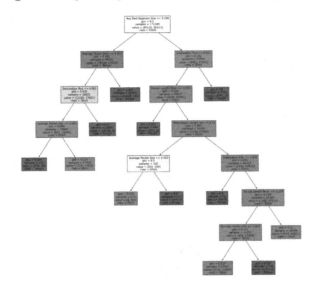

Fig. 3. Fine pruned decision tree

4.3   Training and Validation of Fine Pruned Decision Tree Classifier

Out of the total number of instances,i.e., 255745, 171349 are used to train the decision tree, while the remaining 84396 are utilised for validation. The optimal value of α is 0.025 which is obtained by applying algorithm-1 and five-fold cross validation process. The fine pruned decision tree is illustrated in Fig. 3.

The confusion matrix generated while training and validating the fine pruned decision tree with training instances and validation instances are shown in Fig. 4 and Fig. 5 respectively.

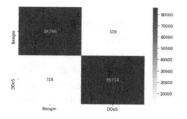
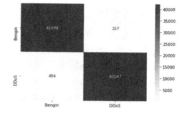

Fig. 4. Confusion matrix for training   **Fig. 5.** Confusion matrix for validation

4.4   The Effect of Complexity Parameter

The effect of complexity parameter on total impurities of leaves (Fig. 6), number of leave nodes (Fig. 7) and depth (Fig. 8) are shown. From these figures, it can be observed that lower value of α is beneficial for pruning process to design a decision tree with better accuracy.

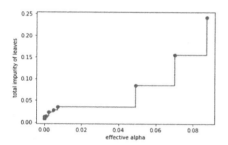
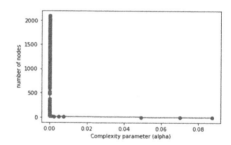

Fig. 6. Total impurities of leaves vs α **Fig. 7.** Number of nodes vs α

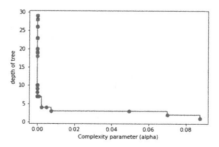

Fig. 8. Depth of the tree vs α

4.5   Comparison

The proposed method is compared against Random Forest(RF), Logistic Regression (LR), Gradient boosting(GB) in terms of training time, accuracy, precision, recall and F1 score (Table 1) over the dataset mentioned earlier. From this table, it can be observed that the proposed method performs better than its counter part methods in terms of training time as well as other performance metrics. In addition to this, the values of different performance metrics when the fine pruned decision tree classifier is used along with PCA are not so appreciable.

Table 1. Comparison of classifiers

Classifier	Training time(sec)	Accuracy	Precision	Recall	F1 score
Proposed method	≤ 1	0.992286	0.988388	0.996280	0.992318
RF	10.70	0.973199	0.968615	0.977891	0.973231
LR	1.57	0.881286	0.90844	0.848071	0.877223
GB	42.60	0.983507	0.988576	0.988555	0.983540
FPDTC+PCA	20.5	0.89334	0.8945	0.8905	0.8923

4.6   Validation of the Proposed Work on Different Dataset

In order to validate the proposed method a different dataset namely Fraud detection in Banks (https://www.kaggle.com/turkayavci/fraud-detection-on-bank-payments/data) is used.

This dataset contains 114 features and 20468 instances. The number of positive instances is 5438 while the negative instances predominates with 15030 number of records. Since, the dataset is highly imbalanced towards negative instances, 11000 instances are chosen with almost equal number of positive (5438 number) and negative instances (5562 numbers). In order to determine the competency of each feature for classification of the target, the proposed linear regression based dimensionality reduction method and Principal Component Analysis method are used for dimensionality reduction. The number of important features generated by both the methods with their statistical significant factors are presented in Fig. 9 and Fig. 10 respectively. By using the above mentioned dimensionality reduction approaches, the dimension of the dataset has been reduced to contain only four selected features. The dataset is then split into training and validation dataset and the proposed fine pruned decision tree classifier is used to classify the target containing two labels(i.e. 0 and 1). The different performance parameters are presented in Table 2. The corresponding confusion matrix are shown in Fig. 11 and Fig. 12 respectively. Table 2 reveals that when PCA is employed with 8 features, the accuracy of the classifier remains 16% lower than when the proposed dimensionality reduction technique is utilised.

These comparison results strongly indicate that the proposed dimensionality reduction technique outperforms PCA in every aspect of performance metrics.

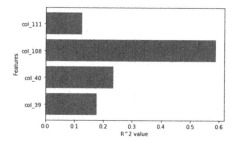

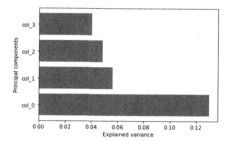

Fig. 9. Features selected by proposed regression model

Fig. 10. Features selected by PCA

Table 2. Performance parameter of classifier w.r.t. the dimensional reduction techniques

Dimensional reduction technique	Accuracy	Precision	Recall	F1 score
Proposed method with 4 features	0.999286	0.999388	0.999280	0.999318
PCA with 4 features	0.814876	0.847608	0.776095	0.810277
PCA with 8 features	0.833609	0.822676	0.848199	0.835243

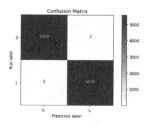

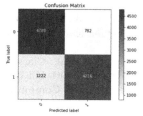

Fig. 11. Confusion matrix of classifier by using proposed method

Fig. 12. Confusion matrix of classifier by using PCA

5   Conclusion

Cloud computing has revolutionized technology with its awe-inspiring and on-demand services. While cloud services are mostly delivered over the internet, their on-demand service makes the availability of computing resources a critical aspect of security. The availability of computing resources is vulnerable to a variety of threats that could result in the exposure of critical data to adversaries. DDoS attack is a cloud-specific attack in which several machines attack a user by sending packets with enormous data overhead. By flooding the network with unnecessary traffic, such attacks render the resources unavailable to the user. Since these attacks are proliferating at an exponential rate, mitigating them has proven to be a difficult task. This paper detects DDoS attacks using a fine pruned decision tree. On comparing the result of the proposed work with random forest, logistic regression and gradient boosting, the proposed method surpasses the other in terms of different metrics such as accuracy, the time required, precision, recall F1 score.

References

1. Somani, G., et al.: DDoS attacks in cloud computing: Issues, taxonomy, and future directions. Comput. Commun. **107**, 30–48 (2017)
2. Zekri, M., et al.: DDoS attack detection using machine learning techniques in cloud computing environments. In: 2017 3rd international conference of cloud computing technologies and applications (CloudTech), pp. 1–7. IEEE (2017)
3. Zhang, B., Zhang, T., Yu, Z.: DDoS detection and prevention based on artificial intelligence techniques. In: 2017 3rd IEEE International Conference on Computer and Communications (ICCC), pp. 1276-1280. IEEE (2017)
4. Cheng, J., et al.: Flow correlation degree optimization driven random forest for detecting DDoS attacks in cloud computing. Secur. Commun. Netw. (2018)
5. Ali, A.A., Osman, S.A.F.: Efficient DDoS attack detection and prevention framework using two-level classification in cloud environment. Int. J. Comput. Sci. Mob. Comput. **7**(8), 1–7 (2018)
6. Amjad, A., et al.: Detection and mitigation of DDoS attack in cloud computing using machine learning algorithm. EAI Endorsed Trans. Scalable Inf. Syst. **6**, 26 (2019)
7. Radivilova, T., et al.: Classification methods of machine learning to detect DDoS attacks. In: 2019 10th IEEE International Conference on Intelligent Data Acquisition and Advanced Computing Systems: Technology and Applications (IDAACS), vol. 1. IEEE (2019)
8. Wani, A.R., et al.: Analysis and detection of DDoS attacks on cloud computing environment using machine learning techniques. In: 2019 Amity International Conference on Artificial Intelligence (AICAI), pp. 870–875. IEEE (2019)
9. Tuan, T.A., et al.: Performance evaluation of Botnet DDoS attack detection using machine learning. Evol. Intell. **13**(2), 283–294 (2020)
10. Bagyalakshmi, C., Samundeeswari, E.S.: DDoS attack classification on cloud environment using machine learning techniques with different feature selection methods. Int. J. **9**(5) (2020)

11. de Miranda Rios, V., et al.: Detection of reduction-of-quality DDoS attacks using fuzzy logic and machine learning algorithms. Comput. Netw. **186**, 107792 (2021)
12. University of New Brunswick. Intrusion Detection Evaluation Dataset (CIC-IDS2017) (2017). https://www.unb.ca/cic/datasets/ids-2017.html. Accessed 6 May 2021
13. Reddy, G.T., et al.: Analysis of dimensionality reduction techniques on big data. IEEE Access **8**, 54776–54788 (2020). https://doi.org/10.1109/ACCESS.2020.2980942

A Survey on Large Datasets Minimum Spanning Trees

Chittaranjan Mohapatra[1,2(✉)] and B. N. Bhramar Ray[1]

[1] Utkal University, Vani Vihar, Bhubaneswar, Odisha, India
[2] Silicon Institute of Technology, Patia, Bhubaneswar, Odisha, India
chitta.mohapatra@gmail.com

Abstract. Spanning trees for large dataset graphs having millions of data points as nodes and almost n^2 edges for a dataset of n points are challenging tasks. Many recent advancements have been made in the design of a spanning tree with millions of points. This is survey work on some recent developments in spanning-tree specific to large data sets. Generally, the efficiency of any design is examined by its time and space complexity. Several partitioning algorithms, clustering models, edge selection techniques, and merging methodologies are examined and evaluated in this paper, along with their respective efficiency. The review spotted a common paradigm, and some strategies, such as Delaunay Triangulation, Hilbert Curve and others, may have research potential for huge datasets.

Keywords: Minimum spanning trees · Large datasets · Partitioning · Delaunay triangulation · Efficiency

1 Introduction

Nowadays, digital platforms are used in most workplaces and businesses for storing and processing data and transaction details. An online shopping site stores the customer's data concerning their choice for their visiting content. This increased data volume has led to Big Data. From the customer's address, networks of local warehouse and delivery locations can be formed. A minimum spanning tree (MST) of these networks may be essential for efficient and optimal transportation of the item [5]. MST is possibly the oldest open topic in computer science, with a long and complex history dating back to Boruvka's work in 1926 [3]. Most textbook MST procedures execute in $O(m \log n)$ time, where the graph consists of n vertices and m edges. It has been seen that a lot of effort has been devoted in the last couple of years to designing MST problems on a graph of voluminous data points. The data can be a network of cities on a map, characters of a text, pins of logic gates in the placement of a VLSI chip and many more. This survey is intended to bring together all the recent developments on MST specific to a large dataset.

The following section is described as follows: Sect. 2 discusses the challenges of designing MST for a large dataset. Section 3 describes the classical algorithms for MST. Section 4 elaborates on the recent work done on MST for large datasets.

A. A. Sk et al. (Eds.): ISAI 2022, CCIS 1695, pp. 26–35, 2022.
https://doi.org/10.1007/978-3-031-22485-0_3

Section 5 tabled the evaluation work. Section 6 discusses some preprocessing techniques of large datasets, and Sect. 7 concludes the survey with some recommendations and future scope.

2 Challenges of MST for Large Dataset

An MST problem is generally applied to a graph data structure. It is necessary to construct and store graphs for additional operations before graph data may be evaluated. In the case of big data analysis in general, the graph data must be retrieved from the original data sources (for example, social networks, web pages, tweets, relational databases, and so on), converted, and cleaned [8]. Peculiar challenges with regard to the minimum spanning tree for a large dataset are described as follows.

a. **Dense Graph.** The number of edges is more than a normal graph, which increases the time complexity to a non-polynomial one.
b. **Determining Edge Cost.** The relationships among the vertices are generally considered the Euclidian distance between two nodes, which might have redundant values.
c. **Memory Space.** Storing a big graph that has n^2 edges may occupy $O(n^2)$ space in memory for an adjacency matrix of a dataset having n data points.
d. **Processing Time.** The processing time for accessing each node and performing matrix operations on it is time-consuming.
e. **Partitioning and Merging.** It is difficult to partition a graph into structure-based subgraphs for any operation, and it is even more difficult to merge the subgraphs with their appropriate neighbours.

3 Classical Minimum Spanning Tree Algorithms

Three classical algorithms are developed by Boruvka [3], Kruskal [10] and Prim [15] where Kruskal and Prim algorithms are very popular and well known.

3.1 The Boruvka's Algorithm

It was developed by Otakar Boruvka back in 1926 to find a minimum spanning tree or forest in a graph. Its nature is parallel. To start with, it finds the total number of forests in the graph. Then it assigns each node to its corresponding forests. Next, it associates the cheapest edge of each node, one by one, with the MST. When all $n-1$ cheapest edges are contracted, the cheapest edge addition process comes to an end.

3.2 The Kruskal's Algorithm

It was developed by Joseph Kruskal in 1956. First of all, it sorts all the edges of the graph. It generates a forest in which each node in the graph is considered a distinct tree. It selects the edge with the smallest edge weight (u, v) from the sorted set. If the vertices u and v belong to distinct trees or sets, then the edge is added and a single tree is formed by a union operation of the two trees based on the disjoint set data structure. This process will continue until all $n - 1$ edges of the spanning tree have been found.

3.3 The Prim's Algorithm

Robert Prim developed it in 1957. It begins with an arbitrary vertex and proceeds as a single node MST. It adds the adjacent nodes having the least weight edge connected to them, which isn't added to the node list of MST. This process continues until all of the nodes are added to the MST. As the shortest edge among all potential nearby edges is added to the MST at each stage, it is greedy in nature. It is also sequential in nature, as each node is added one by one.

4   MSTs for Large Datasets

Irrespective of the difficulties, many studies have been following a common process for designing an MST of a large dataset, as shown in Fig. 1. Generally, the data is partitioned into subsets and MSTs of these subsets are formed, which are finally merged to get the final MST. In most cases, the final MST is an approximation of the exact MST, whose total cost is not the exact minimum.

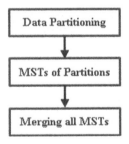

Fig. 1. A common workflow of MSTs for large datasets.

4.1 Divide and Conquer-based Solutions

Zhong et al. Approach [21]. The algorithm produces a two-stage fast approximation of MST using a Divide-and-Conquer methodology. The k-means method is used in the dividing stage to split the dataset into subgroups. Kruskal's or Prim's method is used to generate an exact MST for each subgroup. MSTs of subsets are joined in the Conquer stage to generate a main approximation MST. An obvious technique to combine MSTs from two nearby subsets is to locate the smallest edge between the two subsets and link the MSTs as shown in Fig. 2. Consider two points, a and b, which are part of the clusters S_2 and S_4, respectively. An edge (a, b) can be a connector edge between two clusters if point $a \in S_2$ is closest to the centroid $c_4 \in S_4$ and $b \in S_4$ is closest point to the centroid $c_2 \in S_2$. There may be certain data points on the borders that are susceptible to being incorrectly associated with a cluster. So a refinement step is required where another partition is made centered on the boundaries of the clusters created in the previous step. The aforementioned conquer and combine stages strategies are used to build a secondary approximation of MST. By using Kruskal's or Prim's technique, the two approximation MSTs are combined and a more accurate MST is obtained.

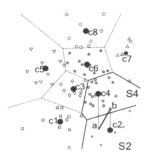

Fig. 2. Detecting the connecting edge between two clusters. (Source: Zhong et al. [21])

Jothi et al. Algorithm [7]. This algorithm uses a recursive Bi-means algorithm in the divide step where the data set is bipartitioned till the size of a sub-cluster is greater than a specific size limit. After the partition phase, the MST generation phase computes the intra-partition and inter-partition edges. An intra-partition edge connects each of the points within a partition. Next, an MST of the cluster's center point is created. The inter-partition edges are computed to connect two boundary points of two neighbouring partitions. A neighbour of a partition is determined by the distance between their centers and the longest edge at the center point MST. If the distance is less than the longest edge length, then the partitions are called neighbors. Finally, a Kruskals or Prims algorithm is run to obtain the approximate MST.

Sandhu et al. Algorithm [16]. It is an enhanced version of the Zhong et al. [21] approach. It uses k-means++ for the divide step, whereas the other steps are similar to Zhong's work. This approach demonstrates that using k-means++ instead of k-means gives a more accurate MST with less complexity and faster convergence.

Mishra et al. Algorithm [14]. This method suggests a hybrid clustering technique for identifying clusters in diverse datasets using the MST approach. It employs a divide-and-conquer strategy to find the clusters. In the divide step, a cluster is moved into a sub-cluster using the highest variance of a vector.

The MST for every sub-cluster is then constructed using the Kruskal or Prim algorithm. Using maximum cohesiveness and intra-similarity among all clusters, neighbouring sub-clusters are found and joined. The time complexity of the proposed approach is $O(N^{\frac{3}{2}})$, where N is the total number of data points in the dataset.

Khan et al. Algorithm [9]. This method is divided into two stages and employs a weighted graph $G(V, E)$, where V and E represent the total number of vertices and edges, respectively. In Phase 1, the weight of each node is initially set to ∞. All the edges of the graph are traversed. During the traversal, if the weight of an edge is greater than its node, the node weight is updated with the edge weight. All the nodes are now traversed to connect to another vertex by the cheapest edge, and sub-graphs (supernodes) are formed. Let S number of supernodes formed, then $S - 1$ edges are required to connect the subsets. In Phase 2, all the subsets are joined. Like in phase 1, all super node weights are initialised to ∞ and all unused edges are traversed. If an unused edge corresponds to the same supernode, it is deleted; otherwise, if the weight of a supernode is greater than the weight of the edge, the supernode's weights are assigned to the edge weight. All the supernodes are now traversed to connect to other supernodes at the cheapest edge.

4.2   Euclidian MST Based Solutions

Lai et al. Method [11]. This paper focuses mainly on the clustering process, but it also creates a MST in its first phase. Points in a higher-dimensional dataset have been mapped to a 1-dimensional linear list using Hilbert Curves [20]. To start, a blank approximate MST(AMST) and an unfilled Link Priority Queue (LPQ) are built. The LPQ describes the vicinity information of each point, which is extracted from a Hilbert list and information from the last AMST. The AMST is expanded by selecting the shortest links from the LPQ. The LPQ is a tuple of three elements, which are two points with the shortest distance between them. The values in LPQ are shifted to AMST in the process. An AMST has the same structure as an LPQ, but the LPQ is sorted based on distance, while the AMST is sorted by coordinate points. A distance matrix is created to store the distance (density) between each point and its nearest neighbor. All densities are initialised to ∞. To begin the algorithm, all data points are moved along the major diagonal by a d-dimensional vector and then sorted into a Hilbert list (HL). The first data point in HL is selected as a visiting point that is to be visited once to avoid a cycle. The k-nearest neighbours of a visiting point are then found using both HL and AMST. A candidate nearest neighbour set is formed by the union of the unvisited nearest neighbour point sets of HL and AMST. The LPQ is updated by the link connecting from the visiting point to all the candidate's nearest neighbors. In LPQ, new links replace existing links if a source point can be reached at a shorter distance than its previously identified source point. An entry is removed from LPQ and added to AMST to form the spanning tree. The process is stopped when the LPQ is empty.

March et al. Approach [12]. A new dual-tree algorithm is presented to generate the Euclidian MST for astronomical data. By amortising some calculations across several locations, it computes all nearest-neighbor pairings at the same time. The Dual Tree Algorithm has been proven as the fastest method for many problems, one of which is the nearest neighbour problem. Two "for" loops are used to compute all pair distances. It takes $O(N^2)$ time, but the kd-tree has shown some improvement. So the dual-tree is applied both to the kd-tree and the cover-tree concepts to find neighbour pairs. Some bounding boxes are maintained for all points in a node of a kd-tree, and the child nodes of the tree are recursively generated by splitting along the midpoint of the parent's bounding box. It has been proven that the neighbour pairs returned by the algorithms are the closest. The algorithm iteratively determines all edges by finding the neighbour pair using either a kd-tree or cover tree. This algorithm's time complexity is approximated to $O(N \log N)$.

Wang et al. Approach [18]. A recursive and parallel approach to Kruskal's algorithm is designed in this paper in a way that is similar to the Euclidian MST (EMST). It first creates an Euler tour, and then WSPD (well-separated pair decomposition) subtree pairs are created using the kd-tree. The kd-tree is traversed to select only the required edges to reduce the number of edges, and Kruskal's algorithm is applied to these edges. A modified Bi-Chromatic Closest Pair (BCCP) method is applied to locate the nearest pair of points within two subtree pairs. The union and find data structures of the set are used to generate dendrograms in the return of the recursive call to merge the subtrees of the EMST.

Delaunay Triangulation Approach [19]. An MST is a subgraph of a Delaunay Triangulation (DT), which is also a sub graph of N points complete graph [6]. A DT is a much reduced set of edges for a complete graph. A Euclidian MST (EMST) can be a faster approach to finding MST in a plane using DT. The algorithm has three steps. First, it generates a planar graph having $O(N)$ edges using DT in $O(N \log N)$ times. Second, the cost/length of each edge are determined. Finally, any MST algorithm, such as Prim's or Kruskal's, is used to calculate the MST of the graph in $O(N \log N)$ times.

5   Evaluation

All the above literature reports on MST are studied, and their complexities are recorded in Table 1. This section explains various time complexities mentioned in the literature, such as the minimum $O(N \log N)$ and the close minimum ($N^{\frac{3}{2}}$). Prim's algorithm [15] is known to be faster for a dense graph. For sparse graphs, Kruskal's algorithm [10] is better and faster. According to the paper [9], the time complexity of the algorithm is $O(E \log E)$ which is the same as Boruvka's Algorithm, Prim's Algorithm, and Kruskal's Algorithm. But it traverses all edges, which may lead to $E = V^2$ for large datasets. Regardless, it demonstrates that $O(E \log V^2)$ is $O(2E \log V)$; that is close to $O(E \log V)$.

In the [11] paper, the cost of creating a Hilbert number for a point is $O(b)$, where b is the bit count of the Hilbert value [29]. In $(d + 1)$ iteration for k

nearest neighbor, N data point, and b bits, the approximate MST is created in $O(dN(b + k + k \log N))$ time and $O(N)$ spaces. In [21], the dataset is evenly partitioned into k clusters. The total partitioning time is $Nkld$, where l is the number of k-means iterations and d is the dataset's dimension. $k(\frac{N}{k})^2$ is the time required to generate MSTs for the k subsets. The approach's overall running time is $O(N^{\frac{3}{2}})$ which is nearly $O(N^{1.5})$. The paper [16] uses k-means++ for the partition process, but the other remains the same as in Zhong et al. [21]. This corresponds to a computation time of $O(N^{1.5})$

In [7], the Bi-means algorithm is used for partitioning data that forms a recursive binary tree. When the size of a cluster equals $\sqrt{N}$, the recursion stops. As a result, the time required for bi-means partitioning is $(N \log N)$. The computation time inter-partition edges and intra-partition edges is $O(N^{\frac{3}{2}}) + O(N^{\frac{3}{2}})$. The MST is generated in $O(N^{\frac{3}{2}} \log N)$. As a result, the time complexity of [7] is calculated to $O(N^{\frac{3}{2}} \log N)$.

The [14] algorithm splits the data into $\sqrt{N}$ sub-clusters. If the partition is a balanced, the partition algorithm takes $O(N)$ otherwise it takes $O(N^{\frac{3}{2}})$. Then, in $O(N)$ times the adjacent sub-clusters are determined. It also takes $O(N)$ times to compute the cohesion and intra-similarity . The worst-case time complexity for clusters merging is $O(\sqrt{N} - k)$. The time required to merge the $O(\sqrt{N})$ intermediate sub-clusters is $O(N(\sqrt{N} - k))$. As a result, the overall complexity of the technique is $O(N^{\frac{3}{2}}) + O(N) + O(N(\sqrt{N} - k))$ which is equal to $O(N^{\frac{3}{2}})$.

In graph operations, the nearest neighbour search is the one that increases the complexity time in most of the problems. In [12], the kd-tree and cover tree are used to improve the nearest neighbor problem in a graph. The cover tree construction takes $O(N \log N)$ time in [2] which runs as a preprocessing step. Including other operations, each finds the nearest neighbour takes $O(N\alpha(N))$ where N union operation is performed in $\alpha(N)$ times. The nearest neighbour algorithm is called $\log N$ times. As a result, the overall time complexity of the DualTreeBoruvka algorithm's [12] is $O(N \log N\alpha(N))$ which is close to $O(N \log N)$. According to the paper [18], an EMST that employs recursion can be completed in $O(N \log N)$ operations. But the article [19] uses Delaunay Triangulation, which can be generated in $O(N \log \log N)$ by using a randomised algorithm [4]. A variant of Boruvka's algorithm [13] can be applied to the Delaunay triangulation to get the MST in a linear time. So the algorithm' expected running time for a two-dimensional dataset is $O(N \log \log N)$ but generally, it takes $O(N \log N)$ time and $O(N)$ space.

6   Discussion

When dealing with enormous datasets, certain issues may arise, such as long processing times, memory (RAM) overflows, longer loading times, and so on. Some techniques, such as data compression and partitioning, are used to tackle such issues without wasting time or money [17]. Data is compressed when it is represented in a new form that uses less memory. This strategy just impacts data loading and has no effect on the code's processing. Lossless and lossy data

Table 1. Time complexities of different approaches on MST.

Approaches	Time complexity	Techniques
The Boruvka Algorithm	$O(E \log V)$	Disjoint-Set
The Kruskal Algorithm	$O(E \log V)$	Disjoint-Set
The Prim Algorithm	$O((E + V) \log V)$	Binary heap
Zhong et al. approach	$O(N^{\frac{3}{2}})$	k-means clustering, Prim's/Kruskal's
Sandhu et el. Algorithm	$O(N^{\frac{3}{2}})$	k-means++, Kruskal
Jothi at al. Algorithm	$O(N^{\frac{3}{2}} \log N)$	Bi-means Algorithm, Prim's/Kruskal's
Mishra et al. Algorithm	$O(N^{\frac{3}{2}})$	Variance, Prim's/Kruskal's, Cohesion
Khan et al. Algorithm	$O(|V| \log |V|)$	Set and Disjoint set
Lai et al. method	$O(dbN + dkN + dkN \log N)$	Hilbert Curves, LPQ, AMST
Wang et al. Approach	$O(N \log N)$	kd-Tree, WSPD, BCCP
March et al. Approach	$O(N \log N)$	DuaulTreeBoruvka algorithm
Delaunay triangulation approach	$O(N \log \log N)$ Expected $O(N \log N)$ Actual	Delaunay triangulation

compression are both possible. Loading particular columns, sparse matrices, and datatype modification of any characteristic are all examples of lossless compression approaches. Lossy compression techniques are analogous to data sampling or numeric value change. Most of the papers reviewed in the previous section use the data partitioning method.

Nowadays, datasets have around 960k rows with 120 features each, where the major issue is memory overflow. Some tricks are there to decrease the memory usage, like changing the feature or column datatype to the smallest possible type. But it may not decrease computation time. Sometimes, loops increase the computation time where vectorization can be used. If the memory requirement is up to 100 GB, then multi-threading can be approached by using a data manipulation library [1]. To achieve one optimum set of edges, the approaches with $n \log n$ time utilise not only the partitioning method but also data compression techniques such as the Hilbert Curves, Delaunay Triangulation, BCCP, and others.

7   Conclusion

The survey has made a significant effort to collect some ideas on recently developed MSTs for large datasets. According to the study, the Delaunay Triangulation approach delivers better time and space complexity for two-dimensional datasets and can be faster than any complete graph to obtain a high level of efficiency in graph-based algorithms. In addition to this, the Hilbert Curve is another way to work easily on high-dimensional datasets. Most of the papers follow the common workflow depicted in Fig. 1, where continuous research such as proper clustering and least-cost bridging between two clusters in such a workflow for massive datasets has yet to achieve an efficiency level, and a comprehensive evaluation such as this can provide an incentive to move forward.

References

1. Bex: How to work with million-row datasets like a pro (2021). https:// towardsdatascience.com/how-to-work-with-million-row-datasets-like-a-pro-76fb5c381cdd. Accessed 19 Jan 2022
2. Beygelzimer, A., Kakade, S., Langford, J.: Cover trees for nearest neighbor. In: Proceedings of the 23rd International Conference on Machine Learning, pp. 97–104 (2006)
3. Borůvka, O.: O jistém problému minimálním (1926)
4. Buchin, K., Mulzer, W.: Delaunay triangulations in o (sort (n)) time and more. J. ACM (JACM) **58**(2), 1–27 (2011)
5. Chazelle, B.: A minimum spanning tree algorithm with inverse-ackermann type complexity. J. ACM (JACM) **47**(6), 1028–1047 (2000)
6. Eppstein, D.: Spanning trees and spanners (2000)
7. Jothi, R., Mohanty, S.K., Ojha, A.: Fast approximate minimum spanning tree based clustering algorithm. Neurocomputing **272**, 542–557 (2018)
8. Junghanns, M., Petermann, A., Neumann, M., Rahm, E.: Management and analysis of big graph data: current systems and open challenges. In: Zomaya, A.Y., Sakr, S. (eds.) Handbook of Big Data Technologies, pp. 457–505. Springer, Cham (2017). https://doi.org/10.1007/978-3-319-49340-4_14
9. Khan, A., Aesha, A.A., Sarker, J.: A new algorithmic approach to finding minimum spanning tree. In: 2018 4th International Conference on Electrical Engineering and Information & Communication Technology (iCEEiCT), pp. 590–594. IEEE (2018)
10. Kruskal, J.B.: On the shortest spanning subtree of a graph and the traveling salesman problem. Proc. Am. Math. Soc. **7**(1), 48–50 (1956)
11. Lai, C., Rafa, T., Nelson, D.E.: Approximate minimum spanning tree clustering in high-dimensional space. Intell. Data Anal. **13**(4), 575–597 (2009)
12. March, W.B., Ram, P., Gray, A.G.: Fast Euclidean minimum spanning tree: algorithm, analysis, and applications. In: Proceedings of the 16th ACM SIGKDD International Conference on Knowledge Discovery and Data Mining, pp. 603–612 (2010)
13. Mareš, M.: Two linear time algorithms for MST on minor closed graph classes. Tech. rep, ETH Zurich (2002)
14. Mishra, G., Mohanty, S.K.: A fast hybrid clustering technique based on local nearest neighbor using minimum spanning tree. Expert Syst. Appl. **132**, 28–43 (2019)
15. Prim, R.C.: Shortest connection networks and some generalizations. Bell Syst. Tech. J. **36**(6), 1389–1401 (1957)
16. Sandhu, S.S., Tripathy, B.K., Jagga, S.: KMST+: A K-Means++-based minimum spanning tree algorithm. In: Panigrahi, B.K., Trivedi, M.C., Mishra, K.K., Tiwari, S., Singh, P.K. (eds.) Smart Innovations in Communication and Computational Sciences. AISC, vol. 669, pp. 113–127. Springer, Singapore (2019). https://doi.org/10.1007/978-981-10-8968-8_10
17. Sara: What to do when your data is too big for your memory? (2020). https://towardsdatascience.com/what-to-do-when-your-data-is-too-big-for-your-memory-65c84c600585. Accessed 19 Jan 2022
18. Wang, Y., Yu, S., Gu, Y., Shun, J.: Fast parallel algorithms for euclidean minimum spanning tree and hierarchical spatial clustering. In: Proceedings of the 2021 International Conference on Management of Data, pp. 1982–1995 (2021)
19. Wikipedia contributors: Euclidean minimum spanning tree – Wikipedia, the free encyclopedia (2022). https://en.wikipedia.org/w/index.php?title=Euclidean_minimum_spanning_tree&oldid=1064995451. Accessed 19 Jan 2022

20. Zaniolo, C., Ceri, S., Faloutsos, C., Snodgrass, R.T., Subrahmanian, V., Zicari, R.: Advanced Database Systems. Morgan Kaufmann (1997)
21. Zhong, C., Malinen, M., Miao, D., Fränti, P.: A fast minimum spanning tree algorithm based on k-means. Inf. Sci. **295**, 1–17 (2015)

Characterization of Simple Sequence Repeats: Evolutionary Implications from Ancient Human Mitochondrial Genome

Poulami Ghosh$^{(\boxtimes)}$ (iD) and Anasua Sarkar (iD)

Department of Computer Science and Engineering, Jadavpur University, Kolkata, India
poulamighosh738@gmail.com

Abstract. Evolution is an extraordinarily long and complex process that all lives on earth undergo. Therefore, studying genetic origins and mutation scans reveal much information about the evolution of life. In this work, we consider the Simple Sequence Repeats (SSRs) of four subspecies of Hominini forms of the taxonomic tribes and derive biological features of the extinct species and search for repeat markers concerning modern humans. We also draw a phylogenetic relationship among the four sub-species from their mitochondrial genomes that had originated during the Pleistocene period and determine the alteration of microsatellite repeats resulting from changes in the formation of protein and, in the long run, leading to evolution.

Keywords: Evolution · Mutation · SSRs · Hominini · Taxonomic tribe · Phylogenetic relationship · Pleistocene period · Microsatellite

1 Introduction

If we travel back in time, Archaic Homo sapiens originated and spread through the Afro-Asian subcontinent during the Pleistocene period. The different sub-species of Archaic humans are the Neanderthals, Denisovans and the Heidelbergensis. The modern *Homo sapiens* emerged close to 20,000 to 45,000 years ago, assumingly in Africa. We have also implied that the *Homo neanderthalensis* or Neanderthals emerged in Africa, and *Homo sapiens sapiens* emerged in Europe and West Asia around the same period.

It has been discovered that Neanderthal-derived DNA can be found in the DNA of possibly all contemporary populations, which vary regionally. The Denisovan ancestry is also called *Homo sapiens Altai*, which emerged during the lower and middle Paleolithic periods. The first identification of Denisovan individuals occurred in 2010 based on the mitochondrial DNA extracted from a juvenile female finger bone from the Siberian Desinovan cave in the Altai Mountains. The DNA indicates a close affinity with the Neanderthal DNA sequence [7].

Another sub-species of Archaic Homo sapiens is the *Homo heidelbergensis*. It is considered a dynamic species that had evolved from an African form of *Homo erectus*. It is the most recent common ancestor between modern humans and Neanderthals [8].

A. A. Sk et al. (Eds.): ISAI 2022, CCIS 1695, pp. 36–43, 2022.
https://doi.org/10.1007/978-3-031-22485-0_4

This study will consider the mitochondrial DNA genomes of the sub-species mentioned above of the tribe Homo and will discuss their distributions as well as in Simple Sequence Repeats characterization, which may imply their evolutionary tree and for a human to escape from extinction.

1.1 The Mitochondrial DNA

Mitochondria is an organelle found in all organisms with nuclei releasing energy from food and storing it as ATP (Adenosine triphosphate) molecules. Mitochondria have their DNA. It was once a free-living bacteria that ancestors of eukaryotes engulfed but could not digest. Bacterial enlarged cells established a symbiotic relationship in which the larger cell protected while bacteria produced food. As a result, the mitochondrial chromosomes store many features like bacteria. They are circular molecules. The human mitochondrial chromosome is around 16,546 base pairs long which is approximate to the size of any bacterial plasmid. Unlike nuclear chromosomes, the mitochondrial chromosome is packed tightly with genes, with a significant region for non-coding DNA between genes. Most mitochondrial genes lack introns which are non-coding information of nuclear genes. Human mtDNA contains 37 genes. 13 are involved in oxidative phosphorylation processes. 22 genes code for tRNA for specific amino acids, whereas 2 regulate the subunit of ribosomes.

The human mitochondrial chromosome has been vastly reduced. Over time, the functionality of genes that the host could provide was lost. Also, some genes needed for respiration were transferred to the nucleus. As a result, millions of years of evolution have resulted in small mitochondrial chromosomes. When an egg and sperm unite, the sperm mitochondria are discarded during fertilisation. MtDNA is, therefore, only inherited from the mother within a family. Unlike the DNA of the nucleus, the mtDNA does not recombine with other chromosomes. Consequently, we can use them to understand the ancestry and evolution of a species [1, 2].

2 Materials and Method

2.1 Genome Sequences

We have considered the whole mitochondrial genome sequences of the species: Neanderthals, *Homo sapiens*, Denisovans and Heidelbergensis. We have downloaded the FASTA files of their reference sequences. We have used sequences with NC 011137.1, NC 012920.1, NC 013993.1, and NC023100.1, respectively, from www.ncbi.nlm. nih.gov.

The lengths of those mitochondrial genomes are 16.9 kb, 16.9 kb, 16.9 kb, and 16.9 kb, respectively.

2.2 Microsatellite Identification and Investigation

Simple microsatellites are extracted with the help of a sliding window algorithm. We have computed the program using Python 3.0 programming language with the assistance of Regular expression package and Biopython modules in Conda environment in Jupyter notebook (version: 6.0.3). For finding the GC content, we have used Bio.SeqUtils package from Biopython module. We have also used the standard Sequence Input/Output interface (Bio.SeqIO) for accessing the FASTA files. We have considered repeat type to be Perfect and motif sizes to vary from 6 to 1, i.e., Hexamer, Pentamer, Quadmer, Trimer, Dimer and monomers. The Considered repeat number is 3,3,3,3,3,6 in the same order, and other parameters are set as default. We have also determined the phylogenetic analysis of the given hominini sub-species with the help of the Molecular Evolutionary Genetics Analysis (MEGA) tool. Version 11.0.10. In the analytical process, we have not found any hexamer and pentamer repeats therefore have considered the repeats that were found.

2.3 Statistical Analysis

We have done the statistical analysis and graphical representations with the help of NumPy and matplotlib libraries in Python 3.

3 Observations and Results

In Table 1, we see that the number of SSRs in Neanderthals mtDNA is 31, which counts to be the highest among the four subspecies. Therefore they have a higher mutation rate than the other species.

Table 1. Overview of the computational results of the whole genome of the four Hominini subspecies.

Sub species	Homo sapiens mitochondrion	Homo sapiens neanderthalensis mitochondrion	Homo sapiens Desinova mitochondrion	Homo Sapiens Heidelbergensis mitochondrion
Length of genome	16568	16565	16570	16568
No. of SSR	26	31	25	28
No. of Tri-mer	9	16	9	9
No. of Di-mer	13	11	12	14
No. of Mono-mer	4	4	4	4
GC Content	44.35	44.39	44.3	43.42

Relative Abundance (RA) in Fig. 1 estimates the biological varieties of a species. RA can be defined as the number of microsatellite repeats divided by genome size in kb. It measures how common or rare a species is comparable to other species in a particular location. According to Fig. 1, the Neanderthals had the highest Relative Abundance of the other species in one specific area. We conclude from this context that Neanderthals were the most diverse, and Denisovans were the least varied in a given location among the given species. Relative Density (RD), shown in Fig. 2, measures the total length contributed by each microsatellite upon the length of the genome in kb. It tells us about the number of a given species expressed as a percentage of all species present.

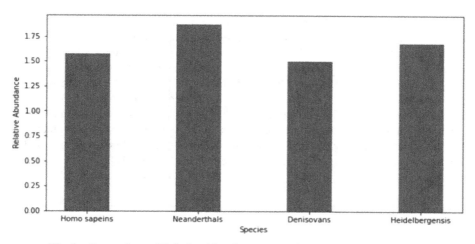

Fig. 1. Comparison of Relative Abundance (RA) of the Hominini sub-species.

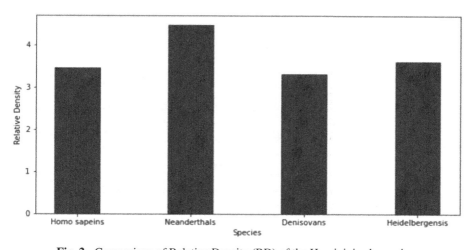

Fig. 2. Comparison of Relative Density (RD) of the Hominini sub-species.

Therefore, according to our observation in Fig. 2, the relative density of Neanderthals is higher than all the given species, and Denisovans have the lowest relative density among the four species. From this angle, we can conclude that Relative Abundance and Relative Density are directly proportional [3, 10].

Moreover, the percentage of GC content showcases the lifespan of a particular species.

Therefore, according to Table 1, we can conclude that Neanderthals had the longest life span and Heidelbergensis the shortest [4, 6]. Figure 3 displays the various simple sequence repeats that show a significant rate of length polymorphism due to mutations of one or more repeat types. The comparison of the common simple sequence repeats in the four species shows that there has been missing and gaining of microsatellites among the four species, which has led to the emergence of one and the extinction of the other. For example, *(ACC)₃* and *(GGA)₃* are gained by all species other than *homo sapiens*. According to Fig. 4, we can see that the *Homo sapiens* and the Neanderthals emerged during the same period, and *Homo Heidelbergensis* is the most recent common ancestor between the two. In contrast, the *Homo sapiens Altai* (Denisovans) emerged a long time after their emergence. While performing the phylogenetic analysis, we had to perform sequence alignment of the mentioned sequences. In the process, we observed mutations in the amino acid sequence that had specifically occurred in the mtDNA sequence of the discussed species, showing some beautiful examples of evolution [4].

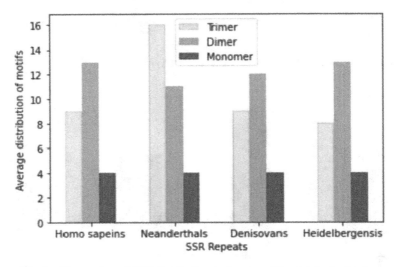

Fig. 3. Observation of SSR distribution in the given Hominini sub-species.

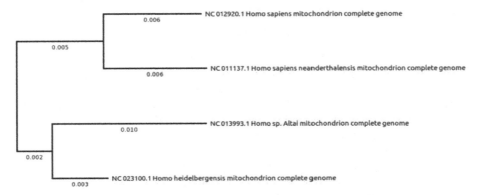

Fig. 4. Observation of the phylogenetic analysis of the Hominini sub-species.

Table 2 displays some of those positions and changes in the amino acid. In Fig. 5, we observe the trimer repeat *(ATC)₃* is gained by *Homo sapiens* and Denisovans, whereas Neanderthals and Heidelbergensis missed it. We also see that the trimer repeat *(ATA)₃* is found in *Homo sapiens*, Neanderthals and Heidelbergensis, but it is missing in the mtDNA of Denisovans. The repeats *(CAG)₃* and *(GCA)₃* are found in all the subspecies except that of Denisovans. *(CCT)₃* is found in *Homo sapiens* and Denisovans, whereas it is missing in Neanderthal and Heidelbergensis. *(ACT)₃* is found in all the subspecies but Heidelbergensis. Trimer motifs *(GGA)₃* and *(ACC)₃* are gained by Neanderthals and Heidelbergensis, whereas missed by the Homo sapiens and Denisovans. *(TTA)₃* is another repeat found in all the subspecies other than the Homo sapiens. *(CAA)₃, (GCC)₃* in Neanderthals and *(CCG)₃, (GAG)₃, (AAC)₃* in Denisovans are the repeats exclusively found in their respective mtDNA sequences. Figure 6 represents the changes that have occurred in the SSRs in the subspecies. We observe that most dimers are present in all the mtDNA sequences except *(GA)₂*, which is missing in Neanderthals and Denisovans. Another repeat *(AG)₂* is present in all the subspecies except the Neanderthals. We have compared our observation with that of the MicroSAtellite Identification tool (MISA), which has led us to the conclusion that the repeats *(ATA)₃, (ACT)₃* and *(CCT)₃* are the SSR markers for Homo sapiens. The presence of *(CCG)₃, (CCT)₃* and *(TTC)₃* confirms that the mtDNA is of the Denisovan subspecies. The presence of *(CAA)₃* and *(ACC)₃* in the mtDNA sequence assures that the mtDNA is of the Neanderthal subspecies. Lastly, the presence of *(GGA)₃, (ACC)₃,* and *(AG)₂* confirms that the mtDNA is of Heidelbergensis.

Table 2. Observed changes in protein sequence after sequence alignment.

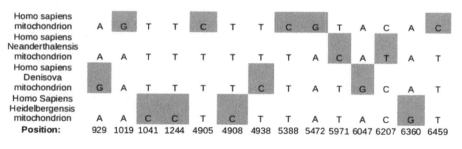

	929	1019	1041	1244	4905	4908	4938	5388	5472	5971	6047	6207	6360	6459
Homo sapiens mitochondrion	A	G	T	T	C	T	T	C	G	T	A	C	A	C
Homo sapiens Neanderthalensis mitochondrion	A	A	T	T	T	T	T	T	A	C	A	T	A	T
Homo sapiens Denisova mitochondrion	G	A	T	T	T	T	C	T	A	T	G	C	A	T
Homo Sapiens Heidelbergensis mitochondrion	A	A	C	C	T	C	T	T	A	T	A	C	G	T
Position:														

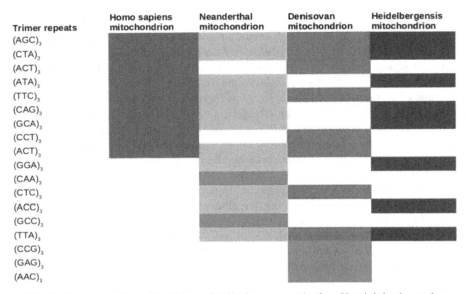

Fig. 5. Representation of the Trimer distribution among the four Hominini sub-species.

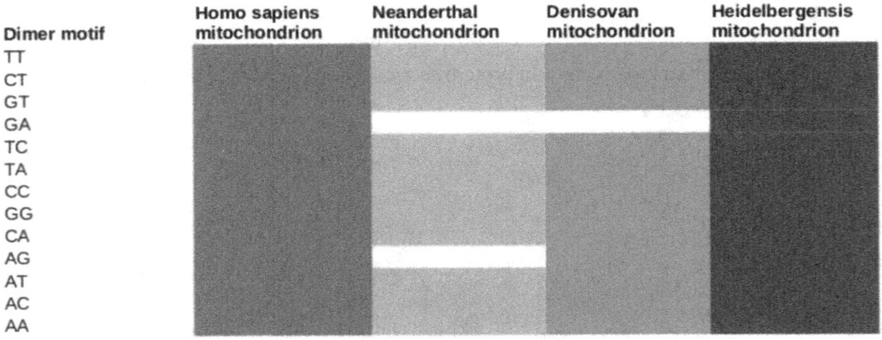

Fig. 6. Representation of the Dimer distribution among the four Hominini sub-species.

4 Conclusion

We can identify the different aspects of evolution in the given subspecies of the Hominini tribe by performing the SSR extraction. From Table 1, we observe that the SSR count in the mtDNA of the Neanderthals is a maximum of 31, and that of the Desinovans is a minimum. The observation concludes that the Neanderthals have maximum relative density and relative abundance, giving us an idea about the vast diversity of the species across a particular location. The high GC content of the Neanderthals also reveals that the species had the longest life span than the rest. Moreover, by extracting the microsatellite sequences, we have tried to understand the alteration of functionalities in the mtDNA sequences. Working more on these data using advanced computational tools will reveal more information about the prehistoric ancestors of humanity to reframe the history of evolution better.

References

1. Khan, S.M., Smigrodzki, R.M., Swerdlow, R.H.: Cell and animal models of mtDNA biology: progress and prospects. Am. J. Physiol. Cell Physiol. **292**(2), C658–C669 (2007). https://doi.org/10.1152/ajpcell.00224.2006
2. Nesheva, D.: Aspects of ancient mitochondrial DNA analysis in different populations for understanding human evolution. Balkan J. Med. Genet. **20**(1), 5–14 (2014)
3. Chaudhary, A., Singh, A., Choudhary, S., Safdar, A.: In-silico analysis of simple and imperfect microsatellites in diverse tobamovirus genomes. Gene **530**(2), 193–200 (2013)
4. Johnathan, A., Robert, P., Corey, C., Aaron, C., David, D.: Finding and extending ancient simple sequence repeat-derived regions in the human genome. Mob. DNA **530**(2), 193–200 (2013)
5. Lehmann, L., Budovsky, A., Khachik, K., Vadimr, E.: Mitochondrial genome anatomy and species-specific lifespan. Rejuven. Res. **9**(2), 223–226 (2006)
6. Lehmann, G., Segal, E., Muradian, K., Fraifeld, V.: Do mitochondrial DNA and metabolic rate complement each other in determination of the mammalian maximum longevity? Rejuven. Res. **11**(2), 409–417 (2008)
7. Gomez, A., Robles, A.: Dental evolutionary rates and its implications for the Neanderthal-modern human divergence. Sci. Adv. **5**(5) (2019)
8. Richter, D.: The age of Hominin fossils from Jebel Irhoud, Morocco, and the origins of the Middle Stone Age. Nature **546**, 293–296 (2017)
9. Barshad, G., Marom, S., Cohen, T., Mishmar, D.: Mitochondrial DNA transcription and its regulation: an evolutionary perspective. Trends Genet. **94**(9), 682–692 (2018)
10. Falkenberg, M., Larsson, N.: DNA replication and transcription in mammalian mitochondria. Annu. Rev. **76**, 679–699 (2007)

Comparative Exploration of Statistical Techniques for Landslide Identification and Zonation Mapping and Assessment: A Critical Review

Sumon Dey$^{(\boxtimes)}$ ⬤ and Swarup Das

Department of Computer Science and Application, University of North Bengal, Darjeeling, India
sumon.csa.nbu@gmail.com

Abstract. Landslides are found to be one of the most dangerous and critical natural hazards, and these are nature's primary ways of slope stability adjustment. For the assessment of landslides, the study of landslide susceptibility, identification of landslides and mapping for the hazardous areas are crucial tasks for the same and it is necessary for the safety of human life and the economic losses that happen each time the natural geo-hazard like landslide occurs in any area throughout the country. There are several methodologies for landslide hazard zonation viz. probabilistic, semi-quantitative, quantitative, and heuristic. However, no method is universally accepted for the effective assessment and management of the same. In recent years, the methodologies have been comprehensively shifted from the heuristic techniques to the data-driven techniques. This paper is aimed to present the review of different statistical techniques for the same. The statistical techniques are found to be more objective and result-oriented as these techniques involve subjectivity in the assignment of weights to the potential factors. The collaboration of statistical and machine-learning techniques with the RS-GIS methods has shown new perspectives for detailed and accurate assessment of landslide hazard mapping and identification.

Keywords: Landslide susceptibility mapping · Hazard zonation · Statistical techniques · Bi-variate statistical analysis · Multivariate statistical analysis · Landslide evaluation

1 Introduction

Landslides are one of the most critical and life-threatening natural disasters having the potential of causing huge economic breakdown especially for the hilly terrains in North-Eastern India. These areas as a consequence, face terrible challenges due to landslide occurrences in the rainy season. Hence the formulation of adequate methodologies to identify the occurrences of landslides is a critical task. Several researches have been carried out that illuminate different ML techniques for landslide identification. For instance, a high-resolution digital elevation model was constructed and its derivatives are exploited

© The Author(s), under exclusive license to Springer Nature Switzerland AG 2022
A. A. Sk et al. (Eds.): ISAI 2022, CCIS 1695, pp. 44–55, 2022.
https://doi.org/10.1007/978-3-031-22485-0_5

for the identification of bedrock landslides [36]. Advanced remote sensing, visual inter-pretation, and perception are collaborated to evaluate remotely sensed images along with topographic surfaces [22]. Researches yield that spectral, shape and contextual infor-mation can be combined together in the OO approaches for the landslide identification and using the multi-temporal images, further exploration can be done in order to iden-tify the historical landslides [33, 35], on which the digital terrain model is used very often [20]. An object-based approach for landslide inventory mapping has been proposed which is optimized by the Taguchi method [40]. The method of data segmentation and SVM can be used to identify the forested landslides with the association of the DTM [60]. Again, the DTM derivatives can be associated with RF along with the SVM to identify the forested landslides [31]. In the field of landslide identification along with many geo-morphological, geotechnical applications, ML and DL methods are found to be efficient and propitious. An integrated method for identifying landslides using ML and DL techniques has been proposed [63], in which the DCNN-11 model and RecLD landslide database were found to be the most promising procedures. An adaptive neural-fuzzy inference system has been proposed for landslide-susceptibility mapping using a geographic information system (GIS) environment [3, 42]. A GIS based SVM model has been proposed for susceptibility mapping of landslides triggered by earthquakes [64]. Studies using DT, ANN, GAM model, CART, LR model, ME model have been carried out [5, 6, 32, 51, 56, 57]. Although the ML techniques are getting importance, each method has its advantages and disadvantages regarding the factors depending on which, the selection of ML methods are carried out [61]. Consequently no one technique or method is universally approved accepted or preferred for landslide hazard and zonation mapping satisfactorily or sufficiently, which results that landslide susceptibility mapping and zonation remain a convoluted and perplexing area of study.

2 Causative Factors for the Occurrence of Landslide

The causative factors for the landslide's occurrences in hilly terrains may be divided into two categories, internal and external. The internal factors such as heavy rainfall, stream erosion, snow melting, ground water-level change, volcanic eruption [9, 16, 26] and the external factors such as expansion of the agricultural area and built-up area, deforestation, clear-cutting, shifting agriculture, poorly planned construction of roadways play an important role in the happening of the landslides and its increase to a fair extent. Undoubtedly, the external factors are mostly human activities. Previous studies indicate that the frequency as well as the magnitude of the landslides occurrence has been on the increasing side due to elevation, slope gradient, slope aspect, slope curvature, rainfall, fault distance, distance to drainage, distance to road, LULC, NDVI, TWI, STI, SPI [17, 45, 58, 59]. Moreover, to the accumulation of the internal and external factors, the climatic extremities in hilly or mountainous regions are also to be considered. In the Indian Himachal Region, the internal factors such as lithology, altitude, slope steepness, fragility of soil, heavy rainfall and many anthropogenic activities like rapid deforestation, agricultural shifting and expansion act as emphatic reasons behind the increased landslides in many of the potentially unstable areas [50]. Consequently, the increment in the landslide occurrence is becoming causative factors for tree losses, forest fragmentation, changes in LULC, slope-instability [1, 38], eventually the natural landscape is vastly affected by the impact of the landslides [14, 52]. Hence, mitigation of frequent landslides occurrence on unstable slopes and assessment of the adverse effects on natural landscapes is one context of this paper.

3 Statistical Approaches for Landslide Susceptibility and Zonation Mapping

For the evaluation of landslide susceptibility and hazard zonation, several techniques have been proposed, including landslide inventories design, statistical modeling techniques, probabilistic methodologies, deterministic methodologies etc. [8, 45, 46, 48]. In the past few years, the landslide susceptibility and zonation mapping approaches have been shifted from heuristic approaches to statistical (data-driven) approaches. The statistical methods can be broadly classified into two categories, namely, bi-variate and multivariate statistical analysis.

3.1 Bi-variate Statistical Methodologies

The bi-variate statistical technique illuminates that if a situation holds in all observed cases, then the situation holds in all cases. There is a general assumption on which the bi-variate statistical techniques depend, "past and present are the key to the future". The common techniques falling under the bi-variate statistical approach are; Weight-of-Evidence (WoE) model [39] and Information Value (IV) model [37]. Apart from these, Frequency Analysis method, known as likelihood ratio method has also been proposed [30]; Fuzzy Logic approach and Weighted Overlay method are proposed respectively [28].

Weight-of-Evidence (WoE) Approach
A quantitative and data-driven approach, used to calculate the causative factors after avoiding the weight's subjectivity. Originally developed for the identification and exploration of mineral deposits, this method came to the application area for the study of landslide susceptibility and with this method, the prior probability, conditional probability, and the positive and negative weights of landslide susceptibility can be determined [11, 54]. The positive and negative weights are:

$$W^{-ve} = ln\frac{\{B|D\}}{\{B|\overline{D}\}} \tag{1}$$

$$W^{-ve} = ln\frac{\{\overline{B}|D\}}{\{\overline{B}|\overline{D}\}} \tag{2}$$

With 'P' denoting the probability, 'B' and '$\overline{B}$' denote the presence and absence of potentially desired landslide causative factors respectively, 'D' and '$\overline{D}$' respectively denote the presence and absence of landslides.

Information Value (IV) Method
Alternatively known as landslide index method, this method is used to compute the

weighted class value through the landslide density with respect to each and every landslide causative factors [37, 66]. The mathematical representation of information value follows:

$$W = ln\frac{Landslide\ density\ with\ a\ potential\ class\ of\ causative\ factors}{Landslide\ density\ in\ the\ area} \tag{3}$$

$$W = ln\frac{N_{pix}(S_i)/N_{pix}(x_i)}{\sum N_{pix}(S_i)/N_{pix}(x_i)} \tag{4}$$

Frequency Ratio Analysis Method

Popularly known as likelihood ratio method, FR is one of the very widely used bi-variate statistical technique, which uses the correlation between the classes of potential causative factors and the spatial distribution of occurred landslides in the area of study [7, 30]. So, $FR > 1$ shows more significant correlation to the landslide occurrence, while $FR < 1$ shows less significant correlation to the same. It can be represented as

$$FR = \frac{Percentage\ of\ landslide\ in\ a\ class}{Area\ of\ the\ factor\ class\ as\ a\ percentage\ of\ the\ entire\ area} \tag{5}$$

The landslide susceptibility index can be thus represented as follows:

$$LSI = \sum_{i=1}^{n} FR_i \tag{6}$$

Weighted Overlay Method

In this method, the landslide hazard can be calculated by assigning the weights based on the correlation of landslide frequency with its causative factors [12]. It is assumed in this method, that if the factors for which landslides occurred in the past, if reoccur in some other area in the future, can again result in the occurrence of landslides. Higher the weight to a potential causative factor or to its class, represents greater significance for the occurrence of landslides [25, 29]. The mathematical representation for the same follows:

$$S = \frac{\sum W * SP}{\sum W} \tag{7}$$

'W' denotes the weight assigned to the respective factor, 'SP' represents the weight to the spatial class and 'S' is the spatial value of the output map.

3.2 Multivariate Statistical Analysis and Methodologies

Multivariate statistical analysis approach for landslide hazard zonation and susceptibility mapping is based on the relative contribution of each potential instability factors to the entire landslide susceptibility of the study area [41]. The multivariate statistical methodologies, determine the percentage of landslide for each and every pixel, and data layer on the presence and absence of landslides is produced and calculated, then the reclassification of hazard is followed with the help of the said methodologies. Logistic regression (LR) analysis, Discriminant analysis are the methodologies that fall under the category of multivariate statistical analysis.

Logistic Regression (LR) Analysis
Using LR method, the occurrence of landslides and the dependability factors can be represented by the following equation:

$$P = \frac{1}{1 + e^{-z}} \tag{8}$$

where, P is the probability of the occurrence of landslide, and z represents a linear combinatorial equation as follows:

$$z = c_0 + c_1 x_1 + c_2 x_2 + \ldots + c_n x_n \tag{9}$$

where x_i (i = 1,2,3,...,n), represents the environmental factors for landslides, c_0 represents the model intercept, c_i (i = 1,2,3,...,n), represents the regression coefficient. Extensive application has been done with this methodology for landslide susceptibility for the Umbria region in central Italy [19]. The LR technique has been used for landslide hazard zonation mapping model for Hong Kong, based on the use of DEM in the GIS perspective [49]. A comparative analysis of different ML techniques along with the heuristic model for predicting landslides has been carried out [23].

Discriminant Analysis Methodology
A frequently used multivariate statistical modeling technique, facilitating to compute the maximum difference for each potential causes segregated in two groups as landslide and non-landslide group. This method assumes all dependent variables to be categorical rather than being continuous [17]. Thus, the weights can be calculated on the basis of the maximum difference. This method can be classified in two categories, (a) Quadratic Discriminant Analysis (QDA), (b) Linear Discriminant Analysis (LDA) [62]. By the use of this method, the Standardized Discriminant Function Coefficient (SDFC) can be calculated and further the relative significance can be represented in terms of discriminant function, acting as a predictor of the instability of slope, eventually considered as one of the most potential factors for landslides occurrence. Using SDFC, the variables having maximized coefficients are correlated strongly to presence or absence of landslide in the study area [21, 44].

4 Pros and Cons of Different Statistical Methodologies for Landslide Susceptibility and Zonation Mapping

Previous studies have suggested that the advantages and disadvantages depend on the application of the technique to the relative context, procurement and/or collection of data and scale of their application [4, 19]. The statistical methodologies are developed based on the correlation between occurred landslides and their causative factors, to which weights are assigned for the measurement of the same, and these weights for the factors are statistically determined. The analysis of the functional relationship between the thematic factors or variables and the distribution of slope deterioration, also termed as the landslide inventory. The statistical techniques are advantageous as these methodologies can be applied over a large area and the past landslide data can extensively be used in the determination, stratification and calculation of the weights for various causative factors for landslides, as it can be witnessed in the WoE model [2]. However, there are some limitations associated with these data-driven techniques. The collection of the past landslide inventory data over large area is considered to be the fundamental disadvantage for the statistical techniques, as the general regulations for landslides susceptibility are formulated based on the past landslides in the area. Consequently, the requirement of a well-defined and distributed landslide inventory data as an input becomes essential for ensuring prompt result. However, there are no fully accepted techniques for the same, which acts as the motivation for the study of landslide susceptibility and hazard zonation mapping in a more extensive way [53].

In addition, to ensure effective and promptness, the collection and validation of the necessary input data are also required, however, the data are rarely available. As a result, large efforts are required to accomplish the same, provided extensive interaction is also a requirement, between the geo-morphologists and statisticians to execute and assess the collected geo-environmental, geo-morphological and landslide data. Apart from these, the study area plays a crucial role as the statistical models are negatively impacted by the study area, which makes it an uneasy task to compute the comparison between the classes of landslide susceptibility from different locations. Moreover, studies are extensively required in the hilly terrains for the future geo-morphological and environmental planning, but very often the mapping techniques based on statistical methodologies happen to be non-understandable by non-specialists which include planners and stakeholders [13, 43, 46, 64]. Research yields that the statistical techniques can extensively be applied for medium scale study in a data scarce environment, however small-scale study for the same can also be done, but the result may not be prompt enough as the data collection in a large geographical area is less feasible, making the statistical methodologies less or practically not feasible for the same.

5 Landslide Susceptibility Assessment and Zonation Mapping Techniques: Literature Survey in Indian Context

The following section contains a summarized literature study about landslide susceptibility and zonation mapping techniques in the Indian Context. An in-depth study along the national highway (NH-39), Manipur has been given about the landslides along with the involvement of various landslides triggering mechanisms and also revealing the fact that the landslides are caused by wedge failure for the slope instability [27]. It is also observed that the terrain comprising soil and rock with a high factor of safety (0.62–1.82) are landslide-prone. The landslide risk and hazard assessment technique using an index value, landslide nominal risk factor (LNRF) and GIS techniques have been proposed [18] from the Ramganga catchment, Himalayas. The heuristic techniques have been proposed, a quantitative methodology has been developed for landslide hazard zonation based on a factor in a numerical rating scheme, called landslide hazard evaluation factor (LHEF). For the Indian mountains, a comparison between BIS and WoE has been drawn [15], which shows that the latter produces enhanced and improved results. A comparative exploration among the BIS, MCA and FR methods was carried out [24] which have shown that FR method is more establishing in nature. Studies were also carried out for establishing the impact of landslides on human lives in the Himalayan region in India [10]. Considering all types of studies altogether, it becomes very clear that the database or inventory related to landslide is insufficient, which may be eradicated by a universally accepted procedure through extensive study.

6   Recent Gaps and Future Directives in the Study of Landslide Susceptibility Mapping and Hazard Zonation

Indian Himalayan Region is highly susceptible to natural disasters, and landslides are one of the same. For the study in landslides, the landslides susceptibility mapping and hazard assessment become very crucial in order to pick out the susceptible areas and assess the risk. This way, the disaster and economic loss may be optimized. The national level organizations and institutions associated with the disaster mitigation and analysis in India include NRSC, IIRS, NIDM, ISRO, GSI, and BMTPC. To obtain landslide susceptibility maps, GSI applies AHP for computing the rating of factors of the classes and assignment of weights to the potential factors with the help of knowledge driven approaches, provided that AHP is a semi-quantitative method which assigns weights through the pair wise relative comparison in the decision process without any inconsistencies. However, AHP does not provide any certainty regarding the selection in ranking of the geo-factors as it may differ from expert to expert. Hence, other quantitative techniques are required to be compared with AHP in order to prepare useful landslide susceptibility maps. The NRSC has a significant role to play with the preparation of landslide inventory using the earth observation data. It has prepared historical landslide inventories using a semi-automatic image analysis algorithmic approach [34]. The historical landslide inventories and landslide susceptibility maps are limited as these are event based such as earthquakes, rainfall. Consequently, the multi-spatial temporal and non-event-based landslide inventories and landslide susceptibility mapping are crucial as these acts as an existing gap in the disaster mitigation.

7   Conclusion

Landslide identification, susceptibility mapping and hazard zonation are comprehensive, crucial and at the same time very critical task in nature as the historical landslide inventories, datasets associated to the existing statistical and knowledge-driven methodologies are very much on the limited side and there are limitations in order to acquire them. The statistical techniques and quantitative methodologies are found to be reliable as these are promising in nature and the landslide identification, prediction and hazard mitigation present the comprehensibility as these are based on the realistic and interpreted data, however the limitations in the availability of credible data makes it effort-worthy techniques. Furthermore, the purpose of investigation, the extent of the study area to be covered, type of landslide, resource availability is to be considered as the potential factors for the same. In the current scenario, the collaboration of quantitative and data-driven techniques has made the landslide susceptibility and zonation mapping a more objective and promising procedure. However, the study for the same is a never-ending process; so good understanding and governing factors are required for the study. The ML techniques are to be collaborated with the remote sensing and GIS methodologies in order to produce comprehensive susceptible maps for the complex natural geo-hazard so that the hazard mitigation and management may be apprehended at local/state/national level.

The following Table 1 gives a comparison among Weight-of-Evidence, Frequency Ratio, Information Value, Logistic Regression for regions in Darjeeling Himalayas

Table 1. Comparison of WoE, FR, IV, LR

Landslide susceptibility classes	WoE		FR		IV		LR	
	Area (in sq. km)	% of Area	Area (in sq. km)	% of Area	Area (in sq. km)	% of Area	Area (in sq. km)	% of Area
Very low	692	21.9	674	21.3	697	22.0	685	21.6
Low	379	12.0	397	12.5	376	11.8	388	12.2
Moderate	813	25.8	811	25.7	820	26.0	828	26.2
High	635	20.2	646	20.5	616	19.6	611	19.2
Very high	630	19.9	621	19.6	640	20.2	637	20.2

References

1. Batar, A., et al.: Assessment of land-use/land-cover change and forest fragmentation in the Garhwal Himalayan region of India. Environments **4**(2), 34–44 (2017). https://doi.org/10.3390/environments4020034
2. Batar, A.K., Watanabe, T.: Landslide susceptibility mapping and assessment using geospatial platforms and weights of evidence (woe) method in the Indian Himalayan Region: recent developments, gaps, and future directions. ISPRS Int. J. Geo-Inf. **10**(3), 114 (2021). https://doi.org/10.3390/ijgi10030114
3. Can, T., et al.: Susceptibility assessments of shallow earthflows triggered by heavy rainfall at three catchments by logistic regression analyses. Geomorphology **72**(1–4), 250–271 (2005). https://doi.org/10.1016/j.geomorph.2005.05.011
4. Casagli, N.: An inventory-based approach to landslide susceptibility assessment and its application to the Virginio River Basin, Italy. Environ. Eng. Geosci. **10**(3), 203–216 (2004). https://doi.org/10.2113/10.3.203
5. Chen, B., et al.: Structural safety evaluation of in-service tunnels using an adaptive neuro-fuzzy inference system. J. Aerospace Eng. **31**(5), 04018073 (2018). https://doi.org/10.1061/(asce)as.1943-5525.0000883

6. Chen, W., et al.: Landslide susceptibility modeling using integrated ensemble weights of evidence with logistic regression and random forest models. Appl. Sci. **9**(1), 171 (2019). https://doi.org/10.3390/app9010171

7. Chimidi, G., et al.: Landslide hazard evaluation and zonation in and around Gimbi town, western Ethiopia – a GIS-based statistical approach. Appl. Geomat. **9**(4), 219–236 (2017). https://doi.org/10.1007/s12518-017-0195-x

8. Corominas, J., et al.: Recommendations for the quantitative analysis of landslide risk. Bull. Eng. Geol. Environ. **73**(2), 209–263 (2013). https://doi.org/10.1007/s10064-013-0538-8

9. Dai, F.C., et al.: Landslide risk assessment and management: an overview. Eng. Geol. **64**(1), 65–87 (2002). https://doi.org/10.1016/s0013-7952(01)00093-x

10. Sunil Kumar, D.E.: Landslides and human interference in Darjiling Himalayas, India. Revista de Geomorfologie **19**(1), 44–57 (2017). https://doi.org/10.21094/rg.2017.014

11. Ding, Q., et al.: Application of frequency ratio, weights of evidence and evidential belief function models in landslide susceptibility mapping. Geocarto Int. **1**, 1–21 (2016). https://doi.org/10.1080/10106049.2016.1165294

12. Erener, A., Düzgün, H.S.B.: Landslide susceptibility assessment: what are the effects of mapping unit and mapping method? Environ. Earth Sci. **66**(3), 859–877 (2011). https://doi.org/10.1007/s12665-011-1297-0

13. Fall, M., et al.: A multi-method approach to study the stability of natural slopes and landslide susceptibility mapping. Eng. Geol. **82**(4), 241–263 (2006). https://doi.org/10.1016/j.enggeo.2005.11.007

14. Geertsema, M., Pojar, J.J.: Influence of landslides on biophysical spanersity – a perspective from British Columbia. Geomorphology **89**(1–2), 55–69 (2007). https://doi.org/10.1016/j.geomorph.2006.07.019

15. Ghosh, S., et al.: A quantitative approach for improving the BIS (Indian) method of medium-scale landslide susceptibility. J. Geol. Soc. India **74**(5), 625–638 (2009). https://doi.org/10.1007/s12594-009-0167-9

16. Glade, T.: Landslide occurrence as a response to land use change: a review of evidence from New Zealand. CATENA **51**(3–4), 297–314 (2003). https://doi.org/10.1016/s0341-8162(02)00170-4

17. Gorsevski, P.V., et al.: Spatial prediction of landslide hazard using logistic regression and ROC analysis. Trans. GIS **10**(3), 395–415 (2006). https://doi.org/10.1111/j.1467-9671.2006.01004.x

18. Gupta, R.P., Joshi, B.C.: Landslide hazard zoning using the GIS approach – a case study from the Ramganga catchment, Himalayas. Eng. Geol. **28**(1–2), 119–131 (1990). https://doi.org/10.1016/0013-7952(90)90037-2

19. Guzzetti, F., et al.: Landslide hazard evaluation: a review of current techniques and their application in a multi-scale study, Central Italy. Geomorphology **31**(1–4), 181–216 (1999). https://doi.org/10.1016/s0169-555x(99)00078-1

20. Guzzetti, F., et al.: Landslide inventory maps: new tools for an old problem. Earth Sci. Rev. **112**(1–2), 42–66 (2012). https://doi.org/10.1016/j.earscirev.2012.02.001

21. Guzzetti, F., et al.: Probabilistic landslide hazard assessment at the basin scale. Geomorphology **72**(1–4), 272–299 (2005). https://doi.org/10.1016/j.geomorph.2005.06.002

22. Haneberg, W.C., et al.: High-resolution LIDAR-based landslide hazard mapping and modeling, UCSF Parnassus Campus, San Francisco, USA. Bull. Eng. Geol. Environ. **68**(2), 263–276 (2009). https://doi.org/10.1007/s10064-009-0204-3

23. Huang, F., et al.: Comparisons of heuristic, general statistical and machine learning models for landslide susceptibility prediction and mapping. CATENA **191**, 104580 (2020). https://doi.org/10.1016/j.catena.2020.104580

24. Kannan, M., et al.: Comparative analysis in GIS-based landslide hazard zonation – a case study in Bodi-Bodimettu Ghat section, Theni District, Tamil Nadu, India. Arab. J. Geosci. **8**(2), 691–699 (2014). https://doi.org/10.1007/s12517-013-1259-9

25. Kanungo, D.P., et al.: A comparative study of conventional, ANN black box, fuzzy and combined neural and fuzzy weighting procedures for landslide susceptibility zonation in Darjeeling Himalayas. Eng. Geol. **85**(3–4), 347–366 (2006). https://doi.org/10.1016/j.eng geo.2006.03.004

26. Keefer, D.K.: Landslides caused by earthquakes. Geol. Soc. Am. Bull. **95**(4), 406 (1984)

27. Kumar, A., Sanoujam, M.: Landslide studies along the national highway (NH 39) in Manipur. Nat. Hazards **40**(3), 603–614 (2006). https://doi.org/10.1007/s11069-006-9024-y

28. Lee, S.: Application and verification of fuzzy algebraic operators to landslide susceptibility mapping. Environ. Geol. **52**(4), 615–623 (2006). https://doi.org/10.1007/s00254-006-0491-y

29. Lee, S., et al.: Determination and application of the weights for landslide susceptibility mapping using an artificial neural network. Eng. Geol. **71**(3–4), 289–302 (2004). https://doi.org/10.1016/s0013-7952(03)00142-x

30. Lee, S., Min, K.: Statistical analysis of landslide susceptibility at Yongin, Korea. Environ. Geol. **40**(9), 1095–1113 (2001). https://doi.org/10.1007/s002540100310

31. Li, X., et al.: Identification of forested landslides using lidar data, object-based image analysis, and machine learning algorithms. Remote Sens. **7**(8), 9705–9726 (2015). https://doi.org/10.3390/rs70809705

32. Li, X., Wang, Y.: Applying various algorithms for species distribution modelling. Integr. Zool. **8**(2), 124–135 (2013). https://doi.org/10.1111/1749-4877.12000

33. Martha, T.R., et al.: Characterizing spectral, spatial and morphometric properties of landslides for semi-automatic detection using object-oriented methods. Geomorphology **116**(1–2), 24–36 (2010). https://doi.org/10.1016/j.geomorph.2009.10.004

34. Martha, T.R., et al.: Landslide hazard and risk assessment using semi-automatically created landslide inventories. Geomorphology **184**, 139–150 (2013). https://doi.org/10.1016/j.geo morph.2012.12.001

35. Martha, T.R., et al.: Object-oriented analysis of multi-temporal panchromatic images for creation of historical landslide inventories. ISPRS J. Photogram. Remote. Sens. **67**, 105–119 (2012). https://doi.org/10.1016/j.isprsjprs.2011.11.004

36. McKean, J., Roering, J.: Objective landslide detection and surface morphology mapping using high-resolution airborne laser altimetry. Geomorphology **57**(3–4), 331–351 (2004). https://doi.org/10.1016/s0169-555x(03)00164-8

37. Filagot Mengistu, K.V., et al.: Landslide hazard zonation and slope instability assessment using optical and InSAR data: a case study from Gidole Town and its surrounding areas, Southern Ethiopia. Remote Sens. Land **3**(1), 1–14 (2019). https://doi.org/10.21523/gcj1.190 30101

38. Meusburger, K., Alewell, C.: Impacts of anthropogenic and environmental factors on the occurrence of shallow landslides in an alpine catchment (Urseren Valley, Switzerland). Nat. Hazards **8**(3), 509–520 (2008). https://doi.org/10.5194/nhess-8-509-2008

39. Mohammady, M., et al.: Landslide susceptibility mapping at Golestan Province, Iran: a comparison between frequency ratio, Dempster-Shafer, and weights-of-evidence models. J. Asian Earth Sci. **61**, 221–236 (2012). https://doi.org/10.1016/j.jseaes.2012.10.005

40. Moosavi, V., et al.: Producing a landslide inventory map using pixel-based and object-oriented approaches optimized by Taguchi method. Geomorphology **204**, 646–656 (2014). https://doi.org/10.1016/j.geomorph.2013.09.012

41. Nandi, A., Shakoor, A.: A GIS-based landslide susceptibility evaluation using bivariate and multivariate statistical analyses. Eng. Geol. **110**(1–2), 11–20 (2010). https://doi.org/10.1016/j.enggeo.2009.10.001

42. Oh, H.-J., Pradhan, B.: Application of a neuro-fuzzy model to landslide-susceptibility mapping for shallow landslides in a tropical hilly area. Comput. Geosci. **37**(9), 1264–1276 (2011). https://doi.org/10.1016/j.cageo.2010.10.012
43. Pachauri, A.K., et al.: Landslide zoning in a part of the Garhwal Himalayas. Environ. Geol. **36**(3–4), 325–334 (1998). https://doi.org/10.1007/s002540050348
44. Pardeshi, S.D., et al.: Landslide hazard assessment: recent trends and techniques. Springerplus **2**(1), 1–11 (2013). https://doi.org/10.1186/2193-1801-2-523
45. Raghuvanshi, T.K., et al.: GIS based grid overlay method versus modeling approach – a comparative study for landslide hazard zonation (LHZ) in Meta Robi District of West Showa Zone in Ethiopia. Egypt. J. Remote Sens. Space Sci. **18**(2), 235–250 (2015). https://doi.org/10.1016/j.ejrs.2015.08.001
46. Raghuvanshi, T.K., et al.: Slope stability susceptibility evaluation parameter (SSEP) rating scheme – an approach for landslide hazard zonation. J. Afr. Earth Sci. **99**, 595–612 (2014). https://doi.org/10.1016/j.jafrearsci.2014.05.004
47. Reichenbach, P., et al.: A review of statistically-based landslide susceptibility models. Earth Sci. Rev. **180**, 60–91 (2018). https://doi.org/10.1016/j.earscirev.2018.03.001
48. Reichenbach, P., Busca, C., Mondini, A.C., Rossi, M.: Land use change scenarios and landslide susceptibility zonation: the briga catchment test area (Messina, Italy). In: Lollino, G., Manconi, A., Clague, J., Shan, W., Chiarle, M. (eds.) Engineering Geology for Society and Territory – Volume 1, pp. 557–561. Springer, Cham (2015). https://doi.org/10.1007/978-3-319-09300-0_104
49. Rowbotham, D.N., Dudycha, D.: GIS modelling of slope stability in Phewa Tal watershed, Nepal. Geomorphology **26**(1–3), 151–170 (1998). https://doi.org/10.1016/s0169-555x(98)00056-7
50. Saha, A.K., et al.: GIS-based landslide hazard zonation in the Bhagirathi (Ganga) valley, Himalayas. Int. J. Remote Sens. **23**(2), 357–369 (2002). https://doi.org/10.1080/01431160010014260
51. Saito, H., et al.: Comparison of landslide susceptibility based on a decision-tree model and actual landslide occurrence: the Akaishi Mountains, Japan. Geomorphology **109**(3–4), 108–121 (2009). https://doi.org/10.1016/j.geomorph.2009.02.026
52. Schuster, R.L., Highland, L.M.: Urban landslides: Socioeconomic impacts and overview of mitigative strategies. Bull. Eng. Geol. Environ. **66**(1), 1–27 (2006). https://doi.org/10.1007/s10064-006-0080-z
53. Shano, L., et al.: Landslide susceptibility evaluation and hazard zonation techniques – a review. Geoenviron. Disast. **7**(1), 1–19 (2020). https://doi.org/10.1186/s40677-020-00152-0
54. Sifa, S.F., et al.: Event-based landslide susceptibility mapping using weights of evidence (WoE) and modified frequency ratio (MFR) model: a case study of Rangamati district in Bangladesh. Geol. Ecol. Landsc. **4**(3), 222–235 (2019). https://doi.org/10.1080/24749508.2019.1619222
55. Sun, D., et al.: Assessment of landslide susceptibility mapping based on Bayesian hyperparameter optimization: a comparison between logistic regression and random forest. Eng. Geol. **281**, 105972 (2021). https://doi.org/10.1016/j.enggeo.2020.105972
56. Tian, Y., et al.: Mapping earthquake-triggered landslide susceptibility by use of artificial neural network (ANN) models: an example of the 2013 Minxian (China) Mw 5.9 event. Geomat. Nat. Hazards Risk **10**(1), 1–25 (2018). https://doi.org/10.1080/19475705.2018.1487471
57. Tien Bui, D., et al.: Spatial prediction models for shallow landslide hazards: a comparative assessment of the efficacy of support vector machines, artificial neural networks, kernel logistic regression, and logistic model tree. Landslides **13**(2), 361–378 (2015). https://doi.org/10.1007/s10346-015-0557-6

58. Tropeano, D., Turconi, L.: Using historical documents for landslide, debris flow and stream flood prevention. Applications in Northern Italy. Nat. Hazards **31**(3), 663–679 (2004). https://doi.org/10.1023/b:nhaz.0000024897.71471.f2

59. Van Beek, L.P.H., Van Asch, T.: Regional assessment of the effects of land-use change on landslide hazard by means of physically based modelling. Nat. Hazards **31**(1), 289–304 (2004). https://doi.org/10.1023/b:nhaz.0000020267.39691.39

60. Van Den Eeckhaut, M., et al.: Object-oriented identification of forested landslides with derivatives of single pulse LiDAR data. Geomorphology **173–174**, 30–42 (2012). https://doi.org/10.1016/j.geomorph.2012.05.024

61. van Westen, C.J., et al.: Landslide hazard and risk zonation – why is it still so difficult? Bull. Eng. Geol. Environ. **65**(2), 167–184 (2005). https://doi.org/10.1007/s10064-005-0023-0

62. Wang, G., et al.: Spatial prediction of landslide susceptibility based on GIS and discriminant functions. ISPRS Int. J. Geo-Inf. **9**(3), 144 (2020). https://doi.org/10.3390/ijgi9030144

63. Wang, H., et al.: Landslide identification using machine learning. Geosci. Front. **12**(1), 351–364 (2021). https://doi.org/10.1016/j.gsf.2020.02.012

64. Xu, C., et al.: GIS-based support vector machine modeling of earthquake-triggered landslide susceptibility in the Jianjiang River watershed, China. Geomorphology **145–146**, 70–80 (2012). https://doi.org/10.1016/j.geomorph.2011.12.040

Enhanced Security and Privacy for IoT Based Locker System Operated at Low Frequency Spectrum Using Blockchain

Soumen Santra[1], Sweta Sharma[1], and Arpan Deyasi[2](✉)

[1] Department of Computer Application, Techno International Newtown, Kolkata 700156, India
[2] Department of Electronics and Communication Engineering, RCC Institute of Information Technology, Kolkata 700015, India
deyasi_arpan@yahoo.co.in

Abstract. Conventional locker system faces continuous threat of breaching of data due to phishing scams, which raises high demand of encryption at server's end. Blockchain based security system provides efficient solution so far either by applying personal signature, or by adopting peer-to-peer network. In the present proposal, security is entrusted by generating new encrypted message from the already received binary information from user's end. The code is incremented at each subsequent step which helps to track the number of times the security door is opened with individual time-stamp along with image capture facility. Corresponding circuit is designed at 433 Hz spectrum where relay is connected with electromagnetic door lock through microcontroller. A novel algorithm is proposed to control cloud-based web server for accessing every HTTP request with NodeJS and a MongoDB database. Enhanced security and privacy can therefore be obtained through low-cost hardware system associated with blockchain feature.

Keywords: Blockchain based security system · Digital signature · Internet of Things · HTTP web server · RF communication · Time-stamp image

1 Introduction

The Internet of Things (IoT) has grown in significance in our data-controlled world as a result of technological innovation [1]. The Internet of Things is essentially a technical amalgamation of intelligent devices with embedded chips, sensors, and actuators that gather information about themselves and their surroundings and communicate it via the Internet [2, 3]. The automation of repetitive chores and subsequent real-time monitoring of equipment and tasks are the biggest benefits that IoTs deliver. These gadgets unfortunately typically have inferior processing capacities, security risks, and are more vulnerable to cyberattacks. Additionally, IoTs produce very sensitive personal data about their users, which is then managed by centralized businesses, raising major privacy and data integrity concerns [4]. Because of the technology that could help IoT devices with their issues, blockchain has just lately become popular [5]. Even in the early stages of its

A. A. Sk et al. (Eds.): ISAI 2022, CCIS 1695, pp. 56–63, 2022.
https://doi.org/10.1007/978-3-031-22485-0_6

development, blockchain has attracted experts from all around the world who recognize the many benefits of this technology.

Smartphones and other embedded devices evolve far more slowly than desktop computers [6]. Due to their weak computing capabilities and small data storage, these quiet devices struggle to process transactions utilizing this blockchain-based system. Instead of using IoT devices for mining, some hardware, such as application-specific microcircuit (ASIC) chips, are created specifically for the purpose. Therefore, while considering the integration of blockchain with IoT, new approaches to overcoming these problems are required. Due to the adoption of blockchain technology, one of the main issues is that IoT devices can only be embedded with so many resources [7, 8]. Work has been carried out using CNN based surveillance model [9] where security is adequately taken care of with image recognition and classification technique. As different applications have different requirements, a replacement or a customized implementation of a blockchain system is required [10].

Design of informative interface is the trend of research for the benefit of civilization which is executed either through voice-controlled mode [11], or for ultra-high frequency sensing purpose [12]. Cloud service is integrated with blockchain for providing secured home service [13]. The same, with IoT enabled circuit, are recently implemented for accident prevention under real-time condition [14]. For visually impaired people, blockchain technology can provide assistance when augmented with microcontroller based low-cost circuit [15] and useful for common people. Secured, data immunable transportation system is very recently proposed with the claim of robust security and transparency [16].

However, implementation of blockchain technology in those cases is difficult owing to the complex circuitry requirement. A few works are reported only in the domain financial transactions [17] and multimedia content protection [18]. In this present work, peer-to-peer security system is investigated and analyzed by designing one smart low-cost system at 433 Hz. To provide an additional security layer, binary information for opening the locker is converted into another cryptic message, and time-stamp will be given for each time when the locker will be opened. For accessing every request, simple yet novel algorithm is proposed with MongoDB database. Results are discussed in the next section along with system architecture, data flow and hardware circuit.

2 System Architecture and Dataflow

Architecture for the proposed smart home security system is described in Fig. 1, It has been found that PIR motion sensor is connected to GPIO pins of microcontroller. LCD monitor is interfaced with Raspberry web server along with mounting of loudspeaker. The Raspberry Pi is connected to a relay driver circuit that uses the IC ULN2003 to control an electromagnetic door lock. On an SD card or USB flash drive linked to the Raspberry Pi, the image that was taken can save the date and time.

Figure 2 shows the flow chart of knowledge communication. Each of the subsequent subsections provides an in-depth explanation of how the devices communicate with one another. The Elegoo board transmits an RF signal from its transmitter to the RF receiver found on the Raspberry Pi at first when the reed switch is open. The Raspberry Pi then issues an HTTP POST request to a cloud-based RESTful web server. The top user can then view the door open events by date and time thanks to this web server, which either pushes information or receives GET requests from an Android application. The following sections mention a number of open-source libraries.

When the door is opened, the reed switch is actuated, and the transmitter sends a 433 Hz RF transmission using the Arduino's RC-switch library. Each time a door is opened after that, a code is sent to the Raspberry Pi receiver, which is increased. This enables the Raspberry Pi to keep track of specific door-opening incidents.

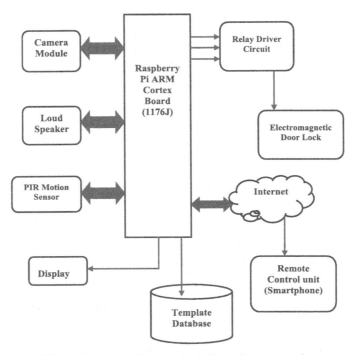

Fig. 1. System architecture for IoT-based smart security

The entire covered area of the home is being monitored by using a simple piece of aluminum (Al) foil as antennas on the receiver and therefore the transmitter when the reed switch is enabled, which sends an uninterrupted stream of binary numbers to the receiver attached to the Raspberry Pi. In order to receive the binary codes, the Raspberry Pi used the 433Utils library and the wiring Pi library. The following stage of the communication process will be carried out by a Python script after it has read the document output containing these codes.

A Python script using the requests library checks the document for brand-new updates every second after the binary codes are received and sent as output to a document. An HTTP web server built with NodeJS and a MongoDB database receives a POST request when replacement code is placed within the page. Door open events will be stored by date and time on this server's RESTful API. The Android application will use GET requests to access the information stored in this database.

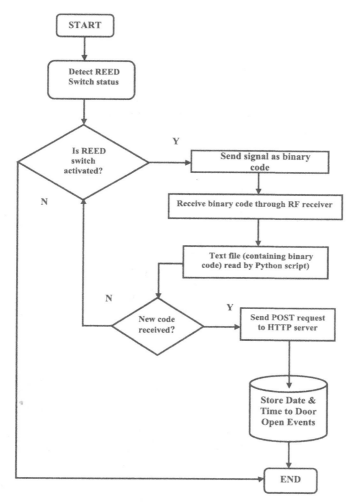

Fig. 2. Flowchart representing data flow through the system

The interaction between internet servers is the last stage of the communication process. But for the purposes of this specific task, the application sends GET requests to the server since it is possible to deliver push notifications whenever a replacement door open event is identified by the online server. The Android application uses a variety of libraries that are accessible through the Android Studio, however the Volley library is the only one that won't process requests.

3 Circuit Design

For the circuit design, Arduino, buzzer, keypad, servo motor, and LCD are considered as major equipments. Arduino is used to control processes like taking a password from the keypad module, comparing passwords, rotating servo motor, driving buzzer, and sending status to the LCD display. The keypad is used for taking passwords. The buzzer is used for indications. The servo motor is used to open the gate while rotating, and the LCD is used for displaying the status or messages on it (Fig. 3).

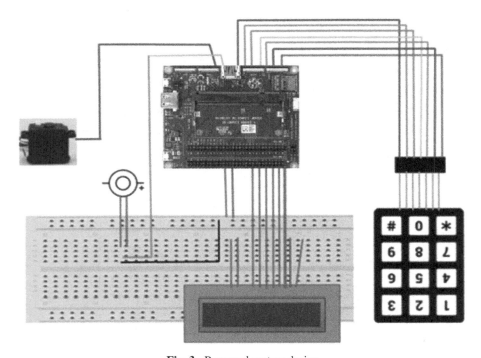

Fig. 3. Proposed system design

4 Proposed Algorithm

The algorithm as proposed is based on the dataflow as mentioned in Fig. 2. In this section, algorithm is described with some arbitrary values, and can be set as per requirement.

STEP 1: Start
STEP 2: Initialize variables
STEP 3: Define a function as unlockdoor()
STEP 4: delay(900), setCursor(0,0), print(" "), setCursor(1,0), print("Access Granted")
STEP 5: setCursor(4,1), print("WELCOME!!"), setCursor(15,1), print(" ")
STEP 6: setCursor(16,1), print(" "), setCursor(14,1), print(" "), setCursor(13,1)
STEP 7: Initialise pos=180
STEP 8: Check for condition(pos>=0)
STEP 9: If condition is true then go to STEP 10 otherwise STEP 13
STEP 10: myservo.write(pos) and delay(5)
STEP 11: Decrease pos by 5
STEP 12: Go to STEP 9
STEP 13: End for loop
STEP 14: delay(2000), delay(1000), counterbeep() and delay(1000)
STEP 15: Initialise pos=0
STEP 16: Check for condition (pos <= 180); pos +=5)
STEP 17: If condition is true then go to STEP 18 otherwise STEP 22
STEP 18: myservo.write(pos), delay(15), lcd.clear() and displayscreen()
STEP 19: Set currentposition=0
STEP 20: Increase pos by 5
STEP 21: Go to STEP 17
STEP 22: End for loop
STEP 23: End function unlockdoor()
STEP 24: Stop

With the aid of this algorithm, we present a decentralised system that enables quick back-and-forth sharing of device information while storing it on a permission-based, secure chain. The suggested architecture would make it easier for the highest user to connect with the blockchain network; different interfaces are developed by leveraging a variety of online front-end technologies. As representational state transfer application programming interfaces (REST APIs), all of the product-specific services offered by the blockchain network can be accessed by both IoT devices and web clients. Users of the gadgets can manage and recall the surrounding environment without being aware of the physical devices beforehand. The smart contract hosts the ledger functionalities over the network and also provides controlled access to the device meta-data. Participants will only be able to access a predetermined number of approved materials or transactions thanks to an access control policy that has been specified within the platform's design.

5   Conclusion

The Hyperledger Fabric, a permission-based decentralized framework created for developing distributed apps (DApps) or distributed ledger solutions on top of it, is used to implement the current blockchain network. A low-cost smart home security system can be created using the current design as a framework. It was able to create an IoT system that allows users of a household to see when a certain door has been opened by using inexpensive components like microcontrollers. The novel algorithm proposed can be applied to any such type of security system at low frequency range through peer-to-peer network with reliable security.

References

1. Khan, M.A., Salah, K.: IoT security: review, blockchain solutions, and open challenges. Future General Computer System **82**, 395–411 (2018)
2. Banerjee, M., Lee, J., Choo, K.K.R.: A blockchain future for the internet of things security. Digit. Commun. Netw. **4**(3), 149–160 (2018)
3. Christidis, K., Devetsikiotis, M.: Blockchains and smart contracts for the web of things. IEEE Access **4**, 2292–2303 (2016)
4. Kuzmin, A.: Blockchain-based structures for a secure and operate IoT, internet of things business models, users, and networks, 23–24 Nov 2017, Copenhagen, Denmark
5. Liu, B., Yu, X.L., Chen, S., Xu, X., Zhu, L.: Blockchain-based data integrity service framework for IoT data. In: IEEE International Conference on Web Services, 25–30 Jun 2017, Honolulu, HI, USA
6. Lee, B., Lee, J.-H.: Blockchain-based secure firmware update for embedded devices in an Internet of Things environment. J. Supercomput. **73**(3), 1152–1167 (2016). https://doi.org/10.1007/s11227-016-1870-0
7. Conoscenti, M., Vetro, A., De Martin, J.C.: Peer to peer for privacy and decentralization in the internet of things. In: IEEE/ACM 39th International Conference on Software Engineering Companion, 20–28 May 2017, Buenos Aires, Argentina
8. Liang, X., Zhao, J., Shetty, D.: Towards data assurance and resilience in IoT using Blockchain. In: IEEE Military Communications Conference, 23–25 Oct 2017, Baltimore, MD, USA
9. Ray, S., Ghosh, S., Bhattacharjee, A., Biswas, R., Ghosh, P., Deyasi, A.: Implementation of semi-autonomous UAV for remote surveillance and emergency reconnaissance using convolutional neural network model. In: 2nd International Conference on Microelectronics, Communication System, Machine Learning & Internet of Things (2021)
10. Pinno, O.J.A., Grigio, A.R.A., De Bona, L.C.E.: Control chain: blockchain as a central enabler for access control authorizations in the IoT. In: IEEE Global Communications Conference, 4–8 Dec 2017, Singapore
11. Santra, S., Mukherjee, P., Deyasi, A.: Cost-effective voice-controlled real-time smart informative interface design with google assistance technology. In: Machine Learning Techniques and Analytics for Cloud Security, Chap. 4 (2022)
12. Nath, A., Roy, L., Shruti, S., Santra, S., Deyasi, A.: Efficient detection of bio-weapons for agricultural sector using narrowband transmitter and composite sensing architecture. In: Convergence of Deep Learning in Cyber-IoT Systems and Security (2022)
13. Liao, K.: Design of the Secure Smart Home System Based on the Blockchain and Cloud Service, Wireless Communications and Mobile Computing, vol. 2022, A. id: 4393314 (2022)
14. Sil, S., Daw, S., Deyasi, A.: Smart intelligent system design for accident prevention and theft protection of vehicle. In: Nath, V., Mandal, J.K. (eds.) Nanoelectronics, Circuits and Communication Systems. LNEE, vol. 692, pp. 523–530. Springer, Singapore (2021). https://doi.org/10.1007/978-981-15-7486-3_47
15. Santra, S., Deyasi, A.: prototype implementation of innovative braille translator for the visually impaired with hearing deficiency. In: Emerging Trends in IoT and Integration with Data Science, Cloud Computing and Big Data Analytics, pp. 272–290 (2022)
16. Das, D., Banerjee, S., Chatterjee, P., Biswas, M., Biswas, U., Alnumay, W.: Design and development of an intelligent transportation management system using blockchain and smart contracts. Clust. Comput. **25**, 1899–1913 (2022). https://doi.org/10.1007/s10586-022-03536-z

17. Hoksbergen, M., Chan, J., Peko, G., Sundaram, D.: Asymmetric information in high-value low-frequency transactions: mitigation in real estate using blockchain. In: Doss, R., Piramuthu, S., Zhou, W. (eds.) FNSS 2019. CCIS, vol. 1113, pp. 225–239. Springer, Cham (2019). https://doi.org/10.1007/978-3-030-34353-8_17
18. Qureshi, A., Jiménez, D.M.: Blockchain-based multimedia content protection: review and open challenges. Appl. Sci. **11**(1), 1–24 (2021)

Genetic Algorithm Based Adaptive PID Tuning of Time Delay Process

Alpana Barman[1], Souvik Dutta[1(✉)], Kamalika Tiwari[2], Soumitra Roy[1], and Santigopal Pain[1]

[1] Haldia Institute of Technology, Haldia, West Bengal 721657, India
souvikdutta77@yahoo.in
[2] Dr. B. C. Roy Engineering College, Durgapur, West Bengal 713206, India

Abstract. Conventional Proportional Integral Derivative controllers are (CPID) unable to provide suitable performance because of large overshoots and oscillations for integrating and nonlinear systems. PID control is extensively used in different control systems, but due to analytically selected parameters K_P, K_I, K_D it is tough to attain parameter optimization. So, it is necessary to use adaptive PID controllers (APID) to get desired performance. Ziegler–Nichols(Z-N) method is a classical method which is used tune the PID parameters in conventional way. It is not easy to tune PID parameters using this method. Ziegler–Nichols tuned PID controller provides better response compare to conventional PID controller. But still there exist some large overshoot and takes more time to damp out oscillations. Natural evolution is represented by Genetic Algorithms (GAs) and for optimization this stochastic global search method is used in this problem. Here, the comparison has been made between PID controller tuned with different standard classical methods along with fuzzy PID (FPID) and proposed genetic algorithm based adaptive PID control (GAPID) technique. It has been found that better response is obtained by adaptive GAPID compare to classical methods and FPID. It is observed that the 2nd order time delay system having delay time L = 0.2 s and L = 0.3 s, GAPID gives minimum rise time and settling time compare to other methods.

Keywords: Time delay process · Adaptive PID · Genetic Algorithm

1 Introduction

The time gap between the starting point of an event and its output in another point is characterized as delay in a control system [1]. It is important to evaluate the performance as well as stability of the system with delay which renowned as transport lag, dead time, time lag etc. Mostly PI and PID controllers are used to get better performance due to their simple construction and less maintenance [2, 3]. It has been observed that in absence of derivative action creates a PID controller simple and less responsive to noise. For more settings of PI controller, usually Ziegler–Nichols proportional Integral Control (ZNPIC) technique is applicable for first and second order system. Sometimes ZNPIC technique is not preferable due to unnecessary oscillation and overshoot [4–6]. PID controllers are widely used in industrial closed loop control now-a-days and ZN tuning is one of the most common approaches for obtaining realistic initial settings for PID controllers. It has been observed that Ziegler-Nichols Proportional Integral Derivative (ZNPID) technique is acceptable for first order system but not able to get suitable performance for high order system [6]. So far several classical methods are implemented to find specific parameters of PI or PID controllers to get desirable output in physical system. It has been seen that Panda et al. [7] proposed a PI controller in which gain values can be scheduled. Here the values of proportional and integral gain can be updated depending on the process error. Weng Khuen Ho et al. (1996) focused on the efficiency and resilience of well-known PID formulas (Ziegler-Nichols, Cohen-Coon, and tuning formulas) for the processes having deadtime between 0.1 and 1 [8]. In 2011, C. Dey et al. reported an auto tuning PID controller All of the PID controller's components are separately updated online by a nonlinear updating factor. In this paper performance and stability robustness of APID are implemented by introducing some disturbances in model and controller parameters [9]. Rajani K. Mudi et al. proposed an augmented Ziegler–Nichols tuned PI controller (AZNPIC) to get better values of system parameters. Because of poor performance of Ziegler–Nichols tuned PI and PID controllers for high order and non-linear system, this AZNPIC is introduced [10]. It is also observed that the performance of AZNPIC is far better than ZNPIC as well as Refined Ziegler–Nichols tuned PI controller (RZNPIC). To resolve this above said issue an improved auto-tuning scheme is implemented for Ziegler–Nichols (ZN) tuned PID controllers (ZNPIDs). To overcome maximum overshoot in high order non-linear system ZNPIDs are upgraded and implemented [11]. In this paper, a comparative study is being observed of augmented Ziegler–Nichols tuned PID controller (AZNPID) for high order linear and non-linear dead-time processes over ZNPID and RZNPID. In spite of quite acceptable output using these classical methods, it will be very difficult to tune for a high order system. It is very complicated to design a suitable PID controller due to large size, more space and huge maintenance for high order system. The complexity of the system is increased due to large structure; nonlinearities present in the system. All the above mentioned conventional classical methodologies are designed for specific type of disturbances and low order system. To overcome above said problems different adaptive control techniques are introduced in days to get satisfactory performance in real life system along with high order system i.e. pure integrating processes with delay (IPD) [12]. Parikshit Kr Paul et al. proposed IMC-PID controller implemented by fuzzy for pure integrating process with delay. Here, the tuning parameters are selected using fuzzy logic to get better performance of a system. It is found that Internal Model Control-PID (IMC-PID) controller delivers an overall enriched performance along with sufficient robustness in its behavior [13]. Solihin, Mahmud et al. [14] employed particle swarm optimization (PSO) technique to enrich the capability of traditional techniques. In this paper, a comparative study has been shown of PSO-PID based technique over ZN-PID. In tune with the above reported PID settings, here a new optimization technique is proposed which will give better result compare to the old techniques of parameter optimization of PID controllers for a linear time delay second order system. These time delay models are often encountered in everyday real life and industrial application especially in process control and others that use a PID controller to control the output. The objective of this work is to show that by employing the GA based PID tuning for a second order time delay system, the best solution can be attained. This is verified by comparing the GAPID optimized plant's outcome to the classically adjusted plant's output like ZNPID, RZNPID, Luyben PID controller (LPID), AZNPI, AZNPID and FPID. It is observed that the adaptive GAPID optimization process gives minimum value of percentage overshoot along with lowest value of settling time having a time delay of L = 0.2 s. Also, by increasing time delay L = 0.3 s, the system performance has been analyzed.

2 PID Controller

Industrial control systems are mainly associated with PID controller. The error value has been calculated by PID controller. The error value is the difference between the desired set point and a measured value and concerns the correction based on proportional, integral and derivative terms. Generally, PID controller is the combination of proportional action, Integral action and Derivative action. PID controller's algorithms are mostly used in feedback systems. The proportional controller compares the desired value with the real value or the value of the feedback process. Whereas, the output is the product of resulting error and proportional constant. It delivers stable operation of a system but always maintains the steady-state error. To eliminate the steady-state error of a system Integral controller is introduced. The error value is integrated over a period of time to make error value zero which introduces a lag in a system. Derivative controller is introduced to predict the future behavior of the error. By compensating lag initiated by P-action, this D-controller improves the stability of a given system.

The PID controller is formed by combining three types of controllers together having the transfer function:

$$C_{PID(S)} = K_D S + K_P + \frac{K_I}{S}. \tag{1}$$

Now the task is to find the optimum value of three parameters: K_P, K_I, K_D by suitable tuning procedure, to build a system which is capable of satisfying the desired performance criteria. This PID controller must be tuned to fit with dynamics of the process to be controlled before the working of the PID controller takes place. In order to achieve the desired output from the controller, many strategies are available such as trial and error, Zeigler-Nichols and several optimization techniques. In this paper, a comparative study is implemented with K_P, K_I and K_D values using different optimization techniques.

Mostly PID controllers are used to their minimal structure and tuning methods. But due to large overshoot and oscillation the conventional PID controllers normally fail to provide satisfactory performance in real life system [15]. To get a desired output of an actual system a number of nonlinear and adaptive PID controllers are being developed and tuning is the most important step for a successful controller design [10]. It has been observed that a good performance of a first order system can be achieved by Ziegler-Nichols tuned PI controller (ZNPIC) but it fails to deliver pleasing output for high order system. Sometimes this ZNPIC of a system is unsatisfactory because of large over-shoot and oscillation [4–6]. It is also observed that Ziegler-Nichols tuned PID controller

(ZNPID) is not desirable in a system due to large overshoot [10]. Similarly, Augmented ZNPID (AZNPID) gives improved performance over ZNPID, refined ZNPID (RZNPID) when it is tested on a second order linear time-delay process.

In this paper the performance of Genetic Algorithm PID controller (GAPID) is experienced and compared with those of ZNPID, RZNPID, AZNPI, AZNPID, FPID and Luyben (LPID) in terms of a number of performance indices like rise time (t_r), percentage overshoot (%OS), Settling time (t_s) and Steady-State Error (SSE).

3 Plant Model

The Plant Transfer Function of time delay process is given as.

$$G_P(s) = e^{-Ls}/(1+s)^2 \tag{1}$$

where L = Delay Time.

Using Padhe's approximation we can write

$$e^{-Ls} = \left(1 - \frac{Ls}{2}\right)/\left(1 + \frac{Ls}{2}\right). \tag{2}$$

and

$$G_P(s) = \left(1 - \frac{Ls}{2}\right)/(1+s)^2\left(1 + \frac{Ls}{2}\right). \tag{3}$$

Here the block diagram of this system with unity negative feedback has been drawn (Fig. 1):

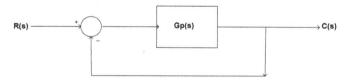

Fig. 1. Block diagram of the plant model with unity negative feedback

The Closed-loop Transfer function by taking L = 0.2 s will be:

$$\frac{C(s)}{R(s)} = \frac{-0.1s + 1}{0.1s^3 + 1.2s^2 + 2s + 2} \tag{4}$$

4 Objective Function or Fitness Function

The objective function has been used for measurement of how individuals have shown performance in the problem domain. When a problem is to be minimized, the fit individuals will have the objective function of minimum numerical value [16]. This raw value of fitness that has been measured is generally used for finding the relative effectiveness of particulars in GA. The objective function value that is transformed into a measure of relative fitness by another function called Fitness Function. In this problem, the maximum fitness values of GA have been calculated for finding the fitter chromosomes. But when it is required to go for the minimization form rather than finding the maximum value, there is need of transformation, a maximization problem to a minimization problem. Here the objective function is inverse of Integral Absolute Error (IAE). The objective function is denoted in Eq. (5). The primary task is to minimize IAE to get optimum solution.

$$F = \frac{1}{\int_0^{\infty} |e(t)| dt} \tag{5}$$

where, F is fitness function and $e(t)$ is error.

5 Proposed Approach

Genetic Algorithms (GAs) are a stochastic global search method that follows the procedure of natural evolution and this method is used for optimization [16]. This method was introduced by John Holland [16]. The genetic algorithm had no starting knowledge of the accurate solution and completely depends on responses from its environment and evolution operators such as selection, crossover and mutation to reach at the exact result. When the algorithm starts at numerous independent points and continue searches in parallel, it doesn't face local minima and sometimes converges to sub optimal solutions [17, 18]. GA have the capability of finding the high-performance areas in complex domains without facing any problem. GAs don't just deal with one possible solution to a problem; they deal with a population of possible alternatives. Chromosomes are the probable solution in the population. Whatever the parameter solution found, these chromosomes are encoded from there. There is a comparison between each and every chromosome in the population and honored by their fitness rating that shows how successful this chromosome to the later [16]. Now to generate new chromosome from the old ones GA will go for crossover and mutation. This is done by either mixing already existed chromosome in the population or by adjusting the current chromosome. The better solution will be achieved when the parent chromosome fitness is taken into account by selection mechanism. It will contribute positive vibes to their offspring. Random population comprising of 20–100 individuals has been considered in GA. Here each chromosome has been represented by a binary string. Every individual has been allotted a corresponding number by the objective function called its fitness. After analyzing the fitness of each and every chromosome, survival of the fittest policy is applied. Here the magnitude of the error is considered to measure fitness of each chromosome. The three important parts of GA are Selection, Crossover and Mutation.

Defining population size is one of the major issues in GA. Sometimes, the population size is decided based on trial and error [19]. The literature survey reveals that in many papers 80 to 100 has been taken as the population size. Here at starting, a population of 100 is considered and the outcome is taken for 50 generation. But, satisfactory result was not found. So, repetition of the process is done with another 50 generations.

Selection: The fitness value is evaluated for each chromosome in selection phase. This value has been applied in the selection process for the individuals to bias which are considered to be fit. As similar to natural evolution, there is a high chance for a fit chromosome to be selected. As a result, the likelihood of an individual being chosen is linked to their fitness, guaranteeing that fitter individuals are more likely to have offspring [20]. Here Stochastic Universal Sampling (SUS) method has been used because of its simplicity. Stochastic Universal Sampling means where individuals are selected randomly from an entire population. Stochastic Universal Sampling method is generally based on Roulette Wheel selection method. Here in SUS multiple pointers has been used for selection. So, by one rotation individuals can be selected.

Crossover: Crossover algorithm will start after selection process is over. In crossover operation there is a swapping of certain parts of two particular strings in a bid to consider better parts of old chromosomes and generate good new ones. Genetic operators directly adjust the behaviour of a chromosome, using the consideration that fitter individuals on average can be produced by certain individual gene codes. The crossover probability shows how frequently crossover operation is executed. A likelihood of 0% indicates that that the offspring will be identical copies of their parents and a probability of 100% implies that each generation will be made up completely of new offspring [16].

Mutation: Selection and crossover will produce a huge quantity of dissimilar strings. Though, two main problems are associated with this:

a) There may not be enough variation in the initial strings to confirm that the GA explores the whole problem space, based on the beginning population chosen. [16].
b) The GA may coincide on sub-optimum strings because of poor starting population selection [16].

So, rectification of these problems may be done by the inclusion of a mutation operator into the GA. In case of a string mutation is the infrequent random change of a value. It is regarded as a contextual operator in the GA. The mutation probability is generally low due to fit strings may be destroyed by a high mutation rate and degrade GA into a random search.

5.1 Genetic Algorithm Summary by Flow Chart

Here the process of GA based adaptive PID tuning method is explained through a flowchart (Fig. 2).

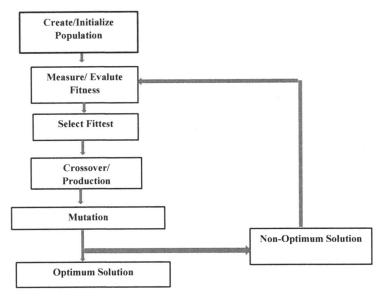

Fig. 2. Genetic Algorithm process flowchart

The steps that are involved in generating and executing the control gains of PID using GA are:

I.   Generate a fixed size initial and arbitrary population of individuals.
II. Assess their fitness.
III. Members that are fittest, selected from the population.
IV. Regenerate chromosomes using a probabilistic method that is roulette wheel, SUS etc.
V.   Apply crossover procedure for the regeneration of chromosomes
VI. Perform mutation procedure having less possibility.
VII. Start repeating from step II until a prespecified convergence criterion is achieved.

GA having the stopping criterion, is a manipulator stated criteria. The optimum solution is obtained when the string fitness value exceeds a specified threshold or when the maximum number of generations is reached.

Elitism: In case of crossover and mutation process, there are huge chances that the best solution can't be achieved. The fittest string will be preserved by these operators, there is no assurance about that. The elitism models are preferred to avoid this. Here, the best individual is saved from a population before taking place of these operations. When a new population is designed and assessed, this model will go for examining to check if this best structure has been well-kept-up and if it is not satisfied the kept copy is reinjected into the population. The Genetic Algorithm will then resume as usual.

6 Result Analysis

In this program the population size of 100 is formed by creating a 2D matrix, taking 100 rows and 24 columns (8 bits for each of the three parameters K_P, K_I, K_D). Actually, this matrix is a decoded version of the real values of K_P, K_I, K_D as Canonical Genetic Algorithm (CGA) is used. Here Strings or chromosomes, which were initially intended as binary illustrations of solution vectors, make up the population members. So, there is a need to make a subroutine which will convert the real set of values into binary digits and vice versa. Here 2nd order linear process having some time delay L = 0.2 s has been considered. The required subroutines are called on for the entire population of 100 rows. This procedure is continued for 50 Generations. Since best solution is still not achieved the whole procedure is repeated for further 50 Generation. Here 2-point crossover with probability of 0.7, and mutation with a probability of 0.01 has been used. Here the plant has high rise time and steady state error.

Comparative study of the newly formed system, PID controller tuned using GA with the system formed earlier by using PID controller tuned with Ziegler Nichol's method is given bellow (Fig. 3, Table 1)).

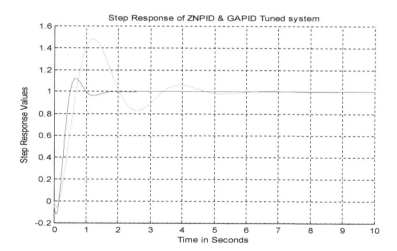

Fig. 3. Comparison of the unit step responses of two systems for L = 0.2 s

Table 1. Different parameters of the plant where PID controller tuned with Z-N method and PID controller tuned with GA method

Specifications	PID tuned with Ziegler Nichol's	PID tuned with GA
Rise time (sec)	0.6900	0.5
% Overshoot	47.97	11.97
Settling time (sec)	5.41	1.47

So, after comparing the performance of the two systems, GA based optimization of PID gives more satisfactory result with respect to PID tuned with Ziegler Nichol's method. There is a decrease in rise time, percentage overshoot, settling time in case of GA-PID (Fig. 4, Table 2).

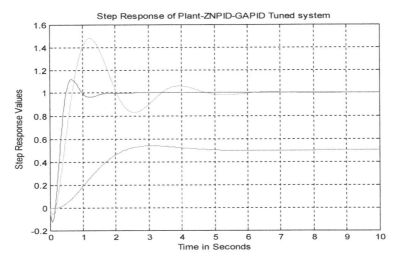

Fig. 4. Comparison of the unit step responses of three systems for L = 0.2 s

Table 2. Different parameters of the plant where PID controller tuned with Z-N classical methods, Fuzzy PID and PID controller tuned with GA method

Specifications	Plant	ZNPID	RZNPID [11]	LPID [11]	AZNPI [11]	AZNPID [11]	FPID [21]	GAPID
Rise time (sec)	2.28	0.69	1.50	1.60	2.30	1.30	2.4	0.5
% Overshoot	7.77	47.97	11.40	0.00	4.04	0.56	30.3	11.97
Settling time (sec)	4.48	5.41	3.90	10.90	2.60	1.60	13.1	1.47
SSE	0.5	0	0	0	0	0	0	0

Here, from the above table it has been observed that the response of the system is improved with the addition of a PID controller tuned with Ziegler Nichol's classical methods, with respect to rise time of the overall system performance (except AZNPI) when subjected to a unit step input. However, this addition of PID controller has introduced high oscillations and instability in the system, which is extremely undesirable. To compensate this or to improve the system performance, the PID controller is tuned with a new technique using Genetic Algorithm. This newly tuned PID controller when added to the existing system shows remarkable improvements in the overall system performance and the drawback of the earlier system i.e. a high percentage overshoot is reduced to a great extent. The settling time is also reduced by a considerable amount. Finally, the efficiency of the system is also improved. In the field of time-delay system the faster the response to reach stability, the better is the design for the plant. Here in case of ZNPID optimum results have been found with control gains $K_p = 6.6$, $K_i = 6.6438$ and $K_d = 1.6401$ and in case of GAPID best result has been found when the value of $K_p = 6.6447$, $K_i = 3.3247$ and $K_d = 3.7153$.

The performance of adaptive GAPID is also studied by taking time delay L = 0.3 s. The result is shown below (Fig. 5, Table 3).

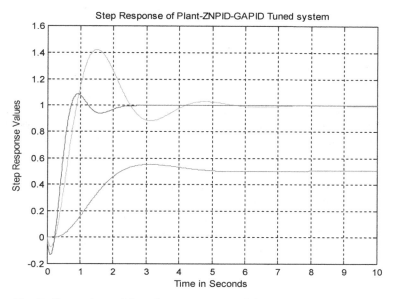

Fig. 5. Comparison of the unit step responses of three systems for L = 0.3 s

Table 3. Different parameters of the plant where PID controller tuned with Z-N classical methods, fuzzy PID and PID controller tuned with GA method

Specifications	Plant	ZNPID	RZNPID [11]	LPID [11]	AZNPI [11]	AZNPID [11]	FPID [22]	GAPID
Rise time (sec)	2.28	0.89	1.30	1.30	2.40	1.10	2.3	0.72
% Overshoot	10.01	42.02	26.40	6.60	5.98	12.27	32.7	8.73
Settling time (sec)	4.59	5.29	5.60	6.60	5.90	4.20	17.2	2.1
SSE	0.5	0	0	0	0	0	0	0

From the above table it has been observed that as the time delay increases from 0.2 to 0.3, there is an increase of percentage overshoot and settling time of the plant. These can be handled sensibly by incorporating PID controller tuned with Ziegler Nichol's classical methods but still the percentage of overshoot and the value of settling time is high. So, system performance has been improved remarkably by incorporating evolutionary adaptive control algorithm that is GAPID. It has been observed from the table that the rise time, maximum overshoot and settling time obtained using GAPID are considerably low compare to different classical ZNPID tuning techniques and FPID. It is also been observed from the response characteristics that the system stability is also improved using GAPID technique.

7   Conclusion

The results reveal that the proposed PID with GA responds substantially faster than the traditional approaches (classical methods). The classical methods are good for determining the PID parameters. Though, the approach for finding the PID values utilizing the classical methods is painful. There are many cumbersome steps need to follow to get the exact PID control gain. In order to see and evaluate how the system responsiveness improves, an optimal method is used to modify the PID parameters. This is accomplished by putting the GA into action. This GA designed PID is much better in terms of the rise time, the settling time and percentage overshoot compared to other methods. Servo-based position control is a common issue in a wide range of industrial operations. This GAPID technique can be implemented on a servo-based position control system to get better performance. This method can also be used in many other time delay processes. The limitation of this algorithm is that the exact values of different controlling parameters may not found. Only optimal solutions are achieved which are good for smooth functioning of the system.

References

1. O' Dwyer, A.: The estimation and compensation of processes with time delays. Ph.D., Thesis, School of Electronic Engineering, Dublin City University (1996)
2. Shinsky, F.G.: Process Control Systems Application, Design, and Tuning. McGraw-Hill, New York (1998)
3. Bissel, C.: Control Engineering. Chapman and Hall, New York (1994)
4. Astrom, K.J., Hang, C.C., Person, P., Ho, W.K. : Towards intelligent PID control. Automatica **28**(1), 1–9 (1992)
5. Basilio, J.C., Matos, S.R.: Design of PI and PID controllers with transient performance specification. IEEE Trans. Educ. **45**(4), 364–370 (2002)
6. Hang, C.C., Astrom, K.J., Ho, W.K.: Refinements of Ziegler-Nichols tuning formula. IEEE Proc-D **138**(2), 111–118 (1991)
7. Panda, S.K., Lim, J.M.S., Dash, P.K., Lock, K.S..: Gain scheduled PI speed controller for PMSM Drive. In: Proc. IEEE industrial electronics society international conference IECON'97, vol. 2, pp. 925–30 (1997)
8. Ho, W.K., Gan, O.P., Tay, E.B., Ang, E.L.: Performance and gain and phase margins of well-known PID tuning formulas. IEEE Trans. Contr. Syst. Technol. **4**(4), 473–477 (1996)
9. Dey, C., Mudi, R.K., Simhachalam, D.: An auto-tuning PID controller for integrating plus dead-time processes. Adv. Mater. Res. **403–408**, 4934–4943 (2011)

10. Mudi, R.K., Dey, C., Lee, T.T.: An improved auto-tuning scheme for PI controllers. ISA Trans. **47**(1), 45–52 (2008)
11. Dey, C., Mudi, R.K.: An improved auto-tuning scheme for PID controllers. ISA Trans. **48**(4), 396–409 (2009)
12. Chidambaram, M., Padma Sree, R.: A simple method of tuning PID controllers for integrator dead-time processes. Comput. Chem. Eng. **27**(2), 211–215 (2003)
13. Paul, P.K., Dey, C., Mudi, R.K.: Design of fuzzy based IMC-PID controller for IPD process. In: International Symposium on Computational and Business Intelligence (2013)
14. Solihin, M., Tack, L., Moey, L.K.: Tuning of PID controller using particle swarm optimization (PSO). In: Proceeding of the International Conference on Advanced Science, Engineering and Information Technology, 1. https://doi.org/10.18517/ijaseit.1.4.93 (2011)
15. Verma, S., Mudi, R.K.: Genetic algorithm-based adaptive PID CONTROLLER. In: Jain, L.C., Patnaik, S., Ichalkaranje, N. (eds.) Intelligent Computing, Communication and Devices. AISC, vol. 308, pp. 57–64. Springer, New Delhi (2015). https://doi.org/10.1007/978-81-322-2012-1_7
16. Meena, D.C., Devanshu, A.: Genetic algorithm tuned PID controller for process control. In: International Conference on Inventive Systems and Control (ICISC-2017)
17. Wang, Q., Spronck, P., Tracht, R..: An overview of genetic algorithms applied to control engineering problems. In: Proceedings of the Second Conference on Machine Learning and Cybernetics (2003)
18. Skogestad, S.: Probably the best simple PID tuning rules in the world. J. Process Control (2001)
19. Luke, S., Balan, G.C., Panait, L.: Population implosion in genetic programming. Department of Computer George Mason University (2003)
20. Giriraj Kumar, S.M., Ravishankar, R., Radha Krishnan, T.K., Dharmalingam, V., Ananthara-man, N.: Genetic algorithms for level control in a real time process, Oct. (2008)
21. Mitra, P., Dey, C., Mudi, R.K.: Dynamic set-point weighted fuzzy PID controller. In: International Symposium on Computational and Business Intelligence (2013)
22. Mitra, P., Dey, C., Mudi, R.K.: Fuzzy rule-based set point weighting for fuzzy PID controller. SN Appl. Sci. **3**(6), 1–34 (2021). https://doi.org/10.1007/s42452-021-04626-0

Hybridization of Sine-Cosine Algorithm with K-Means for Pathology Image Clustering

Krishna Gopal Dhal[1(✉)], Rebika Rai[2], Arunita Das[1], and Tarun Kumar Ghosh[3]

[1] Department of Computer Science and Application, Midnapore College (Autonomous), Paschim Medinipur, , Midnapore, West Bengal, India
krishnagopal.dhal@midnaporecollege.ac.in
[2] Department of Computer Applications, Sikkim University, GangtokSikkim, India
rrai@cus.ac.in
[3] Department of Computer Science and Engineering, Haldia Institute of Technology, West Bengal, Haldia, India

Abstract. The imperative source of diagnostic and prognostic information is pathology image and obtaining an entirely labeled pathology datasets is often challenging. However, with the arrival of whole slide scanner technologies, pathology slides are been digitized making it imaginable and feasible to accumulate and investigate digital pathology images making use of computer systems. Nuclei segmentation is the primary step in quantitative analysis of imaging data and a significant step in cancer analysis, diagnosis and classifying as it extremely hinges on the quality of segmented nuclei. The traditional K-Means algorithm has been gradually mounting since the year 1957 after the partitional clustering procedure was announced. A new era in the field of cluster analysis commenced as the nature inspired metaheuristics were applied and merged with various forms of existing clustering approaches resulting in several novel algorithms that is being widely used and accepted. With this motivation in mind, the proposed work aims in designing and developing improved hybrid procedures for visual information extraction and clustering using Nature Inspired Optimization Algorithm (NIOA) and Machine Learning techniques that takes full advantage of the solving power of underlying Sine Cosine (SC) and K-Means (KM) algorithms. The proposed hybrid Sine Cosine-K-Means algorithm (SC-KM) has been developed to surmount the demerits of SC and KM algorithms in a significant manner for pathology image clustering. Further, the SC-KM is additionally compared with traditional K-Means, Genetic Algorithm (GA), Particle Swarm Optimization (PSO), and Sine Cosine (SC) algorithm and delivers superior results compared to other tested clustering models.

Keywords: Clustering · Image segmentation · Pathology image · Swarm computing · Metaheuristic · Optimization · Machine learning · Sine-cosine · K-means · Genetic algorithm · Particle swarm optimizer

1 Introduction

In disease diagnostic decision-making, digital pathology images showcase a promising role since it is capable of offering priceless data for Computer-Aided Diagnosis (CAD),

A. A. Sk et al. (Eds.): ISAI 2022, CCIS 1695, pp. 76–86, 2022.
https://doi.org/10.1007/978-3-031-22485-0_8

thus permitting numerical investigation of digital images with high throughput processing rate [1, 2]. Image processing-based study of digital pathology facilitates rapid and repeatable image analysis thereby attracting researchers from several research vicinities to explore and exploit the field. Manual image analysis of digital pathology images, in particular, is a tenacious process because of its complexity, which can lead to considerable inter-observer differences. CAD, on the other hand, can significantly lessen bias and provide precise illness classification [1]. Furthermore, critical prerequisite in CAD is nothing but an accurate segmentation, which is traditionally assumed to be the commencement of automated image analysis. It aids in a variety of quantitative studies, including shape, size, texture, and other imagenomics [1, 2]. Efficiently and accurately accomplishing the pathological image segmentation though remains a greater challenge due to several factors such as disturbances, hazy regions, inadequate disparity amid foreground and background, significant differences in cell volume, morphology, and internal brightness variability [1, 2].Amongst several image segmentation technique's including clustering, neural network, thresholding; clustering based methods are gaining utmost importance in recent years due to its efficiency and pleasant performance in considerable and diverse class of image domain.

Clustering being an unsupervised method in the field of Machine learning wherein data with identical properties are analyzed, detected and thereby grouped together [3]. Various clustering approaches, namely Mean Shift, K-means, Hierarchical, and DB Scan clustering, are available in the literature and can be practically implemented. K-means, a hard clustering centroid-based technique wherein one pixel may only fit to one group, is the most straightforward and effectual of all clustering procedures available. Nonetheless, due to the random initialization of centers and it being an efficient local optimizer, K-means has an ultimate drawback of effortlessly getting stuck into local optima. Institutively, Nature-Inspired Optimization Algorithms (NIOA) can be efficaciously employed to overcome the cluster center initialization problem, one of the limitations of the K-means algorithm in determining globally optimum clusters. NIOA based clustering has been proficiently exploited for image clustering specifically for medical image segmentation. For instance, a modified Cuckoo Search (CS) [4] based crisp clustering model had been developed that provided exclusive aftermath when compared to traditional CS, PSO, Bat algorithm (BA), Firefly algorithm (FA), and other prevailing modified CS-based clustering models. Traditional CS [5] also exhibited its operative enactment in the breast histology image clustering domain by surpassing classical K-means. A modified Flower Pollination Algorithm (FPA) [6] based clustering model was correspondingly purported in the area of pathology image segmentation and in that regard, experimental results evidenced that the proposed modified FPA delivered superior outcomes compare to several well-established NIOA like BA, FA, PSO, etc. Stochastic Fractal Search (SFS) based crisp clustering technique had been utilized for the accurate segmentation of White Blood Cells (WBC) from the blood pathology images of leukemia patients [7]. Numerical results illustrated that the SFS offered nonpareil outcomes in contrast to other tested NIOA and various other state-of-the-art image clustering approaches. Dash et. al. [8], alternatively instigated Seeker optimization (SO), Artificial Bee Colony (ABC), Ant Colony Optimization (ACO), and Particle Swarm Optimization (PSO) based on crisp and fuzzy clustering techniques for the optimal lesion segmentation and established pleasing outcomes. In [9, 10], researchers correspondingly suggested and claimed that the NIOA with K-means could be an improved possibility to implement clustering-based image segmentation practices. Das et. al. [11] proposed a histogram-based noise-robust crisp image clustering approach based on SFS and morphological reconstruction. The proposed clustering approach delivered satisfactory outcomes for white blood cell segmentation. Few basic hybrid clustering strategies based on K-means and NIOA has also been developed since NIOA alone suffers from the trade-off between global (exploration) and local (exploitation) search. Essentially, the important factor in NIOA that greatly helps in the global search performance is randomization. Henceforth, KM can be fused with NIOA during clustering as a local search component as KM is famed for its greedy nature [12] and as well-being a competent local optimizer. Therefore, NIOA is offered with a well-balanced exploration as well as exploitation abilities with the help of randomization concept for global search and traditional clustering based local search mechanism. For instance, Li et. al. [13] established a PSO based K-Means algorithm for image segmentation wherein the K-Means algorithm is initialized by feeding the global best solution. Experimental analysis showed outstanding results and also highlighted how the procedure was capable of over powering the limitation of effortlessly getting stuck into local optimum. Nanda et. al. [14] implemented K-Means algorithm keeping the number of iterations fixed, thereby utilizing its output into individual population of the Galactic Swarm Optimization (GSO) algorithm. Investigational results exhibited the supremacy of the proposed approach as and when compared to classical GSO algorithm in the field of image segmentation. Hrosik et. al. [15] established an improvised image clustering technique using the concept incorporated in the Firefly algorithm wherein the solutions obtained are subsequently enhanced making use of K-means clustering algorithm. Experimental results showed that the proposed approach is authoritative over conventional KM and NIOA. Therefore, based on the various paper surveyed, it can be inferred that the hybridization of KM and NIOA shows considerably superior means of clustering. Encouraged from such hybridization approaches, the study highlighted in this paper tends to present a hybrid image clustering technique constructed using KM and one of the competent NIOA called Sine-Cosine (SC) algorithm [16]. The proposed method is used aptly to segment the nucleus from the hematology images. So as to authenticate the efficacy of the proposed strategy, experiments based on real datasets are performed. In the experiments demonstrated in this paper, the anticipated hybridization technique gives superior outcomes to classical SC, PSO, and KM algorithms. The same is emphasized by recording the center values, fitness values, and execution times. Further, ground truth-based performance evaluation parameters namely, Accuracy (AC), Dice Index (DI), Jaccard Index (JI), and Matthews Correlation Coefficient (MCC) [25] are used to evaluate the performance of the tested clustering techniques.

The rest of the paper is systematized as follows: The basic methodology taken into consideration is depicted in Sect. 2 whereas the experimental results are highlighted in Sect. 3. The paper is further concluded in Sect. 4.

2   Methodology

The research interrogation on how finely to group data has constantly been a challenge. K-means (KM) [12] is one of the prevalent exploratory data analysis algorithms that tend to commonly converge towards local optima and at times produce empty clusters. Though considered as one of the powerful local optimizers however, its performance suggestively relies on the initial cluster centers selection. In order to overcome the specified problem, researchers have been fascinated towards Nature Inspired Optimization Algorithms (NIOA) that are designed to work with disparate data points and converges towards global optima. It chiefly possesses global exploration ability and employs the same to solve several problems ranging from medical image processing to Fault Detection of Induction Machines to multi-thresholding image segmentation [17, 18]. However, several NIOA suffers from the trade-off between exploration and exploitation [17–19]. This arises a need of an efficient NIOA, which instead should be an amalgamation of exploration (global search) and exploitation (local search).Thereby, this study focuses deeply on blending NIOA and KM to constitute an influential yet powerful hybrid clustering strategy wherein the major objective of KM will be to perform the local search around the solutions propagated by NIOA. Henceforth, a well-balanced exploration and exploitation will be assimilated in promoting a hybrid strategy.

The Sine Cosine Algorithm (SCA) [16] is a contemporary NIOA and a meta-heuristic algorithm inspired by the trigonometric sine and cosine functions' properties and is extensively used to solve optimization problems thereby gaining lots of attention, attracting several researchers and academician from several research areas. Khrissi et. al. [20] developed a SCA based image clustering model and has acquired acceptable and satisfactory outcomes. However, it is reported in [21] that, though SCA has fine exploration potential but somehow suffers from exploitation capability. Therefore, based on the study and focusing on the flaws of SCA in regard to its exploitation ability, this paper aims to utilize SCA and KM thus performing both exploration and exploitation in the proposed hybrid clustering strategy named as Sine Cosine-K-Means (SC-KM) Algorithm. In the presented clustering framework, the found solutions of SCA are improved by one iteration in each generation using KM. The pseudocode of the SC-KM has been highlighted as Algorithm 1.

Algorithm 1. Pseudocode of Hybrid Sine-Cosine with K-Means Algorithm (SC-KM).

Parameter Used	M *(Total Population size);* N_{iter} *(Maximum number of iterations);* C *(Control parameter);* R_1, R_2, R_3, R_4 *(Random numbers);* t, i, j *(Looping variables);* $P_{i,j}^t$ *(placement of the search agent at the* i^{th} *dimension after the* t^{th} *iteration);* P_i *(Placement of destination point at* i^{th} *dimension);* P_{Best} *(Best Solution of the population);* $|\ |$ *indicates the absolute value;* $F(P_i)$ *(Fitness for the population* P_i *);*
Step 1	**Set initial parameters:** M, N_{iter}, C; $(R_1, R_2, R_3, R_4)=0$;
Step 2	**Generate:** *Population,* $P=P_1, P_2, P_3, P_4, ..., P_M$}; C; R_4
Step 3	**Calculate:** The Fitness $F(P_i)$ and the best solution P_{Best} of the population
(1)	*for* $t=1$: N_{iter}
(2)	$\quad R_1=C\ (1-t\ /\ N_{iter})$
(3)	$\quad for\ i=1$: M
(4)	$\quad\quad for\ j=1$: d
(5)	$\quad\quad\quad R_2=(2^*\Pi)*rand\ ()$
(6)	$\quad\quad\quad R_3=(2-t\ /\ N_{iter})*rand\ ()$
(7)	$\quad\quad\quad if\ (R_4<0.5)$
(8)	$\quad\quad\quad\quad P_{i,j}^t \leftarrow P_{i,j}^t + R_1.sin(R_2).\left|R_3.P_{Best,j}^t - P_{i,j}^t\right|$
(9)	$\quad\quad\quad else$
(10)	$\quad\quad\quad\quad P_{i,j}^t \leftarrow P_{i,j}^t + R_1.cos(R_2).\left|R_3.P_{Best,j}^t - P_{i,j}^t\right|$
(11)	$\quad\quad\quad end\ if$
	Improve solution by using one iteration based K-Means (KM) algorithm
(12)	$\quad\quad\quad\quad P_{i,j}^{KM} = KM\ (P_{i,j}^t)$
(13)	$\quad\quad\quad\quad if\ F(P_{i,j}^{KM}) < F(P_{i,j}^t)$
(14)	$\quad\quad\quad\quad\quad P_{i,j}^t = P_{i,j}^{KM}$
(15)	$\quad\quad\quad else$
(16)	$\quad\quad\quad\quad\quad P_{i,j}^t = P_{i,j}^t$
(17)	$\quad\quad\quad end\ if$
(18)	$\quad\quad end\ for$
	Cross-Border Processing for $P_{i,j}^t$
	Calculate the fitness $F(P_i)$
(19)	$\quad\quad if\ F(P_i) < F(P_{Best})$
(20)	$\quad\quad\quad P_{Best}=P_i$
(21)	$\quad\quad\quad F(P_{Best})=F(P_i)$
(22)	$\quad\quad end\ if$
(23)	$\quad end\ for$
(24)	$end\ for$
Output	P_{Best}: *The best Solution*

The objective function of the proposed crisp clustering approach is developed as follows:

Suppose, an image (I) having N number pixels and L number of gray levels is to be segmented into K clusters wherein the image I is considered as a data point set of pixels, $\mathbf{z}_p$ indicates the d components of pixel p, d designates the number of spectral bands existing in image I i.e. dimension of the problem, then the objective/fitness function is formulated as follows: [For gray and RGB color image, d = 1 and d = 3]

$$J = \underset{K}{argmin} \sum_{i=1}^{N} \sum_{j=1}^{K} u_{ij} \|\mathbf{z}_p^i - \mathbf{m}_j\|^2 \tag{1}$$

where, $\| \cdot \|$ is an inner product-induced norm in d dimensions which measures the distance among i^{th} pixel $\mathbf{z}_p^i$ and j^{th} cluster center $\mathbf{m}_j$. Membership $u_{ij} = 1$ for pixel $\mathbf{z}_p^i$ if it belongs to cluster C_j; otherwise, $u_{ij} = 0$.

Further, minimization is performed using two distinct steps. Firstly, the objective function J w.r.t. u_{ij} by considering the fixed $\mathbf{m}_j$ needs to be minimized. Secondly, the objective function J w.r.t. $\mathbf{m}_j$ by considering the fixed u_{ij} is minimized. The two steps of minimization as discussed above, is depicted below:

$$\frac{\partial J}{\partial u_{ij}} = \sum_{i=1}^{N} \sum_{j=1}^{K} \| \mathbf{z}_p^i - \mathbf{m}_j \|^2$$

$$\Rightarrow u_{ij} = \begin{cases} 1 \text{ if } j = \underset{k}{\operatorname{argmin}} \| \mathbf{z}_p^i - \mathbf{m}_k \|^2 \\ 0 \qquad\qquad \text{otherwise} \end{cases} \tag{2}$$

[Note: The pixels need to be assigned to the closest cluster where the closeness is measured by the distance between the concerned pixel and cluster centers. This is the main idea of KM and its algorithm can be found in [11, 12]].

3 Experimental Results

With the intention to verify the efficiency of the logical model of the proposed novel hybrid clustering strategy, experiment is conducted. 100 blood pathology images are taken into consideration for performing the experiment. Further, MatlabR2018b, Windows-7 OS, x64-based PC, Intel Core i5 CPU with 8 GB RAM are the hardware and software requirements incorporated during the experiment. The proposed algorithm is tested using the images gathered from well-known ALL-IDB dataset [22]. Leukemia is a common type of blood cancer wherein the disproportionate production of leucocytes substitutes normal blood cells causing several problems. Appropriate nucleus segmentation from White Blood Cell of the pathology images is imperative for Acute Lymphoblastic Leukemia (ALL) patients as automatic blood cell morphology analysis in Computer-Assisted Diagnosis (CAD) technique needs to be performed. The two versions (ALL-IDB1 and ALL-IDB2), both of which focuses on segmentation and classification is what ALL-IDB database is divided into. Further, the proposed hybrid Sine Cosine with K-Means (SC-KM) has been compared with classical Sine Cosine algorithm (SCA) [16], Particle Swarm Optimizer (PSO) [23], Genetic Algorithm (GA) [24], and K-Means (KM) [12].

The parameter settings for the above-mentioned clustering algorithms are as follows:

In case of PSO, the consequence of local and global best solution over the current solution is controlled by the acceleration coefficients and the same can be denoted fondly as c_1 and c_2. Here, both c_1 and c_2 are set to 2 with population size of 50.

For SCA and SC-KM, a as 2 and population size of 50 has been taken into account during the experiment.

Similarly, crossover rate of 0.8 with mutation probability of 0.001 and population size of 30 is taken into consideration for GA.

For KM, the procedure needs to be stopped if at all the changes in centroid values is smaller than $\eta = 10^{-5}$. For each NIOA based clustering algorithm the stop criterion has been taken as maximum number of iteration which is set to 200. Number of cluster is set to 4 for the clustering algorithms.

Four ground truth-based performance evaluation parameters namely, Accuracy (AC), Dice Index (DI), Jaccard Index (JI), and Matthews Correlation Coefficient (MCC) [25] are used to calculate to evaluate the performance of the utilized clustering techniques. The higher values of these quality parameters replicate the better segmentation.

The segmentation outcomes for the proposed SC-KM along with other algorithms that has been tested have been highlighted in Figs. 1 and 2. Because of the random nature of the utilized clustering algorithms, they have been executed 30 times for every image and the corresponding best runs are recorded. The center values, fitness values, and execution times for Fig. 1 and Fig. 2 are documented in Table 1. The fitness values generated, indicate the optimization superiority of the SC-KM over SCA, PSO, GA, and KM. Whereas, KM associates with least computational effort among all. It may also be observed that integration of KM into SCA does not make it so computational expensive compare to other tested NIOA based clustering models. The nucleus segmentation efficiency of the employed clustering algorithms has been measured, calculating the ground truth-based quality parameters namely accuracy, MCC, Dice, and Jaccard indices which are tabulated in Table 2. It is to be noted that, the ground truth images for the tested images have been manually prepared by the experts. Visual and numerical analysis of the segmented outcomes clearly demonstrate that the proposed SC-KM provides competitive outcomes compare to other tested NIOA and KM. GA confers worst outcomes among NIOA based segmentation models. Whereas, KM is the worst among all. As a consequence, it can be said that NIOA can be an efficient alternative to classical clustering algorithm. Results also show that classical PSO gives better results than SCA in this image clustering field. But, incorporation of KM into SCA makes it superior to PSO. Therefore, it is also true that hybridization of NIOA make them better in the optimization field however, it solely depends on the way hybridization is performed. A nonparametric significance proof test popularly known as the Wilcoxon's rank test [26] is used to check and verify the superiority of the SC-KM.

Such proof permits evaluating differences in results between two associated methods. Wilcoxon's rank test is basically performed to determine how significantly [with 5% significance level] the results attained by the finest performing algorithm differ from the concluding outcomes of remaining of the competitors. A p-value lesser than 0.05 (5% significance level) strongly supports the rejection of the null hypothesis signifying that the results differs significantly when the best algorithm is compared to other peer algorithms and further the difference has not arisen by chance. The p-values generated by Wilcoxon's test aimed at a pairwise evaluation of the fitness function amongst two groups designed as SC-KM vs. SCA, SC-KM vs. PSO, and SC-KM vs. GA is highlighted in Table 3. All p-values reported in Table 3 are less than 0.05 (5% significance level) which is solid evidence against the null hypothesis, indicating that the SC-KM fitness values for the performance are statistically better, and it has not occurred by chance.

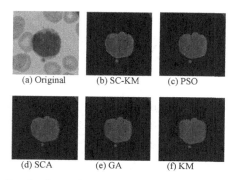

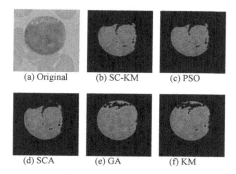

Fig. 1. Results for nucleus segmentation over first ALL image

Fig. 2. Results for nucleus segmentation over second ALL image

Table 1. Fitness and execution time for Fig. 1 and Fig. 2

Algorithms	For Fig. 1		For Fig. 2	
	Fitness	Time (sec.)	Fitness	Time (sec.)
SC-KM	**5.15E+03**	50.66	**5.69E+03**	49.72
PSO	7.48E+03	48.36	5.71E + 03	47.94
SCA	9.79E+03	45.03	5.74E+03	46.88
GA	1.09E+04	54.35	9.63E+03	53.70
KM	–	**8.77**	–	**7.88**

Table 2. Quality parameters for clustering techniques for nucleus detection over 100 images

Method	Accuracy	MCC	Dice	Jaccard
SC-KM	**0.8943**	**0.8747**	**0.8755**	**0.8262**
PSO	0.8931	0.8616	0.8698	0.8259
SCA	0.8925	0.8627	0.8667	0.8241
GA	0.8625	0.8415	0.8507	0.8019
KM	0.8397	0.8175	0.8229	0.7818

* Best results attained are highlighted in bold*

Table 3. p-value comparison among NIOA

Pair	p	h	P	h	p	h
SC-KM vs. SCA	<0.05	1	<0.05	1	<0.05	1
SC-KM vs. PSO	<0.05	1	<0.05	1	<0.05	1
SC_KM vs. GA	<0.05	1	<0.05	1	<0.05	1

4   Conclusion

The proposed hybrid clustering model in this paper, termed as Sine Cosine-K-Means (SC-KM) algorithm is implemented for the appropriate nucleus segmentation using ALL images. Numerical investigation and analysis of the results distinctly disclose that the proposed SC-KM is a perfect blend of exploration and exploitation techniques executed by SC and KM respectively. Further, SC-KM has been judged against or compared with traditional KM, SCA, GA, and PSO based on certain form of analysis such as visual, numerical, and statistical analysis. The experimental results additional-ly reveal that the SC-KM offers superior segmented nucleus than other tested cluster-ing models.

However, the proposed clustering approach might be further investigated in order to carry out future research based on the facts and findings. The major challenge while implementing the proposed module has been to select the proper number of clusters for different images. Though, Davies-Bouldin criterion [27] and Silhouette criterion [28, 29] are two established approaches for determining cluster number however, research suggests that those criterions are not very successful in the domain of image segmenta-tion. Consequently, developing mechanism to identify the cluster numbers could be new research in the image clustering domain. Even though, the noise sensitivity of K-means and their variants is tremendously towering; yet, the proposed clustering model has not been tested in a noisy environment. As a result, developing noise-robust image clustering models that can correctly segment images without knowing the noise type could be an exciting future project to work on with. Numerous NIOA and their enhanced variants have been identified in recent literature thereby paving a way to the researcher to focus on applying spanking new NIOA and improving their performance in the clustering-based image segmentation field.

Acknowledgement. This work has been partially supported with the grant received in research project under RUSA 2.0 component 8, Govt. of India, New Delhi.

Compliance with Ethical Standards.

Conflict of Interest. On behalf of all authors, the corresponding author states that there is no conflict of interest. The authors declare that they have no conflict of interest.

Ethical Approval. This article does not contain any studies with human participants or animals performed by any of the authors.

References

1. Irshad, H., Veillard, A., Roux, L., Racoceanu, D.: Methods for nuclei detection, segmentation, and classification in digital histopathology: a review—current status and future potential. IEEE Rev. Biomed. Eng. **7**, 97–114 (2014)
2. Dhal, K.G., Ray, S., Das, S., Biswas, A., Ghosh, S.: Hue-preserving and gamut problem-free histopathology image enhancement. Iran. J. Sci. Technol., Trans. Electr. Eng. **43**(3), 645–672 (2019). https://doi.org/10.1007/s40998-019-00175-w
3. Dhal, K.G., Das, A., Ray, S., Gálvez, J.: Randomly attracted rough firefly algorithm for histogram based fuzzy image clustering. Knowl.-Based Syst. **216**, 106814 (2021). https://doi.org/10.1016/j.knosys.2021.106814
4. Dhal, K.G., Das, A., Ray, S., Das, S.: A clustering based classification approach based on modified cuckoo search algorithm. Pattern Recognit. Image Anal. **29**(3), 344–359 (2019). https://doi.org/10.1134/S1054661819030052
5. Dhal, K. G., Fister Jr., I., Das, A., Ray, S., Das, S.: Breast histopathology image clustering using cuckoo search algorithm. In: 5th Student Computer Science Research Conference, University of Maribor, Slovenia, pp. 47–54 (2018)
6. Dhal, K.G., Gálvez, J., Das, S.: Toward the modification of flower pollination algorithm in clustering-based image segmentation. Neural Comput. Appl. **32**(8), 3059–3077 (2019). https://doi.org/10.1007/s00521-019-04585-z
7. Dhal, K.G., Gálvez, J., Ray, S., Das, A., Das, S.: Acute lymphoblastic leukemia image segmentation driven by stochastic fractal search. Multimedia Tools Appl. **79**(17–18), 12227–12255 (2020). https://doi.org/10.1007/s11042-019-08417-z
8. Dash, M., Londhe, N.D., Ghosh, S., Shrivastava, V.K., Sonawane, R.S.: Swarm intelligence based clustering technique for automated lesion detection and diagnosis of psoriasis. Comput. Biol. Chem. **86**, 107247 (2020)
9. Khrissi, L., El Akkad, N., Satori, H., Satori, K.: Image Segmentation based on k-means and genetic algorithms. In: Bhateja, V., Satapathy, S.C., Satori, H. (eds.) Embedded Systems and Artificial Intelligence. AISC, vol. 1076, pp. 489–497. Springer, Singapore (2020). https://doi.org/10.1007/978-981-15-0947-6_46
10. Kate, V., Shukla, P.: Image segmentation of breast cancer histopathology images using pso-based clustering technique. In: Shukla, R.K., Agrawal, J., Sharma, S., Chaudhari, N.S., Shukla, K.K. (eds.) Social Networking and Computational Intelligence. LNNS, vol. 100, pp. 207–216. Springer, Singapore (2020). https://doi.org/10.1007/978-981-15-2071-6_17
11. Das, A., Dhal, K.G., Ray, S., Gálvez, J.: Histogram-based fast and robust image clustering using stochastic fractal search and morphological reconstruction. Neural Comput. Appl. **34**(6), 4531–4554 (2021). https://doi.org/10.1007/s00521-021-06610-6

12. Pakhira, M.K.: A fast k-means algorithm using cluster shifting to produce compact and separate clusters. Int. J. Eng. **28**(1), 35–43 (2015)
13. Li, H., He, H., Wen, Y.: Dynamic particle swarm optimization and K-means clustering algorithm for image segmentation. Optik **126**(24), 4817–4822 (2015)
14. Nanda, S.J., Gulati, I., Chauhan, R., Modi, R., Dhaked, U.: A K-means-galactic swarm optimization-based clustering algorithm with Otsu's entropy for brain tumor detection. Appl. Artif. Intell. **33**(2), 152–170 (2019)
15. Hrosik, R.C., Tuba, E., Dolicanin, E., Jovanovic, R., Tuba, M.: Brain image segmentation based on firefly algorithm combined with k-means clustering. Stud. Inform. Control **28**, 167–176 (2019)
16. Mirjalili, S.: SCA: a sine cosine algorithm for solving optimization problems. Knowl.-Based Syst. **96**, 120–133 (2016)
17. Dhal, K.G., Das, A., Ray, S., Gálvez, J., Das, S.: Nature-inspired optimization algorithms and their application in multi-thresholding image segmentation. Arch. Comput. Methods Eng. **27**(3), 855–888 (2020)
18. Dhal, K.G., Das, A., Gálvez, J., Ray, S., Das, S.: An overview on nature-inspired optimization algorithms and their possible application in image processing domain. Pattern Recognit Image Anal. **30**(4), 614–631 (2020). https://doi.org/10.1134/S1054661820040100
19. Dhal, K.G., Das, A., Ray, S., Gálvez, J., Das, S.: Histogram equalization variants as optimization problems: a review. Arch. Comput. Methods Eng. **28**(3), 1471–1496 (2021)
20. Khrissi, L., El Akkad, N., Satori, H., Satori, K.: Clustering method and sine cosine algorithm for image segmentation. Evol. Intel. **15**(1), 669–682 (2021). https://doi.org/10.1007/s12065-020-00544-z
21. Gabis, A.B., Meraihi, Y., Mirjalili, S., Ramdane-Cherif, A.: A comprehensive survey of sine cosine algorithm: variants and applications. Artif. Intell. Rev. **54**(7), 5469–5540 (2021). https://doi.org/10.1007/s10462-021-10026-y
22. Labati, R.D., Piuri, V., Scotti, F.: All-IDB: The acute lymphoblastic leukemia image database for image processing. In: 2011 18th IEEE International Conference on Image Processing, pp. 2045–2048 (2011)
23. Kennedy, J., Eberhart, R.: Particle swarm optimization. In: Proceedings of ICNN'95-international conference on neural networks, vol. 4. IEEE (1995)
24. Maulik, U., Bandyopadhyay, S.: Genetic algorithm-based clustering technique. Pattern Recogn. **33**(9), 1455–1465 (2000)
25. Thanh, D.N., Prasath, V.S., Hien, N.N.: Melanoma skin cancer detection method based on adaptive principal curvature, colour normalisation and feature extraction with the ABCD rule. J. Digi. Imag. **33**, 574–585 (2019)
26. García, S., Molina, D., Lozano, M., Herrera, F.: A study on the use of non-parametric tests for analyzing the evolutionary algorithms' behaviour: a case study on the CEC'2005 special session on real parameter optimization. J. Heuristics **15**(6), 617 (2009)
27. Davies, D.L., Bouldin, D.W.: A cluster separation measure. IEEE Trans. Pattern Anal. Mach. Intell. **2**, 224–227 (1979)
28. Kaufman, L., Rousseeuw, P.J.: Finding Groups in Data: an Introduction to Cluster Analysis, vol. 344. John Wiley & Sons (2009)
29. Rousseeuw, P.J.: Silhouettes: a graphical aid to the interpretation and validation of cluster analysis. J. Comput. Appl. Math. **20**, 53–65 (1987)

Industrial Warehouse Robot Simulation Using ROS

Pratik Padalkar, Pawan Kadam, Shantanu Mirajgave[✉], and Aniket Mohite

Pimpri Chinchwad College of Engineering, Pune, India
shantanu1058@gmail.com

Abstract. This paper presents the simulation of an industrial warehouse robot using ROS (Robot Operating System). In this paper industrial warehouse robot is successfully simulated. This robot can be used to carry the warehouse products from one point to another both manually as well as autonomously. To achieve the real-time autonomous feature SLAM (Simultaneous Localization and Mapping) is used to generate real-time environment maps so that robots can easily get localized in any kind of complex environment. Adaptive Monte Carlo Localization (AMCL) is used for the localization of the robot. Navigation stack is applied to the robot due to which the robot moves autonomously from one point to another.

Keywords: SLAM · TF · Gazebo · URDF · Navigation stack · AMCL · Odometry · Gmapping · RViz

1 Introduction

Robotics and Automation is the branch of science that deals with the process of building intelligent machines called robots to perform repetitive tasks. Earlier lots of research has been done to make robots autonomous. But in today's world as the robot demands are increasing exponentially to perform their daily tasks without any human interruption. So SLAM algorithms can be used to easily localize in any kind of environment so that robots can freely move without any kind of human interference. Industries need robots that can do work more efficiently, accurately, and without any human interaction. In industries, autonomous robots are the most demanding of all the robots.

The main objective of the robot is to self-explore around in the present environment and make smart decisions so that it can localize easily without any interface. The challenges faced in making robots autonomous are the environmental factors that contain numerous complex obstacles and unknown geographical landmarks. Another challenge is robot making, capable of navigating on its own without having any prior knowledge of the environment, trying to generate its own map, making smart decisions based on collected data. The motivation behind this paper is to explore Robot Operating System and use of the tools provided to develop complex robots easily.

A. A. Sk et al. (Eds.): ISAI 2022, CCIS 1695, pp. 87–95, 2022.
https://doi.org/10.1007/978-3-031-22485-0_9

2   ROS - Robot Operating System

ROS is an abbreviation of Robot Operating System. It is an open-source robotics framework. It is a meta operating system, which works on almost all the operating systems like Linux, Windows, etc. [1]. The most commonly used ROS1 distributions are ROS-Indigo, ROS-Kinetic, ROS-Melodic, and ROS-Noetic. ROS has a wide range of community support across the world through its official community support and many other community groups are active in making ROS much stronger and more efficient.

ROS consists of *nodes, topics, clients, services, packages*, etc. through which it communicates with robots and its environment. ROS nodes are the basic working factors in ROS that perform computation [2]. ROS topic acts as a barrier that carries nodes and communicates between them. ROS services are a pair of messages, one for request and the other for replies, which can be sent over to different ROS topics. ROS client is a collection of code that makes writing different publishers and subscribers to the different ROS topics over which data can be passed. ROS package is the directory that contains all the necessary files like launch file, urdf file, params file, etc.

ROS can control multiple robots at the same time. ROS master can be connected to multiple robots at the same time due to which it is possible to control the robot simultaneously.

2.1   Gazebo

A gazebo is an open-source robotics simulation software. Gazebo simulates multiple robots in a 3D virtual environment. The gazebo is officially supported by ROS and is installed by default with certain ROS installations. It can be used for creating a virtual environment with obstacles in Gazebo which can be used with ROS for robot interface and configuration. Gazebo operates in two parts: the server which computes all the physics and the world and the client which is the graphical frontend for the gazebo.

To launch Gazebo, enter the following commands

```
$ roscore
$ rosrun gazebo_ros gazebo
```

2.2   RViz

RViz is an open-source visualization software. It gives us a convenient GUI to visualize our robot's exact position as well as surrounding environment maps. It allows us to view log sensor information from the robot's sensor. With the help of RViz, we can visualize different types of sensor data such as camera, laser, etc. We can give a destination point to the robot through RViz.

To launch RViz enter the following commands on terminal

```
$ roscore
$ rosrun rviz rviz
```

2.3   Simultaneous Localization and Mapping (SLAM)

Simultaneous Localization and Mapping(SLAM) is a technique used in complex robots to generate a map around their present environment. There are various SLAM algorithms available. We can choose them according to our requirements. The map generated using this algorithm is then used by the navigation stack to move from one point to another autonomously [3]. The process of generating maps and localizing the robot is done concurrently where the maps are created dynamically by moving the robot in the present environment.

2.4   Uniform Robot Description Format (URDF)

URDF stands for Universal Robot Description Format. It is a description of a robot CAD model in ROS understandable format. It is an XML file describing the robot's physical attributes [4]. It is used to represent our robot and its physical attributes in simulations such as Gazebo and to visualize in RViz. URDF can be created by converting the CAD model into XML using CAD to the URDF exporter plugin [14].

2.5   Transforms (tf)

tf is a ROS package that is used to create multiple coordinate frames as well as track them over time [5]. tf can be viewed in RViz. It helps us to understand how different links of robots communicate with each other.

There are different frames in the robot which have relative motion between them. And the data between them is constantly changing as it is relative. So tf is used to convert the measurements from one frame to another.

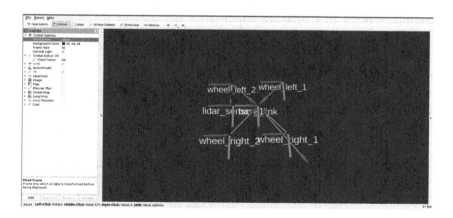

Fig. 1. tf diagram

2.6 Launch Files

Launch files are one of the basic file formats of the ROS. These files are of the format .launch and use a specific XML language format. These files provide users with a convenient way to interact with the ROS environment. Users can set up multiple ROS nodes in a single launch file and can also initialize and alter the various parameters according to the requirements.

3 Methodology

The industrial warehouse robot is designed and created from scratch and simulated in the ROS environment. To simulate a robot in the environment certain steps need to be followed. The steps are as follows:

3.1 Creating URDF from CAD Model

Fusion 360 is software that is used for 3D modeling, making CAD, CAM, CAE, etc. models. The first step for URDF generation is to design a robot model. There are some standard naming conventions to convert the CAD model into URDF [6]. The robot's base model should be given the name base_link which is important for exporting it to URDF. For exporting it to URDF the plugin URDF_EXPORTER is needed. This plugin not only generates urdf files but necessary launch files will be generated for spawning the robot in RViz and Gazebo. For moving the robot in Gazebo, a differential drive plugin needs to be added in URDF. After adding the plugin with the help of *joint_state_publisher_gui* we can simulate the robot in Gazebo and can visualize the same in RViz.

3.2 Creating a ROS Package

In the ROS package, the robot's URDF, all python and C++ script launch files, and also many other files that are required for making our robot autonomous are kept.

To create ROS package launch the below command

```
$ catkin_create_pkg iw_robot rospy roscpp amcl move_base
```

iw_robot is the name of our package and *rospy, roscpp, amcl, and move_base* are the other dependencies that we require for developing the robot.

3.3 Spawn in Gazebo

In order to spawn a robot in a designed environment for simulation purposes, we are using Gazebo. For spawning the robot first the launch files need to be created. As these launch files are coded in XML format, first the default programs need to be added to starting the gazebo, second and the most important thing is to add URDF files in it [7]. As URDF files are broken into multiple .xacro files so main files are to be added. Then the controllers need to be added for controlling the robot. The controllers are usually written in a .yaml file. For spawning the robot in the gazebo, launch the following command. Refer Fig. 2

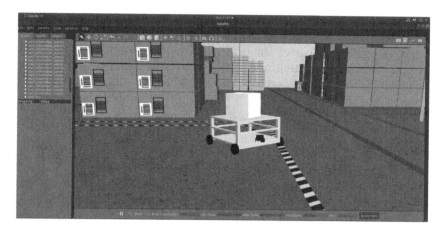

Fig. 2. Spawn in Gazebo

3.4 Spawn in RViz

For visualizing the robot in RViz necessary launch files need to be built. In this display. launch file and URDF file, RViz, and *robot_state_publisher* packages are added. For spawning the robot in RViz, launch the following command. Refer Fig. 3

```
$ roslaunch iw_bot display.launch
```

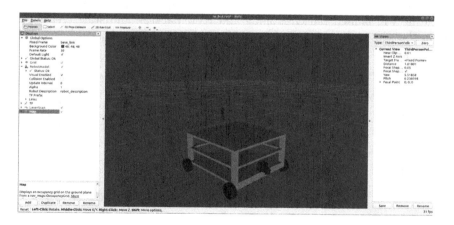

Fig. 3. Spawn in RViz

3.5 Teleoperating the Robot

To control the robot manually then we need to teleoperate it. Teleoperating means controlling the robot with the laptop's keyboard or with a joystick. To teleoperate the robot, first launch the file having the name *iw_robot_teleop*. This launch file contains a *teleop_twist_package* containing a python script that publishes the robot's speed and the angle at which the robot has to travel. For teleoperating the robot there is a differential drive plugin available in iw_robot. URDF subscribes to our *cmd_vel* topic which is published by the *teleop_twist_package* [8].

To launch the *teleop_twist_package* run the following command:

```
$ rosrun iw_bot teleop.launch
```

3.6   Mapping

For creating a map of the environment Gmapping is used. Gmapping is a widely-used open source SLAM algorithm. It is a highly efficient Rao-Blackwellized particle filter-based algorithm which provides laser-based SLAM [9]. Gmapping has its official package to implement Gmapping called *slam_gmapping*. Gmapping acts as a ROS node and takes data from both laser sensor and robot pose and creates a 2D grid map of the environment [10]. This map can be visualized in RViz and retrieved via a ROS topic or service. To save this map we need the ROS map_server package which runs map_server and map_saver as a ROS node that reads the map and saves it to the local computer storage respectively. The map created is stored in a pair of files in the local computer storage. One is a YAML file (map_name.yaml) and the other is a pgm file (map_name.pgm). The YAML file contains the map meta-data and the image file name. Refer Fig. 4

To start the SLAM algorithm launch the following command:

```
$ roslaunch iw_bot gmapping.launch
```

In this launch file, all the necessary gmapping packages are added. This launch file will launch the Gmapping and RViz package and start creating the map in the present environment.

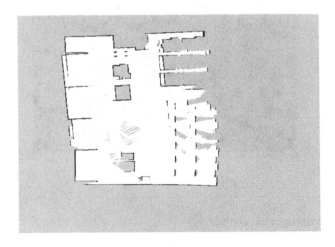

Fig. 4. Map created by Gmapping

3.7   Localization of the Robot

Localization is a process in which a robot tries to locate with respect to its environment. To locate the robot in the environment it needs the robot's odometry which is provided by the gazebo itself. Localization transforms map frames to Odom frames. For localization of the robot, AMCL(Adaptive Monte Carlo Localization) algorithm is used [11]. The robot model uses a plugin of a laser sensor that spreads the particles in all possible directions. But for knowing the probable position of the robot on the map some filtering needs to be done. So it uses particle filters which filter the particle and determine the probable positions in the map. For using the AMCL algorithm, necessary launch files need to be created.

Command to launch the file.

```
$ roslaunch iw_robot amcl.launch
```

This launch file contains the various parameters that are required for this algorithm. These parameter files are configured according to our requirements.

3.8   ROS Navigation Stack

ROS Navigation stack is a ROS package used for navigating a robot autonomously from one location to another. It takes Odometry data, sensor data, and goal pose and gives velocity commands to the robot base. Refer Fig. 5 The Navigation Stack comprises of the following steps -

Local Path Planning. Local Path Planning helps the robot to adapt its movement to a dynamic environment when obstacles are detected [12]. Local Path Planning in ROS is done by a local planner [13]. The local planner helps to move the robot in the environment. This planner calculates and publishes the robot's speed on a certain topic. Although of various local planners, DWA local planner if considered best as this planner gives more performance than any other planners. This algorithm performs forward simulation from the current state and predicts the path where the robot will not collide with the obstacles. This path planner is included in the *move_base.launch*. After launching this file the dwa local planner starts working [14].

Global Path Planning. Global Path Planning is used to find the path between two points. For global path planning, ROS uses a global planner. This planner is included in the *move_base.launch*. After launching this launch file, the global planner starts to plan a path to reach its goal [13].

Navigation Goal. As all the necessary path planning algorithms are provided, it's time to move the robot to its destination. For moving the robot to any desired location there is a tool called 2D nav goal in RViz. Just we need to point

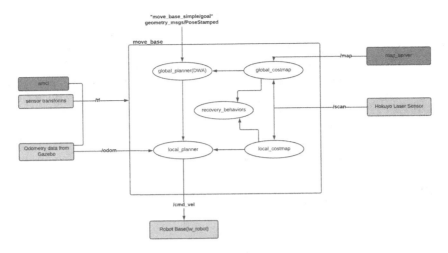

Fig. 5. Navigation stack

at which position and orientation the robot should face on the map from its current position. Once given, the robot will start determining the best-desired path from the current position to the desired location with the avoidance of obstacles.

To start the navigation launch the given command

```
$ roslaunch iw_robot navigation.launch
```

All the launch files that we require such as *move_base, amcl* to run the navigation stack are included in this navigation.launch.

4   Conclusion

This paper describes the simulation of a ROS-based autonomous industrial warehouse robot. This robot can travel manually or autonomously which reduces human efforts. An industrial warehouse robot is spawned in the gazebo for testing purposes. This autonomous robot finds the shortest path which saves time and can be used as industrial robot to move any kind of goods autonomously from one certain place to another, without any human interaction and human effort. Thus, helping in increasing the automation in industrial areas.

Laser-based SLAM is analyzed and simulated on the robot. It uses the robot's Odometry data which is provided by Gazebo itself. By using the gmapping algorithm an incremental map of the environment is created. At last, the robot is localized in the map using AMCL, and a ROS navigation stack is used to implement the robot, due to which the robot moves autonomously from one point to another.

References

1. Kohlbrecher, S., von Stryk, O., Meyer, J., Klingauf, U.: A flexible and scalable SLAM system with full 3D motion estimation. In: 2011 IEEE International Symposium on Safety, Security, and Rescue Robotics, pp. 155–160. IEEE (2011). https://doi.org/10.1109/SSRR.2011.6106777
2. Reid, R., Cann, A., Meiklejohn, C., Poli, L., Boeing, A., Braunl, T.: Cooperative multi-robot navigation, exploration, mapping and object detection with ROS. In: 2013 IEEE Intelligent Vehicles Symposium (IV) 2013 Jun 23, pp. 1083–1088. IEEE.https://doi.org/10.1109/IVS.2013.6629610
3. Teame, W.G., Yu, Y., Zhongmin, W.: Optimization of SLAM Gmapping based on simulation. IJERT Int. J. Eng. Res. Technol. **9**, 74–81. https://doi.org/10.17577/IJERTV9IS040107
4. Johannessen, L.M.G., Arbo, M.H.: Robot Dynamics with URDF & CasADi. In: 2019 7th International Conference on Control, Mechatronics and Automation (ICCMA), pp. 1–6 (2019). IEEE. https://doi.org/10.1109/ICCMA46720.2019.8988702
5. Foote, T.: The transform library. In: 2013 IEEE Conference on Technologies for Practical Robot Applications (TePRA), pp. 1–6 (2013). IEEE.https://doi.org/10.1109/TePRA.2013.6556373
6. Kitamura, T.: Fusion2URDF. https://github.com/syuntoku14/fusion2urdf. Accessed 24 Sept 2021
7. Shimchik, I., Sagitov, A., Afanasyev, I., Matsuno, F., Magid, E.: Golf cart prototype development and navigation simulation using ROS and Gazebo. In: 2016 ResearchGate, p. 09005 (2016)
8. Lee, D., Park, Y.S.: Implementation of augmented teleoperation system based on robot operating system (ROS). In: 2018 IEEE/RSJ International Conference on Intelligent Robots and Systems (IROS), pp. 5497–5502. IEEE (2018). https://doi.org/10.1109/IROS.2018.8594482
9. Xuexi, Z., Guokun, L., Genping, F., Dongliang, X., Shiliu, L.: SLAM algorithm analysis of mobile robot based on lidar. In: 2019 Chinese Control Conference (CCC), pp. 4739–4745. IEEE. https://doi.org/10.23919/ChiCC.2019.8866200
10. KrinKin, K., Filatov, A., Huletski, A., Kartashov, D.: Evaluation of modern laser based indoor SLAM algorithms. In: 2018 ResearchGate, pp. 101–106 (2018). https://doi.org/10.23919/FRUCT.2018.8468263
11. dos Reis, W.P.N., da Silva, G.J., Junior, O.M., Vivaldini, K.C.T.: An extended analysis on tuning the parameters of adaptive Monte Carlo localization ROS package in an automated guided vehicle. In: 2021 ResearchGate (2021). https://doi.org/10.21203/rs.3.rs-225880/v1
12. Kangutkar, R., Lauzon, J., Synesael, A., Jenis, N., Simha, K., Ptucha, R.: ROS navigation stack for smart indoor agents. In: 2017 IEEE Applied Imagery Pattern Recognition Workshop (AIPR), pp. 1–10. IEEE (2017). https://doi.org/10.1109/AIPR.2017.8457966
13. Hussein, A.H., Martin, D.M., Marin-Plaza, P.M., de la Escalera Escalera, A.: Global and local path planning study in a ROS-based research platform for autonomous vehicles. In: ResearchGate (2018). https://doi.org/10.1155/2018/6392697
14. Zhang, X., Lai, J., Xu, D., Li, H., Fu, M.: 2D LiDAR-based SLAM and path planning for indoor rescue using mobile robotss. In: J. Adv. Transp. Hindawi (2020). https://doi.org/10.1155/2020/8867937

Major Challenges and Threats of Blockchain Technology

Milan Kumar Dholey[1] and Ananya Ganguly[2(✉)]

[1] Department of Computer Science and Engineering, Koneru Lakshmaiah Education Foundation, Vaddeswaram, AP, India
[2] SACT Department of Computer Science, AJC Bose College, West Bengal, Kolkata 700020, India
a.ganguly.it@gmail.com

Abstract. Blockchain comes to the market as a distributed, decentralized open ledger or database which is linked with each other using the-hash value of cryptography. Blockchain is bettersecure than other systems but several threats may break the security of the blockchain. Even if blockchain is a more secure and promising aspect of our future, some security concerns and difficulties still surround this ground-breaking method is the important topic now a day and here in this paper we concern about these. It analyzes blockchain architecture containing its immutable transactions in a decentralized manner and including their different security threats, how they can hamper the blocks assets and considerable values of the blocks and security services over it, including their authentications, privacy, and confidentiality taking part of their access control list (ACL). In this article, we tried to find out how the eclipse attack hampers the blockchain distribution and countermeasure.

Keywords: Blockchain · Security threats · Consensus · Miners · Attack · Vulnerability

1 Introduction

Although Bitcoin was the first blockchain claim and operates as a form of digital currency built on blockchain technologies, the current trends are moving toward treating items on the internet as money the same in the actual world we follow it. Recently the achievement of Bitcoin, users can now use blockchain technologies across a wide range of industries and services, including the voting, presentation details generation, Internet of Things (IoT), healthcare, the supply chain, and storage. But as we will be utilizing such products in daily lives, cybercriminals too have a chance to commit cybercrime [1,2]. After going through different attacks and their effects, we tried to develop a proposed algorithm through which an analytical survey of the income variation between honest blocks and affected blocks and how the suffer due to eclipse attack. So how to countermeasure this eclipse attack by our proposed algorithm and their data variation shown in this paper.

A. A. Sk et al. (Eds.): ISAI 2022, CCIS 1695, pp. 96–108, 2022.
https://doi.org/10.1007/978-3-031-22485-0_10

The remaining is as follows. In Sect. 2, we study the fundamental and overview about blockchain. In Sect. 3, we discussed about the different attacks of the blockchain and services. The countermeasure of the Eclipse attack is discussed in Sect. 4 and finally, Sect. 5 is the conclusion followed by the reference.

2   Preliminaries of Blockchain

This section introduces basic concepts of blockchain and blockchain-related other fundamental processes used in blockchain and generates blocks in blockchain by using several consensus mechanisms.

2.1   Basic of Blockchain

Every network node in a blockchain executes and records the identical transactions, which are organized into certain unchangeable blocks. A blockchain is a distributed computing architecture. An open, accessible electronic ledger is a blockchain. Each block consists of three elements: information on the characteristics of that block, its own hash, and a mathematical proof that it follows the previous block in sequence (the preceding block's hash) [3]. Only a block can be supplemented at a time. This is how the blockchain's "distributed database" is kept up-to-date by consensus throughout the whole network. Transactions made by specific users on the ledger are safeguarded by a number of protocols and cryptographic techniques [4].

A block is the building block of a blockchain. The units of data that hold everlastingly recorded data are called blocks in a blockchain technology, together with the hash of the preceding block and current block. In other words, a block is a collection of transactions initially hashed and after that it's added into the blockchain.

Figure 1 explained the basic block diagram of blockchain or the architecture of blockchain containing data of that block with the unique hash value of the preceding block and present block. This previous block's hash value makes the connection of the chain. This block creation is defined in Fig. 2. Where the transaction architecture of each block is explained with proper classification of stored data and the hash value of the existing as well as previous block or transaction is explained and defined properly.

2.2   Mining Pool

The mechanism through which miners pool their resources to process power via the blockchain network is known as a mining pool. In most cases, it is utilized to distribute the reward equally depending on each person's contribution to the labour likelihood needed to determine a block's hash [8–10].

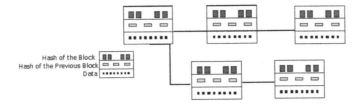

Fig. 1. Structure of Blockchain

Fig. 2. Block or transaction's architecture

2.3 Consensus

A mathematical phrase or technique that pits the nodes against one another in the blockchain cryptographic race to choose which block will add. Despite being a decentralized system, blockchain requires accurate and consistent data even though a third party is not required in this case. Blockchain [11] typically uses the decentralized consensus process for this reason. Numerous blockchain consensus mechanism are at present in use [9], including PoI (Proof-of-Importance), PoS (Proof-of-Stake), PoW (Proof-of-Work), etc.

2.4 Smart Contract Security Threats

A "computerized protocol of transaction that executes the rapports of a contract" is referred to as a smart contract. [22] Every user on the blockchain where a smart contract is based can see it. This results in a situation where problems, such as security holes, are readily apparent to everyone but may not be immediately corrected. [23] In the smart contract, we can get several Vulnerabilities which are also known as Vulnerabilities in solidity. A brief taxonomical analysis of smart contract vulnerabilities is given below (Table 1).

Table 1. Taxonomical analysis of Vulnerabilities of Ethereum smart contracts [24,25]

Vulnerability	Vulnerability the Vulnerability's Cause
Call the unlisted number	Call to function failed
Gas-free send	The reverse call function of the caller is located
Exception disorders	Not consistently handling exceptions
Type casts	If a type error is discovered, no expectation is raised
Reentrancy	Before terminating, re-entry required for a non-recursive methods
Trust secret	Contracts confidential field, confidentiality is not assured
Unassailable bugs	Contracts that are defective or identical cannot be retrieved
Ether misplaced transfer	Unable to find ether delivered to an stray address
Stack size limit	1024 values are present in the stack

3 Security Issues of Blockchain

3.1 Double Spending Issues

Double spending means spending the same money twice. These include double-spending attacks where the same amount or unit of money is simultaneously assigned to a person where the feedback is not yet coming and at that time the same amount is sent to the different person so that both can spend the same coin at the same time. Suppose block1 sends some money to block2 wherefrom the acknowledgment does not come which means the transaction is not yet confirmed so block1 sends the same amount to block3 whereas block2 also accepts that amount. So here, the same amount is involved in both persons. It is known as double-spending.

Double-spending attacks can take many various forms, including the Alternative history attack, Finney attack, Race attack, 51% attack, and Vector76 attack, among others (Fig. 3).

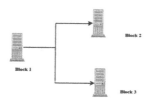

Fig. 3. Double spending problem in Blockchain

3.2 Race Attack

The attacker in this case immediately sends the same coin to numerous targets. And produces contradictory transactions very soon. If the merchant doesn't wait for the confirmation, there is a 50% chance that they will receive the coin that was twice spent. Everyone in this scenario is receiving completed transactions that were not allowed. Next the contradictory operation will [5] also be extracted to the block that can recognized as a genuine transaction whereas, from the sender's aspect it is invalid. In this case, the immediate timing creates the initiation of the double-spending attack.

3.3 Finney Attack

In this case suppose, one person creates a pre-mined block, and in that block that person is trying to find a part of the transaction which sends some of the coins back to that person, and that person keeps that transaction without broadcasting. And when the block is generated then also that person keeps the block without broadcasting it. Instead, [25] that a person spends the same coins to a merchant for some goods or services. After the merchants accept the payment and irreversibly provide the service, the person broadcasts this block. In Fig 4. We can also visualize that, just like a double-spending attack the buyer sends money to sellers A and B simultaneously without any wait of confirmation from the 1st one. And when the confirmation comes from A then B can't able to get that same amount and at that moment the Race Attack occurs.

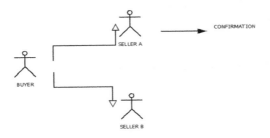

Fig. 4. Race attack problem in Blockchain

3.4 Attack 51% or Greater 50% Attack

All transactions are recorded as blocks in a distributed chaining process on a blockchain. Consensus also states that whenever a vulnerability of 51% or greater appears, it can be used by attackers to take control of and steer the complete blockchain in the wrong direction. More specifically, in the case of a blockchain that are based on PoW, the 51% assault may be conducted if a sole miner's hashing power exceeds 50% of total hashing power of the complete blockchain and it subsequently becomes a trustworthy one. In this, the attacker that gain manage of 51% of the network's or blockchain's hash power, and double spending may also occur here. The computational power employed in the verification of transactions or blocks is referred to "hash power" in this context. Attackers who get control can undo the transaction and create a private blockchain that looks authentic, but this hasn't yet happened because it would be extremely expensive to gain 51% into network's power. Here, if the attacker has run out of blocks, they can try to extend their fork farther in the hopes of catching up to the network [25] Fig. 5.

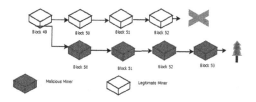

Fig. 5. >50 % or 51 % attack problem in Blockchain

3.5 Alternative History Attack

It calls for a elevated hash speed and runs the hazard of costing the attacking miner significantly more in wasted electricity. The dishonest miners (attackers) send the transaction to the trade or network, which pays the trade, in this sort of double-spending attack. After n commitment, the mercantile transfers item to the attacker after the dishonest miner has secretly created an choice of blockchain fork with a fake double-spending deal. Now, if the intruder discovers additional blocks than 'n', it release the fork and gets back his money. If not, he keeps annoying to expand his fork in the hopes of catching up to the network. To protect against this attack, there is no incoming connection that should allow gregarious links to a well-associated node [25].

3.6 Brute Force Attack

A ¿50 % attack is extremely similar to a brute force attack. Such an attack takes place when an adversarial agent secretly mines a blockchain fork that includes a double-spending transaction in place of the transaction that pays the merchant. Similar to a ¿50 % attack, an attacker can then wait for the merchant to send the product and receive a particular number of confirmations while simultaneously searching for further confirmations in an effort to overtake or pull alongside to the main network. If intruder is never capable to accomplish this, the attack is a failure and the transaction with the merchant is successful. The attacker needs a relatively high hash rate for such an attack. The hash rate of the intruder (expressed percentage of the overall association hash rate) and confirmations of the merchant require determine the likelihood of success.

3.7 Selfish Mining Attacks or Block-Discarding Attack

In this type of attack it is further well described as the exposure in the blockchain which is discredited for one untruthful miners to acquire their unfair reward that

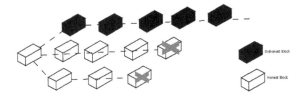

Fig. 6. Selfish mining attack with private miners

concede possibility be higher in amount their share of calculating gone and also involve the different truthful miners and leads bureaucracy to the From Fig. 6 we can see black-colored dishonest blocks when mined than any other honest blocks will be misguided and they entered the wrong path followed by the dishonest miners.

For a new block it is introduced in blockchain, selfish miners remain the new private block to compete with the truthful miners, they release their private block and gain more rewards to win the race. This case is explained in the following Fig. 7. To avoid these attacks miners before publishing the block should randomly allocate miners to their different brushwood of the pool of that blockchain. And for fresh and new blocks should use some unforgettable timestamp by which it can recognize which pool comes very recently and that way it can identify selfish miners.

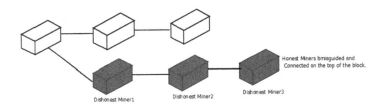

Fig. 7. Selfish mining attack with only one private block

3.8   Eclipse Attack

The aggressor eclipses the bud from the chain in an eclipse attack. The attacker made sure the block couldn't intelligently match with the other blocks on the blockchain. When the block is in risk of one attack, the block digger will rely on a completely different standard of honesty than the rest of the chain. This kind of eclipse attack typically involves miners or sellers acting above-sketch blockchain growth. Calculating freedom investigators Ethan Heilman, Sharon Goldberg, Alison Kendler, Alison Kendler, Aviv Zohar, and others predicted the eclipse attack in 2015. Eclipse Attacks is the title of a Usenix Security study that they have written. The study details the potential for an assault on the blockchain's peer-to-peer network for Bitcoin. Despite being primarily focused on Bitcoin, the attack might also target into peer-to-peer networks of another blockchain application. The viability of an eclipse attack in the Ethereum network was addressed in different research from 2018 for peer-to-peer network (Fig. 8).

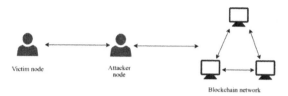

Fig. 8. Eclipse attack and how they control blockchain network

Comparison of these major attacks on the blockchain system and their countermeasures are briefly listed down in the following table (Fig. 9):

Security Threats	Attack Vectors	Primary Targets	Affected Abstract Layers	Reason for the threat	Adverse Effect	Precaution/Counter Measures
Double Spending Threats [5]	Race Attack	Sellers or merchants	Consensus	Transaction Verification mechanism	Seller loses his products, misguide the honest miners	Inserting more observers, create notification and merchants disable the direct incoming Connections
Finney Attack [5,27]	Transaction Verification mechanism	Sellers or merchants	Consensus	Dishonest miner broadcasts pre-mined blocks and receives product	Facilitates double Spending	Wait for multi confirm actions for Transactions
51% Attack [5,28,29]	Consensus mechanism	Bitcoin network, miners, centers, and users	Network, Consensus, Data Model	Adversary controls more than > 50% Hashrate	Drive away single miners from small pools weaken consensus protocol	Inserting more observers, create notification and merchants disincarnate large mining pools
Mining Pools Security Threats [13,12,16]	Selfish Mining/Block-discard Attack	Miners or Mining pools	Consensus mechanism	Dishonest miners get unfair greater rewards &confuse honest miners	Misguided honest miners and entered the wrong path	Before publishing block should randomly assign miners to their different branches
Eclipse Attack[13,23]	Flaws in blockchain protocols - outgoing connections	Pool	Network	Flaws in blockchain protocols - outgoing connections	Network discovery	no practical defense reported so far found
Smart Contracts Threats [27,28]	Vulnerabilities in contracts source code	contract source code	Execution	Program design flaws	Transaction Creations - change of state, Mining	no practical defense reported so far found

Fig. 9. Comparison of the major attacks on the Blockchain

4   Algorithm Analysis and Countermeasure of Eclipse Attack

In the event of an eclipse assault, the perpetrator would need to take advantage of certain weaknesses in order to replace the real path with their own. The following are some of the blockchain's blocks' exploitable vulnerabilities:

The block determines and chooses IP addresses from the victim's path with up-to-date timestamps, increasing the likelihood that the attacker would choose the victim's block.

Every time an IP address of the blocks of a blockchain is filled that address is removed randomly. The attacker might improve the possibilities by lengthening the attack time. The IP address of the intruder gets taken from the blockchain eventually that are submitting it to the block repeatedly because the removed address is random (Fig. 11).

```
START
Step1: Traveler registration for tour
            If flag 1 :
                    Unique traveler_id generates;
                    Add wallet value for traveling cost;
            Else return 0;
Step2: if valid traveler_id found: generate unique luggage_id;
Step3: traveler book for a locate destination;
Step 4: locate destination distance calculated;
       Step 5: if locate destination distance* 10= traveling cost<=
wallet value
                    Wallet value= wallet value- traveling cost
                    Else return 0;
    STOP
```

Fig. 10. Algorithm-1

The attacker can use these stated vulnerabilities. However, these vulnerabilities is again avoidable by changing the activities of the blockchain's block in any platform:

Randomization of the IP address selection from the blockchain's attempted table would make it more difficult to identify an attacker peer's address, even if the peer had just connected. If peer selection is randomized, the attacker will not succeed even following or spending a huge time on the attack.

If a deterministic algorithm or techniques is used to place in the blockchain technology's tackle into a fixed slot, it will also lessen the likelihood that the attacker's deal with will be inserted to a different slot after it is removed from the chain. Repeated address inclusion will not benefit an attack thanks to deterministic insertion (Fig. 12).

No. of IP Address	Value of the Affected Blocks	Value of the Honest Blocks
200	115	200
400	229	400
600	227	600
1100	668	1100
1500	799	1500
2000	890	2000
2200	1770	2200
2500	1890	2500
3000	1990	3000
3500	1999	3800
4000	2100	3800
4500	2110	3813
5000	2114	3815
5500	2115	3816
6000	2118	3818

Fig. 11. Comparison of the values of affected blocks and honest blocks

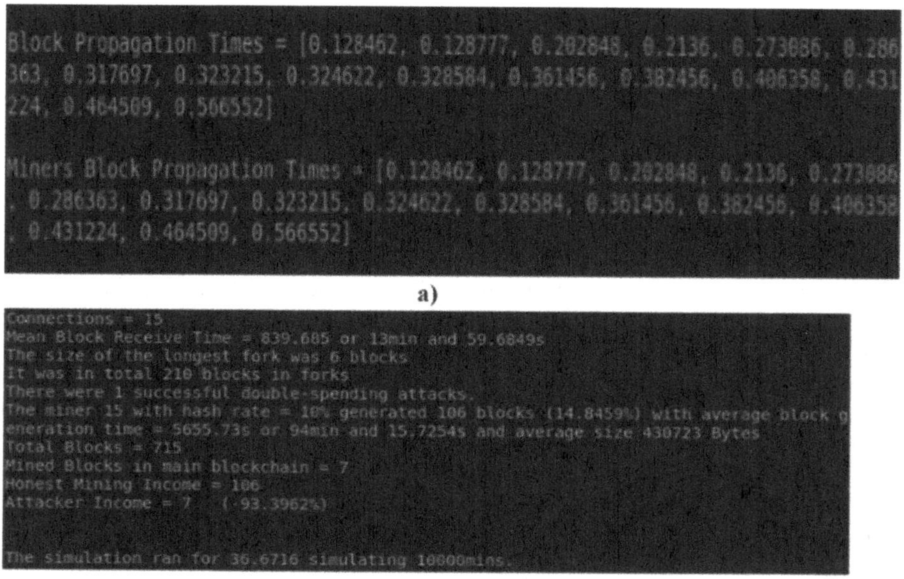

a)

b)

Fig. 12. Screenshots of the tried table Results a) timers propagation tables, b) Effects of Attacks

Based on this proposed algorithm we found the following data given in Table 3. And on basis of this data the graphical analysis of the income variation of honest and victimized affected blocks is shown in Fig. 10 (Fig. 13).

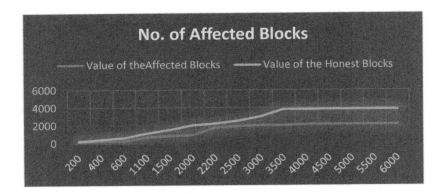

Fig. 13. Comparison of the values of normal and affected blocks

5   Conclusion

Blockchain is intensely estimated and leading upholding foundation and peer-to-peer in character. By examining multiple way and fields of the blockchain in the way that consensus systems, blockchain networks, and smart contracts, benefits of blockchain, and excavating processes use, the study inspected all the existent exposures in the blockchain. However, various types of research concerning the blockchain extent whole are shielded by Bitcoin. But blockchain is a best in range of the fields habit outside limits Bitcoin. Blockchain has proved allure potential for renovation old do business at an establishment of allure key characteristics: decomposition, steadfastness, obscurity, etc. This paper survey the insight of an inclusive survey on blockchain freedom dangers. How eclipse attack influences the profit of the digger's block and the hampering cure to prevent circuit attack. We originally offer an sketch out of blockchain electronics and the traits of blockchain. We before debate and filed and study different issues and challenges that grant permission attack blockchain happening and compiled few existent approaches for verdict these issues.

References

1. Opara, E.U., Soluade, O.A.: Straddling the next cyber frontier: the empirical analysis on network Int. J. Netw. Secur. **19**(5), 653–659 (2017)
2. Singh, J.: Cyber-attacks in cloud computing: a case study. Int. J. Electr. Inf. Eng. **1**(2), 78–87 (2014)

3. Kantur, H., Bamuleseyo, C.: How smart contracts can change the insurance industry: benefits and challenges of using blockchain technology (2018)
4. Akoglu, L., Ferrara, E., Deivamani, M., Baeza-Yates, R., Yogesh, P. (eds.): ICIIT
   2018. CCIS, vol. 941. Springer, Singapore (2019). https://doi.org/10.1007/978-
   981-13-3582-2
5. Cole, R., Aitken, J., Stevenson, M.: Blockchain technology: implications for operations and supply chain management. Supply Chain Manage. Int. J. **24**(11), (2019)
6. Aiko, S.: Blockchain Technologies and Trust Formation in Trade Finance. International Business Management. Masters, University of Oulu (2018)
7. Eyal, I., Sirer, E.G.: Majority is not enough: bitcoin mining is vulnerable. Commun.
   ACM **61**(7), 95–102 (2018)
8. Ittay, E.: The miner's dilemma (pdf). cornel university. archived (PDF) from the
   original on 2017–08-09. Retrieved 2017–05-23. In: The IEEE Symposium on Security and Privacy (Oakland) (2015)
9. Li, X., Jiang, P., Chen, T., Luo, X., Wen, Q.: A survey on the security of blockchain
   systems. Future Gener. Comput. Syst. **107**, (2017)
10. Liu, Z., et al.: A survey on blockchain: a game theoretical perspective. IEEE Access
    7, 47615–47643 (2019)
11. Ghosh, M., Richardson, M., Ford, B. Jansen, R.: A TorPath to TorCoin: Proof-of-
    bandwidth altcoins for compensating relays. Naval Research Lab Washington DC
    (2014)
12. Toyoda, K., Mathiopoulos, P.T., Sasase, I., Ohtsuki, T.: A novel blockchain-based
    product ownership management system (POMS) for anti-counterfeits in the post-
    supply chain. IEEE Access **5**, 17465–17477 (2017)
13. Xu, X., et al.: A taxonomy of blockchain-based systems for architecture design. In:
    2017 IEEE International Conference on Software Architecture (ICSA), pp. 243–252
    IEEE (2017)
14. Bamert, T., Decker, C. Elsen, L., Wattenhofer, R., Welten, S.: Have a Snack, Pay
    with Bitcoins. In: 13-th IEEE International Conference on Peer-to-Peer Computing
    (2013)
15. Heilman, E., Kendler, A., Zohar, A., Goldberg, S.: Eclipse attacks on bitcoin's
    peer-to-peer network. In: Jung, J., Holz, T. (eds.) 24th USENIX Security Sympo-
    sium, USENIX Security 15, Washington, D.C., USA, 12–14 August 2015. USENIX
    Association, pp. 129–144 (2015)
16. Lloyd's London presents a report called emerging risk report (2015)
17. Zohar, A., Vanbever: Bitcoin's Hijacking (2017)
18. Valentino-DeVries, J., Singer, N., Keller, M.H., Krolik, A.: Your apps know where
    you were last night, and they're not keeping it secret. New York Times, 10 (2018)
19. Werbach, K.: Trust, but verify: why the blockchain needs the law. Berkeley Tech.
    LJ **33**, 487 (2018)
20. Piersigilli, F., Bhandari, V.: Biomarkers in neonatology: the new omics of bron-
    chopulmonary dysplasia. J. Matern.-Fetal Neonatal Med. **29**(11), 1758–1764 (2016)
21. Shumway-Cook, A., Ciol, M.A., Yorkston, K.M., Hoffman, J.M., Chan, L.: Mobil-
    ity limitations in the medicare population: prevalence and sociodemographic and
    clinical correlates. J. Am. Geriatr. Soc. **53**(7), 1217–1221 (2005)
22. Böhme, R., Christin, N., Edelman, B., Moore, T.: Bitcoin: economics, technology,
    and governance. J. Econ. Perspect. **29**(2), 213–38 (2015)
23. Galimberti, V., et al.: Axillary dissection versus no axillary dissection in patients
    with sentinel-node micrometastases (IBCSG 23–01): a phase 3 randomized con-
    trolled trial. Lancet Oncol. **14**(4), 297–305 (2013)

24. Bonneau, J.: Hostile blockchain takeovers (Short Paper). In: Zohar, A., et al. (eds.) FC 2018. LNCS, vol. 10958, pp. 92–100. Springer, Heidelberg (2019). https://doi.org/10.1007/978-3-662-58820-8_7

25. Nayak, K., Kumar, S., Miller, A. Shi, E.: Stubborn mining: generalizing selfish mining and combining it with an eclipse attack. In: 2016 IEEE European Symposium on Security and Privacy (EuroS&P), pp. 305–320 IEEE (2016)

SecVT: Securing the Vehicles of Tomorrow Using Blockchain Technology

Amit Kumar Tyagi[✉]

School of Computer Science and Engineering, Vellore Institute of Technology, Chennai, India
amitkrtyagi025@gmail.com

Abstract. Internet of Things (IoT) is one of the fields which has flourished to a great extend over the years because of its varied use cases and versatility. One of the fields which has flourished technologically is the automotive industry where the main focus is not just on improvising the vehicles internally but also to develop communication and interaction between vehicles on the road so as to facilitate a network of interconnected vehicles. However, the exchange of large volumes of data often poses a huge threat to security and privacy and necessitates the incorporation and integration of intense cybersecurity measures to ensure that the system and network is safe from attacks. Blockchain however has proven to be one of the useful techniques in terms of protecting data. This chapter mainly deals with the implementation of securing the information regarding next generation intelligent vehicles.

Keywords: Internet of things (IoTs) · Automotive · Communication · Cyber-security · Blockchain · Next generation vehicles

1 Introduction – Future Vehicles

The development in the transportation and automobile industry has been massive in the recent years. It has acquired new standards with the help of global enhancements and technological growth. This mainly covers concepts such as autonomous vehicles, smart cars, hybrid vehicles, vehicular networks, etc. Computer vision, image processing, sensors, and network-based algorithms are the major arenas that have contributed for such developments [1].

a) Hybrid Intelligent Vehicles and Connected Vehicles
   Connected Automated Vehicles (CAV) are the ones that are instrumented with techniques like vehicle-to-vehicle or vehicle-to-internet networks [2]. They mainly consist of sensory networks to detecting trajectories and objects along with the feature of establishing interconnections with other vehicles. This is extremely useful for traffic forecast, predicting motion in surrounding environment, and to increase the accuracy of such information obtained [3, 4]. This is the foundational logic of cyber physical systems which utilize physical apparent parameters for controls through interaction and forecasting strategies. The supervision and control of CAV's are

done at numerous junctions, freeways, service roads, interjunctions, etc. This definitely helps in improving the efficiency, performance, etc. while also reducing the pollution and fuel consumption [5].

b) Autonomous Vehicles

A step further from the conventional vehicles leads to Autonomous Vehicles (Avs) and is capable of manoeuvring and navigating roads in driverless conditions. This mainly helps in reducing the possibility of human errors, decreases accidents, etc. Many companies and organizations, including tech giants, have invested on AVs so as to reduce the stress and tension caused by driving. However, there's also a sceptical notion about the possibility of such AVs completely losing control on road and causing mishaps [7].

c) Autonomous Intelligent Vehicles (AIV)

Autonomous intelligent vehicles which are intelligent and automated and take action instantly over the road network to avoid any type of accidents or improve the transportation journey. These types of vehicles use Machine Learning, Deep learning, etc., techniques to improve its communication. In near future, AIV will use few emerging technologies like blockchain, edge computing, digital twin, etc., to improve its basic features. Few objectives, scope, etc., of Autonomous Intelligent Vehicles can be discussed in [27]. The possibility of developing a vehicle which is completely automated is highly likely provided it has access to information such the current environment, the route to take, and driving decisions. Robocars or robotaxis are smart vehicles that make use of a combination of sensors, processors, etc. to depict control and supervision over the driving abilities. Vehicles that are integrated with such innovative technologies also have certain unique points of interest. The ultimate aim of such vehicles is to limit accidents and energy consumption while reducing discharges. The key factors that influence such vehicles decisions include:

Perception

a) Motion Preparation - (direction) steering, pace
b) Navigating
c) Behaviour – study of lanes, overtaking

The points mentioned above are targets for real-world users of autonomous vehicles. Now, possible uses of Future Vehicles in near future are (also refer Fig. 1):

- e-healthcare
  Smart and autonomous vehicles are particularly useful in the health sector. In cases of accidents and emergencies, such vehicles can reduce latencies and reach the desired destination with ease in case of unavailability of drivers. Many a times, people affected by accidents are exposed to further critical conditions because of the lack of sufficient care and health support at the right time. Ambulance getting delayed due to heavy traffic, lack of coordination among drivers and hospitals, etc. also contribute to the above-mentioned cause. The fact the smart vehicles can predict traffic, road scenarios, and engage in interconnection networks, are highly efficient to ensure a safe and sound health support being recruited to the patients within very less time. The mini versions

of CAV robots are also utilized for hospital sectors to deliver surgical and medical equipment which are required for surgeries, operations, etc. [8].

- Supply chain

  The process of supply chain is pretty lengthy which starts with extraction and retrieval of raw materials all the way to delivering the products to consumers. The initial stages very often include the transportation of resources such as iron, metal, wood, etc. along with commuting the final goods. This aspect is extremely crucial in supply chains and it's highly important to ensure that the goods are delivered to the customers at the right time, specifically in the food industry. Delays and latencies can often lead to spoilage of food and its wastage. The presence of different sensors in CAVs can make sure that the quality of food is maintained by controlling the ambient temperature and adjusting it as required [9]. This would also motivate consumers to order such products in reduced quantities which in turn decreases the stocks in inventory, benefiting both the employers and customers.

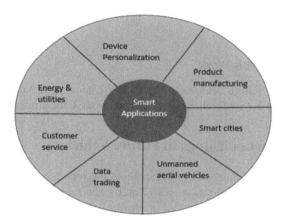

Fig. 1. Smart applications in current scenarios

The detailed description about progress/evolution of connected vehicles (2000 onwards) can be found in [26].

1.1 Blockchain/Distributed Ledger Technology

The infamous decentralized and distributed ledger technology [25, 28, 30] called Blockchain is being heavily used across various application aspects, which is immutable and is used for storing information in block like structures which are encrypted. The possibility of using Blockchain in various disciplines is highly probable in the near future. There are a number of parameters that make Blockchain systems unique and distinctive. Few of the pertinent characteristics are as follows:

- Private, Public, and Permission Blockchain
- Centralization and Decentralization
- Persistency
- Validity
- Anonymity and Identity
- Immutability

Other application of blockchain in this current smart era can be found in [14, 29]. Apart from this, the main advantages of Blockchain are as follows:

- Enhanced transparency and flexibility of shipment procedures
- Development in reliability and loyalty with recorded logs of transactions
- Increased levels of precision and accuracy to combat with IoT
- Users can integrate this to enhance business using IoT applications

With the help of Blockchain technology, it is possible to generate high levels of security and satisfactory levels of trust pertaining to the data stored in the distributed and centralized database.

1.2 Organisation of This Work

Note that in this work, Future Vehicles or Vehicles of Tomorrow or Autonomous vehicles, etc., terms have been used interchangeably (all terms have the similar meaning).

2 Role of Internet of Things in Future Vehicles

IoT is all about the interconnection of devices and gadgets that operate via the internet and is often used in the transportation sector. Intelligent transportation systems basically include a smarter and intelligent way of controlling the automobile sector in fields of traffic and signal management, accident control, road safety, etc. The growing number of vehicles have posed sufficient number of challenges to the people and government from the viewpoint of increasing fuel consumption, pollution and traffic jams. Just like how IoT was easily compatible with various other industries, its integration with the automobile industry would lead to rapid advancements and developments. With the help of IoT, a number of features such ass connectivity, cloud services, smart sensors, etc. could be added which in turn betters the performance and quality control. This powerful combination would lead to an organic interaction between people, roads, and vehicles and can provide a great solution to traffic issues and pollution [10].

3 Motivation

IoT allows for a quicker and safer exposure for pedestrians and drivers because they get sufficient information on road condition, traffic details, performance of vehicles, and energy consumption. However, with increasing usages of IoT for modernizing the vehicular sector, there's an increase in malicious attacks and data breaches. The umbrella term of Internet of Vehicles (IoV), often termed as the future of vehicles, is consolidated with V2V networks and various sensors for information and data gathering. In case of an event where any one of the components fail, it can result in the failure of the whole system [11]. This is a huge vulnerability and when considered along with the lack of succinct privacy techniques to preserve data securely is addressed with the help of Blockchain technology. Protection and preserving privacy of databases and devices in IoT and related applications is one of the areas that is incorporated with this technology [12]. This paper discusses the possible strategies and uses of safe and secure decentralized blockchain environment. We also discuss the challenges in current vehicles and how smart and secure hybrid vehicles can help to solve these issues.

4 Issues, Constraints, Challenges with Current Vehicles

In the Vehicular Adhoc network VANET context [23–26] or current vehicles, we can distinguish several problems/issues:

- Key agreement vs. key transport: Because VANET groups are scattered, key agreement is the most common method for establishing a new key. Each approach requires that all players broadcast numerous rounds of information in succession. While this method can be terminated in one round, it places most of the computational burden on the group leader, which is also a single point of failure, key transport involves allowing a group leader, either chosen by the specific application or chosen at random, to create and broadcast a group key to all members.
- Join/Leave operations: Group membership is subject to rapid change in VANETs. As a result, the effective administration of new members' join and exit procedures is an additional problem in safe group management. Existing keys may be transferred to a new member using simple methods such as key transport, but new keys must be computed and redistributed whenever a member leaves the system. A portion of keys may need to be re-computed for both actions in protocols based on key trees; although this adds complexity, it spreads the computation work better than simple key transfer. Because most VANET cars will have comparable degrees of security, the development of secure groups will simply help reduce security overhead, rather than establishing distinct levels of security across VANET members. This is critical to remember. The usage of secure groups, like digital signatures, secures the network from outsiders, not insiders as stated, just like digital signatures. This means that although it is still essential to renew or transfer current keys when new members join, the group key should not be updated automatically when a member quits.
- Definition of group memberships: The VANET mobility concept, as previously indicated, is very dynamic. Even while some cars may travel close to one other for many

kilometres at a time, others may rapidly overtake them or join the self-formed groups they have created. Group boundaries are exceedingly difficult to establish in these situations. Some members of the platoon may be unaware of a new vehicle joining from behind if the platoon is dispersed across multiple wireless hops. It will be time- and message-consuming and inefficient to perform group rekeying based on tree recomputation and rebalancing or key agreement. Keys might be transferred from the new member's next-door neighbour as a straightforward solution in this instance. But if a group's borders aren't clearly defined, cars that aren't part of the group may be caught up in a critical establishing effort. Additionally, even though these cars lack the group key, they are still required to receive safety warnings, necessitating the continual use of broadcasts with digital signatures. Group borders may be preloaded into vehicles in order to reduce the issue of changing group boundaries. Groups may be constructed based on cell membership, for example, by dividing highways into geographic cells.

- Others: Many attacks like Denial of Service, Distributed Denial of Service (DDoS), Man in Middle Attacks, timing attacks, transition attacks, etc., are mitigate over VANET/current vehicles in Today's scenarios.

5 Proposed System Model – Securing Future Vehicles

To proceed further for proposed work, first we need to explain the problem raised in the recent decade with vehicles or autonomous vehicles.

Problem Definition: One of the various crucial aspects is the leakage of a user's personal data [24–28]. Similarly, preserving the privacy of consumers and building their trust with respect to the service provider can be very tedious in the modern era.

Solution: WE used following algorithms to secure our vehicles over the road network. Which can be explained as:

- Algorithms 1: This algorithm is used to encrypt the communicated data (over the road network) by the sender side.
- Algorithms 2: This algorithm uses Ring signature and public key sharing among users/drivers (over the road network) to encrypted and share the data.
- Algorithms 3: This algorithm is used to decrypt the communicated data (over the road network) by the receiver side.
- Algorithms 4: This algorithm is used to verify signature or shared keys or validate user to access the services (provided by vehicles).

Figure 2 and Figs. 3 show the creation of Blocks, and Blockchain which are written in Java language.

Algorithm 1: Data Encryption

1: **function** ENCRYPTION (data_ file)
2: **if** user confirm data preservation over blockchain **then**
3: Generate a symmetric key ksym
4: C ←Encrypts (data_ file, ksym)
5: Ck ← Encrypts (ksym, rkpub)
6: **else**
7: Do nothing
8: **end if**
9: end function

Algorithm 2: Ring Signature and Public key sharing

1: **function** SIGNATURE (data_ file)
2: **if** user chose anonymity over blockchain **then**
3: Generate an asymmetric public-private key pair sks pub, skspriv
4: hash p← calculate hash of the data_ file
5: Create the **Digital Signature** using hash p and signers private key skspriv
6: Share the public key skspub to the receiver using **Diffie–Hellman key exchange**
7: Mix the signature with another network group to form a ring
8: **end if**
9: end function

Algorithm 3: Data Decryption

1: **Input:** Encrypted file C, Encrypted symmetric key (Ck)
2: **Output:** Decrypted data_ file
3: **function** DECRYPTION (C, Ck, rkpriv, ksym)
4: ksym ←Decryptasym (Ck, rkpriv)
5: data_ file ←Decryptsym (C, ksym)
6: end function

Algorithm 4: Signature Verification

1: **Input:** Encrypted file C, Signers Public key (skspub)
2: **function** VERIFICATION (C, skspub)
3: hashc ← calculate hash of the received encrypted data file C to be verified
4: Using Public key skspub of signer, extract hashp of senders file
5: **if** hashc = hashpthen
6: return C
7: **else**
8: return "Signature incorrect"
9: **end if**
10: end function

```
 1    package blockchain;
 2    import java.util.*;
      import java.text.*;
 4    public class Blockchain {
 5        ArrayList<Block> blockchain = new ArrayList<>();
 6        public static void main(String[] args) {
 7            String[] genesisTransaction = {"Meghna1", "Harika1"};
 8            Block genesisBlock = new Block(0, genesisTransaction);
 9            System.out.println("Hash of Block 1:");
10            System.out.println(genesisBlock.getBlockHash());
11            //digitial signature of the block created
12
13            String[] block2Transaction = {"Meghna2", "Harika2"};
14            Block block2 = new Block(genesisBlock.getBlockHash(), block2Transaction);
15            System.out.println("Hash of Block 2:");
16            System.out.println(block2.getBlockHash());
17
18            String[] block3Transaction = {"Meghna31", "Harika3"};
19            Block block3 = new Block(block2.getBlockHash(), block2Transaction);
20            System.out.println("Hash of Block 3:");
21            System.out.println(block3.getBlockHash());
22
23        }
24    }
```

Fig. 2. Java code for creating a Blockchain

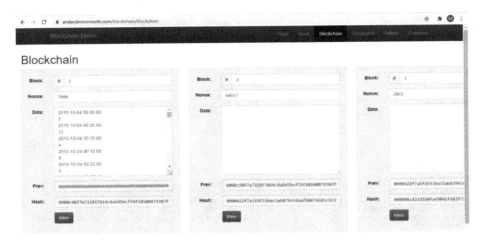

Fig. 3. Simulation of Blockchain after mining all the blocks

6 An Open Discussion on Internet of Things (IoT) – Machine Learning Based Autonomous Vehicles (AV)

Consistent supervision of data from various interconnected Avs and AIVs along with the strategy to compute suitable routes and paths based on environmental factors is what contributed towards the success and evolution of smart vehicles. Incorporating AI with such vehicles led to various patterns which are constantly evolving and they contribute towards identifying a route that smoothen the travel experience. When the AI determines that traffic patterns (using machine learning) are changing, it can even change the course of a journey if necessary. Few other comparisons are summarized here as:

a) Current Vehicles vs Future Vehicles
b) Autonomous Vehicles Vs Autonomous Intelligent Vehicles

In [13, 27], details about Intelligent Vehicles, connected vehicles, Hybrid Vehicles and Autonomous Intelligent Vehicles and raised issues in it have been explained. The majority of previous research on sensory network coverage have been theoretical. Deeper analysis might concentrate on solutions that can be implemented more quickly in the real world. The following is a list of other research issues. These distributed self-organizing networks have three major challenges: high node mobility [25, 26], system scalability constraints, and a wide variety of environmental factors. Automobiles travelling at high speeds in varied situations, such as on highways, provide a unique challenge. The bulk of iterative algorithms meant to optimise channel bandwidth or predefined paths interact with these properties. VANET security and privacy must be managed [27, 28]. The user's privacy concerns may collide with the recipient's desire to know the source of the information. Virtual area networks (VANs) face unique challenges when trying to establish reliable wireless connection.

7   Related Work

As discussed in [26, 27], for a wireless network to function, several general security requirements must be taken into account. These include authenticity, scalability, privacy and anonymity; as well as cooperation, stability, and low communication delay. With respect to this may researchers/scientist have made serious attempts to secure/preserve privacy of vehicles/such transportation system in the previous decades. Which can be summarized here as:

In the case of vehicular ad-hoc networks, the authors of [15] and [16] have worked on a seven-layered secure and reliable technique that utilizes blockchain based Vehicular Adhoc Network (VANETs) system. For applications that relate to gathering vehicular data, car taxes, etc. a combination of Ethereum and blockchain related smart contracts are used. The use of the technology was further enlarged to consist of peer-based interactions and intra-vehicle communication facilities. Furthermore, the author of [17] has put forth a technique using blockchain that is capable of updating the information of the vehicle wirelessly while preserving the details of the vehicle and its users. In [18], the authors have elucidated the use of blockchain via acoustic side channels along with vision empowered light so as to preserve data during intravehicular interactions. The implementation was carried out using a public key for the blockchain, a new key for cryptographic encryption, and a leverage mechanism for both the side-channels. On the other hand, the authors of [19] proposed an idea that utilizes distributed clustering to control the energy demands of IoV which is powered through blockchain facilities. The results obtained saves around 40% of energy and 82% of the transaction numbers needed. In [20], the authors have described the concept of blockchain and have focused on the architectural aspect of the selection process involved in choosing a gas filling station for an autonomous vehicle. The author has emphasized on the different security problems and concerns which prevail due to the existence of data that is transmitted between vehicles.

In [21], the proposal of a blockchain system to validate and verify consent between entities was highlighted. They've given details of using a multi-agent vehicle for communication and have elucidated how the communication can be secured in such cases. Furthermore, the authors of [22] have executed blockchain systems in unmanned aerial vehicles wherein, each vehicle is considered to be an individual node and the controlling mechanism is done by blockchain. Very recently, the authors of [23] had deployed the blockchain concept in terms of transferring data pertaining to traffic jams and scenarios which are transmitted to vehicles in a tamper proof way. The data is gathered through proof-of-event consensus and warnings are initiated through two-phase transaction strategies.

In the last, many other mechanisms like swing and swap, path confusion, l-diversity, encryption-based method, mix zone, etc., have been used in previous decades to preserve the privacy of users during accessing location-based services (LBSs).

8   Conclusion

This paper elaborates on IoT based Blockchain technique which ultimately records and keeps a track of all activities and transactions of users based on their interaction and connections with other nodes/users in the network. Smart contracts are used to help record the transactions and user activities consistently and frequent updates and upgrades of these records are augmented with IoT fragments to escalate the trade invested on the same which is linked with Blockchain systems. User convenience and user efficiency are major issue in transportation sector/future vehicles.

References

1. Bila, C., Sivrikaya, F., Khan, M.A., Albayrak, S.: Vehicles of the future: a survey of research on safety issues. IEEE Trans. Intell. Transp. Syst. **18**(5), 1046–1065 (2017). https://doi.org/10.1109/TITS.2016.2600300
2. Chen, K., et al.: A hierarchical hybrid system of integrated longitudinal and lateral control for intelligent vehicles. ISA Trans. **106**, 200–212 (2020)
3. Piao, J., McDonald, M.: Advanced driver assistance systems from autonomous to cooperative approach. Transp. Rev. **28**(5), 659–684 (2008). https://doi.org/10.1080/01441640801987825
4. Sebastian, A., Tang, M., Feng, Y., Looi, M.: Multi-vehicles interaction graph model for cooperative collision warning system. In: Intelligent vehicles symposium. IEEE, pp. 929–935 (2009)
5. Malikopoulos, A.A., Cassandras, C.G., Zhang, Y.J.: A decentralized energy-optimal control framework for connected automated vehicles at signal-free intersections. Automatica **93**, 244–256 (2018)
6. Haboucha, C.J., Ishaq, R., Shiftan, Y.: User preferences regarding autonomous vehicles. Transport. Res. Part C: Emerg. Technol. **78**, 37–49 (2017)
7. Pedan, M., Gregor, M., Plinta, D.: Implementation of automated guided vehicle system in healthcare facility. Procedia Eng. **192**, 665–670 (2017)
8. M. Gregor, M. Pedan, L. Mizeráková, "SMART" zdravotnícke zariadenia – využitie moderných technológií v zdravotníctve. In: ProIN: dvojmesačník CEIT, vol. 16, no. 5–6, pp. 21–24 (2015). ISSN: 1339–2271
9. Heard, B.R., Taiebat, M., Ming, X., Miller, S.A.: Sustainability implications of connected and autonomous vehicles for the food supply chain. Res., Conserv. Recycl. **128**, 22–24 (2018). https://doi.org/10.1016/j.resconrec.2017.09.021
10. Guerrero-ibanez, J.A., Zeadally, S., Contreras-Castillo, J.: Integration challenges of intelligent transportation systems with connected vehicle, cloud computing, and internet of things technologies. IEEE Wireless Commun. **22**(6), 122–128 (2015). https://doi.org/10.1109/MWC.2015.7368833
11. Sharma, N., Chauhan, N., Chand, N.: Security challenges in Internet of Vehicles (IoV) environment. First Int. Conf. Secure Cyber Comput. Commun. **2018**, 203–207 (2018). https://doi.org/10.1109/ICSCCC.2018.8703272
12. Kim, S.: Blockchain for a trust network among intelligent vehicles. In: Blockchain Technology: Platforms, Tools and Use Cases, pp. 43–68. Elsevier (2018). https://doi.org/10.1016/bs.adcom.2018.03.010
13. Honnery, D., Moriarty, P.: Future vehicles: an introduction. Int. J. Veh. Des. **35**, 1–8 (2004). https://doi.org/10.1504/IJVD.2004.004048
14. Tyagi, A.K., Fernandez, T.F., Mishra, S., Kumari, S.: Intelligent automation systems at the core of industry 4.0. In: Abraham, A., Piuri, V., Gandhi, N., Siarry, P., Kaklauskas, A., Madureira, A. (eds.) ISDA 2020. AISC, vol. 1351, pp. 1–18. Springer, Cham (2021). https://doi.org/10.1007/978-3-030-71187-0_1
15. Yuan, Y., Wang, F.-Y.: Towards blockchain-based intelligent transportation systems. In: 2016 IEEE 19th International Conference on Intelligent Transportation Systems (ITSC), 1–4 Nov 2016

16. Leiding, B., Memarmoshrefi, P., Hogrefe, D.: Self-managed and blockchain-based vehicular ad-hoc networks. In: Proceedings of the 2016 ACM International Joint Conference on Pervasive and Ubiquitous Computing: Adjunct (UbiComp'16), pp. 137–140. ACM, New York, NY, USA (2016)
17. Dorri, A., Steger, M., Kanhere, S.S., Jurdak, R.: Blockchain: a distributed solution to automotive security and privacy. eprint arXiv:1704.00073 (2017)
18. Rowan, S., Clear, M., Huggard, M., Goldrick, C.M.: Securing vehicle to vehicle data sharing using blockchain through visible light and acoustic side-channel. eprint arXiv:1704.02553 (2017). http://arxiv.org/abs/1704.02553
19. Sharma, V.: An energy-efficient transaction model for the blockchain-enabled internet of vehicles (IoV). IEEE Commun. Lett. **23**, 246–249 (2019)
20. Pustišek, M., Kos, A., Sedlar, U.: Blockchain based autonomous selection of electric vehicle charging station. In: Proceedings of the 2016 International Conference on Identification, Information and Knowledge in the Internet of Things (IIKI), Beijing, China, 20–21 Oct 2016
21. Buzachis, A., Celesti, A., Galletta, A., Fazio, M., Villari, M.: A secure and dependable multi-agent autonomous intersection management (MA-AIM) system leveraging blockchain facilities. In: Proceedings of the 2018 IEEE/ACM International Conference on Utility and Cloud Computing Companion (UCC Companion), Zurich, Switzerland, 17–20 Dec 2018
22. Kuzmin, A., Znak, E.: Blockchain-base structures for a secure and operate network of semi-autonomous Unmanned Aerial Vehicles. In: Proceedings of the 2018 IEEE International Conference on Service Operations and Logistics, and Informatics (SOLI), Singapore, 31 Jul–2 Aug 2018
23. Yang, H.-K., Cha, H.-J., Song, Y.-J.: Secure identifier management based on blockchain technology in NDN environment. IEEE Access **7**, 6262–6268 (2019)
24. Krishna, A.M., Tyagi, A.K.: Intrusion detection in intelligent transportation system and its applications using blockchain technology. In: 2020 International Conference on Emerging Trends in Information Technology and Engineering (ic-ETITE), pp. 1–8 (2020). https://doi.org/10.1109/ic-ETITE47903.2020.332
25. Tyagi, A.K., Sreenath, N.: Vehicular ad hoc networks: new challenges in carpooling and parking services. In: Proceeding of International Conference on Computational Intelligence and Communication (CIC), vol. 14. International Journal of Computer Science and Information Security (IJCSIS), Pondicherry, India, pp. 13–24
26. Varsha, R., Nair, M.M., Nair, S.M., Tyagi, A.K.: Deep learning based blockchain solution for preserving privacy in future vehicles. Int. J. Hybrid Intell. Syst. **16**(4), 223–236 (2021). https://doi.org/10.3233/HIS-200289
27. Tyagi, A.K., Aswathy, S.U.: Autonomous intelligent vehicles (AIV): research statements, open issues, challenges and road for future. Int. J. Intell. Network. **2**, 83–102 (2021). https://doi.org/10.1016/j.ijin.2021.07.002
28. Tyagi, A.K., Kumari, S., Fernandez, T.F., Aravindan, C.: P3 block: privacy preserved, trusted smart parking allotment for future vehicles of tomorrow. In: Gervasi, O., et al. (eds.) ICCSA 2020. LNCS, vol. 12254, pp. 783–796. Springer, Cham (2020). https://doi.org/10.1007/978-3-030-58817-5_56
29. Kumari, S., Tyagi, A.K., Aswathy, S.U.: The future of edge computing with blockchain technology: possibility of threats, opportunities and challenges. In: The Book "Recent Trends in Blockchain for Information Systems Security and Privacy", CRC Press (2021)
30. Nakamoto, S.: Bitcoin: A peer-to-peer electronic cash system (2008)

Applied Artificial Intelligence

A Comparative Analysis of Machine Learning Based Sentiment Analysis

Aparajita Sinha$^{(\boxtimes)}$ and Kunal Chakma

National Institute of Technology, Agartala, India
{aparajitacse.sch,kchakma.cse}@nita.ac.in

Abstract. In today's world, everyone expresses themselves through social media. The most popular platforms for sharing opinions on any issue are Twitter, Facebook, Youtube, IMDB, etc. We can examine people's attitudes after evaluating messages, comments, responses, and reviews. Sentiment Analysis is a Natural Language Processing technique for analyzing texts and determining how people feel about them. The purpose of Sentiment Analysis is for the computer to be able to detect and express emotions. This work aimed to apply Machine Learning to discover the best accuracy for text-based sentiment Analysis. We have used two datasets in this project, one is a dataset of tweets, and the other is a dataset of movie reviews. We analyze each Machine Learning algorithm's accuracy and find which algorithm gives the best accuracy in each dataset.

Keywords: Sentiment analysis · Machine learning · Accuracy analysis · TF-IDF

1 Introduction

Sentiment Analysis is the process of identifying subjective expressions inside a text and determining their polarity. An approach for detecting favorable and unfavorable attitudes toward specific topics in vast quantities of papers has a wide range of applications [19]. Sentiment Analysis can be done in a variety of methods, including text-based, sound-based, image-based, or a mix of the two. Sentiment Analysis has risen in popularity in the field of NLP (Natural Language Processing), and it has become a popular issue in business marketing. Positive, negative, and neutral are the three popular forms of Sentiment Labels used in Sentiment Analysis. Online documents now include enormous volumes of data. Researchers have been looking at the problem of automatic text categorization as part of their efforts to better arrange this information for users. In this paper, we performed a Comparative Analysis of various Machine Learning algorithms applied to two different datasets for sentiment analysis. The following steps were followed to conduct the sentiment Analysis: Text is preprocessed, Features are extracted, algorithms are applied, and the sentiment is extracted based on the text. We look at how Machine Learning methods may be used to

A. A. Sk et al. (Eds.): ISAI 2022, CCIS 1695, pp. 123–132, 2022.
https://doi.org/10.1007/978-3-031-22485-0_12

quantify accuracy. We tried Naïve Bayes classification, Support Vector Machine (SVM), Random Forest, and Logistic Regression which are all conventional algorithms. These Four algorithms have very distinct mindsets, yet they all have one thing in common: they all work. In prior text categorization experiments, these algorithms have been demonstrated to be effective. The effectiveness of using Machine Learning approaches to the Sentiment Analysis problem is investigated in this paper. The rest of the paper is organized as follows: researchers' existing Sentiment Analysis work is presented in Sect. 2. The proposed approach is described in Sect. 3. Section 4 covers Experiments on Machine Learning Algorithms. Section 5 presents the experimental findings, whereas Sect. 6 presents the conclusions and suggestions for further research.

2   Related Works

Modern generation people are now using social media sites, blogs, and forums to express their opinions and thoughts with the rest of the world. The range of sentiment values that can be used in sentiment analysis is often binary (positive, negative) or ternary (positive, negative, neutral). The objectives of sentiment analysis are determining polarity and classifying texts as positive, negative, or neutral. However, the sentiment can be classified in more than two ways; it can be classified as strongly disagree, disagree, neutral, agree, or strongly agrees [13]. Reda and Kashfia [12] used three distinct types of Machine Learning Algorithms: SVM, Random Forest, and Naïve Bayes for sentiment analysis on tweets. According to these three algorithms, they discover that Naïve Bayes provides the best accuracy. Ahuja et al. [15] utilized KNN, SVM, Logistic Regression, Naïve Bayes, and Random Forest, five different types of machine learning algorithms. They compare Feature Extraction techniques and find that using TF-IDF (Term Frequency-Inverse Document Frequency), Logistic Regression delivers the best accuracy 57% and using n-gram, Random Forest gives the best accuracy 51%. Pang et al. [14] on movie review datasets, tested three different Machine Learning Algorithms: SVM, Naïve Bayes, and Maximum Entropy Classification. Although the accuracy differences between these algorithms are small, Naïve Bayes and Maximum entropy yield lower accuracy than SVM. They discovered that traditional Machine Learning Algorithms beat human-produced baselines when using movie reviews as data. Soumya and Pramod [17] were utilize Different feature vectors to apply machine learning algorithms like Naïve Bayes and Random Forest to Malayalam Tweets, and it was discovered that Random Forest provides the best accuracy 95.6%. Alexandre Denis et al. [2] explore the Machine Learning (Random Forest Classification) Algorithm on two distinct datasets: Semeval-07 affective task news headlines and Semeval-13 sentiment analysis in Twitter tweets. It relies on simple features like stemmed words and part-of-speech. According to 10-Fold cross-validation results, they reach 64.30% accuracy on Semeval-07 and 60.72% accuracy on Semeval-13. The results demonstrate a considerable discrepancy, which is most likely due to the text length differences between the two datasets.

3   Methodology

We used two independent datasets in this work: the Stanford Test Dataset (Sentiment 140) [8] and the IMDB [1] Dataset. After five Preprocessing techniques, using TF-IDF approaches, we retrieved features, then applied four distinct algorithms. We used the sklearn[1] library's pre-built TF-IDF vectorizer. We are combining matplotlib and seaborn for visualization. Both Seaborn and Matplotlib, a superset of the latter, are necessary for effective visualizations. The Workflow Diagram is shown in Fig. 1, It describes the whole process of Comparative accuracy analysis of this research.

3.1   Dataset

We selected to work with movie reviews and Twitter datasets for our experiments. There are 1,600,000 tweets in the Stanford Test dataset (Sentiment 140) [8], which were gathered using the Twitter API. The tweets have been annotated with 0 as negative, 2 as neutral, and 4 as positive to detect emotion. The tweet hash code is 2087, it was posted on Saturday, May 16, 2009, at 23:58:44 UTC, and the user who posted it was robotickilldozr. Emoticons have been removed from the data, which is in CSV format and comprises six fields. Target, Ids, Date, Flag, User, and Text are the 6 fields. The value becomes NO-Query if there is no query in the tweet. There are 80,000 tweets that are positive and 80,000 tweets that are negative in the Stanford Test dataset (Sentiment 140). An effective technique for understanding model performance is to divide the dataset into a training set and a test set. Stanford Test Dataset(Sentiment 140) has 1,600,000 tweets for training and 498 tweets for the test. The IMDB(Internet Movie Database) dataset [1] comprises 50,000 movie reviews (25,000 positive and 25,000 negative sentiments), all of which are labeled as 0 for negative and 1 for positive. One column contains the text and the other contains a label, 1 for positive and 0 for negative. This dataset is also present in CSV format. We focused solely on distinguishing between positive and negative emotions for the research detailed in this paper. The ratio of the two components of the IMDB Dataset is 70:30. As a result, 30% of the data will be used to test the model, and 70% will be used to train it. The dataset statistics are shown in Fig. 2 and Fig. 3.

3.2   Preprocessing Text

Data processing is the first stage in developing a Machine Learning model, and it marks the start of the process. Pre-processing is a necessary step in the data cleansing process. The quality of the data has an impact on data cleaning as well. We used five preprocessing approaches in this paper: Tokenization, Normalization, Stopword removal, Stemming, and Lemmatization. Tokenization is

---

[1] Shorturl.at/ctwEP.

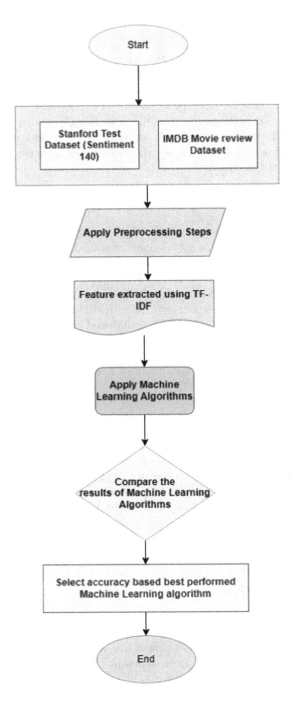

Fig. 1. Workflow diagram of sentiment analysis.

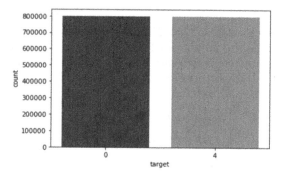

Fig. 2. Stanford test dataset sample.

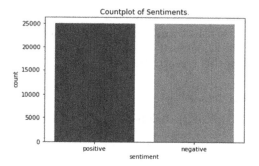

Fig. 3. IMDB dataset sample.

the process of breaking down a text or document into bits of words called tokens. Consider the following sentence: 'NLP is the best subject' before tokenization; after tokenization, it becomes: 'NLP', 'is','the', 'best','subject' [15]. To separate a sentence into tokens or words, we utilize the word_tokenize() method from the NLTK module. Normalization converts our data into a regularised range, making it easier to compare. The NLTK library provides a list of English stop words, which we use here. By truncating suffixes, words are transformed to their root form Stemming. Lemmatization is the process of removing inflectional ends from a token and converting it to the basic word lemma through morphological analysis. We Lemmatize the dataset using the help of Word Net Lemmatizer and perform Stemming using the help of SnowballStemmer.

3.3   Feature Extraction

TF-IDF. "Term Frequency - Inverse Document Frequency" is abbreviated as TF-IDF. The TF-IDF method works by comparing the relative frequency of terms in a single document to the inverse proportion of that word over the whole corpus of documents. Each number quantifies the information contained in these terms in the provided document and acts as a matrix to describe the text. This method is widely used in the disciplines of text mining and information retrieval. All of the text is vectorized so that the computer can better interpret it. The frequency of a term is the number of times it appears in the text. The term's occurrence in all documents is measured by inverse document frequency. We are using a pre-built TF-IDF vectorizer from the sklearn library. In this research we set max_df as 2 and min_df as 0.5.

$$TF(t,d) = count\ of\ t\ in\ d/number\ of\ words\ in\ d \tag{1}$$

$$IDF(t) = log(N/df + 1)) \tag{2}$$

$$TF - IDF = TF(t,d) * log(N/(df + 1)) \tag{3}$$

4   Experiments

In Machine Learning entire dataset is divided into two parts: Training and Testing datasets. First, we used to train the model and then check the performance of the model using the test dataset. Below we described four Machine Learning Models that are used in this research.

4.1   Support Vector Machine

This method is effective for both classification and regression. It creates a hyperplane to distinguish between classes. With regression, this method performs remarkably well, and the impact of SVM increases with the number of dimensions. SVM functions well when the dimension number exceeds the sample number [10]. Support vector machines (SVMs) have been found to outperform Naive Bayes in classical text categorization. Creating a hyperplane, symbolized by a vector w, that not only distinguishes between the document vectors in each class but also has a large separation or margin is the main notion behind the training strategy in the case of two categories. The SVM classifier provided in sklearn is used in this research. We are using Polynomial Kernel. The polynomial kernel can tell if the input space is curved or nonlinear [6]. In both datasets first, we split the data using the train_test_split() function after that we build the SVM Model using Polynomial Kernel in the SVC function. Then, fit our model on the train set using the fit function and predict on the test set with predict function.

4.2   Random Forest

A supervised machine learning system called Random Forest was built utilizing decision tree methods. A random forest algorithm is made up of several different decision trees. The emotion is assessed by creating a decision tree, and this collection of trees provides a more accurate result about a person's emotion. The outcome is determined by the number of decision trees that are satisfied. RandomForestClassifier from sklearn.ensemble given by scikit-learn was used to create the random forest algorithm. We split the data as train and test, After splitting, Using the features from the training set, we will build a model, and using the features from the test set, we will make predictions. [4].

4.3   Logistic Regression

Linear regression and logistic regression are extremely similar. Statistics experts developed the logistic function, commonly referred to as the sigmoid function, to describe how populations expand in ecology and how they eventually reach the carrying capacity of the environment [6]. This predictive analysis technique is based on the concept of probability. Logistic regression is used to model the probability that characterizes how a trial will turn out. Maximum Entropy is another name for this approach. We construct our logistic regression module and create a logistic regression classifier object using the logistic Regression function after partitioning the train-test dataset [7].

4.4   Naive Bayes

This technique is based on the Bayesian theory and operates on probability. It converts unconditional probability to conditional probability, which states that an event may occur based on the condition. The Bayes theorem is used in this model, which is based on the Naive assumption that there is no link between distinct features. The Bayes theorem states that

$$Posterior = likelihood * proposition/evidence. \tag{4}$$

It is known as naive because it assumes that the occurrence of one feature is unrelated to the occurrence of another. The multinomial Naïve Bayes classifier is effective for discrete feature classification. Normally, integer feature counts are required for the multinomial distribution. Tweet d has been assigned to class c_*, where

$$c_* = argmacc PNB(c|d) \tag{5}$$

$$PNB(c|d) := \frac{((P(c) \sum_{i=1}^{m} P(f|c)^{n_i(d)})}{P(d)} \tag{6}$$

In this formula, f stands for a feature, and $n_i(d)$ stands for the number of times feature fi was detected in tweet d.

There are m features in all. Maximum likelihood estimates are used to get the parameters P(c) and $P(f|c)$. In order to classify data using Naïve Bayes, we used MultinomialNB from sklearn.naive_bayes package. We fit the dataset on the classifier using the fit function and perform prediction using predict function [3].

5   Experimental Results

In this research, the TF-IDF feature vector was used to assess the correctness of two datasets. Using the IMDB Dataset, Table 1 obtained the results of four classification algorithms (Logistic Regression, Random Forest, Naïve Bayes, and SVM). On the Stanford Test Dataset (Sentiment 140), Table 2 obtained the results of four distinct algorithms (Logistic Regression, Random Forest, Naïve

Table 1. Accuracy measurement of IMDB dataset

Machine learning Algorithms	f1-score	Accuracy
1st-Logistic Regression	0.90	89.78%
2nd-Naïve Bayes	0.89	89.28%
3rd-Random Forest	0.85	85.08%
4th-Support Vector Machine	0.89	91.13%

Table 2. Accuracy measurement of stanford test dataset

Machine learning Algorithms	f1 score	Accuracy
1st-Logistic Regression	0.79	78%
2nd-Naïve Bayes	0.77	77%
3rd-Random Forest	0.77	78%
4th-Support Vector Machine	0.78	77%

Bayes, and SVM). In Table 1 we have seen that the Support Vector machine gives the best accuracy of 91.13% and in Table 2 we have seen that Logistic Regression and Random Forest give the best accuracy of 78%. Compare to both datasets SVM Works better in IMDB movie review datasets. We obtain validation accuracy of 89.78% using Logistic Regression on IMDB Dataset and 78% accuracy using Stanford Test Dataset (Sentiment 140). A huge number of categorical variables is too much for logistic regression to manage. It's prone to be overfitted. Independent variables that are not associated with the target variable but are very similar or correlated to each other will not perform well in logistic regression. Stanford Test Dataset (Sentiment 140) is larger than the IMDB Dataset so, Logistic Regression works better with IMDB Dataset. We obtain validation accuracy of 89.28% using Naïve Bayes on IMDB Datasets and 77% accuracy using Stanford Test Dataset (Sentiment 140). Comparing both accuracies we have seen that Naïve Bayes works better with IMDB Dataset. We obtain validation accuracy of 85.08% using Random Forest on IMDB Dataset and 78% accuracy using Stanford Test Dataset (Sentiment 140). The Random Forest algorithm also works better with IMDB Datasets. It takes a long time to generate because there are many decision trees involved. The Stanford Test Dataset has 1.6 million tweets, and because there are numerous decision trees generated, the accuracy is affected during the entire process. And Lastly we obtain validation accuracy of 91.13% using SVM on IMDB Dataset and 77% accuracy using Stanford Test Dataset (Sentiment 140). Stanford Test dataset (Sentiment 140) is larger than the IMDB Movie Review dataset, We have demonstrated that the high training time of SVM makes it unsuitable for larger datasets. Overlapping classes are a problem, and the kernel type is also a factor. So, SVM works better with IMDB movie review Dataset. After analyzing each Machine Learning Algorithms separately on two datasets, it is clear that Machine Learning Algorithms work better with IMDB Movie Review Dataset compared to Stanford Test Dataset (Sentiment 140).

6   Conclusion and Future Works

We used Logistic Regression, Naïve Bayes, Random Forest, and SVM to demonstrate the sentiment Analysis techniques in this research. Table 1 shows that the Support Vector Machine provides the highest level of accuracy (IMDB dataset). In addition, we found that logistic regression and random forest provide the best accuracy in Table 2. (Stanford Test Dataset). The novelty of this research is that it analyzes Machine Learning model accuracy using two datasets and concludes which model provides the best accuracy on which dataset. Sentiment Analysis is an increasingly growing research Area. In the future, we would like to try other Machine Learning and Deep Learning Algorithms to improve the accuracy. We also like to work on other aspects of analysis in the future, such as feature engineering comparisons, polarity, word embeddings, and so on.

References

1. Maas, A., Daly, R.E., Pham, P.T., Huang, D., Ng, A.Y., Potts, C.: Learning word vectors for sentiment analysis. In: Proceedings of the 49th Annual Meeting of the Association for Computational Linguistics: Human Language Technologies, pp. 142–150 (2011)
2. Denis, A., Cruz-Lara, S., Bellalem, N.: General purpose textual sentiment analysis and emotion detection tools. arXiv preprint arXiv:1309.2853 (2013)
3. Datacamp Naive Bayes. https://www.datacamp.com/community/tutorials/naive-bayes-scikit-learn
4. Datacamp Random Forest. https://www.datacamp.com/community/tutorials/random-forests-classifier-python
5. Datacamp Logistic Regression. https://machinelearningmastery.com/logistic-regression-for-machine-learning/
6. Datacamp SVM. https://www.datacamp.com/community/tutorials/svm-classification-scikit-learn-python
7. Datacamp. https://www.datacamp.com/community/tutorials/understanding-logistic-regression-python
8. Go, A., Bhayani, R., Huang, L.: Twitter sentiment classification using distant supervision. CS224N project report, Stanford, vol. 1, no. 12 (2009)
9. Hasan, A., Moin, S., Karim, A., Shamshirband, S.: Machine learning-based sentiment analysis for Twitter accounts. Math. Comput. Appl. **23**(1), 11 (2018). Mdpi
10. İşeri, İ., Atasoy, Ö.F., Alçiçek, H.: Sentiment classification of social media data for telecommunication companies in Turkey. In: International Conference on Computer Science and Engineering (UBMK), Antalya, pp. 1015–1019 (2017)
11. Kaggle IMDB Dataset. https://www.kaggle.com/lakshmi25npathi/imdb-dataset-of-50k-movie-reviews
12. Sailunaz, K., Alhajj, R.: Emotion and sentiment analysis from Twitter text. J. Comput. Sci. **36**, 101003 (2019)

13. Nandwani, P., Verma, R.: A review on sentiment analysis and emotion detection from text. Soc. Netw. Anal. Min. **11**(1), 1–19 (2021). https://doi.org/10.1007/s13278-021-00776-6
14. Pang, B., Lee, L., Vaithyanathan, S.: Thumbs up, pp. 79–86 (2002)
15. Ahuja, R., Chug, A., Kohli, S., Gupta, S., Ahuja, P.: The impact of features extraction on the sentiment analysis. Procedia Comput. Sci. **152**, 341–348 (2019)
16. Sentiment 140. http://help.sentiment140.com/for-students
17. Soumya, S., Pramod, K.V.: Sentiment analysis of Malayalam tweets using machine learning techniques. ICT Express **6**(4), 300–305 (2020)
18. Tan, S., Zhang, J.: An empirical study of sentiment analysis for Chinese documents. Expert Syst. Appl. **34**(4), 2622–2629 (2008)
19. Nasukawa, T., Yi, J.: Sentiment analysis: capturing favorability using natural language processing. In: Proceedings of the 2nd International Conference on Knowledge Capture, pp. 70–77 (2003)

ANN-Based Performance Prediction in MoCs

Biswajit Bhowmik$^{(\boxtimes)}$ (iD)

Department of Computer Science and Engineering, National Institute
of Technology Karnataka, Surathkal, Mangalore 575025, India
brb@nitk.edu.in

Abstract. Due to high integration density and technology scaling, the
manycore networks-on-chip (NoCs) often experience higher evaluation
time by traditional simulations for a set of common performance characteristics. Artificial intelligence (AI) is being employed as an altered solution over the simulation-based performance evaluation. However, many
AI techniques' accuracy and estimation time are low and high. This
paper proposes an artificial neural network (ANN) based framework to
quickly and more accurately evaluate mesh-based NoCs (MoCs). Experiments show that the essential performance metrics latency, throughput, and energy consumption are 16.53–40.76 cycles, 7.63–76.46 $\times 10^{-3}$
flits/cycle/IP, and 1417–1625 μJ, respectively. The proposed ANN framework achieves an accuracy of up to 96%. It is around 50% more compared
to many previous works.

1 Introduction

With the rapid advancements in technology, scaling a system-on-chip (SoC) is
continuously altered with a network-on-chip (NoC) because the latter architecture has successfully overcome two significant limitations- scalability and
communication bottleneck of the former architecture [1]. An NoC is a flexible
manycore on-chip communication network. It consists of three primary building
units- IP core, router (switch), and communication channel, interconnected to
build a topology [2]. Mesh-based infrastructures are commonly used in manycore on-chip communication systems. A mesh-based NoC (MoC) is traditionally
evaluated for different standard performance metrics like latency, throughput,
energy consumption, etc., on employing an NoC simulator. An NoC simulator,
e.g., Noxim, BookSim runs an MoC architecture and generates the standard
performance figures. The simulator can provide precise results if the underlying
MoC is simulated at the lower abstraction level or cycle level [3]. Consequently,
simulation time can take much time since a high computation effort is put into
simulating the MoC components at each cycle [4]. For a smaller MoC, this time
is lower and can be acceptable. However, with the increase in the number of
IP cores and interconnect, the MoC size increases. Subsequently, simulating a
higher MoC at the cycle level can take too much time. One can overcome the

A. A. Sk et al. (Eds.): ISAI 2022, CCIS 1695, pp. 133–144, 2022.
https://doi.org/10.1007/978-3-031-22485-0_13

situation by compromising the precise results. In this case, the MoC undergoes a high-level simulation that brings the results faster but with lower accuracy [5,6].

This paper proposes a machine learning approach to evaluate standard performance metrics in MoCs, i.e., mesh-based NoCs. The proposed scheme is based on the artificial neural network (ANN) model. The proposed ANN-model for MoCs (named here *MoCANN*) is first trained on exploiting the simulated data generated for a set of MoCs by the cycle-accurate Noxim simulator [7]. Next, the MoCANN model is executed to evaluate a considerable MoC. The evaluation is accomplished at varying system configurations to predict multiple performance parameters. Finally, the scheduled results for this MoC are validated with its simulated results. A highlight of the expected performance metrics includes 7.63–76.46 $\times 10^{-3}$ flits/cycle/IP as throughput, 16.53–40.76 cycles as global average latency (GAL), and 1417–1625 µJ as total energy consumption. The predicted error lies in the range of 4–6%, resulting in up to 96% accuracy. Compared to many previous works, this accuracy is more by 50%.

The rest of this paper is organized as follows. Section 2 presents the previous works in the literature. Section 3 presents the proposed scheme. Section 4 provides the results. Section 5 concludes this paper.

2   Related Works

Performance accuracy is one of the fundamental requirements for designing a manycore on-chip network because NoCs have a nonlinear behavior and tend to compromise performance accuracy by simulations [3]. On the contrary, designers seek to increase accuracy and reduce the error rate. Further, the accuracy loss could cause resource waste which can be seen more for larger NoCs [4]. One standard method of avoiding a simulation-based NoC evaluation is analytical modeling [8–11]. However, the analytical modeling method has multiple limitations. For instance, the method generally uses the queuing theory that restricts varying packet length and traffic distribution. The analytical modeling cannot be employed for the data, which is difficult to model analytically. On the contrary, NoC-based on-chip communication infrastructures possess this characteristic [12,13].

Machine Learning is a well-preferred technique nowadays broadly used in diverse perspectives such as performance evaluation and prediction of the systems like SoCs and NoCs, novel coronavirus (COVID-19) detection, etc. [14]. Trends in evaluating on-chip networks include various machine learning techniques over a traditional simulation method and an analytical modeling approach. Recent researches in this way are discussed in [4,15–26]. For example, Silva *et al.* [4] have suggested the use of a machine learning technique towards optimization of NoC components during its design phase. The authors have investigated the performance of different NoCs where the employed machine learning techniques achieve accuracy up to 85%. Qian *et al.* [15] have presented a support vector regression (SVR) model for the latency estimation in NoCs. Experimental results of the SVR model provide the prediction error up to 12%; in other words, the performance accuracy is up to 88%. Zheng *et al.* [22] have designed an energy-efficient NoC using a reinforcement learning technique. Evaluation of this technique shows that it can estimate NoC performance up to 93% accurately. Chen *et al.* [16] have addressed the thermal issue as a challenge to the current design of NoC-based complex systems. The authors have employed a proactive and dynamic thermal management (PDTM) technique to control the system temperature. The PDTM can reduce average error by 37.20–62.30%, resulting in 9.16–38.37% system performance. Ping *et al.* [17] presented a latency estimation scheme based on the high accuracy prediction tree method. This tree-based scheme achieves up to 82% accuracy of latency prediction over a mesh network of 120 nodes. Hou *et al.* [20] designed a machine learning-enabled framework targetting performability evaluation of traditional NoCs. The framework applies Markov reward models. Experimental results on an 8×8 mesh NoC show that this scheme achieves communication time accuracy up to 93.32%. Kenarangi *et al.* [23] have used a machine learning technique against on-chip power analysis attacks in NoCs. The simulation result achieves an accuracy of 88%.

The machine learning-based method mentioned above for NoC performance estimation approaches is comparative. However, they are not adequate to the expected level even many previous works offer accuracy below 50%. Their estimation time and performance accuracy still need improvement while a larger NoC or a multimedia application run on an NoC is considered. Thus, it motivates to design an alternate machine learning method that quickly and accurately estimates vagarious performance metrics in NoCs of larger size. Very recently, Bhowmik *et al.* [3] have proposed an SVR framework that predicts the performance of traditional NoCs. In another work [6], Bhowmik *et al.* have proposed a linear regression model to evaluate NoCs' performance. The authors have used the training and test datasets generated using the BookSim simulator in both cases. Current work is an alternative scheme to the strategies discussed above, including [3,6].

3   Proposed Work

Mesh-based NoCs, i.e., MoCs, are the standard manycore on-chip communication networks because they are flexible, regular, and easy to implement. MoCs represent a new paradigm for integrated multiprocessor systems-on-chip (MPSoCs) that support homogeneous and heterogeneous applications. The most common approach to studying MoCs is using an NoC simulator despite it taking higher evaluation time, significantly when the MoC size increases with IP cores and interconnects. This section presents the MoCANN framework as an alternative to the traditional simulation-based MoC evaluation.

3.1   ANN Model

An ANN framework is a computational model based on the belief that human brain workings can be imitated by making the right connections of several processing elements, e.g., silicons and wires. Silicons are treated as neurons, whereas

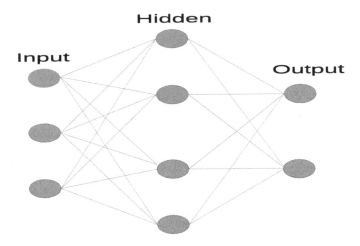

Fig. 1. A typical ANN architecture.

the wires (also known as arcs) are the dendrites. The processing elements receive inputs and deliver outputs concerning their predefined activation functions. Each arc in an ANN model has a weight transferred as the input to the next layer. ANNs are capable of learning. A weight adjusts as learning proceeds. The signal strength at a connection depends on this weight and Consequently increases or decreases.

An ANN model is a layered architecture consisting of three layers- input, hidden, and output. Figure 1 shows a typical ANN Model. The input layer contains the basic information received from external sources, e.g., data files that are later fed to a hidden layer of the system. An ANN model contains multiple hidden layers that evaluate input units and arc weights between hidden and input units. The last and output layer processes the data from the hidden units and provides data points based on the network function.

Hyperparameter Tuning. A hyperparameter is a parameter used to control the learning process. The value of a hyperparameter is set before the learning process begins. A hyperparameter can be independent or dependent. Independent hyperparameters include the number of hidden layers, learning rate, activation function, number of epochs, etc. A few dependent hyperparameters have the size of some layers based on the total number of layers. The values of these parameters are, however, derived via learning. Thus, hyperparameters are the variable that can decide an ANN structure and its training. In this work, multiple hyperparameters are tuned to evaluate the MoCs and improve their performance metrics via prediction. The hyperparameters for the proposed MoCANN model are chosen before introducing its training and adjusted using a random search so that the MoCANN gives the best possible result on the test dataset.

Selection of Hidden Layers. Hidden layer selection is one crucial task in an ANN. Depending on the complexity of the training dataset, the number of hidden layers varies. For example, the ANN uses 1–2 hidden layers if the dataset is simple or less complex. On the other hand, the ANN needs 3–5 or more hidden layers if the dataset is more complex. Subsequently, a learning algorithm at multiple epochs defines the training dataset's works. Different activation functions are used in the hidden and output layers. The role of these activation functions is to convert a weighted sum of input into an out from one node to another. ReLU and linear are two activation functions used in the hidden and output layers of the proposed MoCANN model to get a better result.

Optimizer Selection. An ANN model is expected to work well. Otherwise, the term "loss" defines how the model works poorly. So, the model must be trained such that the loss is minimum. It is possible to change the weights and learning rate of the model by using an optimizer. The MoCANN model uses the adam optimizer as it provides a better result.

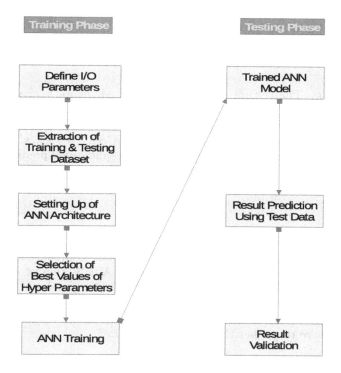

Fig. 2. Proposed MoCANN framework.

3.2   MoCANN Phases

Figure 2 gives a high-level view of the proposed ANN model. The MoCANN works in two phases- training and testing.

Training Phase. Training is a fundamental stage for any ANN framework to predict a parameter. To train the proposed MoCANN model, input and out parameters are first defined. A group of MoCs are simulated to provide both training and test datasets. Then the training dataset is input into the MoCANN framework for learning. The framework learns by processing examples having an input-output relationship. Additionally, the examples store the weights in the net's data structure. The best values of the hyperparameters are selected for better learning, where both weight and bias variables are randomly initialized using the network optimizer. The trained values may differ from the expected output. This difference is known as the error and is measured here as mean square error (MSE) defined in Eq. 1. Here, N = number of data points, y_t is the actual value, and y_t^* is the predicted output [6]. The error is minimized on several iterations and adjusting weights by its learning rule.

$$MSE = \frac{1}{N} \sum_{t=1}^{N} (y_t^* - y_t)^2 \tag{1}$$

Testing Phase. The testing phase is another fundamental stage of an ANN model to validate the predicted results. In this work, the proposed MoCANN framework undergoes testing once its training phase is over. Simulated results from lower-sized MoCs are used for training the MoCANN model, while the same generated from a higher-sized MoC is exploited to validate its predicted results. Thus, the MSE for the MoC validates its accuracy on the predicted results for the simulated results.

4   Results

This section evaluates the proposed MoCANN model to predict standard performance metrics for a set of MoC architectures. A collection of 32-bit MoCs are simulated with the help of a cycle-accurate Noxim simulator that derives the training data for the MoCANN model. The size of the MoCs ranges from $4 \times 4 - 10 \times 10$ whose simulated data are used for training. The trained MoCANN model is used here to predict the 32-bit 11×11 MoC.

4.1   Simulation Setup

Both training and test data are generated by simulating several 32-bit MoCs. Simulations are performed at different environments, including network type and size, channel width, packet injection rate (PIR), routing strategy, buffer

Table 1. Noxim simulation configuration details.

Topology type	2D Mesh
Network size	$4 \times 4 - 11 \times 11$
Channel width	32-bit
Traffic pattern	Random
Routing algorithm	XY Routing
Buffer size	4
Packet size	8 flits
Flit size	32 bits
Simulation period	1000000 cycles
Warmup period	1000 cycles
Injection rate	0.0001–0.01

size, packet size, traffic type, etc. In this work, the PIR = 0.0001–00.01, 32-bit channels, XY routing are considered to simulate $4 \times 4 - 10 \times 10$ MoCs to train the proposed MoCANN model. The simulated data derived at the extended environment for 11×11 MoC is the test data used to validate the predicted results for the MoC. Table 1 summarizes a tentative simulation setup in the Noxim simulator for the MoCs. In every case, experiments are accomplished in a desktop computing system having a basic configuration as Core i7, 3.0 GHz, 64-bit Processor, 16 GB RAM, and Ubuntu 18.04 LTS OS.

4.2   Predicted Results Analysis

Proposed MoCANN framework targets to estimate MoC's performance quickly over a traditional simulation-based evaluation and more accurately over a set of prior works. Figure 3 shows the simulated results by Noxim for the $4 \times 4 - 10 \times 10$ MoCs at the PIR = 0.0005. The simulation is run for 10^6 cycles. The Figure also shows the behavior of the MoCANN model during its training, exploiting these simulated, i.e., training data. The proposed prediction model is trained to evaluate several performance metrics like throughput, latency, dynamic, and total energy consumption. It is observed that the prediction model successfully gets trained with the training data and is ready to predict these metrics for a higher, e.g., 11×11 MoC.

Figure 4 demonstrates the predicted metrics for the 32-bit 11×11 MoC by the MoCANN model. The experiment is run at PIR = 0.001–0.01, each runs for 10^6 cycles. Three fundamental performance metrics are provided here. First, the global average latency (GAL) is shown in Fig. 4a. It shows that the metrics range from 16.53 to 40.76 cycles. The throughput is shown in Fig. 4b. Transferring traffic (packets or flits) from source to destination consumes energy. Both dynamic and total energy consumption are shown in Fig. 4c and 4d, respectively.

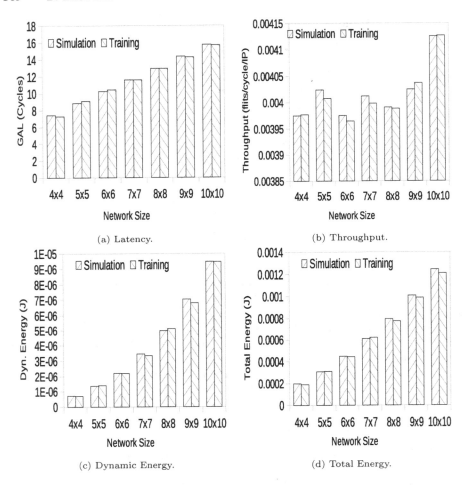

(a) Latency.

(b) Throughput.

(c) Dynamic Energy.

(d) Total Energy.

Fig. 3. Training of MoCANN with noxim simulated results.

It shows that the dynamic energy consumption ranges 23–235 μJ while the total energy consumption ranges as 1417–1625 μJ, respectively.

4.3   Result Validation and Comparison

Predicted results by the proposed MoCANN model need validation. Its validation is done with the simulated results of Noxim for the 11 × 11 MoC. Figure 5 demonstrates the side-by-side comparison between the predicted and simulated results. One can observe that the proposed MoCANN model can predict the performance metrics in the range of 94–96%. This accuracy is up to 50% more compared to many previous works. Although the proposed MoCANN has a minor prediction error (4–6%) over the Noxim simulator, it predicts the performance

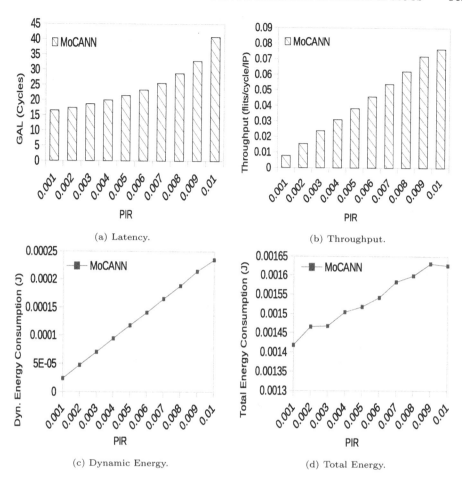

(a) Latency.

(b) Throughput.

(c) Dynamic Energy.

(d) Total Energy.

Fig. 4. Common metrics prediction by MoCANN on 11 × 11 MoC.

metrics more quickly. It is nearly 400× faster than the time needed for the metrics by the Noxim simulator. The proposed MoCANN framework's correctness is achieved by considering several hidden layers and tuning hyperparameters in the framework. Additionally, the proposed MoCANN outperforms many existing schemes. For example, the method discussed in [4] achieves accuracy up to 85%, i.e., 9–11% less than the MoCANN. So, the MoCANN relatively predicts the metrics by 12.50% more accurately. The model used in [17] provides the highest accuracy, up to 82%. Consequently, the proposed MoCANN is about 14%, i.e., relatively 17.07% more accurate.

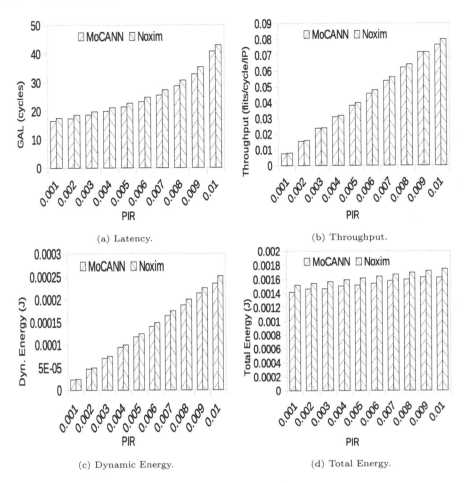

(a) Latency.

(b) Throughput.

(c) Dynamic Energy.

(d) Total Energy.

Fig. 5. Validation of metrics prediction by MoCANN.

5   Conclusion

This paper presented an ANN framework as an alternate solution over a simulation-based method for evaluating MoCs. Experimental results show that the proposed framework has achieved prediction accuracy up to 96% for well-known MoC's performance metrics. This accuracy is nearly 50% more than many existing machine learning-based evaluations of MoCs. Future work includes improving the current accuracy level towards 100%. Scalability is another vital characteristic of the MoCANN. Another future scope consists of the scalability issue of the proposed ANN model concerning MoC's architectural and evaluation features: channel width, network size, and traffic type.

References

1. Bhowmik, B.: Dugdugi: an optimal fault addressing scheme for octagon-like on-chip communication networks. IEEE Trans. Very Large Scale Integr. (VLSI) Syst. **29**(5), 1009–1021 (2021)
2. Bhowmik, B., Deka, J.K., Biswas, S.: Reliability monitoring in a smart NoC component. In: 2020 27th IEEE International Conference on Electronics, Circuits and Systems (ICECS), pp. 1–4 (2020)
3. Jain, S., Kale, P., Hazarika, P., Bhowmik, B.: A machine learning enabled NoC performance evaluation. In: 2021 IEEE 25th High Performance Extreme Computing (HPEC), pp. 1–6, September 2021
4. Silva, J., Kreutz, M., Pereira, M., Da Costa-Abreu, M.: An investigation of latency prediction for NoC-based communication architectures using machine learning techniques. J. Supercomput. **75**(11), 7573–7591 (2019)
5. Qian, Z.-L., Juan, D.-C., Bogdan, P., Tsui, C.-Y., Marculescu, D., Marculescu, R.: A support vector regression (SVR)-based latency model for network-on-chip (NoC) architectures. IEEE Trans. Comput. Aided Des. Integr. Circuits Syst. **35**(3), 471–484 (2016)
6. Bhowmik, B., Hazarika, P., Kale, P., Jain, S.: AI technology for NoC performance evaluation. IEEE Trans. Circuits Syst. II Express Br. **68**(12), 3483–3487 (2021)
7. Catania, V., Mineo, A., Monteleone, S., Palesi, M., Patti, D.: Cycle-accurate network on chip simulation with Noxim. ACM Trans. Model. Comput. Simul. **27**(1), 4:1–4:25 (2016)
8. Ost, L., et al.: Power-aware dynamic mapping heuristics for NoC-based MPSoCS using a unified model-based approach. ACM Trans. Embed. Comput. Syst. **12**(3) (2013)
9. Qian, Z., Juan, D.-C., Bogdan, P., Tsui, C.-Y., Marculescu, D., Marculescu, R.: A comprehensive and accurate latency model for network-on-chip performance analysis. In: 2014 19th Asia and South Pacific Design Automation Conference (ASP-DAC), pp. 323–328 (2014)
10. Bhattacharya, D., Jha, N.K.: Analytical modeling of the smart NoC. IEEE Trans. Multi-Scale Comput. Syst. **3**(4), 242–254 (2017)
11. Qian, Z., Juan, D.-C., Bogdan, P., Tsui, C.-Y., Marculescu, D., Marculescu, R.: SVR-NoC: a performance analysis tool for network-on-chips using learning-based support vector regression model. In: 2013 Design, Automation Test in Europe Conference Exhibition (DATE), pp. 354–357 (2013)
12. Sze, V., Chen, Y.-H., Emer, J., Suleiman, A., Zhang, Z.: Hardware for machine learning: challenges and opportunities. In: 2017 IEEE Custom Integrated Circuits Conference (CICC), pp. 1–8 (2017)
13. Ogras, U.Y., Bogdan, P., Marculescu, R.: An analytical approach for network-on-chip performance analysis. IEEE Trans. Comput. Aided Des. Integr. Circuits Syst. **29**(12), 2001–2013 (2010)
14. Bhowmik, B., Varna, S.A., Kumar, A., Kumar, R.: Reducing false prediction on COVID-19 detection using deep learning. In: 2021 IEEE International Midwest Symposium on Circuits and Systems (MWSCAS), pp. 404–407 (2021)
15. Qian, Z.-L., Juan, D.-C., Bogdan, P., Tsui, C.-Y., Marculescu, D., Marculescu, R.: A support vector regression (SVR)-based latency model for network-on-chip (NoC) architectures. IEEE Trans. Comput. Aided Des. Integr. Circuits Syst. **35**(3), 471–484 (2015)

16. Chen, K.-C.J., Liao, Y.-H.: Adaptive machine learning-based temperature prediction scheme for thermal-aware NoC system. In: 2020 IEEE International Symposium on Circuits and Systems (ISCAS), pp 1–4 . IEEE (2020)
17. Ping, L.B., Kit, C.P., Karuppiah, E.K.: Network latency prediction using high accuracy prediction tree. In: Proceedings of the 7th International Conference on Ubiquitous Information Management and Communication, pp. 1–8 (2013)
18. Chen, K.-C., Wang, T.-Y.: NN-Noxim: high-level cycle-accurate NoC-based neural networks simulator. In: 2018 11th International Workshop on Network on Chip Architectures (NoCArc), pp. 1–5 (2018)
19. Chen, Y., Louri, A.: Learning-based quality management for approximate communication in network-on-chips. IEEE Trans. Comput. Aided Des. Integr. Circuits Syst. 39(11), 3724–3735 (2020)
20. Hou, J., Han, Q., Radetzki, M.: A machine learning enabled long-term performance evaluation framework for NoCs. In: 2019 IEEE 13th International Symposium on Embedded Multicore/Many-core Systems-on-Chip (MCSoC), pp. 164–171 (2019)
21. Zheng, H., Louri, A.: Agile: a learning-enabled power and performance-efficient network-on-chip design. IEEE Trans. Emerg. Topics Comput., 1–13 (2020)
22. Hao, Z., Louri, A.: An energy-efficient network-on-chip design using reinforcement learning. In: Proceedings of the 56th Annual Design Automation Conference 2019, pp. 1–6 (2019)
23. Kenarangi, F., Partin-Vaisband, I.: Exploiting machine learning against on-chip power analysis attacks: tradeoffs and design considerations. IEEE Trans. Circuits Syst. I Regul. Pap. 66(2), 769–781 (2019)
24. Gao, W., Zhou, P.: Customized high performance and energy efficient communication networks for AI chips. IEEE Access 7, 69434–69446 (2019)
25. Choi, W., Duraisamy, K., Kim, R.G., Doppa, J.R., Pande, P.P., Marculescu, D., Marculescu, R.: On-chip communication network for efficient training of deep convolutional networks on heterogeneous manycore systems. IEEE Trans. Comput. 67(5), 672–686 (2018)
26. Joardar, B.K., Kim, R.G., Doppa, J.R., Pande, P.P., Marculescu, D., Marculescu, R.: Learning-based application-agnostic 3D NoC design for heterogeneous manycore systems. IEEE Trans. Comput. 68(6), 852–866 (2019)

Assessment of Shallow and Deep Learning Models for Prediction of Sea Surface Temperature

Susmita Biswas[1]([✉]) [iD] and Mourani Sinha[2] [iD]

[1] Department of Computer Science and Engineering, Techno India University, Kolkata, West Bengal, India
bi.susmita@gmail.com
[2] Department of Mathematics, Techno India University, Kolkata, West Bengal, India

Abstract. Prediction of sea surface temperature is important for the study of marine ecosystems in the oceanic area. The sea surface temperature is a major parameter for analysing extreme atmospheric events. Sea surface temperature determines how heat from the sun is redistributed across the world's oceans and will directly affect large- and small-scale weather and climate patterns. Comparison studies of two different learning (shallow and deep) models are employed for the forecasting of sea surface temperature. In most cases, the deep learning model also manages to overcome the limitations of the prior shallow learning models depending on the complexity of the problem, which helps to impede efficient training and discrete representations of multi-dimensional training data. The deep learning-based LSTM model is considered for the quick prediction of sea surface temperature with higher accuracy than the usual shallow learning-based feedforward model. Two different monthly SST time series data are applied for the estimation of sea surface temperature in the eastern Arabian Sea (AS) as well as Bay of Bengal (BOB) whose grid points are (70°E, 15°N) and (90°E, 15°N) respectively. LSTM and feedforward models are trained with 80% data and tested with different hidden units and epoch values to acquire a minimum error. For the 20% testing set, AS time-series data using the feedforward model gave more error. Performances of the prediction models are assessed by using root mean square error (RMSE). The results suggest that the temporal LSTM model outperforms the feedforward model specifically on sea surface temperature time series forecasting.

Keywords: Sea surface temperature (SST) · Deep learning · Shallow learning · Arabian Sea · Bay of Bengal

1 Introduction

Sea surface temperature (SST) in the Indian Ocean contributes to accelerate global warming, affecting local climate change and the health of the coastal marine ecosystem.

Therefore, SST distribution forecasts in these areas, especially seasonal and annual forecasts, succeed in providing information to understand and evaluate the future consequences of SST changes. [1] Surface temperature is one of the first and the most important ocean parameters examined in the world's oceanic area, whose changes help to have a deep effect on the global climate and can lead to extreme catastrophes like as droughts and floods. Therefore, it is very important to predict the dynamics of future SST which may help [2]. Various techniques are applied for measuring SST. Physics-based or data-driven approaches are used for the prediction of SST. This study essentially combines the numerical and machine learning methods for better SST prediction [3]. In some last decades, different research has been directed to evaluate the sea surface temperature (SST) for appraisement of thermal interchanges between the world's oceans and atmosphere, behavior patterns of aquatic- species, and ocean or tidal currents [7]. Recently, the neural network is the most popular technique for the estimation of SST. Many researchers have applied neural networks to predict the SST. Researcher studied the seasonal forecast of SST across a specific region of the tropical Pacific Ocean [4]. To the author's best knowledge, the neural network is designed to predict SST with long length data values in different geographical locations of India [5]. [2] exhibited the effectiveness of the LSTM network in SST quantification using satellite data and their results showed the most exact predictions to be provided by the LSTM model. In addition, the temporal and spatial information have also been combined for better SST prediction results [6]. Some other researchers introduced a back-propagation neural network (BPNN) technique for determining the subsurface temperature of the North Pacific Ocean by selecting the best input aggregation of sea surface parameters acquired from satellite measurements [14]. Soft computing is another model based on time series modelling that has been employed to predict the SST. Complex and non-linear problems are solved by this model [8]. In another study [9] was employed to assess SST using SVR and LR in the Canadian Berkley Canyon. Several types of input variables such as Latitude, longitude, and depth of water were applied as input variables. These input variables have rarely been used to get accurate prediction results of SST. The outcomes expressed that the SVR provided estimates closer to the observed data than the LR. Another research calculating the capabilities of DGCnetwork models for estimating SST was the one by, [10] who applied DGCnetwork for maintaining good prediction outcomes, better accuracy and stronger stability which has reached the most advanced level. In another research, location-specific SST predictions were formed by putting together deep learning neural networks with numerical estimators at five various localities across India for three distinct time zones (daily, monthly, yearly) [13]. In [12], author developed and compared deep learning and shallow learning models for forecasting wind speed in Indian ocean region. An additional study involving LSTM models was carried through by (11) who employed LSTM, Multi-Layer Perceptron Regression (MLPR), and SVR for modelling the SST in oceans and looked for LSTM to provide the best performance and most exact estimates among the models contemplated. In ocean climatic research, the different learning models play a very important role. So far though, the majority of SST prediction research is based on LSTM techniques adopted on deep learning model, a few studies employed feedforward shallow learning-based model and its hybrid versions.

2   Materials and Method

This present research is used an extended reconstructed sea surface temperature (ERSST) data set which has temporal coverage daily and spatial coverage global sea surface temperature dataset and it is derived from the international comprehensive ocean-atmosphere dataset (ICOADS) and downloaded from https://psl.noaa.gov/data/gridded/data.noaa.ersst.v5.html. Study region covering two SST monthly mean datasets whose grid points one at every AS (70°E and 15°N) and BOB (90°E and 15°N) are chosen for this current experiment. NOAA Extended Reconstructed SST V5 reanalysis data are used here has spatial resolution 2° by 2°. Both AS and BOB data set contains 360 values from the year 1991 to 2020. Both AS and BOB SST time series is prepared for the above two grids. Shallow learning models and deep learning models are chosen for the predictions. To work out the complicated issues in deep learning architectures with several layers like LSTM has been verified to be more fruitful than shallow learning architectures such as feedforward without loops. In present study two learning models namely, Feedforward, and LSTM have been compared and learned. Comparison is driven with respect to root means square error (RMSE) and means square error (MSE). These two network learning algorithms are trained using the 30-years' time-series data.

3   Results and Discussion

Results of time series prediction for both grids (AS and BOB) are compared in terms of tables and different graphs. Monthly SST data is calculated over BOB grids (90°E and 15°N) and AS grids (70°E and 15°N) using feedforward, and LSTM models. Every dataset contains 360 (30 * 12) points for 30 years from 1991 to 2020. Figures 1 and 2 illustrate the plots of the time series during the BOB and AS grid SST data from 1991 to 2020. Time series data is divided into two parts, the training (80%) set, and the test (20%) set. Different hidden units (30, 50, 200, and 250) are tested using values and epochs (50, 100, 200, 500, 1000, 2500, and 4000) to get the best accuracy. The feed-forward model was selected for the BOB and AS time series considering 30,50 hidden units and an

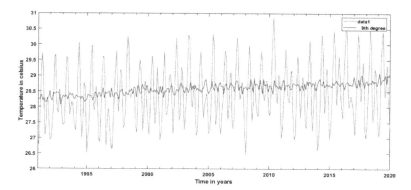

Fig. 1. ERSST monthly SST data of AS grid (70°E, 15°N) from 1991 to 2020

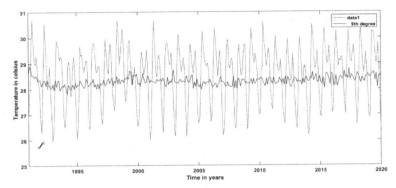

Fig. 2. ERSST monthly SST data of BOB grid (90°E, 15°N) from 1991 to 2020

initial flame rate of 0.005. The learning rate has decreased after 2500 epochs of AS grid and 1000 epoch for the BOB grid.

Figure 3 illustrates, considering AS time series for comparing observed and forecasted values for training by using the feed-forward model. After comparing target and output results, the error value is evaluated. The goal is to input time series and the results are the evaluated value. 0.078764 °C is the calculating MSE value and 0.28065 °C is the RMSE value. The output data is compatible with the target data histogram plot. The error means is computed which is the average of the results of the error and the standard error value is computed using the standardized data error.

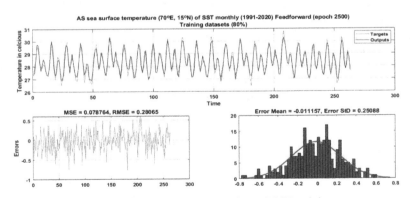

Fig. 3. Feedforward model are used to AS SST training set

Figure 4 depicts a similar plot for the BOB grid. After calculation, it is seen that the RMSE value is 0.19612 °C which is almost nearby the AS RMSE value. Working with the LSTM model, 250 hidden units and a 0.005 elementary learning rate were selected and the learning rate was lowered after 1000 epochs for AS and 500 epochs for BOB grid, respectively.

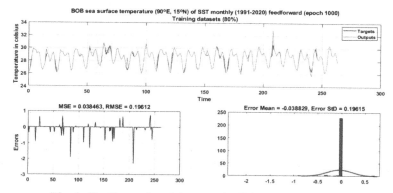

Fig. 4. Feedforward model are used to BOB SST training set

Figures 5 and 6 illustrates Observed and predicted SST values for AS and BOB grids are compared applying the LSTM model. The errors are much lower than in the shallow feed-forward model.

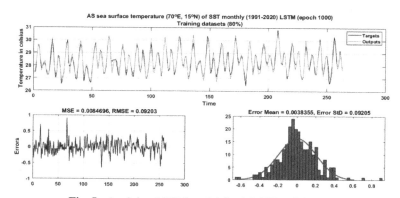

Fig. 5. Applying LSTM model for AS SST training set

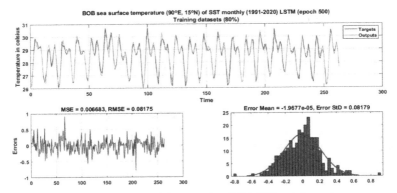

Fig. 6. LSTM model are used to BOB SST training set

Later, the plots for the 10% testing dataset are depicted. Figures 7 and 8 depict the comparison between the observed and forecasted SST values for the AS and BOB grids using the Feedforward network for the 20% testing dataset. Figures 9 and 10 give the same for the LSTM network.

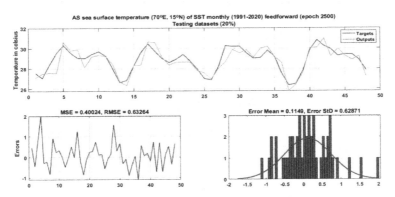

Fig. 7. Application of feedforward model for AS SST testing set

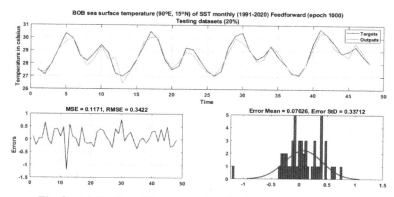

Fig. 8. Application of feedforward model for BOB SST testing set

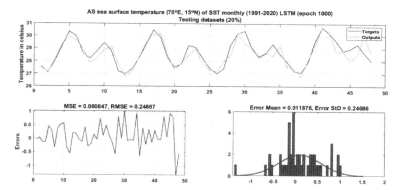

Fig. 9. Application of LSTM model for AS SST testing set

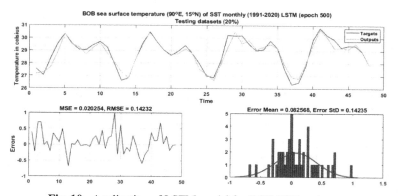

Fig. 10. Application of LSTM model for BOB SST testing set

Tables 1 and 2 depict the values of epoch for the various hidden units for the BOB as well as AS grid testing datasets (20%), respectively. RMSE values are calculated in °C by comparing the feedforward and LSTM models.

Table 1. Error estimation for the application of Feedforward model using AS and BOB grid time series testing set (20%).

Feedforward model		RMSE Values (⁰C)	
Epoch	Hidden layer	AS grid (70⁰ E,15⁰N) from 1991 to 2020	BOB grid (90⁰ E, 15⁰N) from 1991 to 2020
		1.09234	0.41231
50		0.89432	0.39997
100		0.78101	0.39882
250	(30,50)	0.75789	0.41209
500		0.88976	0.37102
1000		0.98782	0.3422
2500		0.63264	0.40012

The error was reduced significantly for the deep learning-based LSTM model. The estimated output time series pursuance the trend of the target or input time series. Considering AS grid, the RMSE error from approximately 0.63264 °C for a shallow network reduces to approximately 0.24667 °C for the LSTM network. There is a momentous improvement in prediction skills. The error means and error standard also reduced substantially as the time series is trained from shallow to deep models. Different hidden units and epoch values are chosen and tested to obtain the minimum RMSE for the 20% testing dataset. In Comparison of the BOB and AS grids there is little bit dissimilation in the trend or pattern of the forecasting strategy but may be sustained for broader applications in the future study. In this research, LSTM and Feedforward learning model have been proposed for the spatio temporal relationship of SST to estimate the future value. To forecast this random time-series data like SST, shallow and deep network models have been assessed in present research. The LSTM model for both grids performed much better than the feedforward model using both previous and subsequent data. LSTM approach needs only to preserve information for the past and future. The architecture suggests that the deep learning-based LSTM model having higher potential performs much better than the shallow learning-based feedforward model. Errors are decreased by some percentage. In the case of the shallow feed-forward model, deep learning models illustrate better prediction accuracy. Considering both grids, The LSTM model provides excellent results.

Table 2. Error estimation for the application of LSTM model using AS and BOB grid time series testing set (20%).

LSTM model		RMSE Values (^{0}C)	
Epoch	Hidden layer	AS grid (70^0 E,15^{0}N) from 1991 to 2020	BOB grid (90^0 E, 15^{0}N) from 1991 to 2020
		0.29801	0.19998
50		0.30061	0.20001
100		0.28970	0.20176
250	250	0.27609	0.19874
500		0.29910	0.14232
1000		0.24667	0.24221
2500		0.39264	0.29879

4   Conclusion

SST is a key physical identity of the interaction of the ocean and the world's atmosphere. This study involves climate change prediction in the AS and BOB region using deep learning and shallow learning models. To assess the sea surface temperature using learning models is an important task for the ocean. To observe the performances of the forecasting models finitely, various error measures including the MSE, RMSE, and error standard are selected as evaluation criteria. These predictions are based on statistical assessment and mathematical modeling. Significant results are generated using statistical assessment. MSE compares the good fit between the observed and predicted value. A high value of MSE proves high efficiency of the model. Details of the MSE, RMSE, and error standard of sea surface temperature are learned and concluded in this paper using both deep learning and shallow models. Error measures of feedforward and LSTM models are also compared including training and testing errors. Considering trial and error method, both models are compared to get desired output in terms of root mean square error. In case of LSTM model, the testing RMSE value of BOB and AS grid are 60% lower than feedforward model. In LSTM model, testing RMSE value of AS and BOB grid are respectively 0.24667 °C and 0.14232 °C and feedforward model RMSE values of AS and BOB are 0.63264 °C and 0.3422 °C respectively. It is observed deep learning models are more accurate than shallow learning models.

References

1. Pravallika, M.S., Vasavi, S., Vighneshwar, S.P.: Prediction of temperature anomaly in Indian Ocean based on autoregressive long short-term memory neural network. Neural Comput. Appl. (2022)
2. Xiao, C., Chen, N., Chuli, H., Wang, K., Gong, J., Chen, Z.: Short and mid-term sea surface temperature prediction using time-series satellite data and LSTM-AdaBoost combination approach. Remote Sens. Environ. **233**, 111358 (2019). https://doi.org/10.1016/j.rse.2019.111358
3. Kalpesh Patil, M.C., Deo, M.R.: Prediction of sea surface temperature by combining numerical and neural techniques. J. Atmos. Oceanic Technol. **33**(8), 1715–1726 (2016). https://doi.org/10.1175/JTECH-D-15-0213.1
4. Tangang, F.T., Hsieh, W.W., Tang, B.: Forecasting the equatorial Pacific sea surface temperatures by neural network models. Climate Dyn. **13**, 135–147 (1997)
5. Kalpesh Patil, M.C., Deo, S.G., Ravichandran, M.: Predicting sea surface temperatures in the north indian ocean with nonlinear autoregressive neural networks. Int. J. Oceanogr. **2013**, 1–11 (2013). https://doi.org/10.1155/2013/302479
6. Yang Y., Dong J., Sun X., Lima E., Mu Q., Wang X.: A CFCC-LSTM model for sea surface temperature prediction. IEEE Geosci. Remote Sens. Lett. **15**(2) (2018)
7. Anding, D., Kauth, R.: Estimation of sea surface temperature from space. Remote Sens. Environ. **1**(4), 217–220 (1970). https://doi.org/10.1016/S0034-4257(70)80002-5
8. Haghbin, M., Sharafati, A., Motta, D., Al-Ansari, N., Noghani, M.H.M.: Applications of soft computing models for predicting sea surface temperature: a comprehensive review and assessment. Prog. Earth Planet. Sci. **8**(1), 1–19 (2021). https://doi.org/10.1186/s40645-020-00400-9
9. Gou, Y., Jiang, Y., Zhang, T., He, L., Bai, H., Hu, C.: High-resolution temperature and salinity model analysis using support vector regression. J. Ambient Intell. Humaniz. Comput. (2018)
10. Yu, X., Shi, S., Xu, L., Liu, Y., Miao, Q., Sun ,M.: A novel method for sea surface temperature prediction based on deep learning. Hindawi Mathematical Problems in Engineering. Volume, Article ID 6387173, pp. 9 (2020)
11. Liu, J., Zhang, T., Han, G., Gou, Y.: TD-LSTM: Temporal dependence-based LSTM networks for marine temperature prediction. Sensors **18**(11), 3797 (2018). https://doi.org/10.3390/s18113797
12. Biswas, S., Sinha, M.: Performances of deep learning models for Indian Ocean wind speed prediction. Model. Earth Syst. Environ. **7**(2), 809–831 (2020). https://doi.org/10.1007/s40808-020-00974-9
13. Sarkar, P.P., Janardhan, P., Roy, P.: Prediction of sea surface temperatures using deep learning neural networks. SN Appl. Sci. **2**(8), 1–14 (2020). https://doi.org/10.1007/s42452-020-03239-3
14. Cheng, H., Sun, L., Li, J.: Neural network approach to retrieving ocean subsurface temperatures from surface parameters observed by satellites. Water **13**(3), 388 (2021)

Bioinformatics Analysis of Oral Squamous Cell Carcinomas and Their Interaction to Identify Molecular Signatures

Bandhan Sarker[1] , Md. Matiur Rahaman[1(✉)] , Suman Khan[1],
Jayashri Deb Sinha[2], and Subhabrata Barman[3(✉)]

[1] Department of Statistics, Faculty of Science, Bangabandhu Sheikh Mujibur Rahman Science and Technology University, Gopalganj-8100, Dhaka, Bangladesh
matiur.stat@gmail.com
[2] Department of Computer Science and Engineering, Bengal Institute of Technology and Management, Santiniketan, West Bengal 721657, India
[3] Department of Computer Science and Engineering, Haldia Institute of Technology, Haldia, West Bengal 721657, India
subha.barman@gmail.com

Abstract. Squamous epithelium is the origin of solid tumor oral squamous cell carcinoma (OSCC). Every year, nearly 400,000 OSCC patients are added to the cancer database. Presently, chemo-radiotherapy is the main important adjuvant treatment for OSCC; nevertheless, clinical resistance (drug resistance) to chemotherapy still leads to a poor prognosis of OSCC patients. Identification of potential genes and drugs might be a significant lead for the analyses of OSCC research. We aimed to identify molecular signatures for the diagnosis of OSCC patients. Statistical methods (ANOVA, limma and SAM) were used to identify differentially expressed genes (DEGs) from two datasets GSE111585 and GSE115119. Considering the cutoff values less than 0.05 and |log FC| greater than 1, we obtained 27 up-regulated and 25 down-regulated common DEGs. Protein-protein interaction (PPI) network determined hub genes (AR, ETS1, MET, PDGFB and VAV3) using STRING database. Other biomolecules: Reporter transcription factors (HIF1A, MYC, FOXP3, E2F4, WT1, PURA, ZEB1 and USF2), microRNAs (hsa-miR-589-3p, hsa-miR-155-5p and hsa-miR-301b-3p) associated with hub-genes were determined. For the hub genes, we also performed GO and KEGG enrichment analysis. We constructed gene-drug interaction using the DGIdb database and identify targeted drugs (IMATINIB, BROMOCRIPTINE, NIFEDIPINE, PIRETANIDE and TRIAMTERENE) for OSCC.

Our study suggested that the biomarkers (hub-genes, TFs and miRNAs) and the discovered drugs might be a therapeutic target of OSCC.

Keywords: Oral squamous cell carcinomas (OSCC) · Differentially expressed genes (DEGs) · Hub-genes · Transcription factors (TFs) · miRNA · Drug discovery

© The Author(s), under exclusive license to Springer Nature Switzerland AG 2022
A. A. Sk et al. (Eds.): ISAI 2022, CCIS 1695, pp. 155–169, 2022.
https://doi.org/10.1007/978-3-031-22485-0_15

1 Introduction

Oral squamous carcinoma (OSCC) is an alarming public health issue that originated from head and neck malignant tumors [1]. Among the oral malignancies its about 90% cases are detected as OSCC [2]. Recently, the number of oral cancer cases increased in Asia and Europe. In Bangladesh, lip and oral vesicle cancers are 2nd most (11.9%) loading cancer for males and 3rd most (6.5%) loading cancer for females [3]. In India, every 12 people are affected by OSCC from 100,000 people [4]. The average survival of oral cancer is more than five years. Beginning phase (I and II) oral malignant growth might be reparable by medical procedure or radiation treatment alone yet progressed tumors (stage III and IV) are the most part treated by a medical procedure followed by radiation treatment [5]. Patients who are reached cutting edge stage have possible change of survive more than 30 months, even those who are early accomplish total clinical abatement [6]. A basic figure is the absence of prognostic improvement is that a critical extent of cancer called asymptomatic injuries which are not analyzed or treated when they arrive at a high level stage. Early revelation of cancer is the best viable means to decrease death from this disease [7]. Also, most patients are prescribed to have radiotherapy and chemotherapy after medical procedure to diminish the chance of repeat. But clinical protection from chemotherapy actually prompts a helpless forecast of OSCC patients. In this analysis, two sets of data were examined to identify a molecular signature for the treatment of OSCC patients. More importantly, our study identified significant hub-genes which might be responsible for clinical resistance of OSCC and suggested candidate drugs might be a therapeutic target of OSCC.

2 Materials and methods

2.1 Conceptual Framework

To achieve the objective of this research, a logical framework was prepared through the organized steps and the methods were used in the analysis shown in Fig. 1.

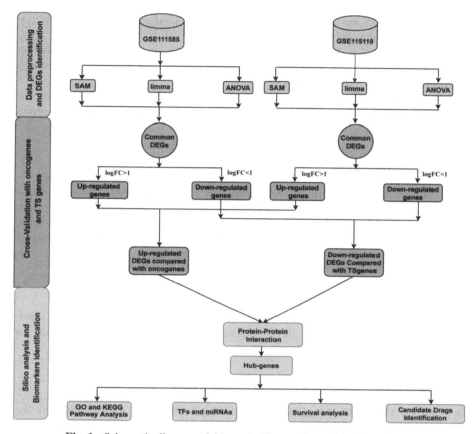

Fig. 1. Schematic diagram of this study (Source Created by the authors)

2.2 Data Description

To identify the biomarkers of OSCC GSE111585 and GSE115119 data sets were downloaded from the NCBI with platforms GPL14715 and GPL16955, respectively. GSE111585 dataset containing six samples of SCC9 cells and 42152 genes which were partitioned into normal group and drug resistance group [8]. Dataset GSE115119 has four samples of CAL-27 cells and 42152 genes which were partitioned into normal group and drug-resistant group.

In this study, additionally we used the list of oncogenes and tumor-suppressor genes which gave a better validation of identified DEGs [9, 10].

2.3 Differentially Expressed Gene Identification Methods

In this analysis we used three different statistical methods to identify differentially expressed genes.

(1) Analysis Of Variance (ANOVA) is a parametric method used to identify differentially expressed genes [11].
(2) Linear Models for Microarray Data (Limma) is a popular method based on Bayesian approach to identifying differentially expressed genes of data arising from microarray experiments [12].
(3) Significance Analysis of Microarrays (SAM) is an efficient technique used for analyzing microarray gene expression data. It was established in 2001 by Virginia Tusher *et. al.* [13]

2.4 Functional Annotation and Pathway Analysis

Gene Ontology (GO) and Kyoto Encyclopedia of Genes and Genomes (KEGG) used for finding biological information of biomarker genes. GO-terms are coordinated into three autonomous controlled ontologies: Biological process, Molecular function and Cellular component. KEGG is used for pathway analysis. We used WEB-based gene set analysis toolkit (WebGestalt) for the GO and KEGG enrichment analysis [14].

2.5 Protein-Protein Interaction (PPI) Network

We constructed a PPI network using the STRING that contains multiple proteins information. Then conceptualize the PPI networks using Cytoscape [15]. We selected a confidence score ≥ 0.4 and maximum interactors $= 0$ for cutoff criteria.

2.6 Reporter Transcription Factors (TFs) and miRNAs

We identified TFs DEGs interactions from HTRIdb [16]. TFs were targeted by the hub genes. For targeting miRNA prediction, we used miRBD to identify a potential miRNA-mRNA interaction network [17]. Then miRNA-mRNA regulatory network was constructed by Cytoscape.

2.7 Survival Analysis of Significance Biomarkers

We completed the prognostic analysis of hub-DEGs using SurvExpress [18]. In Kaplan-Meier plots, we considered log-rank P-value < 0.05 for checking the significant survival output.

2.8 Identification of Candidate Drugs

DGIdb database used to identify desired candidate drugs [19]. In this study, highest degrees of drug-genes network were considered to find candidate drugs for OSCC.

3   Results

3.1   Identification of Differentially Expressed Genes (DEGs)

The methods ANOVA, limma and SAM identified differentially expressed genes (DEGs). The result is shown in the following Table 1. There are 2935 and 2946 common DE genes identified by the three methods for GSE111585 and GSE115119 datasets, respectively (see Fig. 2 A and B). We identified 1380 genes were up-regulated and 1555 genes were down-regulated for cisplatin-safe OSCC from GSE111585 dataset compared with parental OSCC, as like as 2226 genes were up-regulated and 720 genes were down-regulated for cisplatin-safe OSCC from GSE115119 dataset compared with parental OSCC through cluster analysis using cutoff value ($|\log FC| > 1$ and p-value <0.05.

The up-regulated genes of those two datasets were compared with the oncogenes and down-regulated genes were compared with the genes for finding DE genes that might be responsible for tumor. Venn diagram showed that common genes of up or down-regulated from the both datasets with oncogenes or tumor-suppressor genes (TSgenes) used to

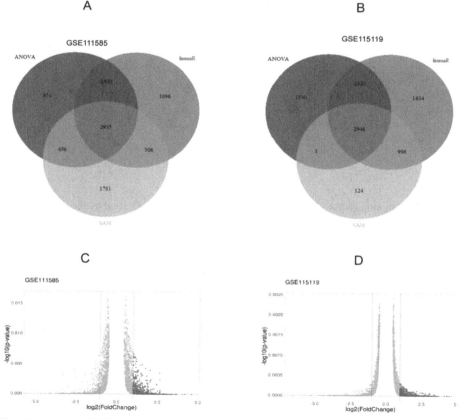

Fig. 2. Common DEGs and volcano plot of common DEGs. A & C for dataset GEO111585 and B & D for dataset GEO115119. (Source Created by the authors)

Table 1. Identified DE genes by using ANOVA, limma and SAM methods.

Dataset	DE genes detected by		
	ANOVA	limma	SAM
GSE111585	6865	6865	5478
GSE115119	7157	7896	4067

(Source Created by the authors).

obtain DEGs in cisplatin-safe OSCC cells. Diagram showed that 27 up-regulated DEGs were intersected between up-regulated genes and the list of oncogenes (see Fig. 3A) and 25 down-regulated DEGs were common between down-regulated genes and the list of TS genes (see Fig. 3B).

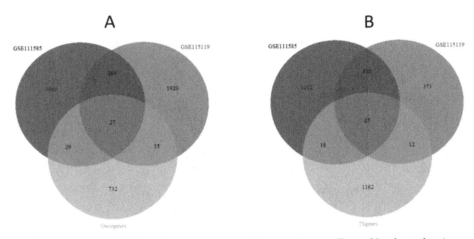

Fig. 3. Common DEGs with oncogenes and TSgenes. (Source Created by the authors)

3.2   Protein-Protein Interaction (PPI) Network for OSCC

To identify central hub protein from differentially expressed genes (DEGs), we construct a PPI network using STRING database and Cytoscape. Figure 4 shows the PPI network for 27 common up regulated DEGs (see Fig. 3A), and hub genes are identified using hub score that has the strong association among other genes. According to high degrees and between closeness, five genes (AR, ETS1, MET, PDGFB and VAV3) are identified.

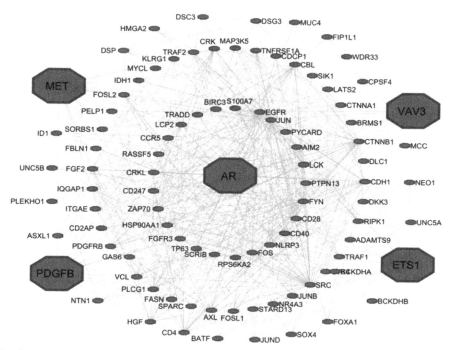

Fig. 4. PPI interaction network of hub DEGs and hub DEGs are highlighted from PPI network. (Source Created by the authors)

3.3 GO and KEGG Pathway Analysis for Hub DEGs

According hub-DEGs, we performed GO and KEGG pathway analysis shown in Fig. 5. The hub-DEGs are mainly involved in positive regulation of endothelial cell migration in BP category (see Fig. 5A), basal plasma membrane in the CC category (see Fig. 5B), and superoxide – generating NADPH oxidase activator activity in MF category (see Fig. 5C). KEGG enrichment analysis showed that these hub-DEGs are involved with renal cell carcinoma, Human T – cell leukemia virus 1 infection and so on (see Fig. 5D).

3.4 Reporter Transcription Factors (TFs) and miRNAs for OSCC

We analyzed significant transcriptional regulatory components for OSCC. We detected TFs are HIF1A, MYC, FOXP3, E2F4, WT1, PURA, ZEB1 and USF2 that are closely targeted as hub DEGs (see Table 2). These hub DEGs are also closely integrated with tumor-related miRNAs. Cytoscape was used to build a miRNA-mRNA network with setting cutoff >70 shown in Fig. 6. Among these miRNAs, some of the miRNAs are connected with multiple genes. These miRNA's are hsa-miR-377-3p, hsa-miR-499a-5p, hsa-miR-34c-5p, hsa-miR-326, hsa-miR-34a-5p, hsa-miR-449b-5p, hsa-miR-449a, hsa-miR-589-3p which are used for next prognostic biomarker analysis.

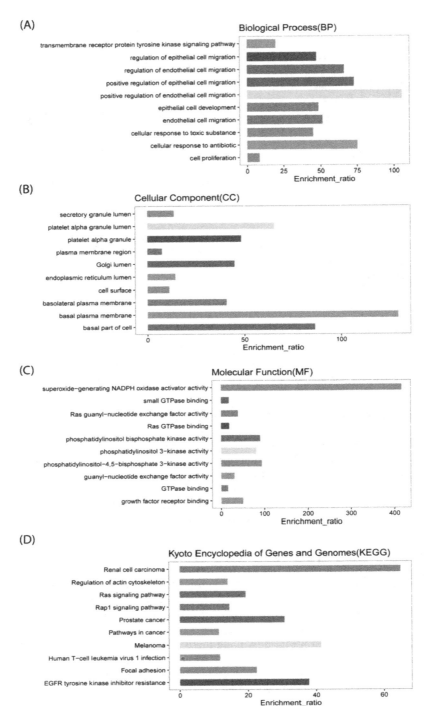

Fig. 5. The GO (BP, CC and MF) and KEGG pathway enrichment analysis of hub-DEGs (Source Created by the authors)

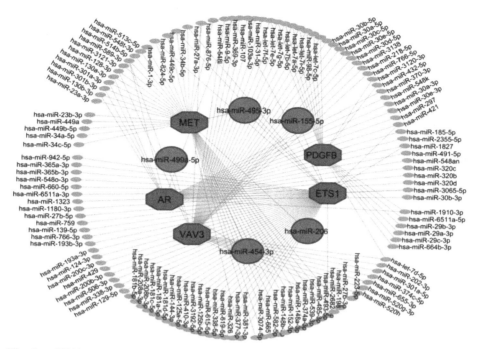

Fig. 6. miRNA–mRNA network identification for hub-DEGs. Highlighted circles predicted the potential miRNAs that can regulate multiple hub-DEGs and miRNAs (Source Created by the authors).

3.5 Overall Survival Significance Biomarkers for OSCC

We also performed an overall survival analysis of hub DEGs, SurvExpress is used to estimate the overall survival probabilities of the hub-DEGs. Figure 7 represents overall survival analysis of hub-DEGs which is statistically significant.

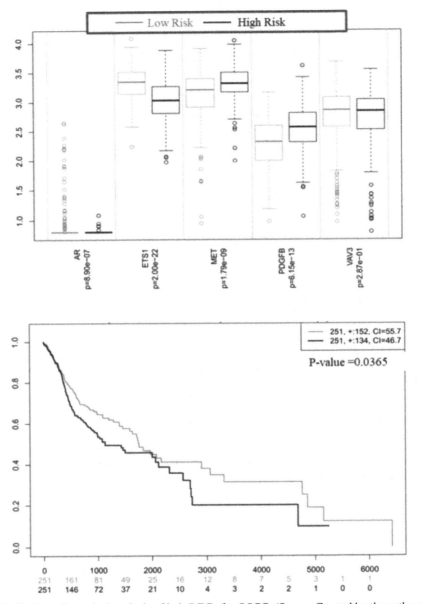

Fig. 7. Overall survival analysis of hub-DEGs for OSCC. (Source Created by the authors)

3.6 Candidate Drugs Identification Through Drug Repositioning for OSCC

We also obtain novel drugs for hub-DEGs and TFs and also constructed a drug-genes network shown in Fig. 8. Which represents the drugs with has the highest degrees (IMA-TINIB, BROMOCRIPTINE, NIFEDIPINE, PIRETANIDE and TRIAMTERENE), and connected with multiple genes.

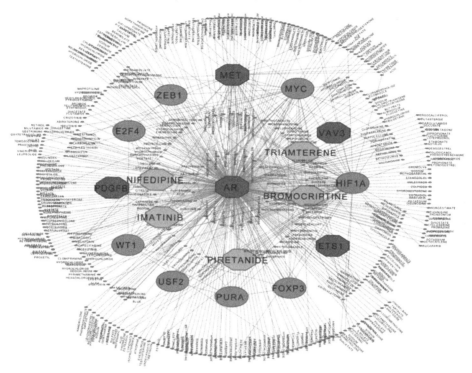

Fig. 8. Drug-gene interaction network for OSCC. Potential drug with multiple connected hub-DEGs and TFs highlighted from the drug-gene network. (Source Created by the authors)

4 Discussion

OSCC is a significant general medical problem with restricted treatment procedures and once again look; foundational drug opposition has disturbed the present circumstance. In this study, significant bioinformatics instruments are utilized to observe 27 up-managed DEGs that are normal with Oncogenes and 25 down-directed DEGs which are normal with TS-genes (see Fig. 3). Cross-over DEGs are utilized to build a PPI organization (see Fig. 4). PPI network recognized as AR, ETS1, MET, PDGFB and VAV3 are the center qualities those are likewise measurably huge and statistically significant (see Fig. 7). AR is related with oral disease [20].

PDGFB is associated with pancreatic cancer risk [21]. MET is associated with the progression of OSCC [22]. ETS1 is also closely related to OSCC and consider as a potential biomarker of OSCC [23]. VAV3 have been identified as important molecules in tumor genesis, tumor growth and cell migration [22].After finding the core genes, GO and KEGG examination of hub genes were performed. In GO examination, BP positively associated with "positive regulation of endothelial cell migration", "cellular response to antibiotic", and so on (see Fig. 5A). CC enrichment showed that hub genes were importantly associated with "basal plasma membrane", basal part of cell", and so on (see Fig. 5B). MF analysis enriched in "superoxide − generating NADPH oxidase activator activity", "phosphatidylinositol − 4, and so on (see Fig. 5C).

Table 2. Reporter Transcription Factors

Symbol	Description	Features
HIF1A	Hypoxia-inducible factor 1-alpha	Promotes human coronavirus SARS-CoV-2 replication
MYC	MYC proto-oncogene, bHLH transcription factor	leads to the development of breast cancer
FOXP3	Forkhead box protein P3	expressed in tumor cells
E2F4	E2F Transcription Factor 4	Control of cell cycle and action of tumor suppressor proteins
WT1	Wilms tumor protein	tumor suppressor
PURA	Transcriptional activator protein Pur-alpha	DNA replication an d in recombination
ZEB1	Zinc finger E-box-binding homeobox 1	Promotes tumorigenicity
USF2	Upstream stimulatory factor 2	binds to a symmetrical DNA sequence

(Source Created by the authors).

KEGG examination described that these hub genes were associated with "Renal cell carcinoma", "Human T − cell leukemia virus 1 infection", and so on (see Fig. 5D). The hub DEGs targeted as reporter TFs are HIF1A, MYC, FOXP3, E2F4, WT1, PURA, ZEB1 and USF2 (see Table 2).These genes promote tumor growth, development of cancer, and are strongly associated with OSCC.

Where HIF1A TFs as an oncogene engaged in OSCC multiplication and cisplatin-safe and may act as a novel remedial objectives for OSCC treatment [24]. It also promotes human coronavirus SARS-CoV-2 replication [25]. MYC is liable for regulated tumor genesis in OSCC [26]. MYC likewise prompts to the advancement of breast cancer. Foxp3 overexpression in cancer cells predicts unfortunate endurance in oral squamous cell carcinoma [27]. E2F4 is a statistical significance gene for OSCC [28]. WT1 can be used as epigenetic oral squamous cell carcinoma biomarkers [29]. Zeb1 is responsible for oral cancer cell invasion and its suppression by resveratrol [30]. USF2 is working as a risk factor for tumor genesis [31]. Hub-DEGs are also associated with miRNAs and are also involved in the cancer cell (see Fig. 6).

hsa-miR-495-3p can be used as a biomarker for the detection of OSCC [32]. Hsa-miR-155-5pis a potential oncogenic in oral squamous cell carcinoma [33]. Hsa-miR-454-3p has been involved in head and neck squamous cell carcinoma invasion [34]. Finally, we detected candidate drugs associated with hub-DEGs such as IMATINIB, BROMOCRIPTINE, NIFEDIPINE, PIRETANIDE and TRIAMTERENE which are mostly connected with multiple genes that have also highest degrees among the other drugs (see Fig. 8). IMATINIB is an oral cancer drug that specifically represses a few protein tyrosine kinases related with human malignancy. IMATINIB is an approved drug for oral cancer [35]. BROMOCRIPTINE is used in the supported medication of metastatic breast cancer and prostate cancer-related hyperprolactinemia [36]. NIFEDIPINE is also an indicator for carcinoma associated fibroblasts (CAFs) in OSCC [37]. PIRETANIDE has a significant effect on oral cancer [38]. TRIAMTERENE is a Photosensitizing antihypertensive drug to lip cancer in non-Hispanic males [39].

5   Conclusion

The survival rate of OSCC patient is very low for its drug resistance. We analyzed cisplatin resistance of OSCC using bioinformatics tools and found hub-genes (AR, ETS1, MET, PDGFB and VAV3), TFs (HIF1A, MYC, FOXP3, E2F4, WT1, PURA, ZEB1 and USF2) and miRNA (hsa-miR-377-3p, hsa-miR-499a-5p, hsa-miR-34c-5p, hsa-miR-326, hsa-miR-34a-5p, hsa-miR-449b-5p, hsa-miR-449a and hsa-miR-589-3p) which may be responsible for cisplatin resistance of OSCC. Furthermore, we discovered candidate drugs (IMATINIB, BROMOCRIPTINE, NIFEDIPINE, PIRETANIDE and TRIAMTERENE) which might be a therapeutic target of OSCC. These molecular signatures are also needed further validation in wet lab.

Acknowledgements. The authors thank the Professor Dr. Md. Nurul Haque Mollah, Bioinformatics Lab. (Dry), Dept. of Statistics, University of Rajshahi, Bangladesh and the reviewers of this work.

Competing Interests. The authors declare that they have no competing interests.

References

1. Siegel, R.L., Miller, K.D., Jemal, A.: Cancer Statistics. CA: Cancer J. Clin. **70**, 7–30 (2020)
2. Neville, B.W., Day, T.A.: Oral cancer and precancerous lesions. CA: Cancer J. Clin. **52**, 195–215 (2002)
3. Hussain, S.M.A.: Comprehensive update on cancer scenario of Bangladesh. South Asian J. Cancer. **2**, 279–284 (2013)
4. Petersen, P.E.: Strengthening the prevention of oral cancer: the WHO perspective. Community Dentistry and Oral Epidemiology 397–3999 (2005). Wiley Online Library

5. Olsen, K.D.: Head and neck cancer: a multidisciplinary approach. Mayo Clin. Proc. **1308** (1999). Elsevier Limited
6. Hill, B.T., Price, L.A.: Lack of survival advantage in patients with advanced squamous cell carcinomas of the oral cavity receiving neoadjuvant chemotherapy prior to local therapy, despite achieving an initial high clinical complete remission rate. Am. J. Clin. Oncol. **17**, 1–5 (1994)
7. Li, Y., et al.: Salivary transcriptome diagnostics for oral cancer detection. Clin. Cancer Res. **10**, 8442–8450 (2004)
8. Lin, Z., et al.: Chemotherapy-induced long non-coding RNA 1 promotes metastasis and chemo-resistance of TSCC via the Wnt/β-catenin signaling pathway. Mol. Ther. **26**, 1494–1508 (2018)
9. Liu, Y., Sun, J., Zhao, M.: ONGene: a literature-based database for human oncogenes. J. Genet Genomics. **44**, 119–121 (2017)
10. Datta, N., Chakraborty, S., Basu, M., Ghosh, M.K.: Tumor suppressors having oncogenic functions: the double agents. Cells. **10**, 46 (2021)
11. Park, T., et al.: Statistical tests for identifying differentially expressed genes in time-course microarray experiments. Bioinformatics **19**, 694–703 (2003)
12. Law, W., Chen, Y., Shi, W., Smyth, G.K.: Voom: precision weights unlock linear model analysis tools for RNA-seq read counts. Genome Biol. **15**, R29 (2014)
13. Tusher, V.G., Tibshirani, R., Chu, G.: Significance analysis of microarrays applied to the ionizing radiation response. Proc. Natl. Acad. Sci. **98**(9), 5116–5121 (2001). https://doi.org/10.1073/pnas.091062498
14. Liao, Y., Wang, J., Jaehnig, E.J., Shi, Z., Zhang, B.: WebGestalt 2019: gene set analysis toolkit with revamped UIs and APIs. Nucleic Acids Res. **47**, W199–W205 (2019)
15. Saito, R., et al.: A travel guide to Cytoscape plugins. Nat. Methods **9**, 1069 (2012)
16. Bovolenta, L.A., Acencio, M.L., Lemke, N.: HTRIdb: an open-access database for experimentally verified human transcriptional regulation interactions. BMC Genom. **13**, 405 (2012)
17. Wong, N., Wang, X.: miRDB: an online resource for microRNA target prediction and functional annotations. Nucleic Acids Res. **43**, D146–D152 (2015)
18. Aguirre-Gamboa, R., et al.: SurvExpress: an online biomarker validation tool and database for cancer gene expression data using survival analysis. PloS One **8**, e74250 (2013)
19. Wagner, A.H., et al.: DGIdb 2.0: mining clinically relevant drug–gene interactions. Nucleic Acids Res. **44**, D1036–D1044 (2016)
20. Tomasovic-Loncaric, C., et al.: Androgen receptor as a biomarker of oral squamous cell carcinoma progression risk. Anticancer Res. **39**, 4285–4289 (2019)
21. Duan, B., et al.: Genetic variants in the platelet-derived growth factor subunit B gene associated with pancreatic cancer risk. Int. J. Cancer **142**, 1322–1331 (2018)
22. Trenkle, T., Hakim, S.G., Jacobsen, H.-C., Sieg, P.: Differential gene expression of the proto-oncogene VAV3 and the transcript variant VAV3. 1 in oral squamous cell carcinoma. Anticancer Res. **35**, 2593–2600 (2015)
23. Arora, S., Ali, J., Ahuja, A., Khar, R.K., Baboota, S.: Floating drug delivery systems: a review. AAPS PharmSciTech **6**, E372–E390 (2005)
24. Wang, F., et al.: LncRNA PVT1 enhances proliferation and cisplatin resistance via regulating miR-194-5p/HIF1a axis in oral squamous cell carcinoma. OncoTargets Ther. **13**, 243 (2020)
25. Codo, A.C., et al.: Elevated glucose levels favor SARS-CoV-2 infection and monocyte response through a HIF-1α/glycolysis-dependent axis. Cell Metab. **32**, 437–446 (2020)
26. Chen, X., et al.: C-MYC and BCL-2 mediate YAP-regulated tumorigenesis in OSCC. Onco. Impact J. **9**(1), 668 (2018)
27. Song, J.-J., et al.: Foxp3 overexpression in tumor cells predicts poor survival in oral squamous cell carcinoma. BMC Cancer. **16**, 1–7 (2016)

28. Diniz, M.G., Silva, J.C., Souza, F.T.A., Pereira, N.B., Gomes, C.C., Gomez, R.S.: Association between cell cycle gene transcription and tumor size in oral squamous cell carcinoma. Tumor Biol. **36**(12), 9717–9722 (2015). https://doi.org/10.1007/s13277-015-3735-1

29. Ribeiro, I.P., et al.: WT1, MSH6, GATA5 and PAX5 as epigenetic oral squamous cell carcinoma biomarkers-a short report. Cell. Oncol. **39**, 573–582 (2016)

30. Kim, J.Y., Cho, K.H., Jeong, B.Y., Park, C.G., Lee, H.Y.: Zeb1 for RCP-induced oral cancer cell invasion and its suppression by resveratrol. Exp. Mol. Med. **52**, 1152–63 (2020)

31. Ganguly, N., Parihar, S.P.: Human papillomavirus E6 and E7 oncoproteins as risk factors for tumorigenesis. J. Biosci. **34**(1), 113–123 (2009). https://doi.org/10.1007/s12038-009-0013-7

32. Shoucair, I.: Extracellular microRNAs as biomarkers for the detection of nasopharyngeal carcinoma [PhD Thesis]. University of British Columbia (2021)

33. Han, H., et al.: TRRUST v2: an expanded reference database of human and mouse transcriptional regulatory interactions. Nucleic Acids Res. **46**, D380–D386 (2018)

34. Jimenez, L., Jayakar, S.K., Ow, T.J., Segall, J.E.: Mechanisms of invasion in head and neck cancer. Arch. Path. Lab. Med. **139**, 1334–48 (2015)

35. Verweij, J., et al.: Imatinib mesylate (STI-571 Glivec®, Gleevec^{TM}) is an active agent for gastrointestinal stromal tumours, but does not yield responses in other soft-tissue sarcomas that are unselected for a molecular target: results from an EORTC Soft Tissue and Bone Sarcoma Group phase II study. Eur. J. Cancer **39**, 2006–2011 (2003)

36. Kulman, G., Lissoni, P., Rovelli, F., Roselli, M.G., Brivio, F., Sequeri, P.: Evidence of pineal endocrine hypofunction in autistic children. Neuro Endocrinol. Lett. **21**, 31–4 (2000)

37. A new indicator for CAFs in oral squamous cell carcinoma

38. Chohan, I.S.: Effects of piretanide on plasma fibrinolytic activity, platelet aggregation and platelet factor-4 release in man. J. Biosci. **10**, 243–249 (1986)

39. Salama, A.: Squamous cell carcinoma of the lip. Lip Cancer 17–23 (2014). Springer

Music Learning Android App Development for Autistic Children

Pragati Ghosh⬤, Sudipta Saha⬤, and Saikat Basu(✉)⬤

Maulana Abul Kalam Azad University of Technology, West Bengal,
Kolkata, West Bengal, India
`saikat.basu@makautwb.ac.in`

Abstract. In this paper, we present a new application named Musica, which is aimed to teach music and improve learning tendencies to children with Autism Spectrum Disorder (ASD). Music is a form of art and a form of Self-expression. The idea of developing such an application is that studies show that children who learn music have better psycho-motor development. Brain development is better with music; music improves memory, makes people happy, teaches them to focus, relieves stress, helps to build emotion, improves social skills, boosts self-confidence. We have done a brief survey on the existing application for children with autism. Some apps include music, but there is no application designed for autistic children to make them learn Indian classical music and instruments. The advantage of this app is that it includes a feature of emotion detection, which will help the child learn facial expressions. The emotion detection component does not seek the parents/therapists' involvement; children can use this alone. It increases the usefulness and effectiveness of this app.

Keywords: Autism spectrum disorder · Music education · Quiz · Android application · Emotion detection

1 Introduction

Our technology has developed so that almost every work can be done through the phone. It is inevitable, and it has played a significant role for therapists and specialists. Computer-based interventions, especially mobile phones, effectively impact children as they have become playing devices and learning devices. Children with autism are not an exception in this matter [1]. ASD is a "neurodevelopmental condition", which causes disabilities to speak, think, communicate. Studies show that children who learn music have better psycho-motor development than others [2,3]. Music helps the brain to develop [2,3], improves social skills [3], teaches to focus and relieves stress [4], improves memory [5], boosts self-confidence [6]. It is a form of self-expression [7]. It makes them happy [7], helps to build emotion [8,9], helps to understand mathematics better [10]. When it comes to children with special needs, like autistic children, they also respond

A. A. Sk et al. (Eds.): ISAI 2022, CCIS 1695, pp. 170–179, 2022.
https://doi.org/10.1007/978-3-031-22485-0_16

to music quite quickly than other things [11]. Several types of research say that children with special needs who are introduced to music show positive and quick growth than other special children [12,13]. Therefore, many children are treated with music therapy. Therapists and teachers use songs and musical instruments to improve cognitive activity to build self-awareness and improve relationships with others [14].

In a brief survey of existing applications that involves music [15–18], we observed that their perspective and design are not such that an autistic child can understand. Also, many of them [15,16,18] are not suitable to make them learn music; instead, the features are more like games, for example, playing music by tapping the screen [18], etc. There is less scope for gathering knowledge in the case of those apps.

This paper describes a brief survey of available applications for children with ASD and the design and development of a mobile application whose purpose is to help autistic children learn the basics of Indian music. The app comprises a brief introduction to musical notes, instruments, sounds, and some related quizzes to measure their progress. Its graphical user interfaces (GUIs) and interaction methods are as simple and straightforward as possible to make it easy for them to learn and practice from home or wherever they prefer.

2   Related Work

After going through several research papers and some applications, it is observed that there are numerous applications available to help these children with ASD in education, learning behavior and emotional outcomes, and social interaction. Each app has its own perspective. There are some applications that involve music as well [15,16], but their perspective and design are quite hard to understand for an autistic child. Also, many of them [15,16,18] are not to make them learn music, instead of using the features for game purposes [18]. There is less scope for gathering knowledge in music from those apps. A comparison has been done between these applications and is shown in Table 1.

3   Methodology

3.1   App Description

The prime objective of "Musica" app is to create a full-fleged android application suitable for children with ASD to learn Indian music. Children will know the basics of musical notes (Swaras), Indian classical instruments, and some western instruments; they can also participate in the quiz to check their knowledge. Also, as learning music has many benefits, it will help those kids in their betterment. It will also increase their abilities. They will be a step towards a normal life and a better future for them. It will also make them happy.

There are four sections in this app which are shown below.

Table 1. Comparison between existing apps for autistic children

Name of the app	Skill/Target	Device/Platform	Remarks
Xylotism [16]	Xylophone	Android	Virtual xylophone playing and identifying colors and sound
FigureNotes [19]	Music therapy course	Web-based	Influences learning skill
Suoniamo [20]	Piano learning	Android	Playing the virtual piano and knowing the notes
Music authoring [21]	Musical game	Android	Making music from notes by tapping the screen
Otsimo [21]	Education	Android	Teaches numbers, emotion and words
Cuedin [21]	Education	Android	Academics, languages, social skills, everyday routines
Fill Me App [21]	Science Education	Android	Science learning, precisely identifying human body part
CaptureMyEmotion [22]	Emotion and well-being	Web-based, Android	Measures emotion and shows emotion intensity
MITA [23]	Social Interaction and well-being	Web-based	Brain training app based on difficulty level. Only for children up to 5 years
TOBY [24]	Therapy	Web-based	Provides timely intensive behavioural interventions

1. **Notes of Music-** It has a brief description of the notes of Indian music. The tune of each note is assigned to a separate button for their ease. Also, there is a keyboard containing an octave of natural notes. Each key shows the assigned notes for ease of learning.
2. **Instruments-** It has a list of popular Indian classical instruments as well as some western musical instruments. Each of the elements contains the view of how to hold that instrument and the sound of the instrument to give a piece of basic knowledge to the child (see Fig. (1a)).
3. **Quiz-** Quiz section contains two distinct categories - Notes quiz, Instrument quiz. Both quiz are of multiple-choice type. For each correct answer, score will be incremented by 1 (no negative marking for wrong attempts). The instrument quiz has image questions to identify the correct name from the options. The quiz is based on a time constraint. The time for answering each question is more than usual because this application is designed for autistic children.
4. **Emotion Recognition-** This section detects the emotion of the person who is in front of the camera. Autistic children are self-focused, repetitive and likes to stay isolated; therefore this tool will be a great start to make them enjoy their own company and learn different emotions. It detects seven types of emotions- happy, sad, surprise, fear, anger, disgust, and neutral. Figure (1b) shows an example of how it works.

(a) Popular Indian classical in- (b) Real-time emotion recog-
struments   nition

Fig. 1. Some features of the application.

This application also includes a screen recorder to record the activity of the child. With the emotion detection and screen recorder, it will be easy to see the expression of the child while playing the app. The interface and contents are designed for easy accessibility for children with autism.

3.2 Application Development

– **Software used:** Android studio, Software Development Toolkit (SDK)- API level 30 (Android 11).
  Machine learning software libraries: OpenCV, TensorFlow
  Database: Firebase real-time database.

3.3 App Structure

The structure of the application is shown below with a page flow diagram (see Fig. 2). It shows how the user can interact with this application. It requires user login details to start. The algorithm for the quiz section is as follows:

Step 1: Show question,
Step 2: Select answer for given question,
    Step 2.1: If ans is equal to correctAns then
    increment score by 1, show the next question, reset the timer,
    Step 2.2: Else change question and reset timer,
    Step 2.3: If timer is equal to limit then change question,
Step 3: If question is equal to limit then show Score, else repeat step 1.

The score for individual quizzes will be saved. The architectural flow of emotion detection method is also described (see Fig. 3).

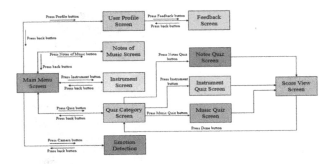

Fig. 2. Page flow diagram of the application

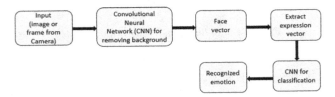

Fig. 3. Architectural flow of emotion detection method

3.4 Participants

Sixteen children were chosen between the age group of 8 to 14 years to study the acceptance of this application. The children were chosen randomly to avoid biases. In this pandemic situation, it has been complicated to conduct the survey. The schools and organizations for autistic children remained closed. Hence, the application has been tested among some new music learners as well as some autistic children. Table 2a shows the number of participants.

The number of male children is 31 percent (frequency(f) = 5), and the number of female children is 69% (f = 11) among all the participants. The average age is 11 years, with a standard deviation of 1.8974. Among all, 44 percent of participants have age of less than or equal to 10 years, and 56% have age above 10 years (see Table 2b).

Table 2. Participant's details

(a) Autistic/Ordinary participants

Children	Frequency	Percentage
Autistic	3	19
Ordinary	13	81
Total	16	100

(b) Age of the participants

Item	Frequency	Percentage	Average
Age<=10	7	44	9.14
Age>10	9	56	12.45
Total	16	100	11

We have taken the children who have no proper knowledge of music. This application will first grow their knowledge and then can test it. The age group is such that they can grasp the lessons quickly. The results are discussed in Table 3a and Table 3b.

4 Experimental Results

We have developed an app that will help children learn music and grow their interest in music. The design provides simplicity in using the application, fully relevant for these targeted users. Each learning unit has proposed an assessment separately to check the learning ability and knowledge.

Before introducing the Musica app, the children were being taught conventionally. It has been observed that most of them prefer learning with this app as it is easy to use and has a compact detail of instruments and notes (Swara). We have analyzed the score for autistic children as well as other children from both the quizzes. Table 3a and Table 3b shows the overall result.

Table 3. Average scores of participants

(a) Autistic participants

Quiz	Average score	Percentage
Notes	3	20
Instruments	8	53

(b) Other participants

Quiz	Average score	Percentage
Notes	10.42	70
Instruments	13.38	89

We have considered a standard score for these participants. For autistic children, it is 5, and for other participants, it is 10. Now, we have analyzed the score for both quizzes accordingly. It is observed that the total result for autistic children (f = 3) is comparatively better than other children (f = 13) based on the standard score. The data interpretations are shown in Fig. 4.

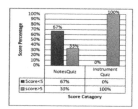 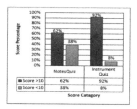

(a) Scores of autistic children   (b) Scores of other children

Fig. 4. Scores of participants in both quizzes.

5   Discussion

The application was built for the betterment and made them learn through it. There can be many obstacles to have a musical instrument at home or appointing a teacher who will make them learn. But this application makes it easy. For the early stages of learning, it only takes the basics to cover, and this app does that correctly. We have tested this application with sixteen children to find its usefulness and acceptance. The children liked the user interface and contents and learned from it. The variation of scores is shown in Fig. 5 to understand it better.

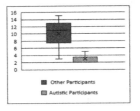 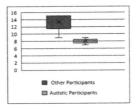

(a) Notes quiz scores   (b) Instruments quiz scores

Fig. 5. Comparison of scores for both participants.

The range of the box is from the first quartile (Q1) to the third quartile (Q3) of the distribution and it is called the interquartile range (IQR). Q1 represents 25 percent of participants; the median, also known as the second quartile (Q2), represents 50 percent, and Q3 shows 75 percent participants.

Figure (5a) shows the distribution of notes quiz scores for autistic children and other children. For other children, the values of the box plot are: Max = 15, Min = 3, Q1 = 7.5, X = 10.076, Q3 = 13. For autistic children, the values of the box plot are: Max = 5, Min = 2, Q1 = 7.5, X = 3, Q3 = 3.5.

Figure 5b shows the distribution of instrument quiz scores for autistic children and other children. For other children, the values of the box plot are: Max = 15, Min = 9, Q1 = 11.5, X = 13.3846, Q3 = 15. For autistic children, the values of the box plot are: Max = 9, Min = 7, Q1 = 7.5, X = 8, Q3 = 8.5. It shows that other children have performed better than autistic children.

6   Novelty of the App

The literature survey shows that those applications (see Table 1) involve music, but none of them possess music education. The app we have built gives a brief idea about Indian classical music and instruments. It offers a compact format for learning that is not usually observed in other applications. With the help of the musical quiz, ASD people can be able to learn and evaluate. This app includes facial expression recognition, which also makes this app unique from other reviewed apps. It will help the children to learn facial expressions. Also, it includes a screen recorder that will record the screen while using the application and corresponding facial expressions will also be recorded. It may help the parent/therapists evaluate the child's progress and the usefulness of this application.

7 Usability Analysis

We took the feedback from each participant to know their perspectives towards this application. Inside the application, there is an option to send feedback. The feedback has been taken through a five point Likert scale [25]. The responses automatically get stored in the database. The following questions were asked in the feedback section to improve the app.

Question 1: How much do you like this application?
Question 2: How useful is this for autistic children?
Question 3: How helpful is this for music education?
Question 4: How much did you learn?
Question 5: How much did your parents like this app?

The response for each question is shown using pie charts (see Fig. 6).

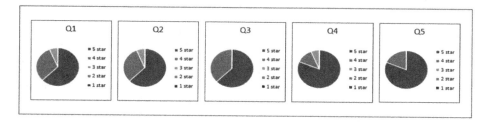

Fig. 6. Feedback analysis for question 1–5.

A five point Likert scale has been used here, where the 1-star implies worst and the 5-star implies excellent. A good rating is observed from the feedback, which implies the acceptance and approval of this app. Overall feedback shows a 70% 5-star rating, 27% 4-star rating, and 3% 3-star rating. There were no rating of 2-star and 1-star.

8 Conclusion

In this paper, we saw the research and related development in treating autism spectrum disorder with the help of technology. Technology, more precisely the touch screen, has offered affordability, accessibility, and portability to reach people easily. It has made education and gathering information more accessible.

Accessing these applications is much simpler than going to any teacher or musician nowadays.

The pandemic situation has reduced the accessibility to more people. Still, for the number of people we have interacted with and tested, it is seen that this application has done its job. The children have learned and performed well and showed interest in the lessons, which includes pictures and sound.

The world is developing so fast, and we aim to make these children with special needs grow as quickly as possible. Much research is going on for their betterment, and this application is another step towards that. We may get to see a more accurate and specified analysis and practical application for these children in the future.

References

1. Hosokawa, R., Katsura, T.: Association between mobile technology use and child adjustment in early elementary school age. PLoS ONE **13**(7), e0199959 (2018)
2. Guhn, M., Emerson, S.D., Gouzouasis, P.: A population-level analysis of associations between school music participation and academic achievement. J. Educ. Psychol. **112**(2), 308 (2020)
3. Hallam, S.: The power of music: its impact on the intellectual, social and personal development of children and young people. Int. J. Music Educ. **28**(3), 269–289 (2010)
4. Zadnik, K., Habe, K.: The developmental benefits of early music education: an evaluation study of the two Slovenian projects. J. Educ. Res. **11**(3) (2017)
5. Musliu, A., Berisha, B., Latifi, D.: The impact of music in memory. Eur. J. Soc. Sci. Educ. Res. **4**(4), 222–227 (2017)
6. Shayan, N., AhmadiGatab, T., Jeloudar, J.G., Ahangar, K.S.: The effect of playing music on the confidence level. Procedia Soc. Behav. Sci. **30**, 2061–2063 (2011)
7. Lawendowski, R., Bieleninik, Ł: Identity and self-esteem in the context of music and music therapy: a review. Health Psychol. Rep. **5**(2), 85–99 (2017)
8. Praise, S.P., Meenakshi, K.: The effect of music on human brain in developing learning skills and physical health. Mediterr. J. Soc. Sci. **6**(2 S1), 244 (2015)
9. Koelsch, S.: Brain correlates of music-evoked emotions. Nat. Rev. Neurosci. **15**(3), 170–180 (2014)
10. Hamilton, T.J., et al.: Teaching mathematics with music: a pilot study. In: 2018 IEEE International Conference on Teaching, Assessment, and Learning for Engineering (TALE), pp. 927–931. IEEE (2018)
11. Bentley, M.M.: Music and attention for children with developmental disabilities (2015)
12. Tomlinson, J.: Music therapist collaboration with teaching assistants for facilitating verbal and vocal development in young children with special needs: a mixed methods study. Br. J. Music Ther. **34**(2), 95–107 (2020)
13. Pelosi, F.: Plato on Music, Soul and Body. Cambridge University Press, Cambridge (2010)
14. Ruksenas, J.: The benefits of music classes for preschoolers: the ABC of Do Re Mi (2014)

15. Lee, L., Lin, H.F.: A study on the application of figurenotes teaching method to music needs of children with special needs. In: Education and Awareness of Sustainability: Proceedings of the 3rd Eurasian Conference on Educational Innovation 2020 (ECEI 2020), pp. 73–76. World Scientific (2020)
16. Elahi, M.T., et al.: *Xylotism*: a tablet-based application to teach music to children with autism. In: Kheddar, A., et al. (eds.) ICSR 2017. LNCS, pp. 728–738. Springer, Cham (2017). https://doi.org/10.1007/978-3-319-70022-9_72
17. Buzzi, M.C., Paolini, G., Senette, C., Buzzi, M., Paratore, M.T.: Designing an accessible web app to teach piano to students with autism. In: Proceedings of the 13th Biannual Conference of the Italian SIGCHI Chapter: Designing the next interaction, pp. 1–12 (2019)
18. Hourcade, J.P., Bullock-Rest, N.E., Hansen, T.E.: Multitouch tablet applications and activities to enhance the social skills of children with autism spectrum disorders. Pers. Ubiquitous Comput. **16**(2), 157–168 (2012)
19. Lee, L., Lin, H.F.: Music educational therapy and the figure notes music pedagogical approach for young children with special needs. Univ. J. Educ. Res. **8**, 2483–2492 (2020)
20. Buzzi, M.C., Buzzi, M., Maugeri, M., Paolini, G., Paratore, M.T., Sbragia, A., Senette, C., Trujillo, A.: Which virtual piano keyboard for children with autism? A pilot study. In: Stephanidis, C. (ed.) HCII 2019. LNCS, vol. 11786, pp. 280–291. Springer, Cham (2019). https://doi.org/10.1007/978-3-030-30033-3_22
21. Xanthopoulou, M., Kokalia, G., Drigas, A.: Applications for children with autism in preschool and primary education. Int. J. Recent Contrib. Eng. Sci. IT **7**(2), 4–16 (2019)
22. Leijdekkers, P., Gay, V., Wong, F.: CaptureMyEmotion: a mobile app to improve emotion learning for autistic children using sensors. In: Proceedings of the 26th IEEE International Symposium on Computer-Based Medical Systems, pp. 381–384. IEEE (2013)
23. Vyshedskiy, A., Dunn, R.: Mental imagery therapy for autism (MITA)-an early intervention computerized brain training program for children with ASD. Autism Open Access **5**(2) (2015)
24. Venkatesh, S., Phung, D., Duong, T., Greenhill, S., Adams, B.: TOBY: early intervention in autism through technology. In: Proceedings of the SIGCHI Conference on Human Factors in Computing Systems, pp. 3187–3196 (2013)
25. Joshi, A., Kale, S., Chandel, S., Pal, D.K.: Likert scale: explored and explained. Br. J. Appl. Sci. Technol. **7**(4), 396 (2015)

NecklaceFIR: A Large Volume Benchmarked Necklace Dataset for Fashion Image Retrieval

Sk Maidul Islam[1(✉)] [ID], Subhankar Joardar[2] [ID], and Arif Ahmed Sekh[3] [ID]

[1] Global Institute of Science and Technology, Purba Medinipur, India
iammaidul@gmail.com
[2] Haldia Institute of Technology, Purba Medinipur, India
[3] XIM University, Bhubaneswar, India

Abstract. In this paper, we present a new necklace dataset related to the fashion domain, namely, NecklaceFIR. In recent years, the retrieval of clothing items has attracted a lot of attention. However, fashion products that are complex in nature, such as jewellery, have not received much attention due to the absence of a proper dataset. To address this problem, we have collected the dataset. The dataset contains over ~4.8K high-definition necklace images collected from various online retailers. The dataset is structurally labeled in 49 categories. To benchmark the dataset, we have used various classical methods and state-of-art deep models. The dataset will be publicly available at: https://github.com/skarifahmed/NecklaceFIR.

Keywords: Fashion image retrieval · Ornament dataset · Image retrieval dataset

1 Introduction

Online shopping is a fast growing market. In recent years, research in the fashion domain is gaining a significant momentum for its substantial possibilities in the fashion industry. Recently, lots of research has been carried out for fashion retrieval [1–3], fashion matching and recommendation [4–6], fashion parsing [6–8], attribute detection [9–11], and many more due to the growing demand of fashion industry. Fashion image retrieval can be performed by using any of the two popular retrieval techniques, TBIR or CBIR. Many fashion sites use TBIR, where fashion images are annotated by text and images are retrieved using a keyword-based search as per user interest. Fashion items have many visual characteristics that cannot be represented by words. Thus, recently, CBIR has got much more attention by the researchers, where similar or identical items are retrieved from the gallery by using the visual contents like color, texture, or shape of a given query image. Applications of CBIR system manifolds such as face detection, fingerprint identification, medical applications, Digital Libraries,

A. A. Sk et al. (Eds.): ISAI 2022, CCIS 1695, pp. 180–190, 2022.
https://doi.org/10.1007/978-3-031-22485-0_17

crime prevention, fashion recognition, fashion recommendation, and remote sensing, etc. In fashion image retrieval, similar fashion items are retrieved from the fashion image gallery based on users' queries. Figure 1 shows the fashion image retrieval process where FIR uses various similarity measurement methods like shape, color, design, and texture similarity to retrieve similar images for a given query. Recently, fashion image retrieval (FIR) has become more popular due to the growing demand for online shopping. Still, FIR has some limitations like the presence of multiple objects in a fashion image, the query image has different viewpoints or captured in low light, and the complex shape, design or texture of fashion image [12].

In the past few years, most of the fashion-related research are on garments. However, the research on ornament retrieval has got less attention due to its complexity in design and lack of proper ornament datasets. It has been noticed that there is a wider variety of jewellery design compared to fashion products such as clothing or footwear.

According to our observations, there is no dataset other than the Ring-FIR dataset [13] that works exclusively with ornament images. This observation inspires us to create a dataset of ornament images.

To address the above challenges, this work has two main contributions. (1) we build a novel fashion image dataset containing ~4.8K high quality nacklace images, namely, NacklaceFIR. (2) State-of-art image retrieval methods are used to benchmark the dataset.

The rest of the paper is structured as follows: the related work in FIR is summarized in Sect. 2; the details of the proposed dataset are explained in Sect. 3; the state-of-the-art benchmarking methods and results are detailed in Sect. 4; finally, Sect. 5 summarizes the conclusion.

2   Related Works

Image retrieval is a challenging issue in computer vision. Various classical methods and deep neural networks are used to solve this problem. Here, we have explained various image retrieval datasets and fashion image retrieval methods.

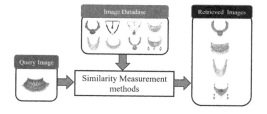

Fig. 1. Fashion image retrieval (FIR) process.

Fashion Image Retrieval Datasets: Huang et al. [14] presents a garment dataset, containing 206,235 cloth images with descriptions. To address the problem of cross-domain image retrieval, Huang et al. [15] proposed a clothing image dataset, containing 453,983 online upper-clothing images from online shopping websites and about 90,000 offline counterpart images of those online images. For exact matching real world clothing images with online shop images, Kiapour et al. [16] introduced a novel dataset, namely, Exact Street2Shop, containing 404,683 online clothing images from different online shops and 20,357 real world street images. Liu et al. [17] constructed a clothing dataset, namely, Multi-view Clothing dataset (MVC), to address view-invariant clothing retrieval problem. Liu et al. [18] introduced a large-scale clothing dataset, DeepFashion, containing over 800,000 fashion images that are annotated with large numbers of attributes, landmarks, and cross-pose/cross-domain image pairs. To retrieve exactly same garments from online shops that appeared in the videos, Cheng et al. [19] proposed a cross-domain dataset Video2Shop, containing 26,352 clothing trajectories from videos and 85,677 online clothing images. Ge et al. [20] introduced a versatile benchmark dataset DeepFashion2 for detection of cloth, estimation of pose, segmentation, and clothing retrieval. For cross-domain clothing image retrieval, Kuang et al. [21] build a benchmarked dataset FindFashion, by revisiting the existing datasets Street2Shop [16], and DeepFashion [18] and contains 565,041 clothing images. For attribute-specific fashion retrieval, Ma et al. [22] created a fashion dataset by rebuilding three fashion datasets, namely, DARN [15], FashionAI [23] and DeepFashion [18] with attribute annotations.

Other Image Retrieval Datasets: In addition to fashion image datasets, image datasets include various types of medical diagnosis, fingerprint detection, landmark detection, crime prevention, face detection, and more.

Deng et al. [24] introduced a database called ImageNet, which contains over ~1.2M annotated images according to the WordNet hierarchy. For sentence-based image description Plummer et al. [25] created a dataset namely, Flickr30k, which contains ~3K images that focus primarily on humans and animals, and ~1.5K English captions. Oh et al. [26] collected a dataset of online products for metric learning, namely, Stanford Online Products (SOP) by crawling eBay.com, and contains 120k images of 23k classes. Weyand et al. [27] introduced a new dataset, Google Landmarks Dataset v2, that includes about 5M images of natural and man-made landmarks all over the world. Van et al. [28] created a unique dataset, iNaturalist, consisting of over 8M images of various species of plants and trees captured around the world.

Some of the image datasets that are used for various image retrieval problems are shown in the Table 1.

Table 1. Some well-known image datasets are used for image retrieval, recognition, and classification problems.

Samples	Dataset	Description	Application	Annotation
	Fashion10000 [29]	A large scale fashion dataset	Fashion recommendation	32,398 fashion outfits
	Multi-view Clothing dataset [17]	View-invariant clothing dataset	Clothing retrieval	161,638 clothing images
	Exact Street2Shop [16]	Clothing items are matched between street and shop images	Image retrieval	~404k online shop and ~20k street images
	DeepFashion [18]	A large scale clothing dataset with annotation	Image retrieval and recognition	800k fashion products
	CIFAR-10 [30]	Gray-scale fashion product images	Classification	70k fashion items
	ImageNet [24]	A large-scale dataset of objects	Object recognition	~100k objects
	Flickr30k [25]	Sentence-based image description dataset	Classification	~3K images with ~ 1.5K captions
	Oxford5k [31]	Benchmarked Oxford landmarks images	Image retrieval	~5K landmark images
	Paris6k [32]	Benchmarked Paris landmarks images	Image retrieval	~6K landmark images
	CUB-200-2011 [33]	A large-scale dataset of bird images	Image retrieval and Classification	~11K bird images of 200 bird species
	Google Landmarks Dataset v2 [27]	Natural and man-made landmarks	Image retrieval and classification	~5M landmark images around the world
	iNaturalist [28]	Images of species of plants and trees	Image retrieval and classification	~8M benchmarked images

According to our observations, there are no datasets available that are exclusively related to ornamental images. This inspires us to build a dataset of ornament images.

State-of-the-Art Fashion Image Retrieval Methods: As fashion e-commerce has grown year after year, there is a high demand for an innovation solution to help customers easily find the fashion item of choice. For Exact Street-to-Shop image retrieval, Hadi et al. [16] introduced three different methods, including two in-depth learning methods and a method to compare the similarity between street and shop fashion images. For in-shop clothing retrieval, Kinli et al. [34] proposed a triplet-based design of capsule network architecture to calculate the similarity between triplets. To train a network that matches fashion item images captured by users with the same item images taken in controlled condition by a professional photographer, Gajic et al. [1] use triplet loss. To retrieve the same or attribute similar clothing images from online shopping, for a user-captured clothing image, Huang et al. [15] developed a Dual Attribute aware Ranking Network (DARN) that integrates feature and visual similarity limitations into retrieval feature learning. For interactive fashion item search, Zhao et al. [35] proposed a memory augmented attribute manipulation network, where the memory block consists of a memory to store a prototype representation of various attributes, and a neural controller, for interactive attribute manipulation. To learn the features of garments with joint predictions of clothing features and landmarks, Liu et al. [18] has developed a novel deep model, namely, FashionNet. A new Match R-CNN framework was proposed by Ge et al. [20] to resolve clothes detection, pose estimation, segmentation, and retrieval problems in an end-to-end manner. Ma et al. [22] proposed a novel Attribute-Specific Embedding Network (ASEN) with two attention networks Attribute-aware Spatial Attention (ASA) and Attribute-aware Channel Attention (ACA), to learn multiple attribute-specific embeddings and to measure fine-grained fashion similarity prediction in the same space. Zheng et al. [36] proposed a weakly supervised contrastive learning framework (WCL) to tackle the class collision problem of contrastive learning. To retrieve weakly-supervised multi-modal instance-level products, Zhan et al. [37] has collected a dataset called Product1M and proposed a hybrid-stream transformer called CAPTURE. To perform weakly supervised classification of unlabeled data, Presotto et al. [38] proposed a rank-based model.

3   Proposed Dataset and Benchmark

There are no datasets available that exclusively deal with ornament images. Ornament images are more complex in nature and a large number of designs are available rather than other fashion image datasets. An earring dataset and its benchmarking have described in [13]. In this paper, we have created an ornament dataset, namely, NecklaceFIR, a collection of high resolution golden necklaces. The datset contains 4,803 images from 49 different classes that are collected from various online shopping sites. Figure 2(A) shows the sample images from our dataset and Fig. 2(B) shows the distribution of images over different classes.

Data Collection: We have collected the dataset by visiting various jewellery chains like Tanishq, Malabar Gold and Diamonds, Kalyan Jewellers, Anjali Jewellers, Senco Jewellers, and PC Chandra Jewellers and from some popular shopping websites such as, voylla, myntra, amazon, and flip-kart. To form the datset, we have marged the images collected from various jewellery chains and online shopping sites. We refine the dataset by deleting the duplicate entry images and low resolution images.

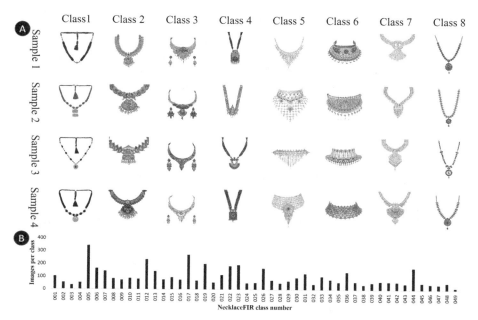

Fig. 2. (A) Samples from the dataset of varied designs are selected randomly to be shown as examples. (B) The images of different classes are also distributed evenly in tabular from.

Image Annotation: Annotation of the dataset is the most crucial part of our work. Here, grouping earrings by visual similarity has been mentioned as an annotation. For this purpose, we have involved 5 female volunteers who have expertise in jewellery and 25 end-user female volunteers. We have also designed a small application for this purpose. The application will show some random query images on the screen and the volunteers will select similar images from the image gallery. The process was repeated for ~1000 times and ~50K arbitrary annotations are collected. Then, based on the maximum vote, the necklace images are grouped into various classes. Finally, we have got 49 different classes of necklace images.

4   Benchmarking Methods and Discussion

To benchmark the NecklaceFIR dataset, we have used various existing classical methods and state-of-art deep models where Histogram similarity using Bhattacharyya distance, Pearson Correlation Coefficient, Chi-Square, and intersection are the classical methods and ResNet50, ResNet101, ResNet152, VGG16, NASNetMobile, MobileNet, DenseNet121, DenseNet169, and DenseNet201 are the deep networking models used for benchmarking.

To extract the features of an image and image retrieval, we have used various deep models. To extract the features of the query and gallery image pair, we have used Imagenet as the baseline image classifier. Then, the feature distance of the query and gallery image pair is calculated using Euclidean distance. The similarity score is calculated using feature distance and based on the similarity score, the ranking of the gallery images are assigned.

We have divided the dataset into train and test sets where 70% of the dataset is the train set used to train the deep network models and remaining 30% is test set used for validation. For validation, 10 images from each class have been separated. Based on the similarity score, the gallery images are sorted images in descending order for a given query image. To record the performance of retrieval, we have used top-k retrieval accuracy. To achieve any true result from the specific test performed by considering any single query image, one item is required to match with the existing gallery. This has to be achieved only within the first k results. At first, the deep models are trained with Imagenet and fine-tuned with our novel dataset NecklaceFIR. Then the features of the query and gallery images

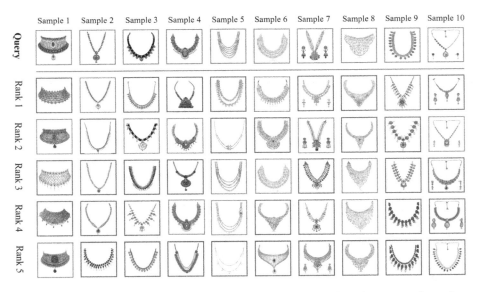

Fig. 3. Some arbitrary retrieval examples using NASNetMobile, where green boundary indicates successfully retrieved images and red boundary indicates failed images.

are extracted using the trained deep model. Finally, feature differences are used as similarities; the less the difference, the greater the similarity. The top-1, top-5, top-10, and top-20 retrieval accuracy's on NecklaceFIR using various methods are summarized in Table 2. The Fig. 3 shows the results of random retrieval using NASNetMobile and Fig. 4 shows the graphical representation of Top-k retrieval accuracy using various methods.

It can be observed that the retrieval accuracy using classical image retrieval methods is not good and state-of-art deep models also perform poorly. And the top-1 accuracy is very low for all methods. It can be also noticed that classical image retrieval methods like Bhattacharyya distance and Chi-Square compete with state-of-art deep models.

From the results, we can conclude that due to less variation in design, color and texture details are the main cause of less retrieval accuracy by the state-of-art deep models and classical methods. We need a custom designed neural network for ornament dataset to achieve better retrieval accuracy.

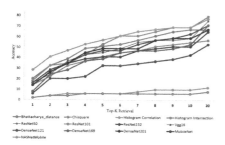

Fig. 4. Top-k retieval accuracy on NecklaceFIR dataset using various state-of-art methods.

Table 2. Accuracy using various state-of-art classical, deep learning methods

Method	Accuracy (%)			
	Top-1	Top-5	Top-10	Top-20
Bhattacharyya [39]	20.41	51.02	67.35	67.34
Correlation [39]	2.04	6.12	10.20	12.24
Chi-Square [39]	18.37	53.06	69.39	79.59
Hist. Intersection [40]	2.04	6.12	6.12	8.16
VGG16 [41]	16.33	44.90	59.18	75.51
ResNet50 [42]	14.29	40.82	55.10	57.14
ResNet101 [42]	14.29	40.82	55.10	57.14
ResNet152 [42]	16.33	40.82	51.02	65.31
DenseNet121 [43]	14.29	46.94	63.27	71.43
DenseNet169 [43]	8.16	38.78	53.06	71.43
DenseNet201 [43]	14.29	48.98	59.18	67.35
NASNetMobile [44]	28.57	57.14	69.39	77.55
MobileNet [45]	6.12	32.65	42.86	53.06

5   Conclusion

In this paper, we have introduced a novel fashion image retrieval dataset featuring large sized gold necklaces, namely, NecklaceFIR containing ~4.8K high-resolution images and labelled in 49 categories. The dataset is also benchmarked using various well-known classical methods and state-of-art deep neural models. As per our observation, the dataset is challenging and the retrieval accuracy using various state-of-art methods is very low. The main challenges of the dataset are: (1) Unlike many other fashion datasets such as shoes and clothing, the idea of matching necklace is abstract because similarity may be based on structure or it may be based on structure and appearance of other material like stone, 2) large interclass variations. We hope that the dataset will make a valuable contribution to the computer vision community and it will attract the researchers. In the future, we will expand the dataset by including other ornaments and will also add textual tags to the ornaments to improve retrieval accuracy.

References

1. Gajic, B., Baldrich, R.: Cross-domain fashion image retrieval. In: Proceedings of the IEEE Conference on Computer Vision and Pattern Recognition Workshops, pp. 1869–1871 (2018)
2. Lang, Y., He, Y., Yang, F., Dong, J., Xue, H.: Which is plagiarism: fashion image retrieval based on regional representation for design protection. In: Proceedings of the IEEE/CVF Conference on Computer Vision and Pattern Recognition (CVPR), June 2020
3. Su, H., Wang, P., Liu, L., Li, H., Li, Z., Zhang, Y.: Where to look and how to describe: fashion image retrieval with an attentional heterogeneous bilinear network. IEEE Trans. Circuits Syst. Video Technol. (2020)
4. Yin, R., Li, K., Lu, J., Zhang, G.: Enhancing fashion recommendation with visual compatibility relationship. In: The World Wide Web Conference, pp. 3434–3440 (2019)
5. Hidayati, S.C., Hsu, C.-C., Chang, Y.-T., Hua, K.-L., Fu, J., Cheng, W.-H.: What dress fits me best? Fashion recommendation on the clothing style for personal body shape. In: Proceedings of the 26th ACM International Conference on Multimedia, pp. 438–446 (2018)
6. Verma, S., Anand, S., Arora, C., Rai, A.: Diversity in fashion recommendation using semantic parsing. In: 2018 25th IEEE International Conference on Image Processing (ICIP), pp. 500–504. IEEE (2018)
7. Khurana, T., Mahajan, K., Arora, C., Rai, A.: Exploiting texture cues for clothing parsing in fashion images. In: 2018 25th IEEE International Conference on Image Processing (ICIP), pp. 2102–2106. IEEE (2018)
8. Dong, H., et al.: Fashion editing with adversarial parsing learning. In: Proceedings of the IEEE/CVF Conference on Computer Vision and Pattern Recognition, pp. 8120–8128 (2020)
9. Ak, K.E., Kassim, A.A., Lim, J.H., Tham, J.Y.: Learning attribute representations with localization for flexible fashion search. In: Proceedings of the IEEE Conference on Computer Vision and Pattern Recognition, pp. 7708–7717 (2018)
10. Ak, K.E., Lim, J.H., Tham, J.Y., Kassim, A.A.: Which shirt for my first date? Towards a flexible attribute-based fashion query system. Pattern Recognit. Lett. **112**, 212–218 (2018)
11. Wang, W., Xu, Y., Shen, J., Zhu, S.-C.: Attentive fashion grammar network for fashion landmark detection and clothing category classification. In: Proceedings of the IEEE Conference on Computer Vision and Pattern Recognition, pp. 4271–4280 (2018)
12. Park, S., Shin, M., Ham, S., Choe, S., Kang, Y.: Study on fashion image retrieval methods for efficient fashion visual search. In: Proceedings of the IEEE Conference on Computer Vision and Pattern Recognition Workshops (2019)
13. Islam, S.M., Joardar, S., Sekh, A.A.: RingFIR: a large volume earring dataset for fashion image retrieval. In: Singh, S.K., Roy, P., Raman, B., Nagabhushan, P. (eds.) CVIP 2020. CCIS, vol. 1377, pp. 100–111. Springer, Singapore (2021). https://doi.org/10.1007/978-981-16-1092-9_9

14. Huang, J., Xia, W., Yan, S.: Deep search with attribute-aware deep network. In: Proceedings of the 22nd ACM International Conference on Multimedia, pp. 731–732 (2014)

15. Huang, J., Feris, R.S., Chen, Q., Yan, S.: Cross-domain image retrieval with a dual attribute-aware ranking network. In: Proceedings of the IEEE International Conference on Computer Vision, pp. 1062–1070 (2015)

16. Hadi Kiapour, M., Han, X., Lazebnik, S., Berg, A.C., Berg, T.L.: Where to buy it: matching street clothing photos in online shops. In: Proceedings of the IEEE International Conference on Computer Vision, pp. 3343–3351 (2015)

17. Liu, K.-H., Chen, T.-Y., Chen, C.-S.: MVC: a dataset for view-invariant clothing retrieval and attribute prediction. In: Proceedings of the 2016 ACM on International Conference on Multimedia Retrieval, pp. 313–316 (2016)

18. Liu, Z., Luo, P., Qiu, S., Wang, X., Tang, X.: DeepFashion: powering robust clothes recognition and retrieval with rich annotations. In: IEEE Conference on Computer Vision and Pattern Recognition, pp. 1096–1104 (2016)

19. Cheng, Z.-Q., Wu, X., Liu, Y., Hua, X.-S.: Video2shop: exact matching clothes in videos to online shopping images. In: Proceedings of the IEEE Conference on Computer Vision and Pattern Recognition, pp. 4048–4056 (2017)

20. Ge, Y., Zhang, R., Wu, L., Wang, X., Tang, X., Luo, P.: Deepfashion2: a versatile benchmark for detection, pose estimation, segmentation and re-identification of clothing images. arXiv preprint arXiv:1901.07973 (2019)

21. Kuang, Z., et al.: Fashion retrieval via graph reasoning networks on a similarity pyramid. In: Proceedings of the IEEE/CVF International Conference on Computer Vision, pp. 3066–3075 (2019)

22. Ma, Z., et al.: Fine-grained fashion similarity learning by attribute-specific embedding network. In: Proceedings of the AAAI Conference on Artificial Intelligence, vol. 34, pp. 11741–11748 (2020)

23. Zou, X., Kong, X., Wong, W., Wang, C., Liu, Y., Cao, Y.: FashionAI: a hierarchical dataset for fashion understanding. In: Proceedings of the IEEE/CVF Conference on Computer Vision and Pattern Recognition Workshops (2019)

24. Deng, J., Dong, W., Socher, R., Li, L.-J., Li, K., Fei-Fei, L.: ImageNet: a large-scale hierarchical image database. In: 2009 IEEE Conference on Computer Vision and Pattern Recognition, pp. 248–255. IEEE (2009)

25. Plummer, B.A., Wang, L., Cervantes, C.M., Caicedo, J.C., Hockenmaier, J., Lazebnik, S.: Flickr30k entities: collecting region-to-phrase correspondences for richer image-to-sentence models. In: Proceedings of the IEEE International Conference on Computer Vision, pp. 2641–2649 (2015)

26. Song, H.O., Xiang, Y., Jegelka, S., Savarese, S.: Deep metric learning via lifted structured feature embedding. In: Proceedings of the IEEE Conference on Computer Vision and Pattern Recognition, pp. 4004–4012 (2016)

27. Weyand, T., Araujo, A., Cao, B., Sim, J.: Google landmarks dataset v2-a large-scale benchmark for instance-level recognition and retrieval. In: Proceedings of the IEEE/CVF Conference on Computer Vision and Pattern Recognition, pp. 2575–2584 (2020)

28. Van Horn, G., et al.: The iNaturalist species classification and detection dataset. In: Proceedings of the IEEE Conference on Computer Vision and Pattern Recognition, pp. 8769–8778 (2018)

29. Loni, B., et al.: Fashion 10000: an enriched social image dataset for fashion and clothing. In: Proceedings of the 5th ACM Multimedia Systems Conference, pp. 41–46 (2014)

30. Xiao, H., Rasul, K., Vollgraf, R.: Fashion-MNIST: a novel image dataset for benchmarking machine learning algorithms. arXiv preprint arXiv:1708.07747 (2017)
31. Philbin, J., Chum, O., Isard, M., Sivic, J., Zisserman, A.: Object retrieval with large vocabularies and fast spatial matching. In: 2007 IEEE Conference on Computer Vision and Pattern Recognition, pp. 1–8. IEEE (2007)
32. Philbin, J., Chum, O., Isard, M., Sivic, J., Zisserman, A.: Lost in quantization: improving particular object retrieval in large scale image databases. In: 2008 IEEE Conference on Computer Vision and Pattern Recognition, pp. 1–8. IEEE (2008)
33. Wah, C., Branson, S., Welinder, P., Perona, P., Belongie, S.: The caltech-UCSD birds-200-2011 dataset (2011)
34. Kinli, F., Ozcan, B., Kiraç, F.: Fashion image retrieval with capsule networks. In: Proceedings of the IEEE International Conference on Computer Vision Workshops (2019)
35. Zhao, B., Feng, J., Wu, X., Yan, S.: Memory-augmented attribute manipulation networks for interactive fashion search. In: Proceedings of the IEEE Conference on Computer Vision and Pattern Recognition, pp. 1520–1528 (2017)
36. Zheng, M., et al.: Weakly supervised contrastive learning. In: Proceedings of the IEEE/CVF International Conference on Computer Vision, pp. 10042–10051 (2021)
37. Zhan, X., et al.: Product1m: towards weakly supervised instance-level product retrieval via cross-modal pretraining. arXiv e-prints, pages arXiv-2107 (2021)
38. Presotto, J.G.C., Valem, L.P., de Sá, N.G., Pedronette, D.C.G., Papa, J.P.: Weakly supervised learning through rank-based contextual measures. In: 2020 25th International Conference on Pattern Recognition (ICPR), pp. 5752–5759. IEEE (2021)
39. Erkut, U., Bostancıoğlu, F., Erten, M., Murat Özbayoğlu, A., Solak, E.: HSV color histogram based image retrieval with background elimination. In: 2019 1st International Informatics and Software Engineering Conference (UBMYK), pp. 1–5. IEEE (2019)
40. Liao, Q.: Comparison of several color histogram based retrieval algorithms. In: 2016 IEEE Advanced Information Management, Communicates, Electronic and Automation Control Conference (IMCEC), pp. 1670–1673. IEEE (2016)
41. Ha, I., Kim, H., Park, S., Kim, H.: Image retrieval using BIM and features from pretrained VGG network for indoor localization. Build. Environ. **140**, 23–31 (2018)
42. Pelka, O., Nensa, F., Friedrich, C.M.: Annotation of enhanced radiographs for medical image retrieval with deep convolutional neural networks. PLoS ONE **13**(11), e0206229 (2018)
43. Zhang, J., Lu, C., Li, X., Kim, H.-J., Wang, J.: A full convolutional network based on densenet for remote sensing scene classification. Math. Biosci. Eng. **16**(5), 3345–3367 (2019)
44. Saxen, F., Werner, P., Handrich, S., Othman, E., Dinges, L., Al-Hamadi, A.: Face attribute detection with MobileNetv2 and NasNet-mobile. In: 2019 11th International Symposium on Image and Signal Processing and Analysis (ISPA), pp. 176–180. IEEE (2019)
45. Ilhan, H.O., Onur Sigirci, I., Serbes, G., Aydin, N.: A fully automated hybrid human sperm detection and classification system based on mobile-net and the performance comparison with conventional methods. Med. Biol. Eng. Comput., 1–22 (2020)

Optimal Sample Size Calculation for Machine Learning Based Analysis for Suicide Ideation

Sudipto Roy[1]([⊠]) and Jigyasu Dubey[2]

[1] Research Scholar, Department of Computer Science, Shri Vaishnav Vidyapeeth
Vishwavidyalaya, Indore, India
sudiptoima@gmail.com
[2] Head of Department of Computer Science, Shri Vaishnav Vidyapeeth Vishwavidyalaya,
Indore, India

Abstract. In the field of Machine Learning and Artificial Intelligence the dataset size and handling plays a vital role in determining the final outcome and prediction accuracy. Since most of the data collection methodology are automated and processing these data are becoming more robust and efficient, the size of data collected for prediction accuracy has become a matter of less important. This has given rise to the field of big data analysis. However, in the field of medical studies and psychological evaluation the data has to be physical collected by a human being and collated in a form which is machine interpretable. This step of manual interaction for data collection cannot be obviated. When compared to automated data collection mechanism, the dataset size is not a significant factor. However, in the case of manual data collection, the optimal size of the data to yield the best machine learning assisted prediction becomes prime importance. All data collection mechanism for medical and psychological studies have been analysed using statistical tool and no study have shown or brought out the optimal dataset requirement to yield the best results when analysing this collected data via machine learning algorithms. In this paper, we look into the domain of optimising the data size so that we can minimise the data collection time without compromising the desired accuracy result. We will draw our inspiration from various medical data collection methodology and build upon the same to work out an optimum data size for analysis through various machine learning algorithm.

Keywords: Machine learning · Psychometric test · Unbalanced dataset · Small dataset · Cross validation · Nested CV · Optimality · Classification · Class imbalance learning · Over fitting · Under fitting

1 Introduction

A general prevailing myth amongst data scientist is the fact that larger the dataset more accurate is the prediction accuracy through Artificial Intelligence or Machine Learning Algorithms. In contrary it is opined that smaller dataset may lead to model overfitting and Machine Learning algorithm may try to adjust the parameters to give a false higher accuracy parameter [1]. In real world scenarios psychological dataset building and collection have several challenges ranging from privacy issues related to patients, medical practitioner's policies, legal limitations [2], etc. In addition most of the medical dataset have a huge nature of being unbalanced, i.e. due to the rareness of the occurrence of any disease, any patient or psychological dataset pertaining to any disease or disorder will display property wherein the non-occurrence of the event will heavily overweight the occurrence of the disease or disorder [3]. Moreover, collection of such a dataset will be time consuming and may run into years before a predictive model of the same can be designed. In this time interval the actual utilisation of the dataset collection time may not be economical as compared to the problem it intends to address.

In spite of extensive research and various deliberations there has not been any consensus in the regard of definition of a small dataset. A break through work in the field has been provided by Shawe-Taylor et al. [4] which has given a mathematical model named as Probably Approximately Correct (PAC) which gives a lot of insight into the dimension of sample size of a dataset with respect to the desired accuracy. The definition in this field has been restricted to as a study of small and unbalanced dataset, however no answer has been provided as to what an optimal sample size should be for the best accuracy using classification or regression model.

Majority of the studies have either concentrated into dealing with either small or unbalanced dataset. When we talk of optimality, then our domain of work is a vertical cross-section over both small and unbalanced dataset. It is of paramount importance and of valid scientific interest to deal with both small and unbalanced dataset at one time to ensure optimally performing machine learning model. It has been noticed that classification algorithm in machine learning have been seen to be performing sub optimally when dealing with limited size dataset [5]. The primary reason for such poor performance in classification models is due to the lack of dimensionality for generalisation of any desired pattern in the training dataset. This lack of data dimensionality and pattern also affect the validation dataset since it is difficult to avoid data overfitting [6] and will eventually lead to biased and unrealistic classification model.

All the studies that have been conducted previously have focused on achieving higher accuracy using classification algorithms on small datasets, however how a small dataset impacts the performance of a classifier have not been studied and remains an area of open research. The approach to solve the issue have been met with a lot of criticism like introduction of noise to the sample dimensions [7], non-scalable model depictions [8], irregular data replication [9], etc.

In addition to small dataset, another major issue that comes in prediction accuracy for any classification model is the unbalanced nature of the data in case of medical and psychological prediction. Certain psychological disorders like suicide make have a completely skewed dataset in which the number of normal people with non-suicidal tendencies may out number people with suicidal tendencies. In certain studies, no dataset have been able to capture suicidal tendencies in the projected demography with high accuracy. This kind of unbalanced nature of the data added to its small size gives rise to multidimensional problem for the use of Machine Learning in the field of the psychological disorders. The use of Machine Learning follows the cognitive brain functioning which are in same lines of cognitive psychology find in human being and is based on the concept of advance human psychology an deep routed neural networks. Limited nature of data available has been treated with the help of statistical tools thus human intervention has overlooked the issues created by dis--balanced or small dataset. However, with the emergence of Machine Learning based approaches, such kind of human interpretation will not be possible and we need to fine tune our algorithm to get the desired result.

In summary we will like to bring out the following few nuances in the field of the optimality study when considering the dataset size for a medical or a psychological dataset which is by nature unbalanced and small in nature. In the first part following the introduction, we will bring out the related study in the field. We will develop on treatment of a small dataset in part three followed by the handling of unbalanced dataset in part four of the paper. Then we will draw some inspiration from the field of medical study and bring out the optimal dataset which we will consider for our research study.

2 Related Study

In this section of the paper we will bring out the nuances in the field of small dataset and imbalanced dataset. We will see the work that have been done in the field before and try to draw inspiration from the same. Though in all the literature we have review, small dataset and imbalanced dataset have been dealt separately. In this paper we will try to bring these two domain under one common point of discussion and try to find out the major challenges that one encounters. From the challenges we will try to deliberate on a methodology which will give us the best accuracy performance based on small and unbalanced dataset. Our major aim of the literature review is to bring out the nuances in determining the optimal dataset.

In the field of unbalanced dataset, the term unbalanced or imbalanced is referred to as the conditions in which the categories under the classification algorithm is not equally represented in any approximation. The ratio of imbalance that is the presence of one majority class against a minority class can be of the magnitude of 1:1000 or 0.01% of majority class may be represented by the minority class [10]. This imbalance nature of the dataset is severely hampering the performance of the designed classifier [11]. The classifiers performance is even deteriorated further due to the fact that the minority class item are the item of interest and the learning task is focused on detection of the same [12]. The most relevance of such dataset are found in the field of medical and psychological disorder classifications [13]. Similar examples are also seen in the field of cyber security and fraud detection, where the fraud occurrence instances are far less than the normal transaction [14].

In the reviewed literature, reinforced algorithms have been designed to better enable classifiers to perform better with unbalanced datasets. Such kind of supervised classifier learning is called Class Imbalance Learning (CIL) Methods. Supervised classifier learning under unbalanced data conditions can be broadly divided into two categories, namely internal and external methods. In internal methods, the learning algorithm is modified to handle the imbalanced dataset whereas in external methodology the imbalanced dataset is treated by pre-processing the training datasets so as to achieve a balanced nature of the dataset [15]. The major advantage that one envisages by the use of the external method is that they have shown better performance irrespective of the underlying classification algorithm or model.

The external method of re-sampling focuses in improving the unbalanced dataset by either focused or random oversampling of minority class or under sampling of the majority class. In oversampling the elements of the minority class are duplicated in a focused or random manner. On the other hand in under sampling the elements of the majority class is removed [16]. The over sampling/ under sampling is carried out till such time a certain percentage is met [17]. However, certain dataset (Sick Dataset) with highly unbalanced data have shown good classification using standard machine learning algorithm. We can clearly deduce that the reduction in performance in accuracy of the learning algorithm is not solely due to unbalance nature of the data. There are other factors also that needs to be looked into. In addition to the imbalance in data, the data distribution within the class also causes the machine learning algorithm to have reduced classification accuracy [18]. Prati et al., also argued that the inefficiency in unbalanced dataset can also be accounted for the degree of data overlapping in the classes [19]. In addition, unbalanced data also poses a lot of other challenges for accurate classification performance. Data duplication, rare case problems and overlapping classes are to name a few of the challenges that an unbalanced dataset imposes.

In this part of the literature review we will deliberate on the issues that a classification algorithm faces when it has a small dataset. Though no clear cut definition has been laid down as a small dataset, however we consider only those dataset whose median size is less than 100. In some literature a 100 point dataset may be enough to give adequate classification results however, we will deliberate on those datasets that have proven to pose challenges to classification algorithm due to their sheer small size.

While experimenting with machine learning classification algorithm it has been noticed that there is a strong co-relation between sample size and reported performance which is suggestive of the fact that a small sample size is directly reported to provide a result that is overoptimistic in nature. Supervised learning is characterised through the ideal learning model which would then use the regularities in the training dataset for building approximate parameters which would then be used in generalising new unseen data. However, one major limitation to the fact is the inbuilt noise in the training data and it may not be sufficient to represent the represented class adequately. Thus such kind of self-adjustment within the used algorithm is termed as overfitting. Though complex and small dataset may lead to overfitting, it has been noticed that simple small dataset may lead to under-fitting. The major focus one intends to achieve in building a classifier model is to ensure that it fits the training data adequately so as to represent the pattern and at the same time be able to avoid the noise which is inbuilt to the training data. In practice, it is easier to deal with under-fitting than with over-fitted data.

Less data can lead to lack of generalisation and raise difficulty in optimisation. Some researchers are of the opinion that this may lead to data imbalance. In Fig. 1 we will summarise the various methods that are available to tackle the problem of small dataset. Lack of generalisation in the data can be tackled with the help of generating additional data, augmenting data points by using different methods like brightness, flips and crops. It can also be achieved by the ridge, elastic net and lasso regularization. Other methods for data generalisation is known as ensemble method and is achieved through two different algorithm known as bagging and boosting. We can overcome the data balancing issue in methods that have been mentioned in para above. For data optimisation we have to rely on the internal adjustment capacity of the algorithms that are being used. We can focus on transferring of learning and try to learn through the use of less data. Meta learning algorithm also provide better learning and optimisation techniques.

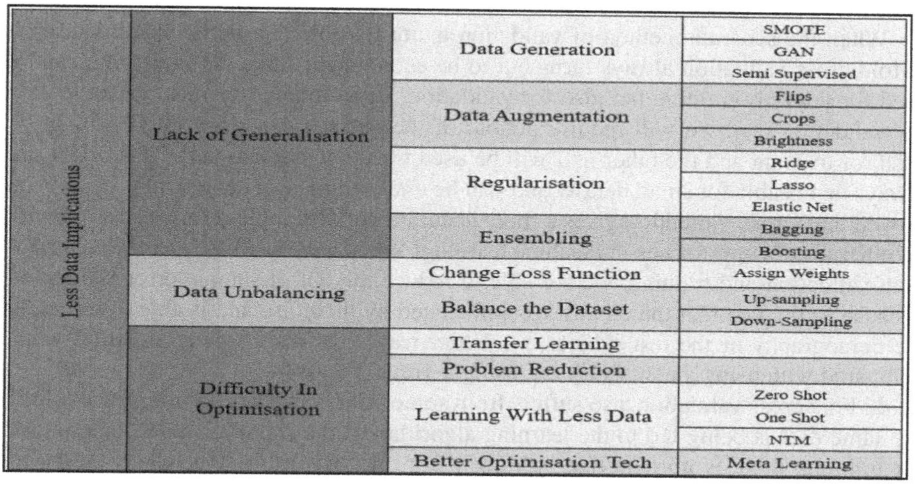

Less Data Implications			
	Lack of Generalisation	Data Generation	SMOTE
			GAN
			Semi Supervised
		Data Augmentation	Flips
			Crops
			Brightness
		Regularisation	Ridge
			Lasso
			Elastic Net
		Ensembling	Bagging
			Boosting
	Data Unbalancing	Change Loss Function	Assign Weights
		Balance the Dataset	Up-sampling
			Down-Sampling
	Difficulty In Optimisation	Transfer Learning	
		Problem Reduction	
		Learning With Less Data	Zero Shot
			One Shot
			NTM
		Better Optimisation Tech	Meta Learning

Fig. 1. Small data set treatment methodology.

3 Data Validation

To validate data in Machine Learning Algorithm, the one of the most reliable methodology is to train the machine learning model with the available data and then to predict the model with new and unseen data. Another methodology is split the dataset into two different parts. One of the part will be used to train the algorithm and for the adjustment of the model parameters for classification. The validation of the performance model will then be performed using the other part of the dataset, in which the actual class will be validated against the predicted resultant class. The best approach is to use new and unseen data for having predictive result that are unbiased in nature thus yield results which will be very close to the accuracy it will obtain on prediction of actual real world data.

The major disadvantage with such an approach is that it requires a huge amount of time and money for collection and holding such a huge additional set of data just for the purpose of validation and such kind of methodology is rarely used when human participants are involved. To overcome this one of the common practice is to use cross validation. In cross validation, we iteratively use the train and the test splitting of the dataset on different random portion of the dataset in the same proportion as has been predetermined. The number of times this iteration is done is predefined and is commonly termed as K-Fold. A well predicting model will go through various steps in which data normalisation will be followed by feature selection followed by parameter tuning and other option additional steps. After a K-Fold cross validation has been used, a portion of the data that have been kept aside is used to validate the model. This is carried out several times by leaving a separate part of the data every time. The performance of the model is then approximated by averaging out the accuracy that has been achieved over the different iterations.

When the separate method of validation is not feasible due to the small dataset, a K-fold cross validation always turns out to be economical since the same data can be used for not only training but also for validation. If we intend to collect separate data for validation then we will require double of the dataset size since one half will be used for training and the other half will be used for the validation part. This might not always be feasible for small dataset and will be uneconomical. Theoretically it has been proved that Cross Validation gives a more accurate out of sample error estimation with all other known approaches in machine learning. When we use all the available data for both validation and training, we are able to reduce the out of sample error estimation because of the fact that the data is less influenced by the noise and is able to represent the demography or the test subject in a better way. This results perform better when compared with using a new dataset or using a Train/ Test split.

K-Fold cross validation also suffers from some criticism. Since in this methodology the same data is being fed to the learning algorithm of the classifier for validation and for training, there is no data that is hidden from the algorithm and it may adjust its internal parameter to overfit the model. Researchers are of the opinion that if sufficient amount of data is available for using K-Fold Cross Validation then one must make it an endeavor to ensure that the data used for model development is different from the data that has been used to train the model and then for model evaluation [20]. Using the same data to train a model and then to use the same data to evaluate and validate the same can give rise to overoptimistic result due to overfitting property of the model [21]. To overcome the same researchers have suggested a new kind of Cross Validation known as Nested Cross Validation, which even though using the same data for both validation and training and gives better performance accuracy without over-fitting thus ensuring economy at the same time [22]. In nested Cross Validation, we use a dataset splitting at the very beginning and in all the different iteration of the cross validation, we train a different model from the scratch which also includes parameter tuning and new feature selection. This step is repeated through all the folds with a different portion of the dataset and training a new model till such time all the data has been used. It has been recorded that such a method always ensure a better unbiased performance estimate.

Another way of treating a small and an unbalanced dataset have been suggested by researchers is by increasing the dataset size by increasing the dimensionality of the data. One such approach is increasing the data dimensionality by adding additional data attributes with the help of fuzzy rules between the different features of the dataset. From the values obtained through the fuzzy rules, it is assigned to each member functions and the same is used to extend the dataset features. It has been noticed that such kind of enhancement have reportedly given better classification results [23]. In case the dataset doesn't provide sufficient data to fill the gaps between the samples, the extended dataset obtained through the fuzzy logic may not provide enough dataset feature extension to provide a better classification result. This is a classical exception when the unavailability of the data may lead to degrading o performance accuracy [24].

4 Determining the Optimum Sample Size

One of the major issues for any clinical study is to determine the adequate sample size so that the number selected is much less than the original represented population but at the same time it represents the total population adequately and one can draw true inferences about the population form the obtained results. It's a laid down statistical norm that we must define the sample size before the start of any clinical trial so that in the interpreted results we can avoid bias. If the sample size is too small, the obtained result will not be generalised to the population since the sample population is not representative of the entire population size. Under such circumstances the research may not be able to detect the differences between the test groups and will be termed unethical.

Similarly, if we include a greater number of test subject in the sample, we will run the risk of intervention with a lot more individuals and will make the research unethical. Also, this will lead to wasting of precious resources and the time of the researcher [25].

The broad parameters on which the sample size of a survey is determined are: Acceptable level of significance, Power of the study, Expected Effect Size, Underlying event rate in the population, and Standard deviation in the population. In addition, there are added factors like unequal allocation ratio, design and objective of study, dropout rates, etc., but these factors contribution are less significant and won't be considered in our sample size determination [26]. We will briefly cover the factors one by one and give the significance of the factor and the value in our research. Before understanding our methodology for calculation of the sample size, we need to understand a few underlying definitions.

4.1 Acceptable Level of Significance (ALS) ('α')

This factor basically lays down the false positive detection. It gives the tolerance of the researcher wherein he is ready to detect a certain percentage of prediction as suicidal where in the actual is non-suicidal ideation.

4.2 Power of the Study

Conversely to the ALS, Power (β) is given by the tolerance of the false negative that a researcher is ready to take as part of his research. A power of the study is given by (1-Power) or (1-β). Since, in Suicide study, false negative plays a very significant role, as we don't want a person with suicide thoughts to be detected as not having suicide thought. So, we will have to keep our Power of study as high as possible.

4.3 Expected Effect Size (Δ)

In statistical term, the difference of the variable value between the training set and the test set is known as the effect size. If the effect size between the train and the test data set is large, we will require a smaller sample set, whereas, if the effect between the train and the test dataset is less, we will require a larger sample set. Since suicide occurrence are very less, so the effect size between the train and the test set will be very less. Thus, it will significantly increase our sample set.

4.4   Underlying Event Rate in the Population

This value is not chosen by convention as with the other cases dealt before. This value is determined from previous studies including observational cohorts. The observed rates of suicide in the population may be affected by our sample size selection since the majority of our training set participants will be healthy individuals or stable people without any comorbidity. One has to take a lot of care to select the event rate, and this may go significant change during the course of the research, if the selected values are seen to be very low [27].

4.5   Standard Deviation in the Population (σ)

This parameter measures the variability or the dispersion in the data. While carry out our research we must keep in mind the variation that is expected in the data. If the data being collected is from a varied population, then we will need a very high sample set since the variance is large and the SD will also be large. Otherwise, the difference between the two groups will be masked by the inherent differences due to the variance. Since in our research, we are focusing on Indian Armed Forces, we are all aware that though ideologically there is not much variance, yet when it comes to background of all soldiers, we have a high variance in our environment and thus will have a high SD value. Since such a SD value couldn't be found in any research field, we will take the SD of Indian population in general [28].

5   Calculation of the Optimal Sample Size

Having seen the various parameters that determine the sample size, now we will see how these parameters determine the overall sample size. There are several ways we can calculate the sample size depending on the design of the study and one blanket formulation for calculation of sample size cannot be used in a standardized way for different research. After understanding the different prerequisites for calculation of the sample size, we reproduce the most logical calculations of sample size for our research. The research proposed in this study is a survey research for representation of collected data for the target population in the whole. Here we will try to gather information for generalizing the findings within the random error limits [29]. The mathematical expression that gives the sample size is given in equation below [30]:

$$N = \frac{2\left(Z_\alpha + Z_{1-\beta}\right)^2}{\Delta^2}\sigma^2$$

where the significance of the figures is as given below:

N = Total Sample Size

Z_α = Constant Value determined by the α level of acceptance

$Z_{1-\beta}$ = Constant value dependent on the Power of the study β

σ = Standard Deviation

Δ = Effect Size Difference

Since we are working with suicide prediction, the effect of false positive will not majorly affect our result output. So, an acceptable level of α will be 5%. The $Z\alpha$ values for a 'α' of 5% will be 1.65.

$Z1-\beta$ is a constant value dependent on the power of study. Since power of study reflects the false negative value, we must be very careful in selecting its value. We must keep the value of β as small as possible. So, the value of $(1-\beta)$ must be as large as possible. The constant value $Z1-\beta$ for the highest possible value of $(1-\beta)$ will be 1.6449.

Effect Size Difference (Δ) has to be calculated based on previous study. The value of the same as reflected in Gen-Min Lin et al., as approx. 5%, i.e., out of every 100-person surveyed only 5 people showed suicide ideation. Since this figure will be small, we will have to take a larger survey size.

The standard deviation for psychological disorder for Indian population in general has been taken as the same is not available for our target population of Indian Armed Forces. Since the Armed Forces represent the Indian population at large, we can assume that the figures can be replicated for the Indian population in general. The SD value for the calculation of sample size is taken at 80%, i.e., 0.8 for the purpose of our calculation.

Substituting the values of variables as shown in para above:

N = Total Sample Size

Z_α = 1.65

$Z_{1-\beta}$ = 1.6449

σ = 0.8

Δ = 0.05

On substituting the values as given above, we get N value as 2779. Catering for a 10% dropout rate, we can say that a sample size of 3000 will be sufficient to make an accurate and correct suicide prediction. The sample size will be split in the form of test and train dataset. For any ML algorithm we can use an 80–20% train test split to train our model for classification prediction.

6 Conclusion

Effective and efficient data mining techniques on small and unbalanced dataset is an open field for further investigation and research. Most researchers have either dealt with small dataset or unbalanced dataset. In our literature review we have not come across any study that have addressed both the issue at the same time. In our paper we have given some direction into calculation of optimal dataset for an unbalance and small dataset having drawn our inspiration on mathematical calculation sample collection tool used in medical field. This is one way of calculation of the sample size which gives a balanced result when accuracy and economy of effort are being considered as the measuring and evaluating parameters. Such kind of mathematical evaluation will give a fair idea about calculating optimal dataset size calculation for small and unbalanced dataset when collection of patient data is costly and time consuming.

References

1. Rahman, M.S., Sultana, M.: Performance of Firth-and logF-type penalized methods in risk prediction for small or sparse binary data. BMC Med. Res. Methodol. **17**, 33 (2017)
2. Floca, R., Bartling, S., Friesike, S.: Challenges of Open Data in Medical Research. In Opening Science. Springer, Cham, Switzerland (2014)
3. Marcoulides, G.A.: Discovering knowledge in data: an introduction to data mining, Daniel T. Larose. J. Am. Stat. Assoc. **100**, 1465 (2005)
4. Shawe-Taylor, J., Anthony, M., Biggs, N.L.: Bounding sample size with the Vapnik-Chervonenkis dimension. Discret. Appl. Math. **42**, 65–73 (1993)
5. Prusa, J., Khoshgoftaar, T.M., Seliya, N.: The effect of dataset size on training tweet sentiment classifiers. In: Proceedings of the 2015 IEEE 14th International Conference on Machine Learning and Applications (ICMLA), Miami, FL, USA, pp. 9–11 (Dec 2015)
6. Rahman, M.S., Sultana, M.: Performance of Firth-and logF-type penalized methods in risk prediction for small or sparse binary data. BMC Med. Res. Methodol. (2017)
7. Coqueret, G.: Approximate NORTA simulations for virtual sample generation. Expert Syst. Appl. **73**, 69–81 (2017)
8. Andonie, R.: Extreme data mining: Inference from small datasets. Int. J. Comput. Commun. Control **5**, 280–291 (2010)
9. Yang, J., Yu, X., Xie, Z.-Q., Zhang, J.-P.: A novel virtual sample generation method based on Gaussian distribution. Knowl. Based Syst. **24**, 740–748 (2011)
10. Wu, J., Brubaker, S.C., Mullin, M.D., Rehg, J.M.: Fast asymmetric learning for cascade face detection. IEEE Trans. Pattern Anal. Mach. Intell. **30**(3), 369–382 (2008)
11. Chawla, N.V., Japkowicz, N., Kotcz, A.: (eds.) Proc. ICML Workshop Learn. Imbalanced Data Sets (2003)
12. Chawla, N.V., Japkowicz, N., Kolcz, A., (eds.) Special issue learning imbalanced datasets. SIGKDD Explor. Newsl. **6**(1) (2004)
13. Kiliç, K., Özge Uncu, I., Türksen, B.: Comparison of different strategies of utilizing fuzzy clustering in structure identification. Inf. Sci. **177**(23), 5153–5162 (2007). https://doi.org/10.1016/j.ins.2007.06.030
14. Mazurowski, M.A., Habas, P.A., Zurada, J.M., Lo, J.Y., Baker, J.A., Tourassi, G.D.: Training neural network classifiers for medical decision making: the effects of imbalanced datasets on classification performance. Neural Netw. **21**(2–3), 427–436 (2008)
15. Batuwita, R., Palade, V.: FSVM-CIL: fuzzy support vector machines for class imbalance learning. IEEE Trans. Fuzzy Syst. **18**(3), 558–571 (2010). https://doi.org/10.1109/TFUZZ.2010.2042721
16. Weiss, G.: Mining with rarity: A unifying framework. SIGKDD Explor. Newsletter **6**(1), 7–19 (2004)
17. Cieslak, D., Chawla, N.: Learning decision trees for unbalanced data. Machine Learning and Knowledge Discovery in Databases. Springer Verlag, Berlin, Germany (2008)
18. Japkowicz, N.: Concept-learning in the presence of between-class and within-class imbalances. In: Stroulia, E., Matwin, S. (eds.) Advances in Artificial Intelligence: 14th Biennial Conference of the Canadian Society for Computational Studies of Intelligence, AI 2001 Ottawa, Canada, June 7–9, 2001 Proceedings, pp. 67–77. Springer Berlin Heidelberg, Berlin, Heidelberg (2001). https://doi.org/10.1007/3-540-45153-6_7
19. Prati, R.C., Batista, G.E.A.P.A., Monard, M.C.: Class imbalances versus class overlapping: an analysis of a learning system behavior. In: Monroy, R., Arroyo-Figueroa, G., Sucar, L.E., Sossa, H. (eds.) MICAI 2004. LNCS (LNAI), vol. 2972, pp. 312–321. Springer, Heidelberg (2004). https://doi.org/10.1007/978-3-540-24694-7_32
20. Whitley, E., Ball, J.: Statistics review 4: sample size calculations. Crit Care **6**, 335–341 (2002)

21. Stone, M.: Cross-validatory choice and assessment of statistical predictions. J. R. Stat. Soc. Ser. B Methodol. **36**(2), 111–133 (1974). https://doi.org/10.1111/j.2517-6161.1974.tb00994.x
22. Varma, S., Simon, R.: Bias in error estimation when using cross-validation for model selection". BMC Bioinform. (Dec 2006)
23. Krstajic, D., Buturovic, L.J., Leahy, D.E., Thomas, S.: Cross-validation pitfalls when selecting and assessing regression and classification models. Journal of Cheminformatics **6**(1), 1–15 (2014). https://doi.org/10.1186/1758-2946-6-10
24. Chen, H.-Y., Li, D.-C., Lin, L.-S.: Extending sample information for small data set prediction. In: Advanced Applied Informatics (IIAI-AAI), 2016 5th IIAI International Congress on. IEEE (2016)
25. Li, D.-C., Lin, W.-K., Lin, L.-S., Chen, C.-C., Huang, W.-T.: The attribute-trend similarity method to improve learning performance for small datasets. Int. J. Prod. Res. **55**(7), 1898–1913 (2017)
26. Kirby, A., Gebski, V., Keech, A.C.: Determining the sample size in a clinical trial. Med. J. Aust. **177**(5), 256–257 (2002). https://doi.org/10.5694/j.1326-5377.2002.tb04759.x
27. Larsen, S., Osnes, M., Eidsaunet, W., Sandvik, L.: Factors influencing the sample size, exemplified by studies on gastroduodenal tolerability of drugs. Scand. J. Gastroenterol. **20**, 395–400 (1985)
28. Altman, D.G.: The revised CONSORT statement for reporting randomized trials: explanation and elaboration. Ann. Intern. Med. **134**(8), 663 (2001). https://doi.org/10.7326/0003-4819-134-8-200104170-00012
29. Prakesh, B., Babu, S.R., Sureshkumar, K.: Response of ayurvedic therapy in the treatment of migraine without aura. Int. J. Ayurveda Res. (2010)
30. Suresh, K.P., Chandrashekara, S.: Sample size estimation and power analysis for clinical research studies. J. Hum. Reprod. Sci. **5**(1), 7 (2012). https://doi.org/10.4103/0974-1208.97779

Query Focused Video Summarization: A Review

Rakhi Akhare[✉] and Subhash Shinde

Lokmanya Tilak College of Engineering, Navi Mumbai, India
rakhiakhare@gmail.com

Abstract. Rapid development in video technologies and easy availability of video capturing devices produces voluminous data which need to handle efficiently to increase the usability of it. Automatic video summarization is a solution to traverse through this data and gives a concise view of it, which is useful in many applications. However, traditional video summarization produces succinct videos without notably qualitative and quantitative loss of information contained in videos. It considers only the important information from the video while generating a summary independent of user interest. Video summarization is a highly subjective task which is not handled by traditional methods and people are more interested in personalized Summary. The solution to handle this problem is multi-model video summarization which helps to produce user-interested summaries by taking two inputs i.e. video and user queries. Different techniques have been explored in previous work based on conventional video summarization. This study presents the reviews of the state-of-the-art query focused video summarization methods to generate the personalized video summary which has not been investigated before. This paper discusses the demand of query-based video summarization in various applications, performance of existing methods and put forward future directions to help the research community to work in this domain.

Keywords: Video summarization · Deep learning · Query-focused video summarization · Multi-model

1 Introduction

Video is an omni-present in various domains like egocentric, surveillance, sports, academics, entertainment, etc. Due to advancement in technology and easily available video recording devices, there is tremendous growth in video data available today which causes network traffic, bandwidth and surfing issues [1].

As the popularity of the video has increased among people, there is an extensive growth in the amount of data daily. It's a very challenging task to navigate through the endless collections of videos and explore the knowledge efficiently. For retrieving useful information from videos, it requires the extraction of semantic information from low level audio or visual data, which is a complex task. Answer to all these questions is automatic video summarization techniques to improve navigation and browsing of large collections of video data on the web [2].

Surfing information on the Internet becomes the popular activity in each domain including education, entertainment, businesses, etc. Efficient content indexing and

© The Author(s), under exclusive license to Springer Nature Switzerland AG 2022
A. A. Sk et al. (Eds.): ISAI 2022, CCIS 1695, pp. 202–212, 2022.
https://doi.org/10.1007/978-3-031-22485-0_19

accessing help user for faster browsing and extract relevant data in less span. Video summarization provides the way to browse a large collection of video data. Video summarization is the process to generate shorter video without losing important information in less time. It helps to give a brief view of larger videos. Another approach for video summarization is taking the users interest in consideration to generate summary. A Personalized video summarization is emerging technique in multi-model summarization.

Due to evaluation of video technologies, video summarization is widely used in various applications to save manpower, storage space management and efficient bandwidth handling. In media organizations, video summarization is used to generate movie trailers and TV serials, highlights of sports videos, News etc. [3]. In surveillance videos tedious labor jobs can be done by creating a short summary of long-term videos, which includes suspicious activity, abnormal behavior, malpractices in examination halls, accidents on roads, etc. People suffering from having dementia or short-term-memory loss disorder mostly use the wearable cameras. Videos captured by these cameras are called Egocentric. A short summary of these videos helps people to monitor daily activities easily [4]. In the medical domain, summarizing lengthy medical process videos, useful to examine the relevant portion and can be used like better teaching aid for medical students. Now a day internet surfing is the most favorable domain among people to learn many things. Figure 1 shows the process of query-based video summarization.

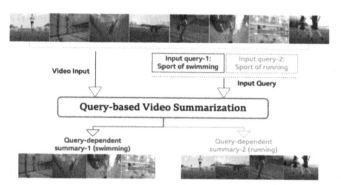

Fig. 1. The basic idea of query based video summarization [5]

As traditional video summarization techniques are not effective to hold the users' interest, query focused video summarization allows to create the users interested summary by giving additional input in terms of text queries. Former works explored the traditional summarization methodology but none other surveyed the query-based video summarization techniques. This gap in literature survey motivates authors to traverse through this area of creating the personalized video summarization and survey the recent development in this domain. The query attentive video summarization is the active area among the researchers since the past few years and efficient algorithms are investigated to solve the problem, but the scope of this domain is very large, there is the huge scope for improvement. This paper presents the survey of the query focused video summarization techniques.

The article is organized as: Sect. 2 explains problem statements containing the basic concept of the video summarization. Section 3 discusses the related work in the area of video summarization and comparative analysis is presented. Section 4 introduces some of the popular datasets and results of different techniques used in query focused video summarization. Section 5 talks about the challenges in query-based video summarization and some solutions to tackle these challenges. Section 5 suggests some future direction in this domain. Lastly, Sect. 6 includes the conclusion and references.

2 Video Summarization

Video is a group of frames which are presented in a sequence which gives the illusion of motion. Video is divided into several segments; further segments are divided into shots and finally shots are the collection of frames. In the video data, many of the frames come with a lot of redundancy and are also irrelevant. Because of the intrinsic characteristic of videos (as a set of many images) has given rise to the need of automatic video summarization techniques. Video summarization is the process of creating a concise view of a complete video without losing important information. Feature extraction is the basic building block of video summarization. Deep learning is a popular technique to retrieve and analyze the contents of the key frames and finally arrange selected keyframes in chronological order to generate a summary.

There are two techniques of video summarization, i.e. Static and Dynamic video summarization. In static summarization, summary is created by extracting the important key-frames which represent the desired content from the video. It is also called key-frame summarization. Dynamic summarization is also called video-skimming, which creates summaries based on important video shots or video segments without changing the meaning and flow of video. The advantage of dynamic video summarization is that it produces a more expressive and natural summary as it includes audio and motion information, but complexity is higher than static summary. Static storyboard offers more flexibility in organizing and synchronizing the frames of the video to generate Summary. Another method for video summarization is to create Multiview summary. The Multiview video captures the video from more than one camera placed at different locations. It is mostly used in surveillance and sports videos [6].

Video summarization is a challenging task as there is a need to select diverse and relevant information from the whole video. To overcome these challenges classical computer vision techniques replaced with the recent deep learning-based video summarization methods. In deep learning methods, visual features are extracted using deep neural network. Researchers prefer Convolution Neural networks and Deep convolution networks [7]. As video summarization is a highly subjective task, a single summary is not enough to handle a users' needs. Vision-language embedding improves the performance of video summarization by adding additional text input along with video data.

The summarization techniques are classified into two categories:

- Single-Model: In this type of summarization, the only video is input and based on important visual, summary is created.

- Multi-Model: Here two modalities are considered i.e. video and text input. Summary has been created by taking text input either from available meta data or from users and extracting the visual contents relevant to the text to create the semantic driven summarization.

3   Related Work and Comparative Analysis

This section provides the systematic review of query-based video summarization techniques. The deep learning-based video summarization are categorized into supervised, unsupervised and weakly-supervised methods. In Weakly-supervised methods, less-expensive weak labels are used instead of full annotated dataset or without ground-truth dataset Supervised techniques are superior to unsupervised and weakly-supervised methods as correct training data is available in it. Summarization can be domain specific, generic and based on queries. In domain specific, summary is created by considering the important part related to that domain. The author proposed the novel framework for domain-specific video summarization [8] and released a dataset to help research community wishes to work in the domain-specific area.

In generic video summarization, important contents from video are considered for creating summary like objects, events, etc. These techniques are having limitation that they have not considered the user's choice in consideration. In the recent past Query focused video summarization has attracted a lot of attention. Plummer et al. [9] proposed the image-language embeddings for generating video summaries, but their method is more relevant in the text domain than the video summarization area. The standard determinantal point Processes (DPP) combine individual importance and collective diversity principles together, but it completely ignores the temporal flow of video [10].

Boqing Gong et al. suggested the sequential determinantal point process (SeqDPP) [11, 12] to overcome the shortfall of DPP It manages the sequential structure in video data, but not able to handle users' queries. Shargi et al. first introduced the Sequential and Hierarchical Determinantal Point Process (SH-DPP) model formulated on DPP for Query-Focused video summarization. It extracts the relevant video contents by taking user queries in the form of one or two concepts. SH-DPP manages long video sequences efficiently but it is computationally extensive [13].

Vasudevan et al. developed a relevance model that computes the relevance between input text queries and frames using the cosine similarity in a learned visual semantic embedding space using LSTM. Model handles query dependent as well as query independent properties like frame quality and submodular mixtures for video summarization. The author released new dataset i.e. Relevance and Diversity Dataset (RAD) with query relevance and diversity annotation [14]. Sharghi et al. [15] proposed a memory network parameterized sequential determinantal point process to handle the query-focused video summarization. Authors evaluated the performance of the model based on novel semantic parameters instead of visual or temporal features. New dataset is released i.e., Query Focused Video Summarization dataset (QFVS).

Zhang et al. [16] proposed a query-conditioned three-player generative adversarial network (GAN). GAN includes combination of generator and discriminator along with the three-player loss function. The three-player loss improves the accuracy of summary.

Zhang performed the query-conditioned video summarization by using reinforcement learning technique which produces personalized summaries by combining relatedness, representativeness and diversity rewards [17].

Jiang et al. [18] explored a well-devised Hierarchical Variational Network called HVAN to create user-diversified & query-focused video summary. HVAN utilized a multilevel self-attention and a variational autoencoder modules to add user diversity in the summarization task. Xiao et al. [19] explained the Convolutional Hierarchical Attention Network (CHAN) which is the combination of a convolutional network and local and global attention mechanism to produce query-based video summary.

Huang et al. [20] introduced the end-to-end deep learning-based model for query-controllable video summarization. Here, author explored the Bag of Words (BOW) concept to manage the input queries. In this work summation, concatenation, and element-wise multiplication are used to fuse query and frame-based features. The author introduced a query-video pair-based dataset. Xiao proposed a hierarchical self-attentive network trained on video caption dataset, and a reinforced caption generator generates a video description to find out the important frames or shots of video. Model efficiently handles the semantic information in the video [21].

Kaushal et al. [22, 23] explained a two-stage method to produce a query-focused summary. In the first stage attention within a segment and across all segments, combined with the query to learn the feature representation of each shot. In the second stage, learned features are again fused with the query across all shots. All the top score shots are combined in chronological order to generate summary.

Sreeja described a framework for instance-driven egocentric video summarization focused on generic as well as query-based summarization along with multi-video summarization. The model used the deep learning techniques for object detection and semantic web technologies to form ontologies for query inference. Novel nameboard detection technique is presented instead of conventional shot boundary detection [24].

Huang et al. [25] introduced a new end-to-end deep model for multi-modal video summarization that integrates a specialized attention network and contextualized word representations. The model is inspired by the natural language processing-based transformer decoder structure, i.e. Generative Pre-trained Transformer-2 (GPT-2). GPT-2 helps to develop the contextualized video summary controller for the text-based query embedding which gives better results than a static word embedding techniques. Narasimhan et al. [26] proposed a language-guided multimodal transformer (CLIP-It) learns to score frames based on relevance of user-defined query (for query-focused summarization) or an automatically generated dense video caption (for generic video summarization). The CLIP-It transformer is presented here for multi-model summarization.

4 Datasets and Performance Analysis

In the realm of query-based video summarization, there are extremely a smaller number of video datasets that incorporate both text and video modalities. One of them is the Query Focused Video Summarization dataset, which is based on the UTE dataset, which contains four egocentric consumer movies ranging in length from three to five hours. For query representation, a set of 48 concepts is employed, and each query is made up of the two concepts (Nouns). [14] also proposes a relevant and diversity dataset, which comprises of 200 videos with query relevance and diversity annotations [29]. Another multimodal dataset that has been proposed 190 videos with a runtime of two to three minutes, each of which is retrieved using a text-based query [20, 30]. Many of the researchers employed Query Focused Video Summarization Dataset (QFVS) and

Table 1. Comparative analysis of related work

Year	Author	Dataset	Approach	Strength	Weaknesses
2016	Sharghi et al. [13]	UT Egocentric, TV Episodes	Sequential and Hierarchical Determinantal Point Process (SH-DPP)	SH-DPP is efficient in modeling extremely lengthy video	SH-DPP is computationally extensive
2017	Vasudevan et al. [14]	Relevance and Diversity Dataset RAD) Query-dependent Thumbnail Selection Dataset (QTS)	Submodular Mixture	Semantic and quality information handled jointly	The temporal flow of the video is totally ignored by submodular functions
2017	Sharghi et al. [15]	Query-focused Video Summarization (QFVS)	A memory network parameterized sequential determinantal point process	Memory network-based video summarizer requires less supervision for training than the hierarchical model like SH-DPP	Query contain two concepts i.e. nouns only
2018	Zhang et al [16]	Query-focused Video Summarization (QFVS)	Query-conditioned three-player generative adversarial network (GAN)	The model is flexible enough to be combined with other GAN structures	GAN training can often be unstable making the model difficult to train

(continued)

Table 1. (*continued*)

Year	Author	Dataset	Approach	Strength	Weaknesses
2019	Zhang et al [17]	Query Focused Video Summarization dataset (QFVS)	A deep reinforcement learning-based	The model focuses on the higher-level semantic information instead of lower-level visual features or temporal overlaps to improve the quality of summary	Complex queries are not handled
2019	Jiang et al [18]	Query Focused Video Summarization dataset (QFVS)	Hierarchical variational network (HVN)	Combination of both supervised and unsupervised is used	Complexity is high
2020	Xiao et al [19]	Query Focused Video Summarization dataset (QFVS)	Convolutional Hierarchical Attention Network (CHAN),	Average running time for the inference phase of each video is less due to its parallel computing ability	Semantic information is ignored
2020	Huang et al [20]	Query-Video pair-based dataset	Deep CNN and Bag of Words (BOW)	End-to-end deep learning reduces pre-processing tasks	Semantic information is not handled properly as individual words are treated

(*continued*)

Table 1. (*continued*)

Year	Author	Dataset	Approach	Strength	Weaknesses
2020	Xiao et al [21]	Video caption dataset Query Focused video summarization dataset (QFVS)	Query-Biased Self-Attentive Network (QSAN)	Can generate generic video summary as well as query-related summary	Lots of preprocessing is required like Sampling, Cleaning the caption information
2020	Kaushal et al. [22]	Query Focused video summarization dataset	Simple attention mechanism	As training can be done parallel, it saves time	Generic queries are not handled
2021	Haung et al [25]	The multi-modal video summarization dataset	Specialized attention network and the contextualized word representations using transformer (GPT-2)	Complex queries can be handled	The word embedding size/dimension affects the training efficiency and model performance
2021	Narasimhan et al. [26]	TVSum and SumMe for generic VS QFVS dataset for query focused VS	language-guided multimodal transformer (CLIP-It)	Handles open ended Natural Language queries	Speech channel is not handled
2020	Sekh Arif Ahmed et al. [27][28]	VIRAT and Sherbrooke Street surveillance video datasets	Tube clustering-based approach	Creates synopsis by preserving long-duration activities of the objects by grouping them together	Only important objects are considered as queries

F1 score metric for computational analysis, as indicated in Table 1. As a result, Table 2 shows a comparison of their performances based on the F1-score.

Table 2. F1-score analysis for QFVS dataset using different techniques

Method	Average F1-score (%)
SeqDPP [11]	30.92
SH-DPP [13]	33.38
Memory-network based sequential DPP [15]	44.19
Query Condition GAN [16]	46.05
Deep Reinforcement learning [17]	47.20
Hierarchical variational network [18]	48.87
Convolutional Hierarchical Attention Network [19]	46.94
Query-Biased Self-Attentive Network [21]	46.59
Local and Global Attention mechanism [22]	49.20
Clip-It [26]	54.55

5 Challenges and Proposed Solutions

The query-focused video summarization is a very vast domain and there is huge scope for improvement. Here, some of the challenges are listed out which help to carry research in the future. These challenges are as below:

- Lack of annotated dataset for query focused video summarization.
  Unsupervised methods or weakly supervised techniques can avoid the need of costly annotated dataset. Also, reinforcement learning and Generative Adversarial Networks (GANs) can tackle this problem.
- Handling the semantic relation between user queries and video frames, to create the diverse, relevant and interesting Summary. Submodular mixture functions and efficient language embedding techniques help to overcome this problem.
- Evaluation of the performance of the produced summary.
  Some of the quantitative parameters are precision, recall, f-measure, reduction rate, and average computation time and qualitative metrics are conciseness, representativeness, diversity, semantic score and overall rating help to evaluate generated Summary. Both need to be used for evaluation of summary.

6 Future Scope

Based on above challenges, the performance of the query-focused video summarization can be improved in the future by considering the following issues:

- In existing work queries are considered in the form of keywords only, generic queries can be handled in future.

- Better language-visual embedding techniques can be explored to refine the performance and quality of summary.
- The user's attention can be considered not only in terms of queries only but in terms of visual coherence, entropy, image memorability score etc.

7 Conclusion

In this paper we highlighted the progress in the area of query-based video summarization domain. Different techniques are explored in this review and comparative analysis is discussed in detail to help the research community to work in this area. We also mentioned the challenges and future scope to improve the performance of existing techniques. The main observation of this work is supervised learning methods give the state-of-the-art performance over unsupervised and weakly supervised methods. The main limitation of previous work is generic queries are not handled and there is huge scope for improvement to handle multi-model video summarization. This is the small contribution in this domain to assist the people for selection of specific technique in the area of personalized video summarization.

References

1. Haq, H.B.U., Asif, M., Ahmad, M.B.: Video summarization techniques: a review. Int. J. Sci. Technol. Res. **9**(11), 146–153 (2020)
2. Workie, A., Sharma, R., Chung, Y.K.: Digital video summarization techniques: a survey. Int. J. Eng. Research & Technol. (IJERT) **9**(01), 8185 (2020)
3. Kwon, J., Lee, K.M.: A unified framework for event summarization and rare event detection from multiple views. IEEE Trans. Pattern Analysis and Machine Intelligence **37**(9), 1737–1750 (2015)
4. Lee, Y.J., Ghosh, J., Grauman, K.: Discovering important people and objects for egocentric video summarization. In: Proceedings of the IEEE Computer Society Conference on Computer Vision and Pattern Recognition (CVPR'12), pp. 1346–1353 (2012)
5. Murn, L., Mrak, M.: Creating automatic video summaries with text queries. BBC publication, UK (2021)
6. Basavarajaiah, M., Sharma, P.: Survey of compressed domain video summarization techniques. ACM Computing Surveys (CSUR) **52**(6), 1–29 (2019)
7. Apostolidis, E., Adamantidou, E., Metsai, A.I., Mezaris, V., Patras, I.: Video summarization using deep neural networks: a survey. J. Computer Vision and Pattern Recognition, under review (2021)
8. Kaushal, V., Subramanian, S., Kothawade, S., Iyer, R., Ramakrishnan, G.: A framework towards domain specific video summarization. In: IEEE Winter Conference on Applications of Computer Vision (WACV), pp. 666–675 (2019)
9. Plummer, B.A., Brown, M., Lazebnik, S.: Enhancing video summarization via vision-language embedding. In: Proceedings of the IEEE Conference on Computer Vision and Pattern Recognition, pp. 5781–5789 (2017)
10. Kulesza, A., Taskar, B.: Determinantal point processes for machine learning. preprint arXiv: 1207.6083 (2012)
11. Gong, B., Chao, W.-L., Grauman, K., Sha, F.: Diverse sequential subset selection for supervised video summarization. International Conference on Neural Information Processing Systems, ACM press **27**(2), 2069–2077 (2014)

12. Gong, B., Chao, W.L., Grauman, K., Sha, F.: Diverse sequential subset selection for supervised video summarization. In: Advances in Neural Information Processing Systems, pp. 2069–2077 (2014)
13. Sharghi, A., Gong, B., Shah, M.: Query-focused extractive video summarization. In: European Conference on Computer Vision, Springer, Cham, pp. 3–19 (2016). https://doi.org/10.1007/978-3-319-46484-8_1
14. Vasudevan, A.B., Gygli, M., Volokitin, A., Van Gool, L.: Query-adaptive video summarization via quality-aware relevance estimation. In: Proceedings of the 25th ACM International Conference on Multimedia, pp. 582–590 (2017)
15. Sharghi, A., Laurel, J.S., Gong, B.: Query-focused video summarization: dataset, evaluation, and a memory network-based approach. In: Proceedings of the IEEE Conference on Computer Vision and Pattern Recognition, pp. 4788–4797 (2017)
16. Zhang, Y., Kampffmeyer, M., Liang, X., Tan, M., Xing, E.P.: Query-conditioned three-player adversarial network for video summarization. arXiv preprint arXiv:1807.06677 (2018)
17. Zhang, Y., Kampffmeyer, M., Zhao, X., Tan, M.: Deep reinforcement learning for query-conditioned video summarization. Applied Sciences 9(4), 750 (2019)
18. Jiang, P., Han, Y.: Hierarchical variational network for user-diversified & query-focused video summarization. In: Proceedings of the 2019 on International Conference on Multimedia Retrieval, pp. 202–206 (2019)
19. Xiao, S., Zhao, Z., Zhang, Z., Yan, X., Yang, M.: Convolutional hierarchical attention network for query-focused video summarization. In: Proceedings of the AAAI Conference on Artificial Intelligence, Vol. 34, No. 07, pp. 12426–12433 (2020)
20. Huang, J.H., Worring, M.: Query-controllable video summarization. In: Proceedings of the 2020 International Conference on Multimedia Retrieval, pp. 242–250 (2020)
21. Xiao, S., Zhao, Z., Zhang, Z., Guan, Z., Cai, D.: Query-biased self-attentive network for query-focused video summarization. IEEE Trans. Image Process. 29, 5889–5899 (2020)
22. Nalla, S., Agrawal, M., Kaushal, V., Ramakrishnan, G., Iyer, R.: "Watch hours in minutes", summarizing videos with user intent. In: European Conference on Computer Vision, Springer, Cham, pp. 714–730 (2020)
23. Kaushal, V., et al.: Demystifying multi-faceted video summarization: Tradeoff between diversity, representation, coverage and importance. In: 2019 IEEE Winter Conference on Applications of Computer Vision (WACV), pp. 452–46 (2019)
24. Sreeja, M.U., Kovoor, B.C.: A unified model for egocentric video summarization: an instance-based approach. Comput. Electr. Eng. 92, 107161 (2021)
25. Huang, J.H., Murn, L., Mrak, M., Worring, M.: GPT2MVS: Generative Pre-trained Transformer-2 for Multi-modal Video Summarization. arXiv preprint arXiv:2104.12465 (2021)
26. Narasimhan, M., Rohrbach, A., Darrell, T.: CLIP-It! Language-Guided Video Summarization. arXiv preprint arXiv:2107.00650 (2021)
27. Ahmed, S.A., et al.: Query-based video synopsis for intelligent traffic monitoring applications. IEEE Trans. Intell. Transp. Syst. 21(8), 3457–3468 (2019)
28. Pritch, Y., Rav-Acha, A., Peleg, S.: Nonchronological video synopsis and indexing. IEEE Trans. Pattern Anal. Mach. Intell. 30(11), 1971–1984 (2008)
29. Müller, H., Ionescu, B., Gînsca, A.L., Boteanu, B., Popescu, A., Lupu, M.: Retrieving diverse social images at MediaEval 2015. In: Working Notes Proceedings of the MediaEval 2015 Workshop (No. CONFERENCE), 14–15 September 2015 (2015)
30. Sigurdsson, G.A., Divvala, S., Farhadi, A., Gupta, A.: Asynchronous temporal fields for action recognition. In: Proceedings of the IEEE Conference on Computer Vision and Pattern Recognition, pp. 585–594 (2017)

Sleep-Wake Classification Using Acceleration Data from Wearable Wrist Worn Sensors: REVIEW

Sayantani Chakraborty[1]([⊠]) [iD], Anasua Sarkar[2] [iD], and Piyali Basak[1] [iD]

[1] School of Bioscience and Engineering, Jadavpur University, Kolkata, India
sayantanic72@gmail.com
[2] Computer Science Engineering, Jadavpur University, Kolkata, India

Abstract. Sleep study has been the most important field of research in recent times. Various works have been published to date that tries to detect the sleep/wake stage differences as well as various stages of sleep. Polysomnography (PSG) is a clinical procedure to score sleep by trained technicians. However, it is not very comfortable for the subject due to its set up and the subject must be placed away from their normal sleeping environment. The identification of wake or sleep stages at home requires the use of the multimodal wearable sensors like ActiGraph, Apple watch, etc. From these devices data is collected for categorization of sleep-wake states as it is easy as well as comfortable method and the subject can use it without going away from his/ her natural sleeping environment. This method also does not require the supervision from trained personnel. These wearable sensors provide the parameters like the acceleration data, heart rate, skin conductance, etc., from which features are extracted that acts as an input used by the different classifiers for detection. Deep learning algorithms like Long Short Term Memory neural networks have been found as a novel application in this classification problem of sleep/wake stages. The validation of various sleep detection systems is either validated against the ground truths like the clinical polysomnography, sleep diaries or can be validated against a self-proposed evaluation metrics. This paper gives a brief overview of the state-of-the-art works that have been done to date in sleep classification.

Keywords: Wearable sensors · Accelerometer data · Deep learning method · Sleep/wake classification

1 Introduction

Sleep is an indispensable part of human life, which has various effects on daily life. It is like a biological life support. It can have effects not only on physical well-being like one's appetite, immunity response, loss in alertness, etc. but also in emotional states. Researchers have found that sleep influences one's longevity as well. So, it can also be said that "Shorter your sleep, the shorter your life". It has been found that poor sleep quality can affect memory decline in aging like Alzheimer's. Thousands of people worldwide suffer from sleep disorders such as insomnia, sleep - apnea, hyposomnia, restless-leg syndrome, and sleep paralysis. It is like a silent sleep loss epidemic, which the 21st century is facing.

Various studies have taken place in the past, that aim to predict sleep/wake stages as well as the different stages of sleep including REM (Rapid – Eye Movement) and NREM (N1, N2 as well as N3) stages of sleep accurately. That is the basis for finding out the quantity and quality of sleep in sleep research. Polysomnography (PSG) is a clinical procedure for detecting the sleep pattern and is used in the diagnosis of sleep disorders. However, the method is cumbersome, expensive, and time-limited [4], along with being uncomfortable for the subject taking the test, where the subject is placed in an environment different from their natural sleeping environment with various wires attached to the body. The subject has to wear electrodes and wires connected to their different parts of the body like the chest straps, Electroencephalogram (EEG) electrodes, Electrocardiogram (ECG) leads, Electromyogram (EMG) electrodes, etc. It is difficult to measure the different parameters accurately due to loosening of the electrode-skin contacts due to movement during sleep and in cognitively impaired subjects.

Wearable devices such as those commercially available wrists worn devices like the Fitbit, ActiGraph, etc. allow smooth measurements of lone time data at home, in the normal sleeping environment. Thus, it will provide more efficient data. The common sensor that is most widely used in sleep detection, embedded in the wearable sensors is the Accelerometer sensor [6]. The sensor is a three-axis motion (acceleration) detection device. The actigraphy data hence helps to provide information about the subject activity, which is widely used in the sleep studies. The actigraphy data features are used by various classifiers and the results are validated then against the PSG results and these show comparable accuracies in both healthy and clinical subjects. However, there are some glitches in the actigraphy technique and hence cannot be used solely for detecting sleep stages accurately as - (1) it may falsely detect the sleep with rest condition of the subject, (2) may possess challenges for the population with irregular circadian rhythms or abnormal sleep distribution. Hence, along with the accelerometer data, data from other parameters like ECG, Heart Rate Variability (HRV), etc. are also used for sleep monitoring from these wearable sensors [8].

Physiological data, such as actigraphy data, is broken down into discrete time intervals called epochs, from which features are extracted. Features such as Mean, Median, Standard Deviation (SD), Root Mean Square (RMS), and others are gathered and employed in both Machine-Learning as well as Deep-Learning algorithms. Decision-Tree (DT), Support Vector Machine (SVM) [1], K-Nearest Neighbors [1, 3], Random Forest (RF) [5, 11] as well as other deep learning algorithms are used including Long-Short-Term Memory (LSTM) neural networks [2, 7], Local Feature-based LSTM (LF-LSTM) [4], Convolutional Neural Networks (CNN) [16], and so on.

Validation of the model is then carried out either by K-fold cross-validation (KCV) [1, 4, 5] or Leave-one-out cross-validation (LOOCV) [3, 8] mainly, to find out the error rate of the algorithm. The results are usually validated against standard PSG, but the sleep diaries are also used for validating the detection accuracy. However, using a sleep diary data is not accurate as the reporting from the subject may not be accurate, especially in the case of proxy reporting. It happens where one subject cannot report directly, like where parents are reporting on behalf of their wards, older population, etc. [9]. The overall sleep classification model is shown in Fig. 1. The outline of the sleep-wake classification is as shown in Fig. 2.

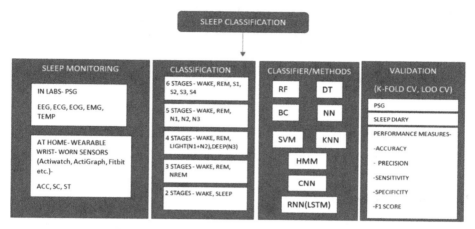

Fig. 1. Existing different sleep classification models

Fig. 2. Flowchart of sleep-wake classification

2   Sleep Monitoring

The sleep monitoring stage will result in the sensor data collection further used for the classification. The sleep monitoring can take place in sleep labs (PSG) or at home by the sensors worn on the body.

2.1   Polysomnography (PSG)

Polysomnography (PSG) is also known as sleep study in the medical domain. The test is widely used in sleep disorders diagnosis. It usually takes place in the sleep laboratory. The PSG records the brain waves (EEG), Eye movement (EOG), Blood oxygen level (Pulse Oximetry), Heart rate, and Breathing rate as well as the leg movement or muscle tone (EMG) during the studies [8]. Overnight, different types of sensors are connected to an individual's body to detect various signals and movement patterns. It records the physiological variations during the night and allows the technician to rate the various stages of sleep. Aside from wearable sensors like ECG leads and EMG leads, non-wearable sensors including videocams, microphones, and light sensors are used in the study. As indicated in Fig. 3, sleep classification can be done using the Rechtschaffen & Kales (RK) as well as the American Academy of Sleep - Medicine (AASM) methods. The scoring in gold standard PSG, on the other hand, is done according to AASM [8]. Th sleep is mainly divided into REM and NREM stages. The REM or Rapid Eye Movement is the final stage of sleep, with rapid ocular movement, after which the cycle repeats from NREM stages. The NREM or Non- rapid eye movement, is further divided into sleep stages S1, S2, S3 & S4 in R & K and N1, N2 and N3in AASM.

R & K METHOD (6 – Stage)	AASM (5- Stage)
Wake	Wake
REM	REM
NREM- S1, S2, S3, S4	NREM- N1, N2, N3

Fig. 3. Sleep classification according to RK method and AASM.

2.2 Wearable Sensors

Wearable sensors especially the wrist- worn sensors are used intensively nowadays for sleep detection at home. These are mainly actigraphy devices, that rely on the accelerometer sensors to detect and calculate the motions, which simply implies wake or sleep in sleep/wake detection. However, the underlying algorithms and their accuracies are not well known and not comparable to the gold standard PSG method for the sleep study. Hence, an extensive study is required to take place in this field for improving the combined usages of sensors to enhance the accuracy for detection of sleep/ wake states. Wearables used in the experiments include wristband sensors like Affectiva Q sensor [1, 2], Zephyr Bioharness chest strap in [5], Motionlogger [2], Apple Watch [3], FAROS in [4], Zeo headband, CamNTech motion-watch and MSR 145B accelerometers for wrist and ankles [5], Move 3 sensors [6] and Philips Actiwatch 2 [7].

3 Feature Extraction

Windowed signal inputs are used to extract features after the data collection. The raw signal (acceleration data) is not given as input, but rather segmented/ windowed signal of certain time is taken from which features (time or frequency) are extracted are provided as input to the classifier. These characteristics features describe the signal's nature. The features are utilized in classifiers and provide information about the signal. Before feature extraction, the signals are pre-processed by using filters, etc. There are several types of features. The most common of them are time domain and frequency domain features. The statistical metrics - Mean, Median, Variance, Standard Deviation, Percentile, and others are included in the time- domain features. It also includes the Zero-Crossing Rate, which gives information about the signal crossing the baseline. It can be derived by taking the mean of the signal in the window taken, which follows the change in signal sign. Similarly, Frequency domain features include extracted features from the Fast Fourier Transform or Z- score from the Power Spectral analysis of the signal. In one recent work [4], Time - domain features, Frequency - domain features, DFA features (3 slopes coefficient), and Poincare plot features from the HRV data are extracted. Handcrafted features or features learning from Deep Learning techniques also can be used by the classifier. Handcrafted features require more time and work. Handcrafted features that are used in [5] are Maximum Frequency, Root Mean Square value of the signal channel, Energy, Standard Deviations, etc.

4 Classification Methods

Classification is the main task in the sleep/ wake detection study. The classification of wake and sleep stages can be categorized as follows: -

- 5 Stages Classification: - This classification is mainly according to the AASM method. The different stages include- Wake, REM, N1, N2, and N3 [5, 17]. However, the classification of N1 from N2 is not accurate and hence, the overall performance is not good enough.
- 4 Stages Classification: - Here, the N1 sleep stage is taken together with the N2 sleep stage into light sleep, while N3 as deep sleep. So, the classification stages are- Wake, REM, Light, and Deep Sleep [18].
- 3 Stages Classification: - The sleep stage classification is into Wake, REM and NREM stage [19, 20].
- 2 Stages Classification: - It is the basis of further deep classification. Here, the sleep is classified into Wake/ Sleep [21–23].

For classification, many ML and DL techniques are utilized. The primary goal of the classification phase is to first thoroughly train the classifier with training data and then to use the trained model to classify additional observations or testing data. Finally, ground truth labels are used to validate the output. K-Nearest - Neighbour (KNN), Random Forest (RF), Support - Vector Machine (SVM), Decision Tree (DT), as well as Neural Networks (NN) are the most used approaches. Neural Networks having more than three hidden layers are used in deep learning. Recurrent- Neural Networks (RNN), such as Long Short-Term Memory (LSTM) and Convolutional Neural Networks (CNN), are commonly employed in sleep research.

- Random Forest (RF): In [5], Random Forest classifier is used to classify the various stages of sleep. The best feature from the subset is used to split the decision tree, which uses a randomly selected feature subset from the total.
- Bagging Decision Tree: In [8], Bagging Decision tree is used for automated classification of sleep stages. Unlike RF classifier the Bagging classifier is different in the way that the bagging classifier uses all features considered for the split of each node and not random features.
- K- Nearest Neighbor (KNN): This supervised machine-learning technique can be used to address both regressions as well as classification issues. It is simple but also has a drawback when used in large datasets. Based on the votes of the neighbors of the data point, the data point is given a label. KNN is used for the sleep detection study in [3],

where features from motion (activity counts), clock proxy, and Heart rate is used for sleep/ wake classification. In [1], features from EEG and multi-modal data are used.

- Recurrent Neural Networks: LSTM Neural nets are Recurrent neural nets, that work on large data points with keeping or forgetting information. Unlike the traditional feed-forward architecture, it has feedback connections and hence can process a sequence of data. In [2], a multimodal data that includes SC, ST, and ACC data are used for sleep/ wake classification as well as sleep onset/ offset detection. In [4], features are extracted from acceleration data using LF-LSTM as well as features extracted from HRV data. The features thus extracted are given as input to a fully connected (FC) layer further to a concatenate layer and finally to a SoftMax output layer for classification.
- Support Vector Machine: It is a linear model for regression and classification problems. It can solve linear practical issues. It creates a hyper-plane and thus separates the data into different classes [1].

5   Validation

The result of the classification of a classifier model is validated against the Ground Truth labels like the gold standard PSG labels, sleep diary labels, or performance metrics, which include accuracy, precision, specificity, sensitivity, Area under ROC - curve (AUC), etc. The confusion matrix is used to construct the performance measures, as shown in Fig. 4. A confusion matrix is a table that shows the true and expected labels in a tabular format. The True Positive – 'TP', True Negative - 'TN', False Positive – 'FP', and False Negative – 'FN' information is provided by the confusion matrix. K- fold cross- validation or Leave -one- out – cross- validation is the validation method employed. In [10], the evaluation is done by using self-evaluation metrics. Different evaluation metrics are used by different studies to understand the ability of a classifier.

Some of the evaluation metrics are as follows, which are commonly used in sleep study:

ACTUAL / PREDICTED	Positives – "1"	Negatives – "0"
Positives – "1"	TP	FP
Negatives - "0"	FN	TN

Fig. 4. Confusion- matrix

- Accuracy: It is the ratio of the correct prediction (TP + TN) by the total.
- Precision: Precision is defined as the ratio of TP to Positives.
- Sensitivity: Sensitivity or Recall or True Positive Rate is the ratio of the TP by Total Positives (TP + FN).

Table 1. Performances of different classifiers in various sleep/wake classification studies.

No	Source	Problem	Population	Sensor	Signal	Feature	Classifier	Performance
[1]	Sano et al. (2014)	Comparison of Sleep-wake classification using EEG and multimodal sensor data	15 College Students	Q sensor (Affectiva)	EEG, SC, ST, ACC	EEG(16 feature), SC(7 feature), ST(5 feature), ACC(7 feature)	SVM with linear kernel, SVM with Gaussian kernel, KNN, Feature selection and SVM with linerar kernel, Feature selection and SVM with Gaussian kernel,Feature selection and KNN	Accuracy: EEG(85%), Wrist worn sensor (74%)
[2]	Chen et al.(2018)	Sleep/Wake detection, sleep on/offset detection	186 students	Q sensor (Affectiva), MotionLogger(AMI)	Wrist sensor data(SC,ST,ACC), Screen on time, SMS sent time, Call duration, Motion Index(Phone location), WiFi connection	SC(Mean, SD, Power with 0–0.5Hz bands, etc.), ACC(Mean, SD), ST(Mean,SD)	Bi-LSTM, Cross Correlation and Peak detection Algorithm	Accuracy: ACC + ST + Time(96.5%), ACC + ST(96.2%), F1 score of sleep onset(0.85),F1 score of sleep offset(0.82)

(continued)

Table 1. (*continued*)

No	Source	Problem	Population	Sensor	Signal	Feature	Classifier	Performance
[3]	Walch et al.(2019)	Sleep/wake detection, REM/NREM	39 subjects	Apple watch	Motion feature (Activity Count), HR, Clock proxy		Logistic Regression, RF, KNN, Multi-layer perception NN (MLP)	Accuracy:True sleep(93%), True wake(60%), REM/NREM difference (72%)
[5]	Reimer et al. (2017)	Sleep stage detection	25 healthy participants	Zephyr BioHarness chest strap, MSR 145B accelerometer	HR, ECG, Breathing Rate, ACC	Handcrafted Features(Energy, RMS, SD, VM, Skewness, Max Freq), DBN Learnt Features	RF	Accuracy: Wake(90.3%), Sleep Stages(82.1%)
[6]	Barouni et al. (2020)	Wear/ Non wear time	98 participants (48 healthy, 50 Sleep disorder)	Wrist sensor(Move 3), Chest sensor(Move 3)	ACC	Power Spectrum of ACC, Zero metrics	Threshold based	Accuracy: Non-wear(wrist sensor = 90.1%, chest 93.5%), Wear(wrist sensor = 92.2%, chest sensor = 97.1%)
[7]	Yildiz et al. (2019)	Sleep/wake detection in older adults	22 older participants	Philips Actiwatch 2	Light Exposure, Activity time		LSTM	Accuracy:67.7%, Specificity:37%, Precession:90.7%
[8]	Boe et al. (2019)	Sleep stages	11 healthy young adults	BioStamprc, Thermochron iButton	ACC,ECG,ST	51 features extracted	Bagging decision tree	Specificity: 74.4%, sensitivity:90%

(*continued*)

Table 1. (*continued*)

No	Source	Problem	Population	Sensor	Signal	Feature	Classifier	Performance
[16]	Cho et al. (2019)	Sleep-wake detection	10 subjects	GT3X(Actilife,USA)	ACC	10 features	Deep-ACTINet	Accuracy: 89.65% Recall: 92.99% Precision: 92.09%
[17]	Zhang et al. (2018)	Sleep/ wake stages	40 healthy subjects	Microsoft Band I	HR, ACC	Low- level features from temporal, frequency features, Mid-Level features from Low- level features	RNN (Bi-LSTM)	Resting Group: Precision-66.6%, Recall-67.7%, F1 – 64.0% Resting/Non-Resting Group: Precision- 64.5%, Recall- 65.0%, F1- 60.5%
[24]	Razjouyan et al. (2017)	Assessment of Sleep Quality	21 subjects	Actiwatch-L,Bio-Patch Zephyrlife	ACC, sleep postures	43 features	CNN	Chest Accuracy: 85.8% Wrist Accuracy: 79.8%

- Specificity: Specificity, True Negative Rate or Selectivity is the ratio of the TN by the Total Negative (TN + FP).
- F1 Score: It is the harmonic - mean of the sensitivity as well as precision.
- Receiver Operating Characteristic curve (ROC): is a graphical representation which shows the trade-off between the True – Positive - Rate, TPR and False – Positive - Rate, FPR.
- Area Under Curve (AUC): It depicts the performance of the classifier. The higher the AUC, the better the performance of the classifier.

Table 1 shows the findings of various study classifiers. Various studies have shown that precision in the sleep/wake or REM/NREM stages is excellent. However, there is still a problem distinguishing the N1 stage from the other stages.

6 Discussion

The sleep – wake detection as well as the detection of different stages of sleep plays an important role in sleep study and research. Traditional gold standard PSG methods are widely used for the same, but its cost and labor extensive procedure, make it a cumbersome process to carry out in the daily sleeping environment of a subject as well as for the older population. Hence actigraphy data from a motion accelerometer embedded in a wearable sensor, like the wristwatch becomes useful. This data along with other parameters like SC, ST, and mobile application usage time, are also used by the various studies in this field for the classification. A combination of multimodal data shows better results in the detection of sleep-wake states. The use of the smartphone applications which collect information about the screen on time, application use time, etc. is used along with the different multimodal data for sleep classifications.

Either Machine or Deep Learning algorithms are used for classification, which shows a promising method for sleep detection in sleep study, not only in the normative subjects but also in non – normative sleep subjects, older population, and the cognitively impaired subjects. Traditional methods which detect the sleep- wake states, have low specificity for detecting the wake state, namely wakefulness. This results in incorrect detection of the wake as sleep states and that result in false detection. The LSTM method, which is used to detect the sleep – wake states [7] detects the waking state with comfortable efficiency. Various features are extracted from physiological signals, that are used by the classification models like SVM, K –Nearest Neighbor, etc. for the sleep classification [1]. The wear and non – wear time are also main concepts to consider while classification. Physiological signals like the respiration wave from the acceleration (ACC) power spectrum signals have been studied extensively for the differentiation of the wear and non – wear period [6]. Figures 5 and 6 demonstrate the results of different sensors and classifiers, respectively.

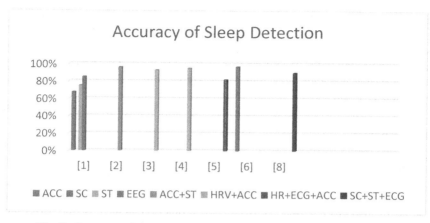

Fig. 5. Accuracy of sleep detection methods using different sensor signals.

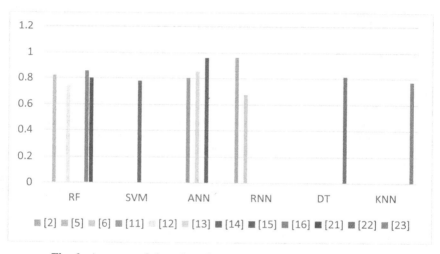

Fig. 6. Accuracy of sleep detection methods using different classifiers

7 Future Works

There are several challenges that the research faces in a sleep study, those include - (1) validation on larger diverse datasets, (2) imbalanced data, (3) inclusion of medical subjects, (4) automating sleep scoring with the accuracy of that of golden standard PSG and (5) generability. The future works lie in addressing these challenges. The different architectures of neural networks should be explored in classification tuning parameters like accuracy and other different architecture hyper-parameters namely epoch length, dropout rates, etc. Using a large cohort for the study will provide us with a greater understanding of the accuracy or precision of the classification method. If the model is trained on one subject dataset, then it should be tested on another subject dataset, to result in generability. Most of the studies to date are focused mostly on healthy subjects for training, so works in the future should include more medical subjects. Future works should focus on the better accuracy of sleep classification with minimum inputs from sleep dairy, therefore considering an automated sleep detection algorithm. The correlation of day behavior with night sleep architecture is also a promising field of study for this problem.

8 Conclusion

In this paper, we have given a brief outline of the recent trends in a sleep study. The field of sleep research is very vast and has great growth. This will give an insight to the researcher into future trends of sleep research. The challenges, which the researcher usually faces, are also given in brief. Solving those problems can increase the performance of classification of sleep stages. The stream of Machine Learning and Deep Learning algorithms is used extensively to date for the classification, which also yields comparable results - still not as accurate as of the gold standard methods. So, the hyper-parameters of the models can be researched further. Also, it is expected that with further development in the field of Artificial Intelligence, further development can be witnessed in the domain of sleep categorization.

References

1. Sano, A., Picard, R.W.: Comparison of sleep-wake classification using electroencephalogram and wrist-worn multi-modal sensor data. In: 36th Annual International Conference of the IEEE Engineering in Medicine and Biology Society ,EMBC, pp. 930–933. IEEE, Chicago, IL, USA (2014)
2. Chen, W., Sano, A., Martinez, D.L, Taylor, S.: Multimodal ambulatory sleep detection. In: IEEE EMBS International Conference on Biomedical & Health Informatics (BHI), pp. 465–468. IEEE, Orlando, FL, USA
3. Walch, O., Huang, Y. , Forger, D.: Sleep stage prediction with raw acceleration and photoplethysmography heart rate data derived from a consumer wearable device. Sleep $42(12)$, zsz180 (2019)
4. Chen, Z., Wu, M., Wu, J.: A deep learning approach for sleep- wake detection from HRV and accelerometer data. In: IEEE EMBS International Conference on Biomedical & Health Informatics (BHI), pp. 1–4. IEEE, Chicago, IL, USA
5. Reimer , U., Emmenegger, S., Maier, E.: Recognizing sleep stages with wearable sensors in everyday settings. In: 3rd International Conference on Information and Communication Technologies for Ageing Well and e-Health, pp. 172–179 (2017)
6. Barouni, A., Ottenbacher, J., Schneider, J.: Ambulatory sleep scoring using accelerometers-distinguishing between nonwear and sleep/wake states. Peer J. (2020)
7. Yildiz, S., Opel, R.A., Elliott, J.E.: Categorizing sleep in older adults with wireless activity monitors using LSTM neural networks. In: Annual International Conference of the IEEE Engineering in Medicine and Biology Society, pp. 3368–3372. IEEE, Berlin, Germany (2019)
8. Boe, A.J., McGee Koch, L.L., O'Brien, M.K.: Automating sleep stage classification using wireless, wearable sensors. Npj Digital Medicine $2(1)$, 19 (2019)
9. Van Hees, V.T., Sabia, S., Jones, S.E.: Estimating sleep parameters using an accelerometer without sleep diary. Scientific Reports $8(1)$, 19 (2018)

10. Chen, S., Perera, R., Engelhard, M.M.: A generic algorithm for sleep-wake cycle detection using unlabeled actigraphy data. IEEE, Chicago, IL, USA (2019)
11. Sundararajan, K., Georgievska, S., Lindert, B.H.W.: Sleep classification from wrist-worn accelerometer data using random forests. Scientific Reports 11(1), 110 (2021)
12. Tilmanne, J., Urbain, J., Kothare, M.V.: Algorithms for sleep-wake identification using actigraphy : a comparative study and new results. J. Sleep Res. 18(1), 85–98 (2009)
13. Karlen, W., Mattiussi, C., Floreano, D.: Sleep and wake classification with ECG and respiratory effort signals. IEEE Trans. Biomedical Circuits Syst. 3(2), 71–78 (2009)
14. Adnanea, M., Jianga, Z., Yanb, Z.: Sleep-wake stages classification and sleep efficiency estimation using single-lead electrocardiogram. Expert Systems with Appl.: An Int. J. 39(1), 1401–1413 (2012)
15. Karlen, W., Mattiussi, C., Floreano, D.: Improving actigraph sleep/wake classification with cardio-respiratory signals. In: Annual International Conference of the IEEE Engineering in Medicine and Biology Society, pp. 5262–5265. IEEE, Vancouver, BC, Canada (2008)
16. Cho, T., Sunarya, U., Yeo, M.: Deep-ACTINet: end-to-end deep learning architecture for automatic sleep-wake detection using wrist actigraphy. Electronics 8(12), 1461 (2019)
17. Zhang, X., Kou, W., Chang, E.I.: Sleep stage classification based on multi- level feature learning and recurrent neural networks via wearable device. Comput. Biol. Med. 103, 71–81 (2018)
18. Fujimoto, K., Ding, Y., Takahashi, E.: Sleep stage detection using a wristwatch-type physiological sensing device. Sleep Biol. Rhythms 16, 449–456 (2018)
19. Matsui, S., Terada, T., Tsukamoto, M.: Smart eye mask: sleep sensing system using infrared sensors. In: ISWC'17: Proceedings of the 2017 ACM International Symposium on Wearable Computers, pp. 58–61. Association for Computing Machinery New York, NY, United States (2017)
20. Renevey, P.: Optical wrist-worn device for sleep monitoring. In: Eskola, H., Väisänen, O., Viik, J. (eds): IFMBE Proceedings, vol-65. Springer, Singapore. https://doi.org/10.1007/978-981-10-5122-7_154
21. Uçar, M.K., Bozkurt, M.R., Bilgin, C.: Automatic sleep staging in obstructive sleep apnea patients using photoplethysmography, heart rate variability signal and machine learning techniques. Neural Comput. Appl. 29, 1–16 (2018)
22. Wolz, R., Munro, J., Guerrero, R.: Predicting sleep/wake patterns from 3-AXIS accelerometery using deep learning. Alzheimer's & Dementia 13(7S), P1012–P1012 (2017)
23. Kuo, C.E., Liu, Y.C., Chang, D.W.: Development and evaluation of a wearable device for sleep quality assessment. In: IEEE Transactions on bio-Medical Engineering 64(7), pp. 1547–1557. IEEE (2017)
24. Razjouyan, J., Lee, H., Parthasarathy, S., Mohler, J., Sharafkhaneh, A., Najafi, B.: Improving sleep quality assessment using wearable sensors by including information from postural/sleep position changes and body acceleration: a comparison of chest-worn sensors, wrist actigraphy, and polysomnography. J. Clin. Sleep Med. 13(11), 1301–1310 (2017)

Understanding Fake News Detection on Social Media: A Survey on Methodologies and Datasets

Debasish Patra[1]([✉]), Biswapati Jana[1], Sourav Mandal[2], and Arif Ahamed Sekh[2]

[1] Department of Computer Science, Vidyasagar University,
West Midnapore 721102, West Bengal, India
logicaldebasish@gmail.com
[2] School of Computer Science and Engineering, XIM University, Harirajpur 752050, Odisha,
India

Abstract. Technological progress opens new ways for us to discover new things every day. Nowadays, we are far too dependent on modern technologies such as social media and digital platforms. The scenario of our daily life has changed drastically within a couple of decades. Just a few decades ago, most people started their morning by looking at the daily newspaper. But the popularity of social media has changed the concept of news consumption. With the ease and popularity of spreading news on social media and online platforms, this has led to some serious problems for our society. The problem that has particularly serious implications in this context is Fake News. In recent years, researchers have tried to solve this complex problem of detecting Fake News. In this review, various aspects of the methods developed so far to detect Fake News are presented. First, we review some previous work on Fake News. Then, we discuss some benchmark datasets available for Fake News detection. Some techniques and methods proposed so far by different researchers are described. All the proposed methods are analyzed in terms of the tools used, the datasets used and the accuracy achieved. Some challenges and future possibilities for Fake News detection are also highlighted and critically discussed.

Keywords: Classification · Data mining · Deep learning · Fake news · Machine learning · Natural language processing · Rumors · Text mining

1 Introduction

Digital social media mainly consists of image, text, audio, and video. News can be composed of all these contents or news can be of any one of these contents. Availability of the low-cost internet is acting as a catalyst to this demand. When we think about social media the first platform that comes to our mind is Facebook. From the inception (2004) this platform has gained people's attention exponentially. As of 2020, Facebook has claimed that they have 2.8 billion monthly active users reaching almost 1/3rd of the world's total population. As the time has progressed (almost 17 years) this social media platform has severely suffered from fake or false news. Although Facebook has revised its algorithm many times to filter out fake and misinformation, today it has become one the most prevalent social media platforms in case of fake news dissipation. The second social media platform that comes in the context of fake news is Twitter because of its power of sharing and resharing of any news. As of February 2019, Twitter has 330 million active users. From the launch (In 2006) this platform has been affected by fake news and misinformation gradually. Although in March 2020 Twitter has announced that it will start marking the tweets which may contain fake news or misinformation and, in some cases, it will provide fact checking page links. But with this step this problem cannot be eliminated. The third platform in this context is one of the most popular platforms which is Instagram. This platform is used for sharing photos and videos. Instagram has 1 billion users as of May 2019. Beside these three platforms, many social media platforms are spreading fake news and misinformation which includes YouTube, WhatsApp, Facebook Messenger, WeChat, Snapchat, LinkedIn etc. When there is no control over the sharing and lack of fact checking tools makes the scenario more miserable.

Another fact that has been making the scenario of fake news more miserable is social bot. A social bot is an autonomous agent that can mimic human interaction on social media without human intervention. This problem has become more evident since the 2016 US presidential election where at least 4 lakh bots tweeted near about 38 lakh tweets. Estimation tells that today 9–15% active twitter accounts can be social bots. Many social media platforms are victims of social bots including Facebook. Many fake news that we find on social media platforms is a result of social bots. It is true that in social media, fake news travels much faster than real news. The travelling speed increases drastically when it comes to political news or hate news. Statistics show (Zhang and Ghorbani 2020) that most of the fake news on social media are political news and news on celebrity personalities. Human behavior also plays a major role as most of the users forward the posts or news articles without checking the fact whether it is true or not.

Though social media has given many positive impacts on our society it has also given some bitter facts which are a concern of our society. The most powerful impact on our society regarding social media is the circulation of fake news or misinformation over the social media. There is lack of control and fact checking on the social media platforms that lead to the major concern for social media platforms and for our society. Fake news has different forms on the social media environment. As the news can take more than one form i.e., it can be of text, image video or combination of them. That has made it more difficult for the researchers to build a convenient tool for the detection of fake news and misinformation. Though it is a very difficult task, over the last few years some very good research work has been done for the detection of fake news.

Both the research community and social media platforms are working on fake news detection and to stop it's spreading. In this paper, we have done an in-depth survey of research work done recently. In Sect. 2, we have discussed some recent survey works done in respect of fake news detection. Section 3 is about different types of fake news. Section 4 is dedicated to some methodologies that are used for fake news detection. Section 5 discusses different fake news detection schemes developed in recent times. In Sect. 6, we have compared different research with their performance, dataset etc. Then we discussed some limitations and future works in Sect.7.

2   Related Survey Works

As fake news detection has been a research attraction for the last few years. The researchers of these works compared the latest research in fake news detection that are based on multimodal frameworks, unsupervised frameworks, and semi-supervised frameworks in Saini et al. (2020). The advantages and disadvantages of each methodology are also available in Saini et al. (2020). In the multi-modal framework, the works are compared to research based on the text-model and image-model used, dataset used, methodology and accuracy. In the semi-supervised framework, the comparisons are based on the dataset they used, with discussion on the labelled and unlabeled data and methodologies. The comparisons are based on the datasets used, methodologies and system accuracy available with the research works in the unsupervised framework.

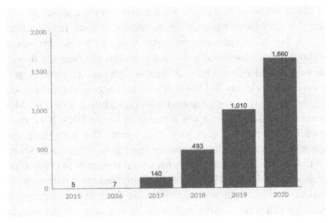

Fig. 1. No of results found about fake news detection in recent years on Google Scholar.

A comprehensive survey of fake news is found (Shu et al. 2017), where the survey has been done from a data mining perspective. From this paper we can find a good overview and discussions on fake news detection. In this paper feature extraction has been categorized by social media using post-based, network-based context. Model construction has been analyzed regarding news content models and social context models. The news content models are sub categorized as knowledge-based and style-based. Social context models are sub categorized as stance-based and propagation-based. Popular fake news datasets like BuzzFeedNews, LIAR is discussed. Related areas like rumour classification, truth discovery, clickbait detection spammer and bot detection have been discussed. But this paper lacks different detection methodologies with critical comparisons.

A detailed presentation on different methods is available with comparisons with respect to fake knowledge and the pattern of propagation with author's credibility in Zhou and Zafarani (2018). Different types of fake news i.e., satire, propaganda, clickbait, hoax is discussed in Sharma and Sharma (2019). The authors describe different characteristics of fake news with little comparison given in respect to machine learning and deep learning methods. Standard tools and datasets like LIAR, FEVER, CREDBANK are discussed in

Sharma and Sharma (2019). Elhadad et al. (2019) did a systematic survey where a brief comparison between terminologies and their references have been given. A summarized discussion on different works is made based on different approaches, platforms, and feature types (Table 1).

Table 1. Some important survey papers on Fake News detection.

Year	Existing work	Broad topics
2017	Shu et al (2017)	Survey on fake news detection from a data mining perspective
2018	Zhou and Zafarani (2018)	A survey of research, detection methods, and opportunities
2019	Bondielli and Marcelloni (2019)	A survey on fake news and rumor detection techniques
2019	Zhang and Ghorbani (2019)	An overview of online fake news: Characterization, detection, and discussion

To see the recent trends in fake news detection over the last 6 years we have used Google Scholar. When the keyword "Fake News Detection" is searched on Google Scholar, the year wise result shows that the number of results increased drastically in the last few years. The result is shown in Fig. 1.

Bondielli and Marcelloni (2019) surveyed various types of fake news, datasets, various techniques with features extraction, and future research directions. A trend has been given on the number papers published over the last 12 years by them. A detailed discussion on data collection of fake news and rumors is also given. Different types of feature extraction methods relevant to content and context have been discussed. They also discussed different approaches in fake news detection using machine learning and deep learning. Some future directions have been given at last.

Zhang and Ghorbani (2020) did a comprehensive review with the negative impacts of fake news. Most of the popular detection methods on existing datasets are discussed with some future directions. The categorization of fake news is done with respect to the science behind news creators and the target users. Online fact checking techniques with some comparisons have been discussed by Zhang and Ghorbani (2020).

3 Types of Fake News

Fake news are the news articles that are written intentionally to misguide or misinform the readers, but it can be verified as fake by means of original sources. Due to easy availability of the internet various types of fake news are creating a major concern over all social media platforms. Nowadays fake news is spreading on social media in several forms. Here we discuss some of these forms.

Misinformation: AN information that is inaccurate or false is called mis information. It has affected our life from all dimensions. The main source of misinformation is social media. As social media is very much liberal in nature it creates a huge probability of misinformation.

Disinformation: AN information that is false or misleading and propagated deliberately to deceive people is called disinformation. All disinformation is part of misinformation. Though the meaning of both misinformation and disinformation may sound the same, the main difference between them is that misinformation can be unintentional, but disinformation is always intentional.

Clickbait: A false or misleading hyperlinked advertisement which is designed to attract the users is called a clickbait. Most of the time it is a headline made with dishonesty. Nowadays we can see many attractive headlines on social media which leads to some information written with dishonesty. It is created to drag user's attention for commercial benefit from social media.

Propaganda: IT is an information which is propagated to impact the target audience with one sided fact for some purpose. Most of the time it is manipulative. After reading that type of information a biased belief may grow.

Hoax: IT is a deception which may be malicious or humorous. It is created to deceive someone intentionally.

4   Fake News Detection Methods

Machine Learning: BY looking at the papers it is quite evident that, major number of works done on fake news detection is based on machine learning algorithms. Many of the machine learning models have generated satisfactory levels of accuracy. Let's have a look at the machine learning techniques used on these papers.

Logistic Regression: Logistic regression is both regression and classification technique. It is used to predict the result of categorical variables. Logistic regression is often used in fraud detection or to classify email. In recent years we can see many fake news detection models have used logistic regression as a classification algorithm. Logistic regression is used (Tacchini et al. 2017) with Boolean level Crowdsourcing (BLC) on the dataset collected from Facebook and the model has achieved 99.4% of accuracy. Logistic regression has been used and also compared with other algorithms in Hiramath and Deshpande (2019). Logistic regression is used with other classifiers Agarwal et al. (2019) and produces almost the same accuracy as SVM. Logistic regression is used in Mahabub (2020) with other classifiers and it has achieved very high mean accuracy. Logistic regression is used with other models (Singh et. al. n.d.) and it achieved an accuracy of 84.43.

SVM: Support vector machine (SVM) algorithms can solve regression problems as well as linear classification. SVM is based on the concept of a hyperplane which is a surface. Hyperplane is a boundary drawn between data instances that are plotted on multi-dimensional feature space. As fake news can be either true or false, this classification model gives us tremendous results in fake news detection. Wang (2017) used SVM on the benchmark dataset LIAR and achieved good accuracy. Jain et al. (2019) used SVM with the combination of Naïve Bayes and semantic investigation. It achieved an accuracy of 93.50%. Gravanis et al. (2019) used SVM with word embeddings and ensemble algorithms that achieved up to 95% accuracy. Hiramath and Deshpande (2019) used SVM which gives a moderate level of results with an accuracy of 79%. Agarwal et al. (2019) used SVM and logistic regression which gives best performance on that dataset. In (Rasool et. al. 2019), SVM is used with Decision Tree and produces accuracy up to 66.29%. SVM gave a cross validation score of 84.75% in Mahabub (2020). SVM achieved accuracy of up to 82.48% on the combination of textual and visual data in Singh et al. (n.d.). Other classification algorithms are outperformed by SVM and Random Forest where SVM gives accuracy of up to 94% in Faustini and Covões (2020). SVM gives an accuracy of 73% in Agarwal and Dixit (2020). SVM gives the best result in Yezdi et al. (2020) when compared to Decision Tree and Naïve Bayes classifiers. In (Hariule et al. 2020) SVM achieved almost 88% accuracy.

Naïve Bayes: IN statistics, Naive Bayes classifiers are simple "probabilistic classifiers" based on the application of Bayes' theorem. It is based on the idea that the outcome of a hypothesis is predicted based on some evidence (E). Naïve Bayes is used on Facebook news posts (Granik and Mesyura 2017) and achieved an accuracy of 74% approximately. Naïve Bayes is combined with SVM in Jain et al. (2019) and produces an accuracy of 93.50%. Naïve Bayes gives an accuracy of 0.881 in Gravanis et al. (2019). A comparison between most common ML classifiers has been done and Naïve Bayes in Agarwal and Dixit (2020) showing some significant performance. Naïve Bayes is giving 89.17% cross validation accuracy in Mahabub (2020). The Naïve Bayes achieved accuracy of up to 78.46% on the combination of textual and visual data (Singh et al. n.d.). Naïve Bayes is compared with other common ML algorithms (Faustini and Covões 2020) but the result is not state-of-the-art. Naïve Bayes in Agarwal and Dixit (2020) provides decent results and is 91%. Naïve Bayes classifier in Yezdi et al. (2020) produces very good outcomes, almost like the other two classifiers-SVM and Decision Tree. In Zervopoulos et al. (2020) Naïve Bayes algorithm produces good results. Naïve Bayes gave the best result at the HongKong event (Nikiforos et. al. 2020) with an accuracy of 99.79%. Naïve Bayes is used as a traditional ML model and compared with popular deep learning approaches like hybrid CNN, RNN (Han and Mehta 2019) and showed good results. The Naïve Bayes algorithm is also used for fake news detection (Harjule et al. 2020) and it has achieved only 72% accuracy.

Decision Tree: A Decision Tree is a kind of supervised learning algorithm that is commonly used in classification problems and has a predefined target variable. The model is built in the form of tree structure. It has a very fast execution time. Decision Tree is used along with other algorithms in Pérez-Rosas et al. (2017) and gives an accuracy of 8.58%. A decision Tree algorithm (Hlaing and Kham 2020) gives an accuracy which is >70%. In Yezdi et al. (2020), Decision Tree is used with SVM and Naïve Bayes and produces good results.

Random Forest: The random forest can be defined as an ensemble classifier as it uses a combination of many decision trees. It can perform dimensional reduction and treat missing values. Large number of trees are using random forest algorithms to get the contribution from each feature to the model. Two Machine Learning algorithms were utilized which are Random Forest and Gradient boosting in Wynne and Wint (2019). However Gradient boosting achieved higher accuracy. A fake news detection system is developed with traditional Machine Learning algorithms in Hiramath and Deshpande (2009) where Random Forest achieves 77% accuracy. Random Forest is used along with other classifiers in Agarwal et al. (2019) and showing good results. Random Forest is giving 83.59% cross validation score in Mahabub (2020). The Random Forest algorithm gives better accuracy (>75%) than the other two algorithms used in Hlaing and Kham (2020) that model, which are Decision Tree and AdaBoost. Random Forest achieved best accuracy (Singh et al. n.d.) of 95.18% on the combination of textual and visual data. Other classification algorithms are outperformed by Random Forest and SVM where Random Forest (Faustini and Covões 2020) gives accuracy of up to 95%. Naïve Bayes (Nikiforos et al. 2020) gives the best result on Hong Kong events with an accuracy of 99.37%.

KNN: The k-Nearest Neighbor algorithm is a very powerful and simple classification algorithm. The main theme of the algorithm is to classify unknown data based on the already trained data set which are like the new element. K-Nearest Neighbors is a lazy learning algorithm used for classification problems. KNN is used along with other traditional Machine Learning algorithms (Gravanis et al. 2019) and KNN achieved a good accuracy of 0.921. KNN is giving a 79.63% cross validation score in Mahabub (2020). KNN achieved the best accuracy of 83.31% on the combination of textual and visual data in Singh et al. (n.d.). KNN is compared with other common Machine Learning algorithms (Faustini and Covões 2020) and gives accuracy of up to 81%. KNN is compared with (Agarwal and Dixit 2020) other common Machine Learning algorithms and it gives an accuracy of 70%.

Deep Learning: AS the time progresses, the availability of large amounts of data is increasing day by day. This results in the rise of Deep Learning algorithms that can achieve more accuracy than the traditional Machine Learning models. In this we have found some very good Deep Learning models with high accuracy. Now we will discuss these Deep Learning models used for fake news detection below.

CNN: Convolutional Neural Network (CNN) is a deep neural network commonly used for image analysis. CNN is commonly made of multilayer perceptron, which are mainly fully connected layers i.e., neurons of one layer are connected to the neurons of the next layer. It is inspired by the neuron's biological process. It consists of one input, one output and multiple hidden layers. Its architecture is made of convolution layer, pooling layer, ReLU layer and fully connected layer. CNN is applied on the benchmark dataset LIAR () and it has outperformed all other models with an accuracy of 27%. CNN is used in a new framework in Karimi et al. (2018) and produces accuracy of 38.81%. A modified CNN model called Text-CNN (Wang et al. 2018) is used on a framework called EANN and produces an accuracy of 0.827 on the Weibo dataset. CNN is used with Random Forest and GAN and the model in He et al. (2019) gives an accuracy of 99.70%. A four-layer Graph CNN with two convolutional layers and two fully connected layers is used by Monti et al. (2019) to predict the fakeness. CNN is used by Liu (2019) with Word embeddings and Bidirectional LSTM and achieved over 90% accuracy. CNN with two layers is applied by Qawasmeh et al. (2019) with Bidirectional LSTM and gives an accuracy of 85.3%. CNN is used with POS tag and LSTM by Balwant (2019) and the model gives an accuracy of 42.2%. CNN is used with RNN and Bidirectional LSTM by Balwant (2019) and achieved a test accuracy of up to 98.75%. A deep CNN network is proposed named FNDNet by Kaliyar et al. (2020). The model predicted test accuracy up to 98.36%. CNN is used with LSTM in Krešňáková et al. (2019) and Agarwal and Dixit (2020) and achieved very good accuracy of 91.2549% and 94.71% respectively. An ensemble learning model is used by Huang and Chen (2020) where 4 different models are combined which are embedding LSTM, depth LSTM, LIWC CNN, and N-gram CNN. CNN is compared with other models in Agarwal and Dixit (2020) where CNN has achieved 94% test accuracy. CNN is used with LSTM by Liu et al. (2020) and achieved an accuracy of 80.38%. In (Antoun et al. 2020) CNN gives a precision of 83% (Table 2).

Table 2. Comparison between some important models.

Methods	Dataset used	Advantage	Limitations
KNN, Decision Tree, Naïve Bayes, AdaBoost, SVM, Bagging	Kaggle, McIntire, BuzzFeed, Politifact, Unbiased	A novel Fake news dataset 'UNBiased'	Mainly Deals with Binary classification
Text Mining, Supervised AI	Buzzfeed, Random Political News, ISOT	23 supervised algorithms have been implemented	Also, a binary classification problem accuracy is not up to the mark
CNN, FNDNet	Fake news dataset	Use of deep learning algorithms that gave very good accuracy	Only one dataset is used
Veracity analysis	PHEME, BuzzFeed, PolitiFact	Text extraction from image	Model is compatible with image text only
Naïve Bayes, K-NN, SVM, Random Forest, ANN, Logistic Regression, Gradient Boosting, Ada Boosting	Various	Use of ensemble classifier and analysis of different ML algorithms	Model works on binary classification and the dataset used is small

(continued)

Table 2. (*continued*)

Methods	Dataset used	Advantage	Limitations
KNN, Random Forest, Naïve Bayes, SVM	TwitterBR, FakeBrCorpus, fakeNewsData1,	Five datasets used and combination of different classifiers gave better result	Binary classification problem
Hybrid CNN	LIAR	Benchmark dataset introduced	Accuracy is low
Attention based LSTM	LIAR	Multiclass classification problem	Combination of CNN and RNN can be used
ELMo with LSTM	LIAR	Attention based deep ensemble model with high accuracy	User credibility score can be used for better accuracy

RNN: A recurrent neural network (RNN) is a class of artificial neural networks that allow the previous outputs to be used as inputs. These models are mainly used in NLP and speech recognition. Most used activation functions of RNN are Sigmoid, Tanh, and RELU. The vanishing gradient problem which is encountered by traditional RNNs is dealt by Gate Recurrent Unit (GRU) and Long Short-Term Memory (LSTM). Recurrent Neural Network is a class of Artificial Neural Network that exhibits temporal dynamic behavior. Mainly RNN is used in handwriting recognition or speech recognition. RNN is used in the Capture module in Ruchansky et al. (2017). The model achieves the highest accuracy of 95.3% on the Weibo dataset. RNN is used by Wang (2017) on the benchmark dataset LIAR in the form of BiLSTM and does not perform well due to overfitting of data. LSTM is used by Long (2017) and the model's accuracy can go to over 41.5%. RNN is used in a new framework called MMFD (Karimi et al. 2018) and produces accuracy of 38.81%. BiLSTM is used by Liu (2019) with CNN and the model can produce accuracy up to 96.1%. LSTM is applied on the FNC-1 Qawasmeh et al. (2019) dataset with 85.3% accuracy. LSTM is used with POS tags and CNN by Balwant (2019). The model gives an accuracy of 42.2%. The FNN model is compared with the LSTM model (Deepak and Chitturi 2020) and the LSTM model is the clear winner with an accuracy of 91.32%. RNN is used by Bahad et al. (2019) with CNN and Bidirectional LSTM and achieved a test accuracy of up to 98.75%. A high dimensional latent space framework is used using BiLSTM by Sadiq et al. (2019) and the accuracy measure showed an accuracy of 89.99%. Some deep learning algorithms applied by Krešňáková et al. (2019) where LSTM's accuracy is 91.8593%. RNN is used in the form of LSTM (Agarwal and Dixit 2020) and the model gives 97.21% precision values. RNN is used in the form of LSTM (Huang and Chen 2020) and the model achieves highest test accuracy of 99.4%. LSTM is compared with CNN, SVM, Naïve Bayes and KNN (Agarwal and Dixit 2020) and LSTM has the highest accuracy with 97% which is highest among all. RNN is used in the form of LSTM by Han and Mehta (2019) and it achieved accuracy up to 82.29%. In (Harjule et al. 2020), RNN is compared with Naïve Bayes, SVM and CNN where RNN achieved the highest accuracy of 93% among all methods. Antoun et al. (2020) used

BiLSTM with attention in combination with hand crafted features which has gained the highest precision of 95% (Kula et al. 2020) LSTM and the accuracy is 99.86%.

Ensemble Learning: IT is the process in which multiple models such as classifiers are combined to solve a particular problem. Commonly used ensemble learning models are Bagging, Boosting, AdaBoost etc.

AdaBoost: IT is the short form of Adaptive Boosting. It is mainly used in combination with other types of learning models to improve a model's performance. Gravanis et al. (2019) used AdaBoost and compared with other models like SVM, KNN, DT, Naïve Bayes and achieved an accuracy of 94.9%, just below the best result. AdaBoost classifier is used for sequential approaches by Hlaing and Kham (2020) to classify authenticity of news. The model achieves an accuracy well over 70% with AdaBoost.

Bagging: Bootstrap Aggregation known as Bagging is an ensemble algorithm used to improve a model's performance. It helps to avoid overfitting by reducing variance. Gravanis et al. (2019) used Bagging and compared with other models like SVM, KNN, DT, Naïve Bayes, AdaBoost and achieved a very good accuracy of 94.4%.

5 Related Datasets

The accuracy of the learning models vastly depends on the size of the datasets. Till date the number of datasets on fake news are very small and out of those only few are publicly available. Here, we will discuss and compare some datasets that are recently used in fake news detection.

LIAR: There are 12,800 news statements collected from PolitiFact.com and labelled manually by the author Wang (2017). The news articles are classified into 6 categories: true, mostly true, half true, barely true, false and pants-fire. The author also proposed a model using hybrid CNN that achieved an accuracy of 27.40%.

BuzzFeed: Published by Horne and Adali (2017) this dataset contained approximately two thousand news articles collected from Facebook. There are four categories: Mostly true, not factual content, mix of true and false and mostly false. The articles are fact checked by Buzzfeed journalists.

Credbank: This dataset is collected from twitter (Mitra and Gilbert 2015) that contains more than sixty million tweets fact checked by 30 annotators (Table 3).

FakeNewsNet: IT contains a total 422 news articles collected from BuzzFeed.com and PolitiFact.com out of which 211 is true news and 211 is fake news. The news articles also associate user information, content, and social engagement information. This dataset is published by Shu et al. (2017).

Table 3. Some important fake news datasets.

Dataset	Num of articles	Description
LIAR	12800	It has 6 categories, collected from PolitiFact.com
BuzzFeed	2000	Collected from Facebook with 4 categories
Credbank	6000000	Fact checked by 30 annotators
FakeNewsNet	422	It includes user info, content and social information
Political news	75	Collected from Business Insider with 3 categories
Satire news	4233	Collected manually by the authors
FEVER	185445	Collected from Wikipedia with 2 categories

Political News Dataset: IT comprises 75 articles which are classified into three categories: fake news, real news, satire. The articles are collected from Zimdar's list (Zimdars 2016) of fake news and most trusted list from Business Insider (Engel 2014).

Satire News Dataset: This dataset consists of 4000 real news articles and 233 satire news articles. The news articles are collected manually by the author Burfoot and Baldwin (2009).

FEVER: FEVER stands for Fact Extraction and VERification (Thorne et al. 2018). It consists of 185,445 articles collected from Wikipedia. There are two categories: Supported, Refuted.

6   Challenges and Future Work

Lack of Dataset: The first challenge is the limited good quality labelled benchmark datasets. The availability of standard labeled datasets may increase the accuracy level.

Data Preparation: AS the collected data are mostly unlabeled, the data preparation is rigorous and time consuming. For this reason, unsupervised learning algorithms can be very beneficial for fake news detection.

Fake News in Regional Language: IN recent years the work has been done on the labelled datasets mostly available in English. In this survey we noticed, there is not much work done on regional languages. In the future work, we anticipate more research on regional languages.

Reusability: IN case of machine learning, most of the time these algorithms are supervised, and the data collected are mostly unlabeled. So, the large amount of data needs to be hand crafted and labelled. That is a time consuming and lengthy process. Also, the machine learning algorithms have very poor ability of transfer learning, re-usability of modules and integration.

Need of Large Dataset: The main limitation of deep learning models is the requirement of a large amount of data. As there is still a lack of large benchmark dataset on fake news it is very difficult to achieve desired accuracy. Other limitations involved with deep learning are overfitting and time consuming.

Higher Computation Time: The computation and design time is very high for ensemble learning. As ensemble learning is a combination of diverse learning algorithms its implementation is difficult in respect to other learning models.

Need of Multi-class Classification: From this survey it is evident that most of the previous works are in the form of binary classification problem, where the data is labelled in the form of true and false. But in practice, the degree of fakeness or trueness is very important in respect to a news article. Very few works are done on fake news detection as a multiclass classification problem. One of the reasons for this is because of the lack of multi-labelled dataset.

7 Conclusion

In this paper, we examined and analyzed some recent research on fake news detection. We know that fake news has a very big impact on our society, and research on fake news detection is still in its early stages. We discussed and compared some very recent results and found some commonly used datasets. Some research results are very promising and have achieved very good accuracy.

From this review, instead of using a single algorithm, combining classifiers, i.e., ensemble learning, can be very beneficial. And with the availability of large benchmark datasets on fake news, deep learning algorithms also see a promising future for fake news detection. Since real-time detection of Fake News is still lacking, more research is needed to compare large datasets in this direction with new feature extraction techniques. A common interface for social media users to report or detect Fake News may be beneficial to society. Work on Fake News in regional languages is also on the horizon, as research on processing low-resource languages moves forward.

From both a societal and scholarly perspective, we can expect that the topics covered in this study will become increasingly common in social media discourse. Therefore, we believe that further studies are needed in this area, as such contributions will undoubtedly have a major impact on the outcome of online communication.

Acknowledgements. This study is **funded** by the **Department of Science and Technology – Science and Engineering Research Board (DST-SERB), Govt. of India** under the research project entitled "Fake Image and News Detection on Social Media Through Trustware Based Community Portal". (**No-EEQ/2019/000317**). The authors are thankful to the Vidyasagar University for providing infrastructural facilities required for carrying out the project.

References

Agarwal, A., Dixit, A.: Fake news detection: an ensemble learning approach. In: 2020 4th International Conference on Intelligent Computing and Control Systems (ICICCS), pp. 1178–1183. IEEE (2020)

Agarwal, A., Mittal, M., Pathak, A., Goyal, L.M.: Fake news detection using a blend of neural networks: an application of deep learning. SN Comput. Sci. 1(3), 1–9 (2020). https://doi.org/10.1007/s42979-020-00165-4

Agarwal, V., Sultana, H.P., Malhotra, S., Sarkar, A.: Analysis of classifiers for fake news detection. Procedia Comput. Sci. 165, 377–383 (2019)

Antoun, W., Baly, F., Achour, R., Hussein, A., Hajj, H.: State of the art models for fake news detection tasks. In: 2020 IEEE International Conference on Informatics, IoT, and Enabling Technologies (ICIoT), pp. 519–524. IEEE (2020)

Bahad, P., Saxena, P., Kamal, R.: Fake news detection using bi-directional LSTM-recurrent neural network. Procedia Comput. Sci. 165, 74–82 (2019)

Balwant, M.K.: Bidirectional LSTM based on POS tags and CNN architecture for fake news detection. In: 2019 10th International Conference on Computing, Communication and Networking Technologies (ICCCNT), pp. 1–6. IEEE (2019)

Bondielli, A., Marcelloni, F.: A survey on fake news and rumour detection techniques. Inf. Sci. 497, 38–55 (2019)

Burfoot, C., Baldwin, T.: Automatic satire detection: are you having a laugh? In: Proceedings of the ACL-IJCNLP 2009 Conference Short Papers, pp. 161–164 (2009)

Cao, J., Qi, P., Sheng, Q., Yang, T., Guo, J., Li, J.: Exploring the role of visual content in fake news detection. arXiv preprint arXiv:2003.05096 (2020)

Cook, J., Ecker, U., Lewandowsky, S.: Misinformation and how to correct it. In: Emerging Trends in the Social and Behavioral Sciences: An Interdisciplinary, Searchable, and Linkable Resource, pp. 1–17 (2015)

Deepak, S., Chitturi, B.: Deep neural approach to fake-news identification. Procedia Comput. Sci. 167, 2236–2243 (2020)

Elhadad, M. K., Li, K. F., Gebali, F.: Fake news detection on social media: a systematic survey. In: 2019 IEEE Pacific Rim Conference on Communications, Computers and Signal Processing (PACRIM), pp. 1–8. IEEE, August 2019

Fallis, D.: What is disinformation? Libr. Trends 63(3), 401–426 (2015)

Faustini, P.H.A., Covões, T.F.: Fake news detection in multiple platforms and languages. Expert Syst. Appl. 158, 113503 (2020)

Gaglani, J., Gandhi, Y., Gogate, S., Halbe, A.: Unsupervised WhatsApp fake news detection using semantic search. In: 2020 4th International Conference on Intelligent Computing and Control Systems (ICICCS), pp. 285–289. IEEE, May 2020

Garrido-Merchán, E.C., Puente, C., Palacios, R.: Fake news detection by means of uncertainty weighted causal graphs. arXiv preprint arXiv:2002.01065 (2020)

Gilda, S.: Evaluating machine learning algorithms for fake news detection. In: 2017 IEEE 15th Student Conference on Research and Development (SCOReD), pp. 110–115. IEEE, December 2017

Granik, M., Mesyura, V:. Fake news detection using naive Bayes classifier. In: 2017 IEEE First Ukraine Conference on Electrical and Computer Engineering (UKRCON), pp. 900–903. IEEE, May 2017

Gravanis, G., Vakali, A., Diamantaras, K., Karadais, P.: Behind the cues: a benchmarking study for fake news detection. Expert Syst. Appl. 128, 201–213 (2019)

Han, W., Mehta, V.: Fake news detection in social networks using machine learning and deep learning: performance evaluation. In: 2019 IEEE International Conference on Industrial Internet (ICII), pp. 375–380. IEEE, November 2019

Harjule, P., Sharma, A., Chouhan, S., Joshi, S.: Reliability of news. In: 2020 3rd International Conference on Emerging Technologies in Computer Engineering: Machine Learning and Internet of Things (ICETCE), pp. 165–170. IEEE, February 2020

He, P., Li, H., Wang, H.: Detection of fake images via the ensemble of deep representations from multicolor spaces. In: 2019 IEEE International Conference on Image Processing (ICIP), pp. 2299–2303. IEEE, September 2019

Hiramath, C.K., Deshpande, G.C.: Fake news detection using deep learning techniques. In: 2019 1st International Conference on Advances in Information Technology (ICAIT), pp. 411–415. IEEE, July 2019

Hlaing, M.M.M., Kham, N.S.M.: Defining news authenticity on social media using machine learning approach. In: 2020 IEEE Conference on Computer Applications (ICCA), pp. 1–6. IEEE, February 2020

Horne, B., Adali, S.: This just in: Fake news packs a lot in title, uses simpler, repetitive content in text body, more similar to satire than real news. In: Proceedings of the International AAAI Conference on Web and Social Media, vol. 11, No. 1, May 2017

Huang, Y.F., Chen, P.H.: Fake News detection using an ensemble learning model based on self-adaptive harmony search algorithms. Expert Syst. Appl. **159**, 113584 (2020)

Jain, A., Shakya, A., Khatter, H., Gupta, A.K.: A smart system for fake news detection using machine learning. In: 2019 International Conference on Issues and Challenges in Intelligent Computing Techniques (ICICT), vol. 1, pp. 1–4. IEEE, September 2019

Jain, V., Kaliyar, R.K., Goswami, A., Narang, P., Sharma, Y.: AENeT: an attention-enabled neural architecture for fake news detection using contextual features. Neural Comput. Appl. **34**(1), 771–782 (2021). https://doi.org/10.1007/s00521-021-06450-4

Kaliyar, R.K., Goswami, A., Narang, P., Sinha, S.: FNDNet–a deep convolutional neural network for fake news detection. Cogn. Syst. Res. **61**, 32–44 (2020)

Karimi, H., Roy, P., Saba-Sadiya, S., Tang, J.: Multi-source multi-class fake news detection. In: Proceedings of the 27th International Conference on Computational Linguistics, pp. 1546–1557 (2018)

Kong, S.H., Tan, L.M., Gan, K.H., Samsudin, N H.: Fake News detection using deep learning. In: 2020 IEEE 10th Symposium on Computer Applications & Industrial Electronics (ISCAIE), pp. 102–107. IEEE, April 2020

Krešňáková, V.M., Sarnovský, M., Butka, P.: Deep learning methods for Fake News detection. In: 2019 IEEE 19th International Symposium on Computational Intelligence and Informatics and 7th IEEE International Conference on Recent Achievements in Mechatronics, Automation, Computer Sciences and Robotics (CINTI-MACRo), pp. 000143–000148. IEEE, November 2019

Kula, S., Choraś, M., Kozik, R., Ksieniewicz, P., Woźniak, M.: Sentiment analysis for fake news detection by means of neural networks. In: Krzhizhanovskaya, V.V., et al. (eds.) ICCS 2020. LNCS, vol. 12140, pp. 653–666. Springer, Cham (2020). https://doi.org/10.1007/978-3-030-50423-6_49

Kunbaz, A., Saghir, S., Arar, M., Sönmez, E.B.: Fake Image detection using DCT and local binary pattern. In: 2019 Ninth International Conference on Image Processing Theory, Tools and Applications (IPTA), pp. 1–6. IEEE, November 2017

Little, A.T.: Propaganda and credulity. Games Econom. Behav. **102**, 224–232 (2017)

Liu, H.: A Location independent machine learning approach for early fake news detection. In: 2019 IEEE International Conference on Big Data (Big Data), pp. 4740–4746. IEEE, December 2019

Liu, H., Wang, L., Han, X., Zhang, W., He, X.: Detecting Fake News on social media: a multi-source scoring framework. In: 2020 IEEE 5th International Conference on Cloud Computing and Big Data Analytics (ICCCBDA), pp. 524–531. IEEE, April 2020

Long, Y.: Fake News Detection through Multi-perspective Speaker Profiles. Association for Computational Linguistics (2017)

Mahabub, A.: A robust technique of fake news detection using ensemble voting classifier and comparison with other classifiers. SN Appl. Sci. **2**(4), 1–9 (2020). https://doi.org/10.1007/s42 452-020-2326-y

Mishra, R.: Fake news detection using higher-order user to user mutual-attention progression in propagation paths. In: Proceedings of the IEEE/CVF Conference on Computer Vision and Pattern Recognition Workshops, pp. 652–653 (2020)

Mitra, T., Gilbert, E.: Credbank: a large-scale social media corpus with associated credibility annotations. In: Ninth International AAAI Conference on Web and Social Media, April 2015

Monti, F., Frasca, F., Eynard, D., Mannion, D., Bronstein, M. M.: Fake news detection on social media using geometric deep learning. arXiv preprint arXiv:1902.06673 (2019)

Zimdars, M: False, misleading, clickbait-y, and satirical 'news' sources, Google Docs (2016)

Ni, B., Guo, Z., Li, J., Jiang, M.: Improving generalizability of fake news detection methods using propensity score matching. arXiv preprint arXiv:2002.00838 (2010)

Nikiforos, M.N., Vergis, S., Stylidou, A., Augoustis, N., Kermanidis, K.L., Maragoudakis, M.: Fake News detection regarding the hong kong events from tweets. In: Maglogiannis, I., Iliadis, L., Pimenidis, E. (eds.) AIAI 2020. IAICT, vol. 585, pp. 177–186. Springer, Cham (2020). https://doi.org/10.1007/978-3-030-49190-1_16

Okoro, E.M., Abara, B.A., Umagba, A.O., Ajonye, A.A., Isa, Z.S.: A hybrid approach to fake news detection on social media. Niger. J. Technol. **37**(2), 454–462 (2018)

Ozbay, F.A., Alatas, B.: Fake news detection within online social media using supervised artificial intelligence algorithms. Phy. A **540**, 123174 (2020)

Park, K., Rim, H.: Social media hoaxes, political ideology, and the role of issue confidence. Telemat. Inform. **36**, 1–11 (2019)

Engel, P.: Here are the most-and least-trusted news outlets in America. Business Insider. Business Insider. Business Insider, Inc, 21 (2014)

Paul, S., Joy, J. I., Sarker, S., Ahmed, S., Das, A.K.: Fake News Detection in Social Media using Blockchain. In: 2019 7th International Conference on Smart Computing & Communications (ICSCC), pp. 1–5. IEEE, June 2019

Pérez-Rosas, V., Kleinberg, B., Lefevre, A., Mihalcea, R.: Automatic detection of fake news. arXiv preprint arXiv:1708.07104 (2017)

Potthast, M., Kiesel, J., Reinartz, K., Bevendorff, J., Stein, B.: A stylometric inquiry into hyperpartisan and fake news. arXiv preprint arXiv:1702.05638 (2017)

Qawasmeh, E., Tawalbeh, M., Abdullah, M.: Automatic identification of fake news using deep learning. In: 2019 Sixth International Conference on Social Networks Analysis, Management and Security (SNAMS), pp. 383–388. IEEE, October 2019

Qazi, M., Khan, M.U., Ali, M.: Detection of fake news using transformer model. In: 2020 3rd International Conference on Computing, Mathematics and Engineering Technologies (iCoMET), pp. 1–6. IEEE, January 2020

Rasool, T., Butt, W.H., Shaukat, A., Akram, M.U.: Multi-label fake news detection using multi-layered supervised learning. In: Proceedings of the 2019 11th International Conference on Computer and Automation Engineering, pp. 73–77, February 2019

Roy, A., et al.: A deep ensemble framework for fake news detection and classification. arXiv preprint arXiv:1811.04670 (2018)

Rubin, V.L., Conroy, N., Chen, Y., Cornwell, S.: Fake news or truth? Using satirical cues to detect potentially misleading news. In: Proceedings of the Second Workshop on Computational Approaches to Deception Detection, pp. 7–17, June 2016

Ruchansky, N., Seo, S., Liu, Y.: CSI: a hybrid deep model for fake news detection. In: Proceedings of the 2017 ACM on Conference on Information and Knowledge Management, pp. 797–806, November 2017

Sabeeh, V., Zohdy, M., Al Bashaireh, R.: Enhancing the Fake news detection by applying effective feature selection based on semantic sources. In: 2019 International Conference on Computational Science and Computational Intelligence (CSCI), pp. 1365–1370. IEEE, December 2019

Sadiq, S., Wagner, N., Shyu, M.L., Feaster, D.: High Dimensional latent space variational autoencoders for fake news detection. In: 2019 IEEE Conference on Multimedia Information Processing and Retrieval (MIPR), pp. 437–442. IEEE, March 2019

Saikh, T., De, A., Ekbal, A., Bhattacharyya, P.: A deep learning approach for automatic detection of fake news. arXiv preprint arXiv:2005.04938 (2020)

Saini, N., Singhal, M., Tanwar, M., Meel, P.: Multimodal, semi-supervised and unsupervised web content credibility analysis frameworks. In: 2020 4th International Conference on Intelligent Computing and Control Systems (ICICCS), pp. 948–955. IEEE, May 2020

Shahi, G.K., Nandini, D.: FakeCovid--a multilingual cross-domain fact check news dataset for COVID-19. arXiv preprint arXiv:2006.11343 (2020)

Shao, C., Ciampaglia, G.L., Varol, O., Flammini, A., Menczer, F.:The spread of fake news by social bots. arXiv preprint arXiv:1707.07592, 96, 104 (2021)

Sharma, S., Sharma, D.K.: Fake news detection: a long way to go. In: 2019 4th International Conference on Information Systems and Computer Networks (ISCON), pp. 816–821. IEEE, November 2019

Shu, K., Bernard, H.R., Liu, H.: Studying fake news via network analysis: detection and mitigation. In: Agarwal, N., Dokoohaki, N., Tokdemir, S. (eds.) Emerging Research Challenges and Opportunities in Computational Social Network Analysis and Mining. LNSN, pp. 43–65. Springer, Cham (2019). https://doi.org/10.1007/978-3-319-94105-9_3

Shu, K., Sliva, A., Wang, S., Tang, J., Liu, H.: Fake news detection on social media: a data mining perspective. ACM SIGKDD Explor. Newsl. **19**(1), 22–36 (2017)

Shu, K., Wang, S., Liu, H.: Beyond news contents: the role of social context for fake news detection. In: Proceedings of the Twelfth ACM International Conference on Web Search and Data Mining, pp. 312–320, January 2019

Singh, V.K., Ghosh, I., Sonagara, D.: Detecting fake news stories via multimodal analysis. J. Assoc. Inf. Sci. Technol. **72**, 3–17 (2021)

Tacchini, E., Ballarin, G., Della Vedova, M.L., Moret, S., de Alfaro, L.: Some like it hoax: automated fake news detection in social networks. arXiv preprint arXiv:1704.07506 (2017)

Thorne, J., Vlachos, A., Christodoulopoulos, C., Mittal, A.: Fever: a large-scale dataset for fact extraction and verification. arXiv preprint arXiv:1803.05355 (2018)

Tschiatschek, S., Singla, A., Gomez Rodriguez, M., Merchant, A., Krause, A.: Fake news detection in social networks via crowd signals. In: Companion Proceedings of the the Web Conference 2018, pp. 517–524, April 2018

Vishwakarma, D.K., Varshney, D., Yadav, A.: Detection and veracity analysis of fake news via scrapping and authenticating the web search. Cogn. Syst. Res. **58**, 217–229 (2019)

Wang, W.Y.: Liar, liar pants on fire: a new benchmark dataset for fake news detection. arXiv preprint arXiv:1705.00648 (2017)

Wang, Y., et al.: EANN: event adversarial neural networks for multi-modal fake news detection. In: Proceedings of the 24th ACM SIGKDD International Conference on Knowledge Discovery & Data Mining, pp. 849–857, July 2018

Wang, Y., et al.: Weak supervision for fake news detection via reinforcement learning. Proc. AAAI Conf. Artif. Intell. **34**(1), 516–523 (2020)

Wu, L., Rao, Y.: Adaptive interaction fusion networks for fake news detection. arXiv preprint arXiv:2004.10009 (2020)

Wynne, H.E., Wint, Z.Z.: Content based fake news detection using N-Gram models. In: Proceedings of the 21st International Conference on Information Integration and Web-based Applications & Services, pp. 669–673, December 2019

Yang, S., Shu, K., Wang, S., Gu, R., Wu, F., Liu, H.: Unsupervised fake news detection on social media: a generative approach. In: Proceedings of the AAAI Conference on Artificial Intelligence, vol. 33, pp. 5644–5651, July 2019

Yazdi, K.M., Yazdi, A.M., Khodayi, S., Hou, J., Zhou, W., Saedy, S.: Improving fake news detection using K-means and support vector machine approaches. Int. J. Electr. Commun. Eng. **14**(2), 38–42 (2020)

Zervopoulos, A., Alvanou, A.G., Bezas, K., Papamichail, A., Maragoudakis, M., Kermanidis, K.: Hong Kong protests: using natural language processing for fake news detection on Twitter. In: Maglogiannis, I., Iliadis, L., Pimenidis, E. (eds.) AIAI 2020. IAICT, vol. 584, pp. 408–419. Springer, Cham (2020). https://doi.org/10.1007/978-3-030-49186-4_34

Zhang, J., Dong, B., FakeDetector, P.Y.: Effective fake news detection with deep diffusive neural network. In: 2020 IEEE 36th International Conference on Data Engineering (ICDE) (2020)

Zhang, J., Dong, B., Philip, S.Y.: Deep diffusive neural network based fake news detection from heterogeneous social networks. In: 2019 IEEE International Conference on Big Data (Big Data), pp. 1259–1266. IEEE, December 2029

Zhang, X., Ghorbani, A.A.: An overview of online fake news: characterization, detection, and discussion. Inf. Process. Manage. **57**(2), 102025 (2020)

Zhou, X., Zafarani, R.: Fake news: a survey of research, detection methods, and opportunities. arXiv preprint arXiv:1812.00315 (2020)

Zhou, X., Zafarani, R.: Network-based fake news detection: a pattern-driven approach. ACM SIGKDD Explor. Newsl. **21**(2), 48–60 (2019)

Zhou, X., Wu, J., Zafarani, R.: SAFE: Similarity-aware multi-modal fake news detection. arXiv preprint arXiv:2003.04981 (2020)

Freshness Quality Detection of Tomatoes Using Computer Vision

Sikha Das[1]([✉]), Prabir Mondal[2], Md Iqbal Quraishi[3], Samarjit Kar[4], and Arif Ahmed Sekh[5]

[1] Haldia Institute of Technology, Purba Medinipur, India
sikhad.123@gmail.com
[2] ArrayTree, West Bengal, India
[3] Kalyani Government Engineering College, Nadia, India
[4] NIT Durgapur, Durgapur, India
samarjit.kar@maths.nitdgp.ac.in
[5] XIM University, Bhubaneswar, India

Abstract. Grading and classification of fruits and vegetables has a major role in storage and supply chain. Manual grading is difficult and time-consuming. Therefore, this study employs computer vision (CV) and machine learning algorithms to detect the freshness quality of tomatoes during storage. The freshness quality is classified into 10 grades, where grade 1 is fresh and grade 10 denotes rotten. Image prepossessing and handcrafted feature extraction combined with a shallow artificial neural network (ANN) is employed for the task. Results from the proposed ANN outperform several state-of-the-art methods, including imaging-based deep neural networks. We construct a large volume dataset containing −70 days, day-by-day degradation for the task. We hope that the dataset will attract researchers and add a valuable contribution to the community.

Keywords: Vegetable freshness detection · Vegetable quality measurement · Vegetable grading

1 Introduction

Agriculture is one of the largest economic sectors, and it plays a major role in economic development [1]. Grading vegetables and fruits based on freshness is important in the store and sales cycle. Fresh items can be stored for a long time, whereas degrading items need to sell earlier. Similar grading methods are also useful to decide the value of the items. Manual grading of vegetables and fruits based on freshness is a Herculean task. While purchasing fresh fruits and vegetables from the supermarket, we need to check each item visually or picked up in our hands because there is no established vegetable freshness classification system. It is quite time-consuming and impossible when we go for large quantities to purchase. Recent development in computer hardware and artificial intelligence

© The Author(s), under exclusive license to Springer Nature Switzerland AG 2022
A. A. Sk et al. (Eds.): ISAI 2022, CCIS 1695, pp. 243–255, 2022.
https://doi.org/10.1007/978-3-031-22485-0_22

(AI) methods has opened up new possibilities in many sectors and agriculture is one of them [2]. Various computer vision (CV) techniques are applied for grading based on shape, size, and color. Although grading based on shape, texture, damage, etc. are popular and used in different fruits and vegetable grading [3], none of the methods has been applied for identifying the freshness of vegetables or fruits [4]. The main challenges of such a system are:

- Grading based on day-by-day degradation demands a systematic dataset that includes everyday pictures of the same vegetable/fruit for a long duration. Such a dataset is unavailable publicly.
- Day-by-day degradation is a slow process, and changes between two consecutive dates are nominal. State-of-the-art neural networks using only images as the input are not suitable (see the results section).

The objective of this research is to implement the vegetable classification system based on its quality and freshness. This system will show us how old the vegetable/fruit is and identify how long the vegetable/fruit will be healthy or unhealthy. People will be able to identify the freshness of fruits and vegetables very quickly using this application. Figure 1 demonstrates the proposed methods used for different grading of vegetables and fruits as an example using tomato based on the quality. In this paper, we have solved the above problems by constructing a suitable dataset of tomatoes and extracting some handcrafted features which are excellent for overcoming the challenge after feeding them to our proposed ANN model. We have captured 70 days of degradation images of a set of tomatoes on average. Next, we have designed an artificial neural network (ANN) with a set of handcrafted features. We consider color features, statistical features, combined with the geometry, and some basic features. The result shows that the proposed method can be a useful tool for grading the freshness of tomatoes.

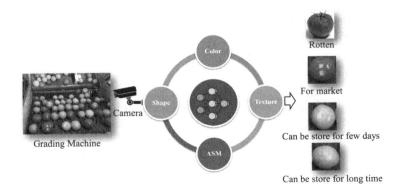

Fig. 1. Application of the proposed method. The method can be used to grade tomatoes based on the quality.

The paper has four sections. Section 1 elaborates the related work of this domain. In Sect. 2, the proposed method has been described. Section 3 discusses the resulting part of the proposed method along with a comparative study with others existing CNN architectures, and Sect. 4 concludes the paper.

1.1 Related Work

Automatic grading of fruits and vegetables became emerging and got attention for many potential applications [5]. The applications include disease classification [6], post-harvest grading [3], bruised fruit identification [4], etc.

Capizzi et al. [7] proposed a method for automatic classification based on co-occurrence matrix and neural networks of fruit defects. The authors considered various type defects of fresh orange surface including stab wounds, bruises, abrasion, sunburn, injury, hail damage, cracks, insect pest, etc. Numerous image based datasets of Orange are applied in the proposed classifier. Prince et al. [8] the proposed method starts for capturing fruit or vegetable images. Then, features are extracted from the sample images. Finally, the fruit or vegetable is classified by artificial neural network and identify the quality. Hossain et al. [9] proposed a deep learning model which is more efficient network for fruit classification in industrial applications. The authors have used two deep learning architectures, i.e. one have six CNNs layers a light model and another is Visual Geometry Group (VGG)- 16 deep learning model. Kaur et al. [10] proposed an ANN based quality evaluation process which detects the quality of fruits accurately. Bhargava et al. [5] evaluates the quality of fruits and vegetables by determining the color, texture, size, shape and defects. Image preprocessing, segmentation, feature extraction, and classification have been considered in their proposed methods. Maksimenko et al. [11] proposed a method which measured the ripeness and quality of watermelon using techniques of image processing and artificial neural network. The authors collected a dataset of watermelon and applied preprocessing, segmentation, and feature extraction before ANN was used. An ANN is used to find the ripeness accuracy. Shijin et al. [12] proposed two types of methods, i.e. gray level co-occurrence matrix and connected regions, for extracting texture and shape features. The texture features are extracted by gray level co-occurrence matrix, whereas connected region was used for shape feature extraction. Finally, these features were used in the classification algorithms. Liu et al. [13] proposed a computer vision technique for grading tomatoes based on color, size, and shape. The histograms of HSV color model and first-order FD method were used for extracting the features. Opeña et al. [14] proposed an automated tomato maturity grading system based on artificial neural network and the artificial bee colony (ABC) algorithm. Luna et al. [15] classifies tomato into different classes based on size. Machine learning (SVM, KNN, and ANN) and deep learning models (VGG16, InceptionV3, and ResNet50) have been implemented in their proposed methods. Semary et al. [16] proposed a classification method for infected/uninfected tomato based on its external surface. Gray level co-occurrence matrixes (GLCM) have been used along with color moments, wavelets, energy, and entropy in preprocessed images for feature extraction. The tomato images are classified into 2 classes using Min-Max and Z-Score normalization methods and Support vector machine (SVM) are used as a classifier. Wan et al. [17] proposed that the color features were recognized in concentric circles on the tomato surface with equal area, and made a maturity grading model based on color features and backpropagation neural network (BPNN).

2   Proposed Methods

The proposed method of this work for detecting the freshness of fruit consists of three steps. The method consists of (1) Preparing the image dataset, (2) preprocessing and feature extraction, and (3) Implementing the ANN for classification. The method is depicted in Fig. 2. In this paper, each module of the proposed method has been discussed in detail.

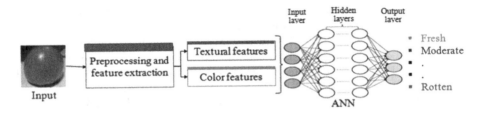

Fig. 2. The proposed system.

2.1   Preparing the Image Dataset

We have proposed a new domain of research where we measure a day-by-day degradation of the vegetable. Hence, the data collection is the most crucial part of the work, as it sets the tune for the whole work. In this paper, first, we have considered 12 number tomatoes for an experiment. We have collected it from the nearby market and placed the items at room temperature. 8 different images from 8 different angles of each sample have been captured daily using Sony DSC-W190 camera. Next, the dataset is divided into 10 classes according to the freshness. A random example of the dataset has been shown in Fig. 3.

2.2   Preprocessing and Feature Extraction

We note that the raw images are not suitable for the classification task (see the results section). We have preprocessed the collected images for handcrafting feature extraction. Different texture and color feature extraction methods were implemented for meeting the purpose. The steps involved in preprocessing and feature extraction are shown in Fig. 4. Next, the applied preprocessing steps have been discussed in detail.

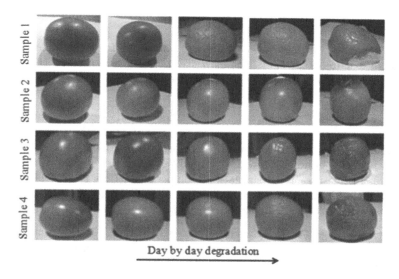

Fig. 3. Collection of original samples

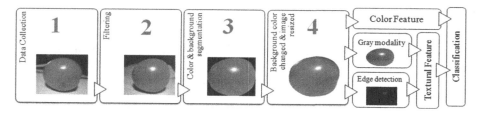

Fig. 4. Flow of the preprocessing and feature extraction mechanism in the proposed system.

Non-local Means Denoising: Non-local means [18–20] is an image denoising algorithm in image processing. The non-local means denoising follows mainly two steps, first, how to find similar pixels for the target pixel and how to average these pixels. In this technique, a pixel is replaced with an average of the neighborhood pixels. This technique takes a target pixel and makes a small window around that pixel. All window sizes (like 5×5 or 7×7) are the same in the input image. We search the similar pixel windows all over the images and calculate the average of all similar windows.

Color Segmentation: Segmentation is essential for preprocessing. The image segmentation is to divide an image into meaningful regions for different purposes. Before they process the object, the raw images are segmented using the grab cut algorithm.

2.3   Feature Extraction

After segmentation of images, the samples are obtained from the region of interest through feature extraction. The extracted features are used as the input to the proposed classifier. These features are discussed below:

Texture Features. In texture analysis technique, the textural features have been extracted from preprocessed images by using the Gray level co-occurrence matrix [12,21]. The matrix elements are normalized for making the element simple and easy to handle. From the normalized gray level co-occurrence matrix the features like Contrast, Dissimilarity, Homogeneity, Energy, Correlation, and Angular Second Moment have been extracted and are fed as input to an Artificial Neural Network (ANN). The extracted features are defined as follows:

Contrast: Contrast of an image is the difference in color that makes a difference between objects or regions. Here in the gray-level co-occurrence matrix of image to measure the local intensity variations the contrast is used.

Dissimilarity: The dissimilarity is the numerical measurement of the degree between two objects which are different, or we can say dissimilarity is the pixel to pixel distance in the region.

Homogeneity: The homogeneity comes from homogeneous functions which have the same kind of components. In this experiment, the closeness of the distribution of elements to the gray level co-occurrence matrix diagonal in the gray level co-occurrence matrix of the entire image is measures by a value that is homogeneity.

Correlation: Correlation means a relationship or connection between two variables. In other words, we can say that the correlation measures how two variables move in relation to each other in the entire image. In GLCM, its range is [1,–1], where 1 refers to the positive correlation which increases the two values in the same direction and –1 refers to the negative correlation which increases one value and decreases the other value in different directions of the input image.

Angular Second Moment (ASM): ASM is the sum of squares of entries in the gray level co-occurrence matrix. ASM measures the image homogeneity. When the pixels of input images are very similar or when the entire image has excellent homogeneity, the ASM value is large.

Energy: Energy measures homogeneity of an image. It is derived from the Angular Second Moment (ASM). It is the square root of the Angular Second Moment.

Entropy: Entropy measures the loss of information of the input image or the measurement of randomness of images. To characterize the texture of the input image, entropy is used.

Mean of Image: Here, the mean [22] of an image is calculated by taking the sum of the pixel intensities of an image and dividing it by the number of pixel intensities.

Standard Deviation of Image: Standard deviation [23] is used for showing how measurements for a group of numbers are spread out from the average value of the entire image. If the numbers are more distributed from the average value that is called High standard deviation and if the numbers are close to the average value that is called Low standard deviation.

Variance of Image: The summation of the squared differences of every item in the distribution from the mean (μ) and obtained result is divided by the total number of items in the distribution (N) is defined as variance (σ^2) of the image.

Median and Mode: The middle value of set pixels, arranged in ascending or descending order of pixel intensity values, is called median [22]. In this paper, we have input images of 87,500 numbers of pixels. So here N = 87,500. The mode [22] in our experiment is the intensity value of the pixel of an input image occurring with the largest frequency.

Connected Components of an Image: In connected components [24] of an image, a set of pixels are clustered with the same value or the same type of pixels which are connected to each other. In 2D images, the same type of pixel value is connected to each other by 4-pixel, or 8-pixel connectivity. Pixels that are connected one with another by any of their four faces would group by 4-pixel connectivity, whereas pixels that are connected with any face or corner would group by 8-pixels.

Structural Similarity of Image: A method is defined as Structural similarity (SSIM) which measures the similarity between two images. The SSIM can be considered a quality measure of the images. In our paper, we have selected one of the images which is compared to the rest of the images for checking the changes in the structure day-by-day in our dataset.

Edge Length (in pixel) of Image: In this work, the canny edge detection algorithm has been used to detect the edge in images. Next, we have converted the images into binary digital images and counted the number of white pixel intensity values in the binary image. These numbers of white pixel intensities are considered as a feature of the input images. Here, we have used 36 such features for the classification task.

Color Features. To extract color feature, RGB color model is used. First, the image is segregated in R, G, and B channels. The histogram of the pixel intensity in each channel is computed.

Table 1. Image extracted features and description

Features name	Number of features	details
Gray level co-occurrence matrix	28	Consist of the contrast, homogeneity, energy, correlation, dissimilarity, Angular Second Moment (ASM) and Entropy
Mean and standard deviation	2	Pixel-level mean and standard deviation of images
Variance, Median, and Mode	3	Pixel-level variance, median, and mode of images
Connected components	1	Number of connected components in the segmented images
Number of pixel intensity	1	Number of white pixel intensity in edge extracted image
Structural similarity	1	Structural similarity was calculated between two images
Color	1	RGB values

2.4 Classification and Validation

The final stage of the proposed method is to classify the quality of the tomatoes. We have considered 10 such classes, where class 1 is fresh and class 10 denotes fully rotten. First, the above-mentioned features are extracted from the images. Next, an artificial neural network (ANN) [10, 11] is used to classify.

3 Results and Discussion

3.1 Dataset

In this work, we have focused only on tomatoes' images while preparing the dataset. The tomato images were collected with a fixed resolution of 360×250 as JPG format. First, a set of tomatoes are stored at room temperature. We collected 12 numbers of tomatoes. Every day, eight different images from eight different orientations have been captured for a single tomato. The images have been captured using Sony DSC-W190 camera. The data are captured until the tomatoes get fully rotten (70 days). We collected 6450 numbers of such images in total. Finally, the dataset is grouped into 10 classes according to the capture date. The dataset is randomly divided into (60% and 40%), (70% and 30%), and (80% and 20%) for training and testing, respectively.

3.2 Experimental Setup

Proposed Artificial Neural Network and its Pearameteres: Artificial neural network is used in our proposed architecture where the extracted features have been fed. The architecture consists of 6 fully connected layers, among them one input layer, four hidden layers, and one output layer. Relu has been used in the input layer and all hidden layers as activation function, and we have used Softmax as activation function in the output layer of our proposed ANN architecture. The L2 regularization has been considered for keeping the parameters regular or normal in all fully connected layers of the network. Initialize is a method that has been used to initialize random values of the weights of the layers. During compiling the model, we have used categorical cross entropy for loss function and an optimizer has also been applied to change the attributes such as weights, learning rate to reduce the losses of ANN for getting accurate results. In the training phase, the model takes 10 as batch size. The network consists of 63,5946 trainable parameters. For determining the optimal structure of the neural network, four hidden layer network structures have been used with a fixed output layer having ten neurons.

3.3   Baseline Comparison

We have evaluated the proposed method using state-of-the-art classification methods i.e. Support Vector Machines (SVM) [25], Random Forest [26], and K-Nearest Neighbors (KNN) [27]. We have also evaluated the proposed dataset by state-of-the-art convolutional neural networks (CNN) of three different architectures using the color image as input. We have used different variations of CNN for evaluation. In state-of-the-art CNN, all the layers in the models except output layer used ReLU for activation which is nonlinear function and softmax function is used in output layer. Fixed-sized kernels of 3×3 in size have been used and a dropout layer with the probability of 30%. The first architecture is a shallow neural network [28,29] consisting of 10 convolution layers, 3 fully connected layers along with a 2×2 size max pooling kernel. The Second architecture is a dual CNN. It is also a shallow CNN [30] containing 8 convolution layers, 3 fully connected layers, and a 2×2 size max pooling kernel for color input images. In this architecture has two inputs, i.e., one input is RGB and another is segmented. In the same architecture, a gray image is also passed where a 2×2 size average pooling kernel is considered instead of max pooling. Third, architecture [31] is an encoder-decoder framework consisting of 10 convolution layers for the encoder, 6 convolution layers for the decoder, and 3 fully connected layers. The decoder is one type of upsampling network which is mapped to the low-resolution encoder's features. We have also applied the state-of-the-art ResNet50 [32], VGG16 [33], MobileNets [34] on our proposed dataset. The classification results are summarized in Table 2.

Table 2. Performance of the different methods

Method	Feature	Accuracy (%)
ResNet50 [32]	Image	55.59
VGG16 [33]	Image	63.52
Shallow CNN [9]	Image	63.11
Dual CNN [30]	Image	69.28
Encoder-Decoder [31]	Image	59.20
MobileNets [34]	Image	64.47
SVM [25]	Proposed feature	70.21
Random forest [26]	Proposed feature	81.70
KNN [27]	Proposed feature	78.11
Proposed	Proposed feature	83.13

3.4 Discussion of the Results

We have compared the results of some classical machine learning algorithms such as SVM, random forest, and KNN after applying them on our dataset. We have used 37 hand-crafted features for classification. We have also benchmarked the dataset using state-of-the-art shallow CNN [28], dual CNN [30], ResNet50 [32], VGG16 [33], MobileNets [34] and encoder-decoder framework [31]. In this study, we have used the color and gray scale images as the input. It is observed that in our objective, inputting our extracted features to our proposed ANN architecture performs better than passing images directly to CNNs. Figure 5 shows the loss and accuracy over epochs of ANN architecture.

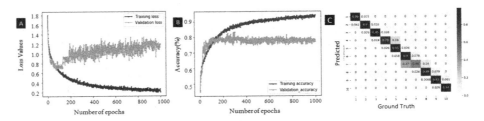

Fig. 5. Performance of ANN over epochs: (a) Compare between training loss and validation loss, (b) Compare between training accuracy and validation accuracy. (c) Confusion matrix for the 10 class classification using proposed ANN.

Performance Evaluation: Different types of metrics are used for evaluating a model's predictive performance. The predictions can be categorized into different types, i.e., True Positive (TP), False Positive (FP), False Negative (FN), and True Negative (TN). However, True Negative (TN) is not considered for multiclass classification problems. We have also extensively analyzed the testing result evaluation of our proposed architecture in phrases of class wise accuracy, precision, recall, and f1 scores based on True positive, false positive, false negative. The confusion matrix for the above-mentioned 10 class problems using proposed ANN is shown in Fig. 5(c).

4   Conclusion

This paper presents a novel method for grading tomatoes according to the freshness. Grading fruits and vegetables based on the quality is common. The quality depends on the visual features such as size, shape, color, etc. Grading fruits and vegetables according to the freshness is getting less attention by the researchers. Hence, we have not found a suitable dataset for the task. Here, we have proposed a new dataset for the task and opened up new challenges to the computer vision community. We assume that tomatoes will degrade at room temperature ($35°C$) and day by day the degradation will increase. Based on the assumption, we have collected a large volume tomato dataset for continuous -70 days. We have proposed to use ANN combined with handcrafted features. The method used to classify the tomatoes into 10 classes, where Class 1 is the most fresh and Class 10 is rotten. The proposed method outperforms state-of-the-art image-based neural networks. There are many applications of such classifiers. The method can be used in agricultural decision-making in fruits and vegetable supply chains. Where, fruits and vegetables can be sorted according to their freshness and can be used intelligently for selling or storing.

There are many avenues of the method. First, we will extend the methods to different vegetables and fruits. Next, we will investigate how to improve image-based neural networks for the task.

References

1. Antle, J.M., Ray, S.: Sustainable Agricultural Development. PSAEFP, Springer, Cham (2020). https://doi.org/10.1007/978-3-030-34599-0
2. Longsheng, F., Gao, F., Jingzhu, W., Li, R., Karkee, M., Zhang, Q.: Application of consumer rgb-d cameras for fruit detection and localization in field: a critical review. Comput. Electron. Agricul. **177**, 105687 (2020)
3. Ucat, R.C., Cruz, R.C.D.: Postharvest grading classification of cavendish banana using deep learning and tensorflow. In: 2019 International Symposium on Multimedia and Communication Technology (ISMAC), pp. 1–6. IEEE (2019)
4. Zilong, H., Tang, J., Zhang, P., Jiang, J.: Deep learning for the identification of bruised apples by fusing 3D deep features for apple grading systems. Mech. Syst. Sign. Process. **145**, 106922 (2020)
5. Bhargava, A., Bansal, A.: Fruits and vegetables quality evaluation using computer vision: a review. J. King Saud Univ.-Comput. Inf. Sci. **33**(3), 243–257 (2018)
6. Saha, R., Neware, S.: Orange fruit disease classification using deep learning approach. Int. J.,**9**(2) (2020)

7. Capizzi, G., Sciuto, G.L., Napoli, C., Tramontana, E., Wozniak, M.: Automatic classification of fruit defects based on co-occurrence matrix and neural networks. In: 2015 Federated Conference on Computer Science and Information Systems (FedCSIS), pp. 861–867. IEEE (2015)

8. Prince, R., et al.: Identification of quality index of fruit/vegetable using image processing. Int. J. Adv. Res. Ideas. Inno. Tech. **4**, 1–6 (2018)

9. Hossain, M.S., Al-Hammadi, M., Muhammad, G.: Automatic fruit classification using deep learning for industrial applications. IEEE Trans. Ind. Inform. **15**(2), 1027–1034 (2018)

10. Kaur, M., Sharma, R.: Quality detection of fruits by using ANN technique. IOSR J. Electron. Commun. Eng. Ver. II **10**(4), 2278–2834 (2015)

11. Maksimenko, V.A., et al.: Artificial neural network classification of motor-related EEG: an increase in classification accuracy by reducing signal complexity. Complexity (2018)

12. Shijin Kumar, P.S., Dharun, V.S.: Extraction of texture features using GLCM and shape features using connected regions. Int. J. Eng. Technol. **8**(6), 2926–2230 (2016)

13. Liu, L., Li, Z., Lan, Y., Shi, Y., Cui, Y.: Design of a tomato classifier based on machine vision. PloS one **14**(7), e0219803 (2019)

14. Opeña, H.J.G., Yusiong, J.P.T.: Automated tomato maturity grading using ABC-trained artificial neural networks. Malays. J. Comput. Sci. **30**(1), 12–26 (2017)

15. de Luna, R.G., Dadios, E.P., Bandala, A.A., Vicerra, R.R.P.: Size classification of tomato fruit using thresholding, machine learning, and deep learning techniques. AGRIVITA J. Agri. Sci. **41**(3) (2019)

16. Semary, N.A., Tharwat, A., Elhariri, E., Hassanien, A.E.: Fruit-based tomato grading system using features fusion and support vector machine. In: Filev, D., et al. Intelligent Systems 2014. Advances in Intelligent Systems and Computing, vol. 323, pp. 401–410. Springer, Cham (2015)

17. Wan, P., Toudeshki, A., Tan, H., Ehsani, R.: A methodology for fresh tomato maturity detection using computer vision. Comput. Electr. Agri. **146**, 43–50 (2018)

18. Buades, A., Coll, B., Morel, J.-M.: Non-local means denoising. Image Process. Line **1**, 208–212 (2011)

19. Buades, A., Coll, B., Morel, J.M.: A non-local algorithm for image denoising. In: 2005 IEEE Computer Society Conference on Computer Vision and Pattern Recognition (CVPR'05), vol. 2, pp. 60–65. IEEE (2005)

20. Baozhong, L., Jianbin, L.: Overview of image noise reduction based on non-local mean algorithm. In: MATEC Web of Conferences, vol 232, p. 03029. EDP Sciences (2018)

21. Haralick, R.M., Shanmugam, K., Dinstein, H.: Textural features for image classification. IEEE Trans. Syst. Man Cybern. **6**, 610–621 (1973)

22. Griffin, L.D.: Mean, median and mode filtering of images. In: Proc. R. Soc. London Ser. Math. Phys. Eng. Sci. **456**(2004), 2995–3004 (2000)

23. Kumar, V., Gupta, P.: Importance of statistical measures in digital image processing. Int. J. Emerg. Technol. Adv. Eng. **2**(8), 56–62 (2012)

24. He, L., Ren, X., Gao, Q., Zhao, X., Yao, B., Chao, Y.: The connected-component labeling problem: a review of state-of-the-art algorithms. Pattern Recogn. **70**, 25–43 (2017)

25. Chao, C.F., Horng, M.H.: The construction of support vector machine classifier using the firefly algorithm. Comput. Intell. Neurosci. (2015)

26. Denil, M., Matheson, D., De Freitas, N.: Narrowing the gap: random forests in theory and in practice. In: International Conference on Machine Learning, pp. 665–673 (2014)
27. Indriani, O.R., Kusuma, E.J., Sari, C.A., Rachmawanto, E.H., et al.: Tomatoes classification using k-nn based on GLCM and HSV color space. In: 2017 international conference on innovative and creative information technology (ICITech), pp. 1–6. IEEE (2017)
28. Mureşan, H., Oltean, M.: Fruit recognition from images using deep learning. Acta Universitatis Sapientiae, Informatica **10**(1), 26–42 (2018)
29. Nishi, T., Kurogi, S., Matsuo, K.: Grading fruits and vegetables using RGB-d images and convolutional neural network. In: 2017 IEEE Symposium Series on Computational Intelligence (SSCI), pp. 1–6. IEEE (2017)
30. Zeng, G.: Fruit and vegetables classification system using image saliency and convolutional neural network. In 2017 IEEE 3rd Information Technology and Mechatronics Engineering Conference (ITOEC), pp. 613–617. IEEE (2017)
31. Yasrab, R.: Ecru: an encoder-decoder based convolution neural network (cnn) for road-scene understanding. J. Imaging **4**(10), 116 (2018)
32. He, K., Zhang, X., Ren, S., Sun, J.: Deep residual learning for image recognition. In: Proceedings of the IEEE Conference on Computer Vision and Pattern Recognition, pp. 770–778 (2016)
33. Simonyan, K., Zisserman, A.: Very deep convolutional networks for large-scale image recognition. arXiv preprint arXiv:1409.1556 (2014)
34. Howard, A.G., et al.: Mobilenets: Efficient convolutional neural networks for mobile vision applications. arXiv preprint arXiv:1704.04861 (2017)

Facial Gesture Recognition Based Real Time Gaming for Physically Impairment

Anjali Agarwal and Ajanta Das[(✉)]

Amity Institute of Information Technology, Amity University, Kolkata 700135, India
cse.dr.ajantadas@gmail.com

Abstract. Technology has refined online gaming by introducing new engagement modes that are being created at a rapid pace in today's society. Eye blinking and facial movement is a basic nonverbal interaction that is increasingly evolving in the next generation. This eye-gazing technology and facial feature movement create a communication bridge for individuals with impairments. With the aid of a highly efficient library, OpenCV intended to handle Computer Vision issues and PyAutoGUI, which enables the Python scripts to manage the mouse and keyboard to automate interactions with other programs, developers can automate the game by blinking the eyes and other facial gestures.

This paper is written to illustrate a Python alternative to commercial systems like Tobii and Kinect, so that the code may be used in mobile devices and apps with limited CPU power. Our research focuses on the virtual keyboard, which not only triggers keys through facial gestures but may also give help to those who are physically impaired. To do this, we have used the built-in camera on our computer/laptop, which identifies the face and features of the face. This makes detecting the face far more straightforward than before. A mouse click on the virtual interface can be replaced by an eye blink or lip movement. The ultimate goal is to enable a computer-human connection based solely on the movement of facial features, allowing physically handicapped persons to communicate with the computer and play games easily using a facial based interface.

Keywords: Computer vision · Dlib · Eye aspect ratio · Facial landmarks · OpenCV · PyAutoGUI · Threshold

1 Introduction

Games are rapidly being used to entertain the general audience but also to educate people in several areas. Instead of pushing keys on a keyboard or using a mouse, gestures are utilized as instructions in vision-based interfaces for video games. Gesture recognition, an emerging concept of Human Computer Interaction [1] is now used in a wide range of applications, from simple home automation to navigation and gaming. Unintentional motions and continuous gestures must be enabled in these interfaces to give the user a more natural experience.

The development in this discipline has the potential to make the lives of handicapped persons with neuromotor disorders easier. This sort of invention is a blessing for those

© The Author(s), under exclusive license to Springer Nature Switzerland AG 2022
A. A. Sk et al. (Eds.): ISAI 2022, CCIS 1695, pp. 256–264, 2022.
https://doi.org/10.1007/978-3-031-22485-0_23

who suffer from neuromotor problems. To utilize this technology, all that is required is good eye and vision control. Adults and children alike can utilize it. We can increase the possibilities for controlling this game by leveraging the application's interaction elements, called Interacts, and employing haar cascade through OpenCV [2]. As a result, in addition to a keyboard and mouse, a traditional video camera may be used to operate the game.

A camera is installed on the display to watch the user's face as they are positioned in front of it. This equipment may be placed in front of a wheelchair user so that when the user wants to control the game, all they have to do is blink and the actions will be triggered automatically. The user must blink to begin, and they must double blink to end. We've recorded the lip movement in the same way that we've captured the eye motions to go right and left. To shift to the right, the user must close his or her lips; to move to the left, the user must open his or her mouth. It might be exhausting, but capturing and monitoring their eye and lip movement can help them focus on the game rather than their physical limitations. The actions triggered can be measured using the time frame or frame rate supplied by the software, in which the key is pushed after a certain number of frames, or else it isn't regarded blink of the eye or lip movement. This is a communication system that is controlled by vision and lip movement. People who are unable to move their hands or speak may be able to overcome this.

The novelty of this paper is to access a car racing game that is an endless racing game where the user may utilize their facial motions such as eyes and lips to play the game with ease to accomplish our proposed algorithm and idea. The game may be easily played without a keyboard or mouse by utilizing a vision-based virtual interface using the OpenCV and dlib libraries to trigger facial movement. Existing related research study is presented in Sect. 2. Section 3 presents proposed framework for eye and lip movement detection followed by the detailed methodology of the proposed framework in Sect. 4. Section 5 presents experimental results and discussion. The paper concludes in Sect. 6.

2 Related Work

Based on the initial centroid analysis methodology, this study [3] suggested a novel method for estimating eye location and orientation. Tracking eye location in high and low occlusion conditions was used to validate the suggested technique. They describe an approach for reliably detecting eye blinking in a real-time context in this study. On the OpenCV platform, which is open source and created by Intel they utilized the linked component approach and the centroid method to track and blinking of eyes.

A real-time prototype computer vision system for measuring driver attentiveness is described in this paper [4]. The technology was put to the test in a simulated setting with people of various ethnic origins. The major component is to test driver vigilance using computer vision algorithms in real-time through a video camera.

In this paper [5] is based on a hardware device that uses an active IR illuminator to capture pictures of a driver in real time, as well as a software application that monitors specific visual characteristics that describe a driver's level of attentiveness. To infer the driver's inattentiveness, these characteristics are integrated using a fuzzy classifier. Utilizing many visual characteristics and fusing them together produces a more robust and accurate inattention characterization than using only one. Different sequences captured in night and day driving situations were used to evaluate the technology.

In this paper [6], a vision system for monitoring a driver's face characteristics is provided. To begin, the input video sequence is searched for the driver's face. It's then followed throughout the next few photos. Face tracking continues to recognize facial characteristics such as eyes, mouth, and head. The feature detection and tracking are done in parallel to increase the precision. To show the performance of the proposed system, a variety of video sequences with drivers of all ages and genders were used in varied lighting and road conditions.

In this paper [7] offers a novel detection technique in this work that incorporates many of the fundamental features of REMs while requiring minimum parameter changes. A single parameter may be utilized to regulate the REM detection sensitivity and specificity tradeoff in the suggested approach. The technique is being developed using manually rated training data. The method's performance is compared to hand scoring of individual REM episodes, and validation findings are shown using a different data set.

Until far, these applications have only been useful for drivers monitoring their dizziness, but with our novel technique, it will be useful for physically challenged persons as well, who will be able to interact with the computer purely by facial motions.

3   Proposed Framework

The proposed framework uses the HOG and SVM Classifier to recognize face gestures in real time via web cam as input, and then processes it to activate a keyboard functionality using facial motions, allowing physical challenged persons to communicate with computers without using their hands or other ways.

When the user is playing games, the camera records images in real time, and these frames of the webcam constitute the image input sequence. This system recognizes the face followed by the eye and the lips using a Haar based Histogram of Oriented Gradients (HOG) and a linear SVM classifier. Following that is the eye blink, which requires the user to blink to begin and double blink to stop. We captured the lip movement in the same way that we captured the right and left eye movements. The user must shut his or her lips to move to the right, and open his or her mouth to go to the left.

In general, the system is set to propose a protocol when the eye aspect ratio and lip ratio are said to be greater than their respective thresholds, at which point the keys are triggered using the PyAutoGUI library; otherwise, if the ratio is less than the threshold, there is no movement and no further computation is done. This is entirely dependent on the ratio in which the movement is performed and whether or not it is a blink or a movement of the lips. The operation is so easy that even physically challenged individuals can understand it, and the key feature is the blink detection as well as the lip and mouth opening and shutting. The entire proposed architecture is depicted in diagram form in Fig. 1.

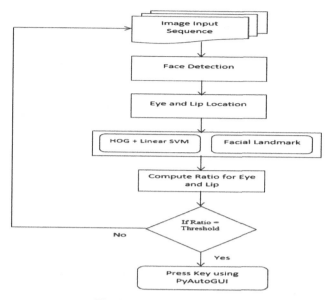

Fig. 1. Proposed architecture

4   Methodology

4.1   Face Detection

It's a system that can recognize human faces in any picture or video. OpenCV and dlib are commonly used to recognize faces using a variety of techniques. The detector consists of a linear classifier and a standard Histogram of Oriented Gradients (HOG) feature [9]. Inside dlib, a facial landmarks detector is implemented to identify face characteristics such as eyes, ears, and nose.

4.2   Facial Landmark Extraction

Face landmark detection is a subset of the shape prediction issue [10]. A shape predictor attempts to pinpoint key points of interest along a shape given an input picture (and typically an ROI, Region of Interest that identifies the item of interest).

Our objective is to use shape prediction algorithms to discover key facial features on the face. As a result, detecting face landmarks is a two-step process:

Step 1: Identify the face on the camera.

Step 2: On the face ROI, find the major facial structures.

The dlib library's pre-trained facial landmark detector is used to estimate the position of 68 (x, y)-coordinates that correspond to facial structures. These annotations are from the 68-point iBUG 300-W dataset, which was used to train the dlib face landmark predictor. The 68 coordinates' indices can be seen in Fig. 2 beneath.

Fig. 2. 68 Facial Landmarks Co-ordinates.

4.3 Eye and Lip Detection

Following the detection of the face, the eye and lip area is identified using facial landmark characteristics. We can identify 68 landmarks on the face using the facial landmarks dataset [10]. An index is allocated to each landmark. The target area of the face is identified using these indices. It is then processed to identify eye blinks and lip movement once the eye area has been extracted. The eye and lip index can be extracted from the 68 facial landmarks coordinates depicted in Fig. 2 above.

For two eyes index –
Left eye: (37, 38, 39, 40, 41, 42), *Right eye:* (43, 44, 45, 46, 47, 48)
For both lip index - *Upper Lip*: (63), *Lower Lip*: (67)

4.4 Eye Aspect Ratio

Eye aspect ratio (E.A.R) is a single scalar number that indicates whether or not the eye is closed. The eye aspect ratio function is used to determine the distance between vertically aligned eye landmarks and horizontally aligned eye landmarks [11]. Now, for each video frame, we must compute the Euclidean distance between the facial landmarks points in order to calculate the eye aspect ratio. As a result, when the eye is open, the value obtained for the eye aspect ratio is approximately constant. The value will then rapidly fall until it reaches zero in the event of an eye blink. When the eye is closed, the eye aspect ratio reaches a near-constant value that is significantly less than when the eye is open. As a result, the dip in the aspect ratio shows that the eyes are blinking.

$$E.A.R = \frac{||p2 - p6|| + ||p3 - p5||}{2||p1 - p4||}$$

where p1, p2, p3, p4, p5, and p6 are the 2D landmark locations, depicted in Fig. 3 below. Because there are only two sets of vertical points, the numerator of this equation estimates the distance between vertical eye landmarks, while the denominator represents horizontal eye landmarks, correctly weighting the denominator [12].

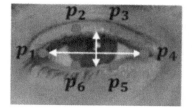
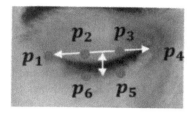

Fig. 3. Eye landmark co-ordinates.

4.5 Eye Blink and Lip Movement Monitoring

With the assistance of two lines, we can identify blinks in the exact eye area. One is drawn horizontally, while the other is drawn vertically, forming a divide between the eyes. Blinking is the temporary closure of the eyes along with the movement of the eyelids which is a quick natural process. We need to figure out what occurs when one of the eyes blinks. When the eyeball is not visible or the eyelid is closed, we might assume that the eye is closed/blinked. If these motions last for (roughly 0.3 s to 0.4 s), we may infer they are blinks; if they last longer, we can believe they are closed eyelids. Both vertical and horizontal lines are nearly similar with an open eye, but in a closed eye, the vertical line becomes much smaller or disappears entirely. A ratio is determined with regard to the vertical line, using the horizontal line as a point of reference. We'll need to specify a threshold number here, and if the ratio is larger than that, we'll presume the eye is closed; otherwise, we'll assume it's open. The threshold value is computed by the Eye Aspect Ratio (E.A.R).

Similarly, we can identify the lip area as well. Here, we have just considered the vertical line. To activate the left and right keys, the distance between the upper and lower lip indexes must be larger than the threshold. As shown in Fig. 4 below, the threshold is equal to the absolute value of upper lip index value minus lower lip index value.

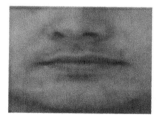
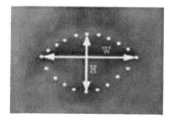

Fig. 4. Lip landmark co-ordinates.

4.6 Access Keyboard

PyAutoGUI is a package that lets you control the mouse and keyboard to do a variety of tasks. It's a Python GUI automation module for humans that works across platforms. To press the respective keys in the keyboard, call the press() function and pass it a string from the PyAutoGUI [13]. The keyDown(), keyUp(), left(), and right() methods, which simulate pressing and then releasing a key, are wrapped in the press() function. When the user must shut his or her lips then using PyAutoGUI library, we are calling the right() method to move to the right, similarly left() method while opening the mouth to go to the left. The Up Key is always triggered for the car racing game for the car to move forward.

5   Experimental Results and Discussions

The author has tested the system through its trials in real-time and analyzed the outcomes. Our computer vision-aided algorithm was put to the test in a real-life situation, and the results were recorded. Our system is completely efficient and user-friendly. We utilized a low-cost, lightweight Python alternative to commercial systems so that the code could be run on any device and apps with limited computational resources. Though eye blinks and lip movement are more precise in triggering the keys on the keyboard, natural blink can sometimes be detected instead of voluntary blink. These drawbacks can be mitigated by utilizing a high-resolution camera.

5.1   Eye and Lip Movement Detection

Within seconds of starting the application, the camera begins capturing your facial movements, mostly eye blink and lip movement, and begins providing a live feed to the application through OpenCV, a computer vision library. The face is identified using the Haar based Histogram of Oriented Gradients (HOG) and a linear SVM classifier using the video as the source. Following the detection of the face, the eye area is identified using dlib library 68 facial landmarks feature detector. Using the PyAutoGUI library, we were able to control the mouse and keyboard keys to shift left and right, as well as the start and stop keys.

5.2   Facial Movement Monitoring

The main purpose of the system is to play the games through facial movement. After the eye region is recognized, we apply the threshold to the eyeball to capture more accurately. To differentiate the normal and the voluntary eye blinks we use a variable called eye aspect ratio. If the observed ratio is greater than the threshold for a frame then the respective key is triggered. We set the eye threshold to 0.26 for our system but it may vary depending on the quality of the webcam and the environment it works. Similarly, for lip movement, if the difference between the upper coordinates of the lip and lower coordinates of lip is greater than the threshold then the key is triggered respectively. We have applied the lip threshold of 0.30 for our system to record whether the mouse is closed to press the right key or open for the left key.

6 Limitations

1. *Adequate Lighting* - The framework is occasionally unsuited to recognize the eyeballs due to bad lighting situations. As a result, it produces an incorrect outcome that must be controlled. To avoid bad illumination situations, 56 circumstance infrared setting enlightenments should be utilized continuously.
2. *Optimum Range* - When the distance between the face and the webcam isn't quite right, problems arise. The framework is unsuited to perceive the face from the image when the face is excessively close to the camera (less than 25 cm). When the face is more than 80cm away from the camera, the setting light is not there to properly edify the face. As a result, eyes are unrelated to high precision, resulting in a loss in recognizable evidence of sluggishness.
3. *Face Orientation* - The face is generally perceived when it is slanted to a particular degree, but beyond that, the framework is unable to recognize the face. When the face isn't recognized, the eyes aren't recognized either. If the webcam recognizes more than one face, the framework will produce an erroneous result.
4. *Spectacles* - The system may not identify eyes if the user is wearing spectacles, which is the most significant drawback of these systems. This issue has yet to be resolved, and it is a test for nearly all eye detection systems now in use.

7 Conclusion

We have discussed the functionality and operation of the system extensively in this paper using OpenCV, PyAutoGUI and, dlib library. This method allows persons with neuro-motor disorders to enjoy games and accomplish other activities with ease, especially since it may be utilized with relatively inexpensive equipment. Gaming is a method for everyone to unwind from time to time, but when you have a disability, it takes on a whole new meaning. It might be one of the factors that give you a sensation of power and control. They are no longer hindered by their physical limitations. This computer vision-aided technology does not require a person to operate and requires very little maintenance thus it is cost and time-efficient.

This algorithm aids disable people in communicating with the system effectively. The suggested system, a computer or laptop, and a webcam sum up the entire concept. The eye blink frame rate is used to distinguish between voluntary and natural eye blinks. The system may be utilized in a variety of settings, including hospitals, residences, non-profit organizations, and special schools for the disabled. This technology opens up new possibilities in the lives of disabled individuals who can move their eyes and faces. The goal of this technology is to use a facial gesture algorithm to help disabled persons convey their thoughts. This device will undoubtedly give a remedy for those who are severely paralyzed and are suffering from neuromotor disorder. Experiments related to the proposed system would be utilized immensely for physical impairment in future.

References

1. Bradski, G., Kaehler, A.: Learning OpenCV Computer Vision with the OpenCV Library, O'Reilly (2008)

2. Laganiere, R.: OpenCV 2 Computer visionApplication Programming Cookbook. PACKT-publication (2011)
3. Pimplaskar, D., Nagmode, M.S., Borkar, A.: Real time eye blinking detection and tracking using opencv. Technology **13**(14), 15 (2015)
4. Ji, Q., Yang, X.: Real-time eye, gaze, and face pose tracking for monitoring driver vigilance. J. Real-Time Imaging **8**(5), 357377 (2002). ISSN: 10772014. https://doi.org/10.1006/rtim.2002.0279
5. Bergasa, L.M., Nuevo, J., Sotelo, M.A., Barea, R., Lopez, M.E.: Real-time system for monitoring driver vigilance. Intelligent Transportation Systems, IEEE Transactions on March **7**(1), pp. 63–77 (2006). ISSN: 1524–9050
6. Wang, M., Chou, H.P., Hsu, C.F., Chen, S.W., Fuh, C.S.: Extracting driver's facial features during driving. In: 2011 14th International IEEE Conference on Intelligent Transportation Systems Washington, DC, USA. October 5–7 (2011)
7. Agarwal, R., Takeuchi, T., Laroche, S., Gotman, J.: Detection of rapid-eye movement in sleep studies. IEEE Trans. on Biomedical Eng. **52**(8), 1390–1396 (2005)
8. Adrian Rosebrock, OpenCV Haar Cascades (2021). https://www.pyimagesearch.com/2021/04/12/opencv-haar-cascades/
9. Adrian Rosebrock, Facial landmarks with dlib, OpenCV, and Python (2021). https://www.pyimagesearch.com/2017/04/03/facial-landmarks-dlib-opencv-python/
10. Vignesh, C.P., Sriram, R.: Eye blink controlled virtual interface using opencv and dlib. European J. Molecular & Clinical Med. **7**(8), 2119–2126 (2020)
11. Soukupova, T., Cech, J.: Eye blink detection using facial landmarks. In: 21st computer vision winter workshop, Rimske Toplice, Slovenia (2016)
12. AlSweigart, PyAutoGUI. https://pypi.org/project/PyAutoGUI/

Deep Learning Approaches for Analysis and Detection of Tomato Leaf Diseases

Shaon Bandyopadhyay[1]([✉]), Abhijit Sarkar[2], Abhirup paria[2], and Biswajit Jana[2]

[1] St.Thomas College of Engineering and Technology, Kolkata, India
shaon.bandyopadhyay@gmail.com
[2] Haldia Institute of Technology, Haldia, India

Abstract. Recent advances in computer vision, facilitated by deep learning, have opened the way for detecting plants' leaves by capturing photos with a camera and utilising them as a foundation for distinguishing several plant types. This study provided a new-fangled method for identifying various plant category. The system was developed to detect and identify a variety of Tomato leaf diseases. Deep Learning models were trained in the approach for detecting Tomato leaf diseases using 2598 photographs from PlantVillage dataset (PVD). Our trained model achieved an accuracy level of 96.37% which can be considered to be competent.

Keywords: InceptionV3 · CNN · Transfer learning · Leaf detection

1 Introduction

Diagnosis of plant diseases is critical for effective crop production. Several plant diseases including black rot, black measles adversely affects the quality as well as growth of agronomy trade. To curtail the leaf diseases influence on agriculture field, farmers typically employ costly techniques including the usage of pesticides. Chemical means are detrimental in plants environs. Additionally, this strategy increases the cost of production and results in significant financial losses for farmers. The only goal of disease detection is to obtain real-time data that assists in monitoring large farms of corps, identifying pests and infections, and ensuring that the quality is maintained. Manual disease identification by human specialists is a common method in agriculture [1]. Computer vision and AI - powered technologies have enabled the automated diagnosis of plant diseases from uncooked photos [2]. In this paper, tomato leaf diseases have been inspected and detected using various deep learning means and methodology.

Computer vision are currently widely used in agriculture for weed identification and recognition [3,4], fruit grading [4,5], detecting and quantifying crop diseases infections [5,6], and plant genetics [7].

Deep learning is a more sophisticated variety of machine learning which uses the subsidy of neural networks functioning correspondingly alike brains of humans [8]. Traditionally, categorization is accomplished through the use of

ⓒ The Author(s), under exclusive license to Springer Nature Switzerland AG 2022
A. A. Sk et al. (Eds.): ISAI 2022, CCIS 1695, pp. 265–273, 2022.
https://doi.org/10.1007/978-3-031-22485-0_24

semantic characteristics [9]. In accordance with LeChun et al., as a characteristics of deep learning, involuntary retrieval of graphical configuration features is probable [10]. Image processing procedure tries to exploits an arrangement of deep learning viz. Convolutional Neural Networks (CNNs). Lee et al. [11] conferred about a amalgam model for the task of extraction and also categorizing leaf traits using CNN. Ferentinos, K.P.'s work identifies plant illnesses using basic and infected plant leaf photos and a pre-trained CNN model [12].

2   Convolutional Neural Network

Deep learning which is a subfield of Machine Learning and Artificial Intelligence, practices Artificial Neural Networks. Deep learning models are trained by isolating the feature extraction process and extracting their classification features. Deep learning has several applications, comprising computer vision, image categorization, restoration, voice recognition, and video exploration. A convolutional neural network with a trifling process is proficient of straightforward detection and categorization. Through its multi-layered edifice, it is effective in assessing graphical pictures and mining their key elements. CNN comprises of 4 layers explicitly input picture, convolutional besides pooling layer, fully connected layer with output layer as exhibited in Fig. 1.

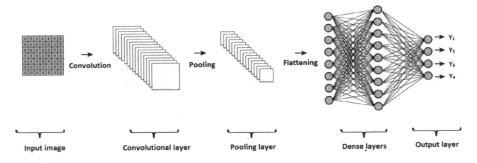

Fig. 1. CNN (Convolutional Neural Network) Structural Design

2.1   Convolutional Layer

The convolutional layers encompass the outputs of the cores from the previous layer, counting the pre-learned weights and offsets The optimization function's objective is to construct kernels that precisely reflect the data. This layer implements a series of mathematical procedures over input images to procure the feature map [16]. Figure 2 and Fig. 3 depicts this which is using 5×5 and another 3×3 input photograph images and produces a condensed magnitude filter of 3×3 [17]. Additionally, graphic image exemplifies in what way the filter is budged from topmost left junction of the input image. Filter values are used to burgeoned values for each step which yields additional values. The supplied picture is transformed into a new matrix with a lower extent.

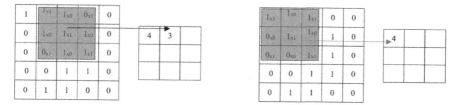

Fig. 2. Convolution layer operation with 5 × 5 inputs

Fig. 3. Convolution layer operation with 3 × 3 inputs

2.2 Pooling Layer

The layer of pooling curtails overfitting as well as shrinkages neuron magnitude used in down-sampling level. The pooling procedure is seen in Fig. 4. This layer minimises the size of the feature map, the number of parameters, the training time, and the pace of computation, and it also thwarts overfitting [20]. If a model attains 100% accuracy on the dataset of training nonetheless only a 50% over the test data, then it is considered to an overfitting. The size of feature maps were abridged using reLU and max pooling [21].

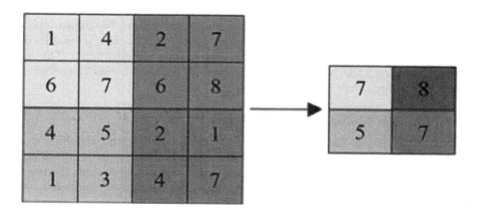

Fig. 4. Operation of pooling.

2.3 Activation Layer

A non-linear activation layer viz. ReLU i.e. Rectified Linear Unit is used by individual convolution layer for the processing. Overfitting is eluded by this layer by the practice of dropout layers.

2.4 Fully Connected Layer

Class level likelihoods are inspected by fully connected layer in addition to it, corresponding output assists as the input of classifier. The Softmax classifier is a well-known input classifier, and this layer is used to distinguish and classify plant diseases. Softmax is a recognized input classifier, and this layer is used to extricate and categorize plant diseases.

3 Proposed Method

The purpose of this research is to provide a technique for classifying tomato leaf illnesses and to recommend the best approach for overcoming them. This was accomplished successfully with the use of image processing techniques and the most recent niche model (Inception-v3), as well as the open source programming language Python. The suggested method's procedure is depicted in Fig. 5.

3.1 Dataset

To our knowledge, the PlantVillage dataset (PVD) is the only publicly available dataset for plant disease identification. Because the photos in the PlantVillage collection were collected in laboratory settings rather than in actual agricultural fields, their efficacy in the real world is likely to be low. PlantVillage is a collection of pictures made in controlled environments. This dataset has limitations in terms of disease detection since, in fact, plant photos may contain several leaves with changing background conditions and illumination circumstances. The collection comprises 2,598 photographs representing 27 classes across 13 species. A selection of photos from the dataset are shown in Fig. 6.

3.2 Inception Model

The Inception model has been extensively validated on picture classifications. The model is essentially composed of several convolution filters that are performed in parallel to a constant input with some pooling. After that, the result area unit is concatenated. Prior to conception, all architectures conducted convolution on abstractions and channel-wise domains. The inception structure enables cross-channel correlations, execution on lower-resolution input, and circumvention of spatial dimensions. We classified leaves using inception-v3. Inception v3 has been trained on a huge dataset. The inception v3 model requires days or weeks to train on a machine equipped with eight Tesla K40 GPUs and is reportedly priced at $32,000. As a result, it is difficult to train a model on a common computer. The architecture of the inception model is depicted in the image below (Fig. 6)

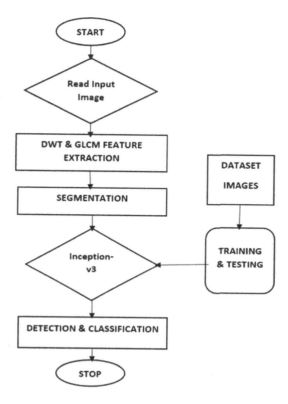

Fig. 5. Process diagram of the proposed method

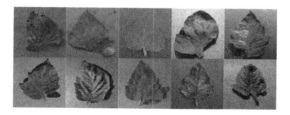

Fig. 6. Sample dataset images

3.3 Transfer of Knowledge

Transfer learning is a technique for reducing the number of parameters in a model by reusing a piece of the trained model on a familiar task in the new model. Transfer learning is a type of machine learning technique that makes use of a previously trained neural network. Thus, when we evaluate our original dataset using the new model, we are essentially utilising previously extracted features and training the model on our data. The advantage is that you may train the model with the fewest possible resources, datasets, and time, as we do not need to train the feature extraction component [4] (Fig. 7).

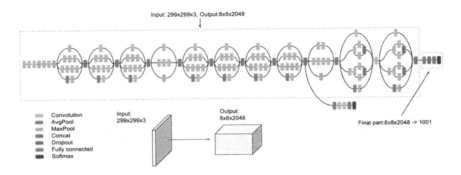

Fig. 7. Inception model architecture.

3.4   Experiments

The suggested solution was validated against OpenCV, one of the most used libraries for computer vision applications. OpenCV-Python is the OpenCV API that is both quick and optimal for implementing the Image Processing principles of leaf disease detection. This article discusses how to diagnose tomato leaf disease and how to differentiate between afflicted and normal leaves. A larger sample size is required to conduct a survey on various illness classifications. For the suggested technique, tomato leaf image datasets linked with important illnesses were used for detection and classification. The suggested technique is extremely computationally efficient and yields optimal results, demonstrating the efficacy of the proposed method of tomato leaf disease detection by producing a high accuracy rate for classification and recognition of tomato leaf illnesses. The training and validation datasets' loss and accuracy graphs are shown in Figs. 8 and 9 (Table 1).

Table 1. Comparison average performance measures of tomato leaf disease detection.

S. no	Method	Accuracy (%)
1	**Deep NN (AlexNet)** [17]	95.75
2	**Artificial NN technique** [18]	92.94
3	**Tomato leaf diseases Detection using Deep learning (proposed method)**	96.37

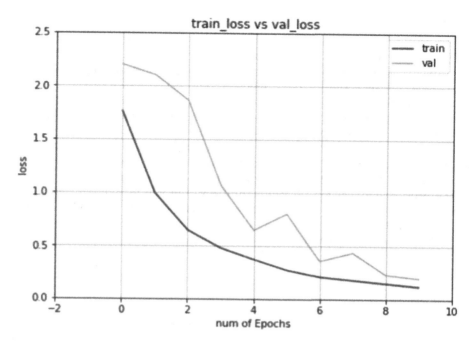

Fig. 8. Train VS validation loss.

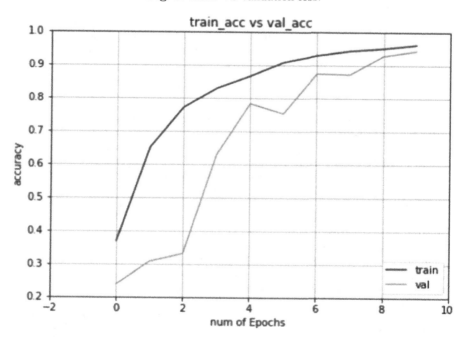

Fig. 9. Train VS validation accuracy.

4   Conclusion

The agricultural industry is perilous to the global economy, since crops are the principal source of food. The agronomic business be contingent on early unearthing and detection of these illnesses. The perseverance of this research is to exhibit in what way a convolutional neural network can be used to identify and distinguish distinct Tomato plant illnesses. Additionally, sundry models were matched and compared in this study. The expert model may be used to gauge real-time photos for illness detection and recognition. Supplementary plant kinds and new varieties of different plant diseases may perhaps be added to current dataset in future to augment the number of models which are well trained by the process. Further CNN architectures possibly will be experimented with numerous learning proportions as well as optimizers, so that model's accuracy can be checked and performance can also be compared to the existing scenario. The advocated models accuracy viz. 96.37% empowers farmers to ascertain and diagnose plant illnesses.

References

1. Park, H., Eun, J.S., Kim, S.H.: Image-based disease diagnosing and predicting of the crops through the deep learning mechanism. In: IEEE 2017 International Conference on Information and Communication Technology Convergence (ICTC), pp. 129–131 (2017)
2. Elangovan, K., Nalini, S.: Plant disease classification using image segmentation and SVM techniques. Int. J. Comput. Intell. Res. **13**(7), 1821–1828 (2017)
3. Vibhute, A., Bodhe, S.K.: Applications of image processing in agriculture: a survey. Int. J. Comput. Appl. **52**(2), 34–40 (2012)
4. Militante, S.: Fruit grading of Garcinia Binucao (Batuan) using image processing. Int. J. Recent Technol. Eng. (IJRTE) **8**(2), 1829–1832 (2019)
5. Garcia, J.G.B.: Digital image processing techniques for detecting, quantifying and classifying plant diseases. Springer Plus **2**, 660 (2013). https://doi.org/10.1186/2193-1801-2-660
6. Mutka, A.M., Bart, R.S.: Image-based phenotyping of plant disease symptoms. Front. Plant Sci. **5**, 1–8 (2015)
7. Mohanty, S.P., Hughes, D.P., Salathé, M.: Using deep learning for image-based plant disease detection. Front. Plant Sci. **7**, 1419 (2016)
8. Benuwa, B., Zhao Zhan, Y., Ghansah, B., Wornyo, D., Banaseka, F.: A review of deep machine learning. Int. J. Eng. Res. Afr. **24**, 124–136 (2016). https://doi.org/10.4028/www.scientific.net/JERA.24.124
9. Su, Y., Jurie, F.: Improving image classification using semantic attributes. Int. J. Comput. Vis. **100**(1), 59–77 (2012). https://doi.org/10.1007/s11263-012-0529-4
10. LeChun, Y., Bengio, Y., Hinton, G.: Deep learning. Nature **521**, 436–444 (2015). eprint https://doi.org/10.1038/nature14539
11. Lee, S.H., Chan, C.S., Mayo, S.J., Remagnino, P.: How deep learning extracts and learns leaf features for the plant classification. Pattern Recognit. **71**, 1–13 (2017)
12. Ferentinos, K.P.: Deep learning models for plant disease detection and diagnosis. Comput. Electron. Agric. **145**, 311–318 (2018)

13. Durmus, H., Gunes, E.O., Kirci, M.: Disease detection on the leaves of the tomato plants by using deep learning. In: IEEE 6th International Conference on Agro-Geoinformatics, pp. 1–5 (2017)
14. Atabay, H.A.: Deep residual learning for tomato plant leaf disease identification. J. Theor. Appl. Inf. Technol. **95**(24), 6800–6808 (2017)
15. Hughes, D.P., Salathé, M.: An open access repository of images on plant health to enable the development of mobile disease diagnostics. arXiv:1511.08060 (2015)
16. Tumen, V., Soylemez, O.F., Ergen, B.: Facial emotion recognition on a dataset using convolutional neural network. In: 2017 International Artificial Intelligence and Data Processing Symposium (IDAP) (2017)
17. Krizhevsky, A., Sutskever, I., Hinton, G.H.E.: ImageNet classification with Deep convolutional neural networks. In: Advances in Neural Information Processing Systems (2012)
18. Iandola, F.N., Han, S., Moskewicz, M.W., Ashraf, K., Dally, W.J., Keutzer, K.: Squeezenet: AlexNet-level accuracy with 50x fewer parameters and ¡0.5MB model size. eprint arXiv:1602.07360v4, pp. 1–13 (2016)

Prediction of Impact Energy of Steel Using Artificial Neural Network

S. Rath[1]($\boxtimes$), S. K. Gond[2], P. Kumar[1], P. Sahana[1], S. K. Thakur[1], and P. Pathak[1]

[1] R&D Centre for Iron & Steel, Steel Authority of India Limited, Ranchi, India
srath@sail.in
[2] Rourkela Steel Plant, Steel Authority of India Limited, Rourkela, India

Abstract. The impact energy of steel depends upon the chemical composition of steel and rolling mill parameters. It is difficult to predict the impact property of steel from the fundamental theory of micro-structural evolution during the rolling process. This paper discusses the prediction of Charpy impact energy of steel by regression analysis and artificial neural network models. The feed-forward neural network was trained using the back-propagation algorithm. The R-value of the trained neural network model is about 1.3 times the R-value of the linear regression model. A user-friendly Excel sheet has also been developed to calculate the Charpy impact energy using the weights and biases obtained from the training module of the neural network model. Sensitivity analysis was also carried out using the trained neural network model. It was recommended that waiting thickness and finishing temperature during the rolling process should be maintained at higher side when Si in steel composition is high.

Keywords: Charpy impact energy · Rolling mill · Linear regression · Artificial neural network

1 Introduction

The product mix of an integrated steel plant consists of many different grades of steel as per the requirements of customers. IS2062-E350 is a high tensile steel grade used for structural applications. As per IS2062:2011 standard published by the Bureau of Indian Standards, IS2062-E350 grade steel must have yield stress of a minimum of 350 MPa, the tensile strength of a minimum of 490 MPa and elongation of a minimum of 22%. This grade is subdivided into 4 sub-qualities based on the Charpy impact property. For sub-quality A, there is no requirement of testing for Charpy impact energy. For sub-quality BR, the impact test is optional but if the customer requires this property, then it is tested at room temperature. For sub-qualities B0 and C, the samples are tested for Charpy impact energy at 0°C and -20°C respectively. Whenever there is a Charpy impact test, the minimum value of Charpy impact energy must be 27J. If the Charpy impact property is less than 27J, the material is not accepted by the customer. Therefore, the present study was conducted to find out the effect of different parameters on Charpy impact energy using machine learning algorithms and to formulate suitable recommendations.

A. A. Sk et al. (Eds.): ISAI 2022, CCIS 1695, pp. 274–283, 2022.
https://doi.org/10.1007/978-3-031-22485-0_25

There have been attempts by different researchers to correlate impact properties with chemical composition and process parameters. However, there is no evidence of correlation of Charpy impact energy with chemical composition and rolling mill parameters. The objective of the present study is to develop an artificial neural network (ANN) model to correlate the Charpy impact property of IS2062-E350 grade C sub-quality steel with chemical composition and rolling mill processing parameters. The objective also includes sensitive analysis using the trained model to find out the effect of different input parameters on Charpy impact energy.

This paper describes the application of ANN for correlating chemical composition and rolling mill parameters to impact energy of steel using ANN. Sensitive analysis has also been carried out to identify the process parameter which can be changed during the process in order to achieve desired charpy impact property.

This paper is divided into 6 sections. Related work on prediction of impact and other properties of steel is described in section 2. Section 3 describes the process of rolling. The experimental procedure is described in Section 4. Results and discussion is described in section 5 and conclusions are given in Section 6.

2 Related Work

Different researchers have tried to develop artificial neural network (ANN) models for material science applications. Bhadeshia et al. [1] have predicted the impact toughness of C-Mn steel arc weld using Bayesian neural network analysis. Dunne et al. [2] have developed an artificial neural network (ANN) model for the prediction of the impact toughness of steel. Tan et al. [3] have used ANN modelling for the energy absorption of hot rolled Plates in Charpy impact Tests. Faizabadi et al. [4] have developed an ANN model for predictions of toughness and hardness by using chemical composition and tensile properties in microalloyed line pipe steels. Bhadeshia [6] states that neural networks have been used in quantitative design and control. To discover something novel using a neural network is particularly rewarding because the method has its background in empiricism. Cottrell [7] developed a neural network (NN) model for the Charpy transition temperature shift (DDBTT) in irradiated low activation martensitic (LAM) steels. Colas-Marquez [8] predicted Charpy impact energy for alloy steels ANN trained with different sets of data. Bhadeshia [9] has described the prediction of the toughness of ferritic steel welds using neural networks. The Charpy toughness was expressed as a function of the welding process, the chemical composition, the test temperature and the microstructure. Pak et al. [10] have tried to use a scheme used in kinetic theory to create a bounded neural network for predicting Charpy toughness of steel welds. Bhadeshia [11] has described a neural network model for the prediction of Charpy toughness of steel welds with 22 input variables in more than 1900 experimental datasets. Singh et al. [12] predicted two mechanical properties, yield strength and ultimate tensile strength, using ANN. Thankachan and Sooryaprakash [13] developed an ANN model for the prediction of impact energy of cast duplex stainless steel using chemical composition as input parameters. Tong et al. [14] developed an ANN model of the Charpy impact toughness of deposited metals of welding materials with chemical composition and diameter of welding wire as input parameters

3 Process Description

The layout of a typical plate rolling process is shown in Figure 1. Steel slabs enter the reheating furnace, where it is heated. The heated slab is passed through a primary descaler where the scales are removed from the surfaces of the slab. It is then rolled in the reversing rolling mill in a number of rolling passes. The rolled plate is then passed through an accelerated cooling system where is subjected to water cooling. The plate passes through a hot plate leveler and a marking machine and is finally cooled in a cooling bed.

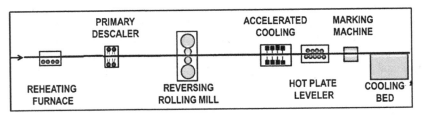

Fig. 1. Layout of a plate rolling mill

Samples are cut from the finished plates for testing in the laboratory for mechanical properties like yield stress, ultimate tensile strength, percentage elongation and Charpy impact energy. The chemical composition of steel slabs, measured at the upstream continuous casting process, is available in the rolling mill automation system. The process parameters like reheating furnace parameters, rolling mill parameters and accelerated cooling parameters are recorded from rolling mill sensors.

4 Experimental Procedure

The experimental procedure includes generation of industrial data, pre-processing of industrial data, development of linear regression and ANN models and sensitivity analysis using the trained ANN model.

4.1 Generation of Industrial Data

The industrial data for each dataset consists of input variables of the chemical composition of steel and rolling mill parameters and output variable Charpy impact energy (J) at −20°C. The chemical composition variables are percentages of C, Mn, P, S, Si, Al, Nb and V in the steel composition.

A large number of rolling mill parameters can be considered as input parameters to the model. However, based on the domain expertise, 14 important parameters have been selected for analysis and model development. Two reheating furnace parameters discharge temperature in °C and heating time measured in hour are selected. The temperature after the primary descaler is measured by an infrared pyrometer. The recorded average temperature along slab length of the pyrometer measured in °C, is considered as one of the input variables for model development.

While a slab is rolled in a reversing rolling mill, it has two stages: roughing stage and finishing stage. In the roughing stage, the average temperature of slab measured in °C and reduction in last roughing pass measured in percentage are input variables to the models. Before entering of the semi-rolled slab to finishing passes, it waits for some time due to its thermo-mechanical processing requirement. The thickness of slab during waiting in mm, time for waiting in seconds and temperature before restarting of rolling in °C are 3 important parameters selected for model development. In the finishing stage, reduction at first finishing pass in percentage, the reduction in the last pass measured in percentage, the temperature before last pass in °C and the temperature after last pass in °C are considered as inputs to the model. The total number of passes in the reversing rolling mill and the final thickness of plates in mm are also two other input variables selected for model development.

The variables mentioned above are recorded in the mill automation system from different sensors and stored in the ORACLE database in the industrial rolling mill for which the model has been developed. The corresponding Charpy impact energy, the output of the model, was collected from the laboratory where the testing is carried out. The plate number is the key for matching the data between the mill automation system and laboratory storage system. Datasets of 440 number of plates of ISO2062-E350-C grade of steel were generated initially for model development.

4.2 Pre-processing of Industrial Data

The data collected from the industrial rolling mill were analysed first through box plots. Industrial data contains a lot of noise. Sometimes there may be recording errors. Datasets having more than one extreme explainable outliers were eliminated completely. Datasets having one outlier were modified and included in the database for model development. If the outlier is less than the median, then the outlier value was modified to lower whisker. If the outlier is more than the median then the outlier value was modified to upper whisker. After the reduction of outliers, 412 datasets were finally selected for model development. After the box plot, the descriptive statistics parameters of the data were calculated. Then histograms of the pre-processed data were generated. Before the use of data for training and validation of models, correlation coefficients of all the input and output variables were also determined using the formula,

$$R = \frac{n(\sum xy) - \sum x \sum y}{\sqrt{\left[n \sum x^2 - (\sum x)^2\right]\left[n \sum y^2 - (\sum y)^2\right]}} \tag{1}$$

where, x and y are two correlating parameters and n is the number of datasets for which both x and y values are available.

4.3 Development of Models

A linear regression (LR) model was developed as the base model for correlating Charpy impact energy with input parameters. The hypothesis for linear regression model is given by,

$$h_\theta(x) = \sum_{i=0}^{n} \theta_i x_i \text{ (with } x_0 = 1)$$ (2)

where, x_i is the ith input feature and θ_i is the ith coefficient. In this equation, n is the number of input variables. The coefficients of the linear regression model were calculated by minimizing the cost function of the sum square of errors between the hypothesis values and measured values of Charpy impact energy.

After development of the LR model as the base model, the ANN model was developed. The structure of the ANN model for the prediction of Charpy impact property is shown in Figure 2. The feed-forward neural network model consists of 22 nodes in the input layer and Charpy impact energy as the output node. Different structures of neural network were tried during the training of the model. In some structures, one hidden layer was tried while in some other structures two hidden layers were tried. Different structures of neural network were trained using back-propagation algorithm [13] with datasets recorded from the industrial rolling mill. The data were divided into 3 groups: training data (about 60% of datasets), test data (about 20% of datasets) and validation data (about 20% of the datasets). The R-values between the predicted and measured Charpy impact energy value were calculated for all three datasets.

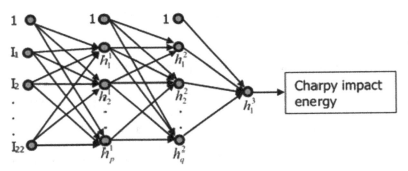

Fig. 2. Structure of feed-forward neural network

The training of the ANN model was initiated with a 22–2-1 structure in which 2 nodes were selected in one hidden layer. With one set of network structures, the program was run 200 times, each time with different random initialization of weights and biases. The run in which the R-value was found to be maximum was selected as the best run. In a similar way, different structures with one and two hidden layers were tried and the network structure having the highest R-value was selected as the final model.

It may be mentioned here that an optimum epoch was found out as the epoch where the difference between training error and testing error is minimum. A model trained with epochs lower than the optimum epoch is considered as under-trained whereas models with higher epochs than the optimum epoch is considered as over-trained.

4.4 Sensitivity Analysis

Sensitivity analysis of the final trained ANN model was carried out to study the effect of each input parameter on the Charpy impact energy. Each of the input variables was varied from its minimum to maximum value in certain steps, keeping all other input parameters at their median values. The output variable was calculated using the final trained ANN model. The input parameters for which variation of output parameters is higher are considered as important parameters affecting Charpy impact energy.

5 Results and Discussions

The parameters of descriptive statistics of all the 22 input variables and Charpy impact energy were calculated. Though the 3 central tendency parameters, mean median and mode are almost the same for some variables, there is a significant difference in these parameters for few variables like heating time and restart temperature.

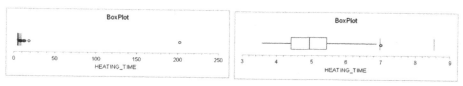

Fig. 3. Boxplot of heating time before and after data filtering

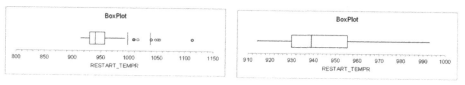

Fig. 4. Boxplot of Restart Temperature before and after data filtering

Box plots of all the input variables and Charpy impact energy were also generated. However, two plots where outliers are significant are shown in Figure 3 and Figure 4. In the left part of Figure 3, there is only one outlier which shows the heating time of 200 h. Practically, slabs are not heated for so many hours in a reheating furnace. So, clearly, this data is wrongly recorded by the mill automation system. The dataset containing the outlier was deleted. The modified boxplot after deletion of the dataset is shown in the right part of the figure.

Figure 4 shows the box plot of restart temperature. In the left figure, there are a number of outliers. The temperature values of these outliers are very high which is not practically possible. The measurement of the temperature values by pyrometers may be sometimes erroneous due to the presence of water and steam. So, the datasets with the outlier values were deleted. The plot of restart temperature after data filtering is shown in the right side of the figure.

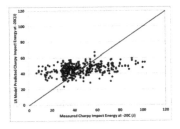

Fig. 5. Plot between LR model-predicted and measured Charpy impact energy

After pre-processing of data, a linear regression (LR) model was developed with 22 input parameters and Charpy impact energy as output parameter. A plot between the Charpy impact energy predicted by the linear regression model and measured values of Charpy impact energy is given in Figure 5. This plot shows that there is a low correlation between the model predicted and measured values of Charpy impact energy. The R-value calculated using Equation-1 was found to be 0.35, which is very low. The linear regression model acts as a base model for assessing the performance of the ANN model.

Neural network models with different structures were tried. The model which gives the best R-value was found out. It is found that the ANN model with 22-8-1 structure, in which there is only 1 hidden layer with 8 nodes gives the highest R-value in 200 runs with different initial weights and biases. Figure 6 shows the performance of the ANN model. The R-value for training data is found to be 0.93, that of test data was found to be 0.48 and that of the validation data was found to be 0.60. The overall R-value was

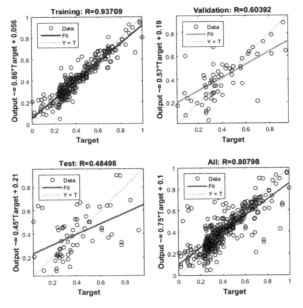

Fig. 6. Performance of ANN model

found to be 0.807. This is much higher than the R-value of 0.35 calculated using the LR model. The R-value of the ANN model is 1.3 times that of LR model.

The weights and biases of the final ANN model were transferred to a Microsoft Excel Sheet and the formula was written for the prediction of Charpy impact energy. The Excel sheet was handed over to the industrial rolling mill operators.

Sensitivity analysis was carried out to find the effect of each of the 22 input variables using the finally selected ANN model. It is found that 3 input variables have a very high effect on Charpy impact energy which are discussed below.

Figure 7 shows that with the change in finishing temperature, Charpy impact energy increases significantly. Charpy impact energy increases by about 50J when finishing temperature increases from 720 to 970°C. This is the most important rolling mill parameter affecting Charpy impact energy. Therefore, it should be maintained at higher side. Charpy impact property increases by about 28J when waiting thickness changes from 24 to 96 mm. However, it is possible to always maintain higher waiting thickness as it adversely affects mill productivity. So, it should be maintained as high as possible without affecting mill productivity significantly (Fig. 8).

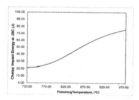

Fig. 7. Sensitivity of finishing temperature on Charpy impact property

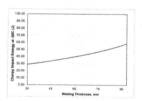

Fig. 8. Sensitivity of waiting thickness on Charpy impact property

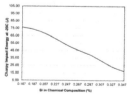

Fig. 9. Sensitivity of Silicon in steel composition on Charpy impact property

From the different elements in the chemical composition of the steel grade, it is found that the silicon content affects Charpy impact energy most adversely as shown in Figure 9. When silicon percentage increases from 0.167% to 0.347% in the steel composition, Charpy impact energy reduces by about 60J. So, it should be maintained as low as possible.

6 Conclusions

Linear regression (LR) and artificial neural network (ANN) models have been developed for an industrial application of predicting Charpy impact energy of steel. Before the development of the models, industrial data was collected and pre-processed, The R-value of the ANN model was found to be 1.3 times that of the LR model. A Microsoft Excel sheet was developed for the prediction of Charpy impact energy using weights and biases of trained ANN model. Sensitivity analysis was carried out and it is found that the percentage of silicon in steel composition has the most adverse effect on Charpy impact energy. Waiting thickness and finishing temperature have the most favorable impact on Charpy impact energy though these two factors adversely impact mill productivity. It is recommended that waiting thickness and finishing temperature should be maintained at the higher side when Si in steel composition is high.

References

1. Bhadeshia, H.K.D.H., MacKay, D.J.C., Svensson, L.E.: Impact toughness of C-Mn steel arc welds – Bayesian neural network analysis. Mater. Sci. Technol. 11(10), 1046–1051 (1995). https://doi.org/10.1179/mst.1995.11.10.1046
2. Dunne, D., Tsuei, H., Sterjovski, Z.: Artificial neural networks for modelling of the impact toughness of steel. ISIJ Int. 44(9), 1599–1607 (2004). https://doi.org/10.2355/isijinternational.44.1599
3. Tan, W., Liu, Z.Y., Wu, D., Wang, G.D.: Artificial neural network (ann) modeling for the energy absorption of hot rolled plates in charpy impact tests. Multidiscip. Model. Mater. Struct. 4(1), 37–46 (2008). https://doi.org/10.1163/157361108783470423
4. Faizabadi, M.J., Khalaj, G., Pouraliakbar, H., Jandaghi, M.R.: Predictions of toughness and hardness by using chemical composition and tensile properties in microalloyed line pipe steels. Neural Comput. Appl. 25(7–8), 1993–1999 (2014). https://doi.org/10.1007/s00521-014-1687-9
5. Azimzadegan, T., Khoeini, M., Etaat, M., Khoshakhlagh, A.: An artificial neural-network model for impact properties in X70 pipeline steels. Neural Comput. Appli. 23, 1473–1480 (2013). https://doi.org/10.1007/s00521-012-1097-9
6. Bhadeshia, H.K.D.H.: Neural networks and information in materials science. Statistical Analy. Data Mining 1, 296–305 (2009). https://doi.org/10.1002/sam.10018
7. Cottrell, G.A., Kemp, R., Bhadeshia, H.K.D.H., Odette, G.R., Yamamoto, T.: Neural network analysis of Charpy transition temperature of irradiated low-activation martensitic steels. J. Nuclear Materials, 367, 603–609 (2007). https://doi.org/10.1016/j.jnucmat.2007.03.103
8. Colas-Marquez, R., Mahfouf, M.: Data mining and modelling of charpy impact energy for alloy steels using fuzzy rough sets. IFAC-PapersOnLine 50(1), 14970–14975 (2017). https://doi.org/10.1016/j.ifacol.2017.08.2555
9. Bhadeshia, H.K.D.H.: Neural networks in materials science. ISIJ Int. 39(10), 966–979 (1999). https://doi.org/10.2355/isijinternational.39.966

10. Pak, J., Jang, J., Bhadeshia, H.K.D.H., Karlsson, L.: Optimization of neural network for charpy toughness of steel welds. Mater. Manuf. Processes **24**(1), 16–21 (2009). https://doi.org/10.1080/10426910802540232

11. Bhadeshia, H.K.D.H., Dimitriu, R.C., Forsik, S., Pak, J.H., Ryu, J.H.: Performance of neural networks in materials science. Mater. Sci. Technol. **25**(4), 504–510 (2009). https://doi.org/10.1179/174328408X311053

12. Singh, S., Bhadeshia, H.K.D.H., MacKay, D., Carey, H.C., Martín, Í.L.: Neural network analysis of steel plate processing. Ironmaking Steelmaking **25**, 355–365 (1998)

13. Thankachan, T., Sooryaprakash, K.: Artificial neural network-based modeling for impact energy of cast duplex stainless steel. Arab. J. Sci. Eng. **43**(3), 1335–1343 (2017). https://doi.org/10.1007/s13369-017-2880-9

14. Tong, L.G. et al.: Prediction model of the charpy impact toughness of deposited metals of welding materials. Applied Mechanics and Materials **130**, 1001–1004 (2012). https://doi.org/10.4028/www.scientific.net/AMM.130-134.1001

15. Yegnanarayana, B.: Artificial Neural Networks, Prentice-Hall of India, New Delhi (2004)

A New Method of Galaxy Classification Using Optimal Convolution Neural Network

Goutam Sarker[✉] [iD]

National Institute of Technology, Durgapur 713209, India
goutam.sarker@cse.nitdgp.ac.in

Abstract. A galaxy classification system using Optimal Convolution Neural Network has been designed and developed. Broadly there are five different types of galaxies. They are elliptical, spiral, disk, lenticular and irregular. We have proposed an Optimal Deep Convolution Neural Network which learns the features of the different types of galaxies in the form of a set of filters and after the learning is over recognizes the type of the unknown galaxies. With this, the optimal point with data size as well as number of filters of neither overshooting nor undershooting is found out to get the optimal network complexity – which highly improves the performance evaluation. The performance evaluation of the CNN architecture used for galaxy classification in terms of its accuracy, precision, recall and f-score is quite satisfactory. Also the training and testing time is affordable.

Keywords: Deep learning · Convolution Neural Network · Galaxy · Types of galaxies · Performance evaluation · Holdout Method · Confusion matrix

1 Introduction

Previously galaxy classifications were done through visual inspection of two-dimensional images of galaxies and appearance based classification [1, 9, 10]. Even if we assume that accurate and correct classification of abnormally huge quantity of data done by experts of astronomy is far more reliable, it is too much time consuming which is totally unaffordable. Thus there is a tremendous need to separate those images of terrestrial bodies like the different types of galaxies by an automatic procedure especially a neural network based machine learning approach [5–8] like deep learning or convolution neural network.

2 Theory of Operation

According to Hubble Classification, galaxies are most commonly classified [1–4] according to either their shape as Elliptical, Spiral, Irregular Disk and Lenticular (Fig. 1).

A. A. Sk et al. (Eds.): ISAI 2022, CCIS 1695, pp. 284–293, 2022.
https://doi.org/10.1007/978-3-031-22485-0_26

a Elliptical Galaxy	**b** Spiral Galaxy

c Irregular Galaxy

d Disk Galaxy   **e** Lenticular Galaxy

Fig. 1. Different types of galaxies

2.1 Over Fitting and Under Fitting Problems in Convolution Neural Networks

Over Fitting in CNN. This problem is likely to occur in CNN [11–16] when the training data size (no. of data) is small compared to the network complexity, such that the network is able to "memorize" all the given data instead of "learning" them through optimum generalization. The system is unable to recognize test data (Fig. 2).

Under Fitting in CNN. This problem is likely to occur in CNN [11–16] when the training data size is large enough compared to the network complexity, such that network "maximally generalizes" without performing effective or fruitful learning. The system is unable to recognize both training and test data.

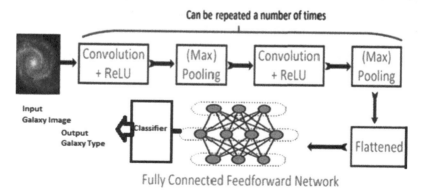

Fig. 2. CNN model for galaxy classification

2.2   Algorithm for Preprocessing and Learning

Galaxy Image Preprocessing Algorithm
Input: 300 Stratified Raw Image of each of size 300 * 300
Output: 300 Pre-processed Image.
Steps:

1. Crop the color images to 180 × 180 pixels, thus removing the noise in the outer part of the galaxy images.
2. Perform Rotation, Translation and Flipping of the images for data augmentation.
3. Scale the image by dividing each element by 255.
4. Save the 300 Stratified Pre-processed Image for training and validation.

Learning Algorithm
Input:

i)   Pre-processed Stratified Image data set of size 300.
ii) Keras CNN Model for training.

Output: Trained Keras Model for Galaxy Classification.
Steps:

1. Divide the dataset into train/test split of 2:1 of Holdout Method for training and validation respectively.
2. Vary both the number of filters as well as the size of the training data set together. Initially start from a very small training data size and huge number of filters.
3. Step by step increase training data size and at the same time decrease the number of filters. At each step, calculate the performance evaluation (accuracy) of the system.
4. When the total amount of data has been used up as training/ validation data and the corresponding minimum number filter has been attained, plot (data size, no. of filters) vs. accuracy.
5. Find the optimal point where the accuracy is found maximum for the test data set.

3   Results

3.1   Platform Used

Implemented in Python Framework used – Tensorflow
Editor/IDE – Google Colab/Jupyter Notebook
Librarires used – Keras-CNN, Numoy, Pandas, Sklearn, Seaborn, Matplotlib etc.
Specifications Used – 12 GB Ram/Nvidia T4 GPU.

3.2   Sample Benchmark Dataset

(See Fig. 3).

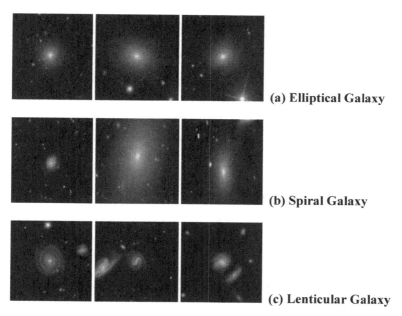

(a) Elliptical Galaxy

(b) Spiral Galaxy

(c) Lenticular Galaxy

Fig. 3. Sample benchmark galaxy dataset

3.3   Model Summary

The more is the number of dense layers the better is the clarity to differentiate among the different output types. We found that use of 5 dense layers is the optimal one (Fig. 4).

Layer (type)	Output Shape	Param #
conv2d (Conv2D)	(None, 180, 180, 110)	3080
max_pooling2d (MaxPooling2D)	(None, 90, 90, 110)	0
conv2d_1 (Conv2D)	(None, 90, 90, 120)	118920
max_pooling2d_1 (MaxPooling2	(None, 45, 45, 120)	0
conv2d_2 (Conv2D)	(None, 45, 45, 130)	140530
max_pooling2d_2 (MaxPooling2	(None, 22, 22, 130)	0
flatten (Flatten)	(None, 62920)	0
dropout (Dropout)	(None, 62920)	0
dense (Dense)	(None, 100)	6292100
dense_1 (Dense)	(None, 200)	20200
dense_2 (Dense)	(None, 300)	60300
dense_3 (Dense)	(None, 400)	120400
dense_4 (Dense)	(None, 5)	2005

Fig. 4. Model summary

3.4   Training and Testing Results

There are total 12 steps and all were run for 200 epochs. No of Starting Point Filters and Dataset:

Filters – 240
Dataset – 25.
No of Ending Point Filters and Dataset:
Filters – 20
Dataset – 300.

The confusion matrix and the accuracy results are shown in a tabularized form below in Table 1 and Table 2 respectively.

Table 1. Confusion matrix

	Actual Class ->				
		0	1	2	3	4
	0	8	1	1	0	0
	1	0	7	0	2	0
Predicted Class ∨	2	0	0	12	0	0
	3	0	1	0	10	8
	4	0	0	0	0	4

In the above table confusion the numbers 0–4 has the following interpretations:
0 - Disk Galaxy
1 - Elliptical Galaxy
2 - Irregular Galaxy
3 - Lenticular Galaxy 4 - Spiral Galaxy

Table 2. Results indicating no of filters corresponding training and testing accuracy

Serial No.	No of Filters	Stratified Dataset Used	Training Accuracy	Test Accuracy
1	240	25	95	69
2	220	50	100	64
3	200	75	100	74
4	180	100	100	80
5	160	125	100	83
6	130	150	100	90
7	120	175	100	85
8	100	200	100	78
9	80	225	100	67
10	60	250	99	62
11	40	275	99	60
12	20	300	98	58

The classification report is presented below in Table 3.

Table 3. Precision, recall, F1-score and support

	Precision	Recall	F1-Score	Support
0	1	0.89	0.89	10
1	0.78	0.78	0.78	9
2	0.92	1	0.96	12
3	0.83	0.91	0.87	11
4	1	1	1	8

Estimated time taken to run the model in the optimal point (130 filters in each layer and 150 Dataset Size) for 200 epochs was 1 h and it is presented below in Table 4. 33% Train/Test Split in Dataset.

Table 4. Training & testing time taken at optimal point

Serial No	Training Time	Validation Time	Testing Time for 1 image
1	68 mins	0.125 s	0.1 s

3.5 Optimal Point

From Table 2 we find that in the sixth step, with 150 stratified data, accuracy of 90% was reached with 130 filters in the convolutional layer (Figs. 5 and 6).

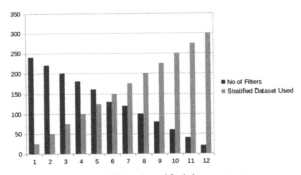

Fig. 5. No of filters/stratified dataset vs step.

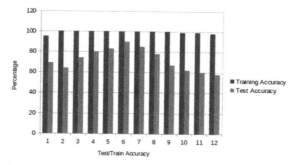

Fig. 6. Training/testing accuracy vs step

Optimal Point for Testing Accuracy

The model reaches an optimal point at step no 6. Far from the point of overshooting and undershooting, with 130 filters in each convolutional layer and 150 stratified dataset.

It achieved an accuracy of 90% when run for 200 epochs. It is presented in the Fig. 7 below.

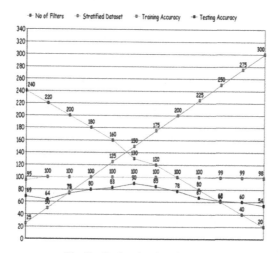

Fig. 7. Optimal point detection

4   Conclusion

In the present paper we have proposed and developed a galaxy classification system using optimal deep CNN model. The system finds out on its own, the optimal size of the training benchmark data set and at the same time the optimal number of filters with that training data for the given deep CNN. Thus the system model would be able to find out the exact combination of training data size and number of filters of the CNN such that the system is not prone to either overshooting or undershooting which is a basic problem in CNN like other ANN. The performance evaluation of the present CNN architecture used for galaxy classification in terms of its accuracy, precision, recall and f-score is quite satisfactory. Also the training and testing time is affordable.

Acknowledgment. The author wishes to acknowledge his B.Tech Project Students of the final year 2021–22 for coding the algorithm of the entire work.

References

1. Hawking, S.: A Brief History of Time – From Big Bang to Black Holes. Bantom Books, New York (1995)
2. Sarker, G.: On the change in entropy due to accretion and collision of black holes. Int. J. Appl. Phys. (IJAP) **8**(2), 5–15 (2021)
3. Sarker, G.: A treatise on astronomy and space science. Int. J. Appl. Phys. (IJAP) **8**(2), 47–58 (2021)
4. Basu, B.: An Introduction to Astrophysics, 1st edn. PHI, Delhi (2006)
5. Sarker, G.: A learning expert system for image recognition. J. Inst. Eng. (I) Comput. Eng. Div. **81**, 6–15 (2000)
6. Sarker, G., Ghosh, S.: Biometric-based unimodal and multimodal person identification with CNN using optimal filter set. In: Mandal, J.K., Mukhopadhyay, S. (eds.) Proceedings of the Global AI Congress 2019. AISC, vol. 1112, pp. 17–31. Springer, Singapore (2020). https://doi.org/10.1007/978-981-15-2188-1_2
7. Sarker, G.: Some studies on convolution neural network. Int. J. Comput. Appl. (IJCA) Found. Comput. Sci. N. Y. **182**(21), 13–22 (2018)
8. Sarker., G.: A survey on convolution neural networks. In: IEEE Region 10 International Conference 2020, pp. 923–928 (2020)
9. Elfattah, M., Bendary, N., Elsoud, M., Hassanien, A., Tolba, M.: An intelligent approach for galaxies images classification. In: 13th International Conference on Hybrid Intelligent Systems, p. 167172 (2013)
10. Calleja, J., Fuentes, O.: Machine learning and image analysis for morphological galaxy classification. Mon. Not. R. Astron. Soc. **349**(1), 87–93 (2004)
11. Sarker, G.: A Treatise on Artificial Intelligence, 1st edn. Copyright ©2018 from Registrar of Copyrights, Goverment of India (2018). ISBN 978-93-5321-793-8
12. Sarker, G.: An unsupervised natural clustering with optimal conceptual affinity. J. Intell. Syst. **19**(3), 289–300 (2010)
13. Kundu, S., Sarker, G.: A programming based boosting in super-classifier for fingerprint recognition. In: Sahana, S.K., Saha, S.K. (eds.) Advances in Computational Intelligence. AISC, vol. 509, pp. 319–329. Springer, Singapore (2017). https://doi.org/10.1007/978-981-10-2525-9_31
14. Kundu, S., Sarker, G.: A super classifier with programming-based boosting using biometrics for person authentication. In: Sahana, S.K., Saha, S.K. (eds.) Advances in Computational Intelligence. AISC, vol. 509, pp. 331–341. Springer, Singapore (2017). https://doi.org/10.1007/978-981-10-2525-9_32

15. Kundu, S., Sarker, G.: A person identification system with biometrics using modified RBFN based multiple classifier In: International Conference on Control, Instrumentation, Energy & Communication (CIEC) © 2016, pp. 125–129. IEEE (2016)
16. Kundu, S., Sarker, G.: A person authentication system using a biometric based efficient multilevel integrator. In: 2nd International Conference on Sustainable Computing Technique in Engineering, Science and Management (SCESM – 2017), Belagavi, India, pp. 261–270 (2017)

Early Detection of Pneumonia Using Deep Learning Approach

Prathiksha P. Pai[✉] and Sarika Hegde

NMAM Institute of Technology, Nitte, Karnataka, India
prathikshapai77@gmail.com

Abstract. Pneumonia is a lung disease caused by a variety of bacteria and viruses. Pneumonia will spread quickly from person to person, when a person is coughing or sneezing and this will lead to death if early treatment is not taken. WHO predicted that millions of people die every year across the globe due to these infectious diseases like pneumonia. Therefore, there is an urgent requirement to do research and develop an automatic system to detect pneumonia. It is easy to detect pneumonia is present or not in the lungs but identifying the bacterial and viral pneumonia is a challenging task. So, this research work also focuses on identifying bacterial and viral pneumonia along with classification and calculates the accuracy of bacteria and virus present in the lungs. In the proposed research work the simplest deep learning technique used for classification is Convolutional Neural Network (CNN) along with that K-Means clustering and watershed algorithm is used to extract the important features from chest x-ray images. At the end, the system can detect the cases of pneumonia and calculate the percentage of bacteria and viruses present in the lungs. The model gives 85.6% accuracy on test datasets. Thus, the early diagnosis of the lung abnormalities like pneumonia can reduce the rate of death worldwide by enabling faster and more efficient treatment.

Keywords: Deep learning approach · Pneumonia detection · Early diagnosis of pneumonia

1 Introduction

Pneumonia is a lung disease in which air sacs become filled with pus or other liquid [1] and they are caused by variety of bacteria and viruses. Signs and symptoms of pneumonia are high fever, shaking chills, cough, nausea, vomiting or diarrhea, shortness of breath (dyspnea), chest pain when breathing deeply, increased breathing rate, fatigue and muscle aches, dusky or purplish skin color from the poorly oxygenated blood [2]. In bacterial pneumonia, breathing sounds are normal on one side but absent on other side of the chest. Most of the time bacteria affect only one side of the lungs. In viral pneumonia, breathing sounds are not clear on either side of the chest. Most of the time virus affect both sides of the lungs [3]. Chest X-Ray images will show the presence of bacteria and viruses in the lungs.

Pneumonia will spread quickly from person to person, when a person is coughing or sneezing and this will cause the death. WHO predicted that millions of people die

A. A. Sk et al. (Eds.): ISAI 2022, CCIS 1695, pp. 294–304, 2022.
https://doi.org/10.1007/978-3-031-22485-0_27

every year across the globe due to these infectious diseases like pneumonia [4]. Most of the time pneumonia is found in children below 5 years and adults above 65 years [5]. Therefore, there is an urgent requirement to do research and develop an automatic system to detect pneumonia. It is easy to detect pneumonia is present or not in the lungs but identifying the bacterial and viral pneumonia is a challenging task. So, this research work focuses on identifying bacterial and viral pneumonia and finds the accuracy of virus and bacterial present in the lungs. The motivation behind this research is to diagnose the lung abnormalities like pneumonia to reduce the death rates in the individual to a great extent. Medical images of the patient are used to diagnose lung abnormalities at the early stage.

Deep learning technique has contributed largely to diagnose lung abnormality diseases at the early stage and it will give an accurate result. The simplest deep learning technique used for classification is CNN. The main feature of CNN is to extract the essential elements from the entire image and to separate the nodule. Most of the image classification task in the medical domain is carried using CNN gives the better accuracy in classifying the medical images based on its features [6].

2 Literature Survey

Chest X-Ray images and CT Scan images are used to detect pneumonia in the lungs. Kundu and Das [7] developed computer aided diagnosis system for detecting Pneumonia. Three CNN models: GoogLeNet, ResNet-18 and DenseNet121 is used to handle scarcity of datasets. These models perform better than other ensembled techniques. Eishesawy and Ibrahim [8] describe that four deep learning models are used to detect pneumonia, among them two are pre-trained models ResNet15V2 and MobileNetV2. CNN and LSTM are the two main models used. The performance of ResNet15V2 model is less when compared with other three models. Hashmi and Katiyar [9] describe that a weighted classifier is used to update the weights from the pre-trained models like ResNet18, DenseNet21, Inception V3, Xception and mobileNetV2. A weighted classifier will classify the pneumonia cases as normal or abnormal. The network will predict the results based on quality of dataset. So the model is not so efficient when compared to other models. Tatiana and Dmytro [10] say that the model will detect pneumonia in X-Ray chest images. Data augmentation has been applied to the database to make the CNN model more powerful. Asnaoui and Idri [11] compared recent deep convolutional neural network with turned version of pre-trained model. CNN will display low performance and model yields the accuracy of 84%. Maulana and Kurniawan [12] proposed a smart medical device that is designed for the initial treatment of the lung condition based on the fingernail color and body temperature. Lung diseases like pneumonia and tuberculosis are detected at an early stage by the smart device. The temperature sensor and the color sensor are used to collect the temperature of the body and nail color. The naïve bayes method will classify the condition of lungs on the basis of collected data. Urey and Saul [13] describes that the classification method uses the CNN and residual neural network architecture for classifying the chest X-Ray image as normal or infected from pneumonia. The model yields the accuracy of 78.73%. Stephen and Sain [14] describe, CNN is used to diagnose pneumonia using X-Ray images of a patient.

Data augmentation technique is used to improve the classification accuracy. Antin and Kravitz [15] proposed the model to detect pneumonia in chest X-Ray images using SVM and deep learning methods. The CNN model will provide more accuracy and the model will be trained. The SVM model will provide 60.9% accuracy and the CNN model will provide 82.8% accuracy. Rajpurkar and Irvin [16] say chest X-Ray14 is an implant given to the XNet121 model of a CNN to differentiate the image as normal or infected with pneumonia. According to Bejan and Xia [17] ICU follow-up reports of 426 patients are provided as inclusion data for pneumonia. Mathematical selection algorithms are used for text classification to improve section accuracy. Only pneumonia identified problem reports was taken separately instead of using all patient reports. Mendonca and Haas [18] describe NLP-based monitoring system is used to address health-related pneumonia in neonates. The automated system that uses NLP is inexpensive as a manual method and is a very important tool that can be used to improve surveillance. Ponnada and Srinivasa [19] proposed an integrated system that is used to detect lung cancer and pneumonia using CT scan images. Two different CNN models used are the pneumonia data model and lung cancer data model to detect the diseases. An integrated system gives 85% of accuracy on test set data. Bhandary and Prabhu [20] describe lung abnormalities like pneumonia and lung cancer are examined using a deep learning framework. A Deep Learning method, Modified AlexNet (MAN) is used to diagnose pneumonia using x-ray chest images. SVM is used for clustering. The accuracy obtained by deep learning method is greater than the SVM. Khobragade and tiwari [21] says the system will detect lung diseases like pneumonia, lung cancer, and tuberculosis using chest radiographs. Lung diseases are detected using a feed-forward artificial neural network. This method is not robust when position and size of input dataset changes.

3 Methodology

Figure 1 shows the flow of the system in which chest x-ray images are processed and classify images into different categories. Step by step procedure is followed to classify the images using different techniques is shown.

A. *Data Collection:* Chest X-Ray datasets used to detect pneumonia are collected from Kaggle [22] and Spandana healthcare Karkala. The folder consists of 3 subfolders train, test, and validation. Again these 3 folders consist of 2 subfolders of normal and pneumonia. The normal folder consists of normal images and the pneumonia folder consists of bacterial pneumonia and viral pneumonia infected images (Table 1 and Fig. 2).

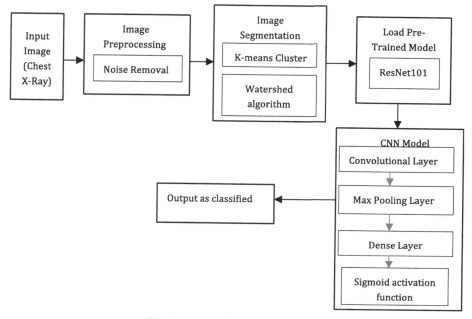

Fig. 1. Proposed system architecture

Table 1. Shows the count of chest X-Ray image datasets for pneumonia

	Normal	Pneumonia	Total
Train	1,791	4,455	6,246
Test	538	492	1,030
Validation	8	8	16

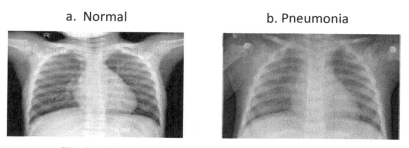

Fig. 2. Chest X-Ray image dataset samples for pneumonia

The images in the train folder consists of different size and dimensions, so all the images in the folder are resized to 200 × 200 before processing it into Convolutional Neural Network (CNN) model.

B. Image Pre-processing
Noise removal - The noise removal technique used are morphological operations they are used as the tool in image processing for extracting the useful content like region and shape. Open morphological operation is used to break down the narrow joints, to smoothen the contour of objects and it will also eliminate the thin protrusions in the image. It is used when the image region consists of many numbers of noise. Close morphological operation is used to fuse the narrow joints, smoothen the sections of contour and also fills the contour gaps. It eliminates the smallest holes in the image and restores the connectivity between objects.

C. Image Segmentation: Image segmentation techniques used to find objects and borders (lines, curves, etc.) to extract useful content from an image that will be easy to analyse. In this phase, k means clustering algorithm and watershed segmentation algorithm are used to segment the chest x-ray images.

K means clustering algorithm - It is used when the unlabeled data is present (i.e. data without defined categories or the groups). It partitions the given data into k-clusters or k-centroids. The aim of clustering algorithm is to minimize the sum of squared distances between all the points and the cluster center.

Watershed segmentation algorithm - It is a region-based technique that will select one or more marker points for every object. The background is included as a separate object. The marker images are super imposed on the original image to find the segmented points in the original image.

D. ResNet-101 (Residual Network): IT is a Convolutional Neural Network (CNN) which is 101 layers deep. Resnet model is pre-trained from the ImageNet database. ResNet model will solve the problem of training very deep networks and it will improve the accuracy and performance. They are also useful in solving complex problems.

E. Convolutional Neural Network (CNN) Model
Convolution layer - It is the main and the very important building block of the CNN model. This layer performs the dot product of the kernel and the required portion of the respective field. The output of this is called an activation map. The output of this layer is fed as input to next layer.

Max pooling layer - The composite layer will reduce the size of the feature map. The output of the convolution layer is given as an insert in this layer. The maximum intensity value for each patch of the feature map is calculated by this layer.

ReLu (Rectified Linear Unit) - This activation function is applied to each field. After applying this function there will be a backpropagation and the weights will be updated and the output changes. This activation function will ignore all the negative weights and useful in classification.

Fully connected layer - Fully connected layer is popularly known as a dense layer. This has 3 layers they are input layer, hidden layer, and output layer. All layers have neurons and neurons of each layer are connected. This layer helps in extracting the important features from the image and forwards them to the output layer to classify the image.

Sigmoid activation function - This function is used to classify the images. So, the sigmoid activation function is called a classifier. In this function, the output ranges between 0 and 1. If the output neuron ranges between 0.5 to 1 the neurons will be activated and helps in classification.

The proposed CNN model is divided into different layers to classify the image. The input image size of $200 \times 200 \times 3$ is processed into various layers for classification. The layers for feature extraction consist of 3×3, 32, 3×3, 32, 3×3, 64, 3×3, 128, 3×3, 256, 3×3, 512, and ReLu activation function is present in between the layers to convert the negative values into non-negative values. The output obtained from convolution layers and max-pooling layers are converted into 2D planes are called as features maps. The Sigmoid activation function acts as a classifier and performs the image classification as shown in Fig. 3. Scikit learn python package is used to calculate the accuracy of bacteria and viruses present in the given chest x-ray image input [23].

$$\text{Accuracy}(y, \hat{y}) = \frac{1}{n} \sum_{i=0}^{n-1} 1(\hat{y} = y_i) \tag{1}$$

The normal cases are indicated with green colour and bacterial pneumonia and viral pneumonia cases are indicated with yellow colour as shown in Fig. 7. The train folder consists of two images named as goodlungs.png and badlungs.png. Image goodlungs.png indicates green colour chest x-ray image and this image will be superimposed on the input image after classifying image as normal case. Image badlungs.png indicates yellow colour chest x-ray image and this image will be super imposed on the input image after classifying image as pneumonia case.

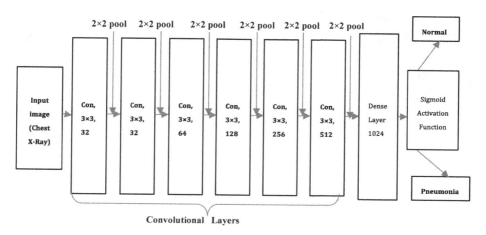

Fig. 3. Representation of CNN model

4 Results and Discussion

This project focuses on early detection of pneumonia to reduce the death rate in the world. We developed a model to detect and classify the pneumonia using chest x-ray images. We used python programming language to develop this work and to design a frontend, most popular python web framework flask is used to develop a web application framework. After pre-processing step, the images are segmented using k-means clustering and watershed algorithm. In the next step, all the important features are extracted from the segmented image using the CNN model, and the images are classified. All the procedures are shown below in the snapshots (Figs. 4, 5 and 6).

Fig. 4. After applying morphological open operation for chest X-Ray images

Fig. 5. After applying morphological close operation for chest X-Ray images

Fig. 6. After applying segmentation operation for chest X-Ray images

Finally, the CNN model will detect the pneumonia and gives the percentage of bacteria and viruses infected to the lungs. Scikit learn python package is used to calculate the accuracy of bacteria and viruses present in the given chest x-ray image input. The normal cases are indicated with green colour and bacterial pneumonia and viral pneumonia cases are indicated with yellow colour as shown in Fig. 7.

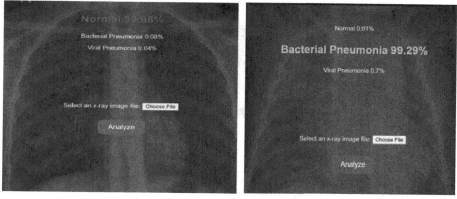

Fig. 7. Shows the accuracy of bacteria and viruses infected to normal and pneumonia cases (Color figure online)

CNN model is trained using chest X-Ray images and model accuracy and loss is shown in the Table 2.

Table 2. Shows the accuracy and loss for the pneumonia model

Epochs	Dropout	Learning rate	Batch size	Training accuracy	Training loss	Validation accuracy	Validation loss
1 (750)	0.5	0.0002	5	0.7974	0.5021	0.7994	0.4077
2 (375)	0.5	0.0001	10	0.8332	0.3671	0.9274	0.2225
5 (250)	0.6	0.0001	15	0.8647	0.3139	0.7866	0.4121
10 (188)	0.4	0.0004	20	0.8954	0.2659	0.7962	0.4679
15 (125)	0.4	0.0001	30	0.9141	0.2194	0.9200	0.2131

Table 3. Shows the performance results of the pneumonia

Model	Confusion matrix & Performance results (%)							
	TP	TN	FP	FN	Recall	Precision	F1-score	Accuracy
Pneumonia	214	214	34	38	84.92	86.29	85.6	85.6

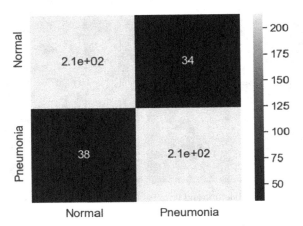

Fig. 8. Confusion matrix for pneumonia

The abbreviations in Table 3 are: TP (True Positive), TN (True Negative), FP (False Positive), FN (False Negative). The standard notation for 214 in Fig. 8 is denoted as 2.1e+02. The accuracy yield by the model on training datasets was 91.41% and on testing datasets was 85.6%. Our system detects and classify the cases of pneumonia and calculate the accuracy of bacteria and virus present in the lungs. So, our model is more efficient than existing research work.

5 Conclusion and Future Work

This work proposes an automatic system for detecting pneumonia using CNN model. Other research works have only developed model to detect pneumonia in the lungs but our model can detect bacterial pneumonia and viral pneumonia cases and calculate the percentage of bacteria and viruses present in the lungs. So early diagnosis of this lung abnormalities can reduce the death rate across the globe.

The proposed work can be extended as types of bacterial pneumonia and viral pneumonia can be detected and the output given by the system can be sent as a notification to end-users via email and audio by developing application.

References

1. Johns Hopkins Medicine, Pneumonia. https://www.hopkinsmedicine.org/health/conditions-and-diseases/pneumonia. Accessed 31 Dec 2019
2. Taina, J., Olli, R., Jussi, M.: Symptoms and signs of community-acquired pneumonia in children. Scand. J. Prim. Healthcare **21**, 52–56 (2003). ISSN 0281-3432
3. Contou, D., Claudinon, A., Pajot, O.: Bacterial and viral co-infections in patients with severe SARS-CoV-2 pneumonia admitted to a French ICU. Ann. Intensive Care **10**, 119 (2020)
4. World Health Organization: Household Air Pollution and Health [Fact Sheet], WHO, Geneva, Switzerland (2018). http://www.who.int/newa-room/fact-sheets/detail/household-air-pollution-and-health
5. Rudan, I., Pinto, B.: Epidemiology and etiology of childhood pneumonia. Bull. World Health Org. **86**, 408–416 (2008)
6. Samir, S., Shivajrao, M.: Deep convolutional neural network based medical image classification for disease diagnosis. J. Big Data **6**, 113 (2019). Yadav and Jadhav
7. Kundu, R., Das, R.: Pneumonia detection in chest X-Ray images using an ensemble of deep learning models. PLoS ONE **16**, e0256630 (2021). https://doi.org/10.1371/journal.pone0256630
8. Eishesawy, N.M., Ibrahim, D.M.: Deep pneumonia framework using deep learning models based on chest X-Ray images. Diagnostics **10**, 649 (2020)
9. Hashmi, M.F., Katiyar, S.: Efficient Pneumonia detection in Chest X-Ray images using deep transfer learning. Diagnostics **10**, 417 (2020)
10. Gabruseva, T., Poplavskiy, D., Kalinin, A.A.: Deep learning for automatic pneumonia detection, 28 May 2020 (2020)
11. Asnaoui, K.E.L., Idri, A.: Automated methods for detection and classification pneumonia based on X-Ray images using deep learning (2020)
12. Maulana, R., Kurniawan, D.: Smart devices for self-diagnosing of lung condition based on body temperature and fingernail color. IEEE (2020)
13. Urey, D.Y., Saul, C.J., Taktaloglu, C.D.: Early diagnosis of pneumonia with deep learning, 01 April 2019 (2019)
14. Stephen, O., Sain, M.: An efficient deep learning approach to pneumonia classification in healthcare, 27 March 2019 (2019)
15. Antin, B., Kravitz, J., Martayan, E.: Detecting pneumonia in chest X-Rays with supervised learning (2018)
16. Rajpurkar, P., Irvin, J.: CheXNet: radiologist - level pneumonia detection on chest X-Rays with deep learning, 25 December 2017 (2017)
17. Bejan, C.A., Xia, F.: Pneumonia identification using statistical feature selection. J. Am. Med. Inf. Assoc. **19**, 817–823 (2012)

18. Mendonca and Haas: Extracting information on pneumonia in infants using natural language processing of radiology reports, 5 March 2005 (2005)
19. Ponnada, V.T., Naga Srinivasu, S.V.: Integrated clinician decision supporting system for pneumonia and lung cancer detection. IJITEE **8**(8) (2019). ISSN: 2278-3075
20. Bhandary, A., Ananth Prabhu, G.: Deep learning framework to detect lung abnormality - a study with chest X-Ray and lung CT scan images. Elsevier (2019)
21. Khobragade, S., Tiwari, A.: Automatic detection of major lung diseases using chest radiographs and classification by feed-forward artificial neural network. IEEE (2016)
22. Bian, X.: https://www.kaggle.com/therealcyberlord/pneumonia-detection-using-deep-learning. Accessed 01 Sept 2021
23. Pedregosa, F., Varoquaux, G., Gramfort, A.: Scikit-learn: machine learning in Python. J. Mach. Learn. Res. **12**, 2825–2830 (2011)

Concrete Crack Segmentation Using Histogram Based Fast Clustering and Morphological Operators

Daipayan Ghosal, Rajdeep Kanjilal, Partha Pratim Roy, Abhisekh Nayek, Saraswati Dutta, and Krishna Gopal Dhal[✉]

Department of Computer Science and Application, Midnapore College (Autonomous), Paschim Medinipur, West Bengal, India
{saraswati.dutta,krishnagopal.dhal}@midnaporecollege.ac.in

Abstract. The problem of routinely detecting complicated cracks on coarse concrete surfaces using image processing is tough activity. Clustering is an efficient and easy unsupervised technique in the image segmentation area. Fuzzy C-Means and K-Means are the most efficient partitional clustering techniques. But, the computational effort of the image clustering substantially relies upon on image size because they consider the entire pixels. To overcome this problem, this paper devised a histogram based fast K-Means clustering method for the correct segmentation of the crack area within less computational effort due to the fact variety of grey levels in the histogram is a lot less than quantity of pixels present within the image. To enhance the segmentation quality, unsharp masking and morphological operations have been incorporated in the stated technique. The proposed technique has been in comparison with classical KM, FCM, Otsu method, and canny edge detector. Performance of the devised and other utilized techniques has been measured by computing well-known quality metrics. Investigational study exhibits that the devised technique provides better segmented crack area than other tested models.

Keywords: Clustering · Crack detection · Image processing · Image segmentation

1 Introduction

Engineered structures such as concrete surfaces, beams are frequently subjected to fatigue stress, cyclic loading, which causes cracks that generally begin on the surface of the structure at the microscopic level. Structure cracks result in material discontinuities and reduced local stiffness [1, 2]. Early analysis here enables the implementation of preventative actions to avoid potential failure and future damage [3]. Fracture/crack finding is the procedure of employing one of the machining processes to find flaws in a structure. There are two ways to detect cracks. A destructive test and a non-destructive test are involved. Deficiencies in the surface situation are evaluated by combining visual

A. A. Sk et al. (Eds.): ISAI 2022, CCIS 1695, pp. 305–313, 2022.
https://doi.org/10.1007/978-3-031-22485-0_28

inspection and detecting techniques [3]. The first degree of decay and the bearing capacity of the concrete structure are indicated by the type, width, number, and length of cracks on the surface of the structure [4]. Automatic crack detection has been developed to replace the slower conventional human subjective inspection processes for quick and accurate examination of surface faults. This allows for the adaptation of safer investigation approaches [5]. Non-destructive testing is quite successful with automatic fracture detection. Manual inspection makes it far more difficult to accurately assess the damage [6]. Several non-destructive testing methods, such as radiography testing, infrared and thermal testing, ultrasound testing, and laser testing, can be used for computerized crack detection [6].

Image-based fracture detection for non-destructive inspection is becoming more and more fascinating. Random crack shapes and widths, in addition to numerous noises including choppy lighting conditions, shadows, smudges, and concrete chips in the scanned image, contribute to some of the challenges in image-based detection [7]. Numerous image processing detection approaches were offered due to how easily it could be processed. Those techniques are mainly grouped into 3 types depending on the utilized methods, specifically (i) threshold-based approach (ii) neural network-based approach and (iii) clustering-primarily based approach.

Convolutional neural community (CNN) is a way which is extensively used in signal processing and image classification. A quicker region-based convolutional neural network is included into Kang et al. devised hybrid crack localization method [8] and performed better than deep learning methods under consideration. It also performs effectively in various difficult environments with complicated visual backgrounds. However, preparing a sizable volume of the ground truth for a dataset that is pixel-level categorized takes a lot of effort and resources. Liu et al. [9] proposed a strong crack segmentation approach using image patches to detect. This model had vast improvement in phrases of accuracy and robustness over previous work. In the same manner, some other efficient CNN models [10–17] had also been developed for crack detection and provided satisfactory results. Therefore, it can be said that although CNN has the great impact in crack segmentation and detection, but it also has some drawbacks like it is a supervised approach and hence requires training, need large image dataset with corresponding ground truth which is critical in crack segmentation domain. For the training, GPU is needed.

Therefore, researchers also employed thresholding and clustering techniques for crack detection which are unsupervised, simple, and effective. For example, a model for detecting concrete fractures was put forth by Dinh et al. [18] by considering histogram thresholding to detach areas of interest. The created technique is then applied to the smoothed image's grey-scale histogram for automated detection of large peaks. When cracks can be identified without the need of heuristic reasoning, the evaluation of the proposed method worked better on a variety of test photos. This method does, however, incorporate several deep learning techniques that are typically computationally and structurally demanding. Cao [19] also performed a comparative study of thresholding techniques for crack detection. Whereas, Nnolim [20] combined the thresholding and clustering techniques for the crack detection. Spectral clustering was applied by Vedrtnam et al. [21] for crack detection. Noh et al. [22] employed fuzzy c-means (FCM) for the right segmentation of the crack area and provided satisfactory result. Here authors also used dilation morphological operation and filtering techniques to improve the results. Therefore, clustering and thresholding attracts researchers for the accurate crack detection.

However, the classical clustering techniques like k-means and FCM consider all the pixels of the images and hence the computational complexity of the clustering technique considerably relies on the image size. However, thresholding makes use of the histogram of the image and hence, time complexity depends on number of gray levels and is not influenced by image size. By considering this idea, this study develops a histogram based fast K-means like crisp clustering strategy for the proper segmentation of the crack area. Unsharp masking based filtering and morphological operations have also been considered for the better results.

The other parts of the research are organized in the following way: Sect. 2 explains the methodology, and Sect. 3 discusses the outcomes. The conclusions are provided in Sect. 4.

2 Methodology

The proposed crack area segmentation method consists of three major steps. In the pre-processing step, at to begin with the color image is change over to gray scale image by using "RGB2GRAY" inbuilt function of the MATLAB software. Then the unsharp masking has been applied to make the image sharp. After that, histogram based fast clustering approach then applied over the preprocessed image for crack area segmentation. In the final step, the morphological operations have been performed to enhance the segmentation standard. The flowchart of the devised technique is presented in Fig. 1.

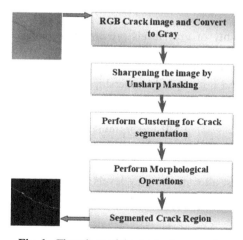

Fig. 1. Flowchart of the devised approach.

2.1 Unsharp Masking

This [23, 24] method is predicated on a publishing field method of sharpening an image by subtracting an obscured (unsharp) form of the concerned image. The blurred form of the image is computed by utilizing Gaussian low pass filter in this study. The STD (Standard deviation) value for the Gaussian low pass filter has been taken as 1. Another parameter called Strength of the sharpening effect has been taken as 0.8. Lastly the Minimum contrast threshold parameter for crack images is set to zero. These three parameters set from the experience for better outcomes.

2.2 Histogram Based K-Means Clustering

K-means (KM) [25–27] is a powerful clustering technique which partitioned the image into K numbers of clusters having high and low intra- and inter-cluster relationship, respectively. But KM has one notable problem which is that, its time complexity depends on its size. The tedious distance between each of the N pixels in the image and each of the K cluster centers are calculated during the clustering process. As a result, when image size and cluster count are increased, a significant amount of computing work is required. Generally, the time complexity of the KM is O(N × K × d × t) [28, 29]. N, K and d indicate the number of pixels, clusters, and dimension, respectively. It is fact that usually, d, K ≪ N. Hence, image size is a massive issue. Last of all, t shows iterations to finish the process.

  To get over the difficulty of the high temporal complexity, the Histogram based K-Means (HBKM) [28] technique performs clustering on the grey level histogram rather than the pixels of the image. The fact that the grey levels are typically substantially less than the total number of pixels in the image contributes to the short calculating time. The following equation represents the objective.

$$J = \underset{K}{\arg\min} \sum_{i=1}^{L} \sum_{j=1}^{K} \gamma_i u_{ij} \left\| gl_i - m_j \right\|^2 \tag{1}$$

L denotes the quantity of grey levels present in the image. An 8-bit image, for instance, has 256 distinct shades of grey. $\|.\|$ indicates inner product-induced norm, gray level is gl_i, cluster center m_j and γ_i is the total number of pixels with gl_i gray level. Hence, $\sum_{i=1}^{L} \gamma_i = N$ and $1 \leq i \leq L$. Membership $u_{ij} = 1$ for pixel gl_i if it belongs to a cluster C_j; otherwise $u_{ij} = 0$. Scientifically, it is as follows:

$$u_{ij} = \begin{cases} 1 \text{ if } j = \underset{k}{\arg\min} \| gl_i - m_k \|^2 \\ 0 \text{ otherwise} \end{cases} \tag{2}$$

As a result, we must allocate the grey levels to the closest cluster. The following equations are used to compute the cluster centers.

$$\frac{\partial J}{\partial m_j} = 2 \sum_{i=1}^{L} \gamma_i u_{ij} \left(gl_i - m_j \right) = 0$$

$$\Rightarrow m_j = \frac{\sum_{i=1}^{L} \gamma_i u_{ij} gl_i}{\sum_{i=1}^{L} u_{ij}} \tag{3}$$

In order to make the updated grayscale allocations visible to the clusters, recalculation of cluster centers is required. In Algorithm 1, we describe the HBKM procedure based on the above discussion.

Algorithm 1: The of Procedure Histogram based K-Means
1. Initialize K cluster centers at random.
2. **while** (*Stopping condition does not met*)
3. For each histogram's gray level (gl_i), computes membership u_{ij} to every center m_j.
4. Again calculate the m_j of each cluster by using Eq.(3).
5. **end of while**
6. **output:** Segment the input image into K number of regions by utilizing final centers.

We can use the various termination conditions in HBKM just like in traditional KM. K-Means' poor overall performance across a very large image collection can be attributed primarily to its high time complexity. Essentially, in the developed method, $1 \leq gl_i \leq L$, where L is the total gray levels of concerned image and $L \ll N$ normally. Then time complexity of HBKM is $O(L \times K \times t)$, which is independent of image size. Hence, much less than classical pixel-based KM.

2.3 Morphological Operations

A broad range of image processing techniques known as morphology transform images depending on shapes [30]. Each pixel in the image is changed during a morphological operation according on how distinctive pixels in its vicinity are valued. Two morphological operations on a binary edge picture have been carried out in this study. To remove the background's eight-connectivity, we first utilize diagonal fill. Then, if a pixel has nonzero neighbors who are not linked, bridge unconnected pixels, which converts the pixel's value from zero to one. The MATLAB software's built-in functions were used to complete the two tasks [31].

3 Experimental Results

The test was run on 458 crack pictures using MatlabR2018b and Windows-10 OS on a computer with an x64 architecture and an Intel core i5 CPU and 16 GB of RAM. The website link is https://data.mendeley.com/datasets/jwsn7tfbrp/1, and the photographs were taken from [32]. Here, the algorithms Histogram-based K-Means (HBKM) with Morphological Operations (Proposed Method), Classical K-Means (KM) [26, 28, 36], Fuzzy C-Means (FCM) [33], Canny method [34], and Otsu Thresholding Method [35] were utilized. The parameter setting for the mentioned clustering algorithms is as follows:

For proposed method, classical KM, FCM, number of clusters (k) has been considered as 4. Fuzzification parameter of FCM is set to 2 and if maximum refinement, between two progressive partition matrices U is much less than minimal error threshold η then stop the corresponding set of rules and $\eta = 10^{-5}$. For proposed histogram-based clustering and KM, KMMF, stop the process if the difference in centroid values is lower than η. In Otsu thresholding, number of thresholds has been taken as 1. So, binary thresholding is performed for finding the crack area.

The effectiveness of the clustering approaches used has been assessed by generating the performance assessment parameters namely Accuracy (AC), Dice Index (DI), Jaccard Index (JI), and Matthew's correlation coefficient (MCC) [29]. The higher values of these quality parameters reflect the better segmentation.

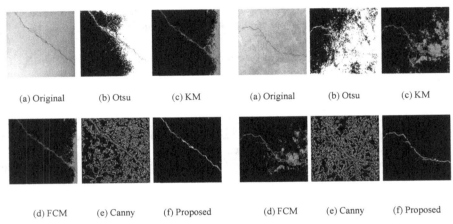

(a) Original   (b) Otsu   (c) KM   (a) Original   (b) Otsu   (c) KM

(d) FCM   (e) Canny   (f) Proposed   (d) FCM   (e) Canny   (f) Proposed

Fig. 2. Result for crack segmentation over first image

Fig. 3. Result for crack segmentation over second image

The segmentation results of the proposed approach and other tested algorithms have been presented in Figs. 2 and 3. As the utilized clustering algorithms are random in nature, they were run 10 times for every image and the corresponding best runs are recorded. The crack segmentation efficiency of the employed clustering models has been measured by computing accuracy, MCC, Dice, and Jaccard indices which are given in Table 1. The ground truth images for the tested images have been prepared by the experts manually and have been included with the aforementioned dataset. Visual and numerical analysis of the segmented outcomes clearly demonstrate that the proposed HBKM with Morphological Operators provides better outcomes compare to other tested Edge-Based, Thresholding based and classical Clustering-based Segmentation Methods. The Proposed Histogram-based K-Means Method with Morphological Operations confers the best outcomes among all the segmentation models including pixel-based clustering models. Whereas, the Otsu and Canny based are the worst among all. As a consequence, it can be said that the proposed Histogram-based K-Means Method with Morphological Operations can be an efficient alternative to classical clustering, edge-based and threshold-based segmentation algorithms. Results also show that Classical FCM gives better results than Classical K-Means in this image clustering field. But, usage of histogram-based method instead of the classical pixel-based ones into K-Means makes it superior to all the others including FCM.

Table 1. Quality Parameters for clustering techniques for nucleus detection over 458 images

Method	Accuracy	MCC	Dice	Jaccard	Execution time
Otsu	0.58361	0.10837	0.08526	0.05700	0.24 s
K-Means	0.93333	0.28231	0.26663	0.19372	7.15 s
FCM	0.95261	0.25456	0.22883	0.22371	10.20 s
Canny	0.79310	0.00509	0.03018	0.01540	**0.10 s**
Proposed method	**0.96558**	**0.37411**	**0.36635**	**0.28371**	0.19 s

bold indicates best outcomes

4 Conclusion

This study represents a Histogram based fast clustering strategy with morphological operation for the proper segmentation of the crack from concrete structure. The proposed method utilizes the unsharp masking technique for preprocessing the input image. The proposed method has been compared to classical KM, FCM, Otsu, and canny operator. The visual and quality metrics clearly illustrate the prevalence of the devised method over rest used techniques. The major merit of the proposed methods is the method is basically utilizing the gray level of the histogram for clustering in the place of pixels. Hence, the computational time is reduced to some great extent. As it is an unsupervised method, therefore, the critical training is not needed like deep learning-based techniques. Whereas, the main limitations are: (i) The method is not noise robust and (ii) the problem of local optima trapping is not tackled in the study. As a consequence, in future, researchers can incorporate the noise immunity ability to the proposed method. Nature-inspired optimization algorithms can also be employed for performing the histogram-based clustering which can tackle the local optima trapping problem. Deep learning-based strategies [37] can also be compared with the proposed technique.

Funding.   There is no funding associate with this research.

Ethical Approval.   This article does not contain any studies with human participants or animals performed by any of the authors.

Conflict of Interest.   On behalf of all authors, the corresponding author states that there is no conflict of interest. The authors declare that they have no conflict of interest.

References

1. Budiansky, B., O'connell, R.J.: Elastic moduli of a cracked solid. Int. J. Solids Struct. **12**(2), 81–97 (1976)
2. Aboudi, J.: Stiffness reduction of cracked solids. Eng. Fract. Mech. **26**(5), 637–650 (1987)
3. Dhital, D., Lee, J.R.: A fully non-contact ultrasonic propagation imaging system for closed surface crack evaluation. Exp. Mech. **52**(8), 1111–1122 (2012)
4. Shan, B., Zheng, S., Ou, J.: A stereovision-based crack width detection approach for concrete surface assessment. KSCE J. Civ. Eng. **20**(2), 803–812 (2016)
5. Oliveira, H., Correia, P.L.: Automatic road crack detection and characterization. IEEE Trans. Intell. Transp. Syst. **14**(1), 155–168 (2012)
6. Wang, P., Huang, H.: Comparison analysis on present image-based crack detection methods in concrete structures. In: 2010 3rd International Congress on Image and Signal Processing, vol. 5, pp. 2530–2533. IEEE (2010)
7. Fujita, Y., Hamamoto, Y.: A robust automatic crack detection method from noisy concrete surfaces. Mach. Vis. Appl. **22**(2), 245–254 (2011)
8. Kang, D.H., Benipal, S., Cha, Y.-J.: Hybrid concrete crack segmentation and quantification across complex backgrounds without a large training dataset. In: Madarshahian, R., Hemez, F. (eds.) Data Science in Engineering, Volume 9. CPSEMS, pp. 123–128. Springer, Cham (2022). https://doi.org/10.1007/978-3-030-76004-5_14
9. Qu, Z., Chen, W., Wang, S.Y., Yi, T.M., Liu, L.: A crack detection algorithm for concrete pavement based on attention mechanism and multi-features fusion. IEEE Trans. Intell. Transp. Syst. **23**, 11710–11719 (2021)
10. Yamane, T., Chun, P.J.: Crack detection from a concrete surface image based on semantic segmentation using deep learning. J. Adv. Concr. Technol. **18**(9), 493–504 (2020)
11. Han, C., Ma, T., Huyan, J., Huang, X., Zhang, Y.: CrackW-Net: a novel pavement crack image segmentation convolutional neural network. IEEE Trans. Intell. Transp. Syst. **23**, 22135–22144 (2021)
12. Tang, Y., Zhang, A.A., Luo, L., Wang, G., Yang, E.: Pixel-level pavement crack segmentation with encoder-decoder network. Measurement **184**, 109914 (2021)
13. Ali, R., Chuah, J.H., Talip, M.S.A., Mokhtar, N., Shoaib, M.A.: Automatic pixel-level crack segmentation in images using fully convolutional neural network based on residual blocks and pixel local weights. Eng. Appl. Artif. Intell. **104**, 104391 (2021)
14. Lee, D., Kim, J., Lee, D.: Robust concrete crack detection using deep learning-based semantic segmentation. Int. J. Aeronaut. Space Sci. **20**(1), 287–299 (2019)
15. Piyathilaka, L., Preethichandra, D.M.G., Izhar, U., Kahandawa, G.: Real-time concrete crack detection and instance segmentation using deep transfer learning. In: Engineering Proceedings, vol. 2, no. 1, p. 91. Multidisciplinary Digital Publishing Institute (2020)
16. Choi, W., Cha, Y.J.: SDDNet: real-time crack segmentation. IEEE Trans. Ind. Electron. **67**(9), 8016–8025 (2019)
17. Kalfarisi, R., Wu, Z.Y., Soh, K.: Crack detection and segmentation using deep learning with 3D reality mesh model for quantitative assessment and integrated visualization. J. Comput. Civ. Eng. **34**(3), 04020010 (2020)
18. Dinh, T.H., Ha, Q.P., La, H.M.: Computer vision-based method for concrete crack detection. In: 2016 14th International Conference on Control, Automation, Robotics and Vision (ICARCV), pp. 1–6. IEEE (2016)
19. Cao, J.: Research on crack detection of bridge deck based on computer vision. In: IOP Conference Series: Earth and Environmental Science, vol. 768, no. 1, p. 012161. IOP Publishing (2021)

20. Nnolim, U.A.: Automated crack segmentation via saturation channel thresholding, area classification and fusion of modified level set segmentation with Canny edge detection. Heliyon **6**(12), e05748 (2020)

21. Vedrtnam, A., Kumar, S., Barluenga, G., Chaturvedi, S.: Early crack detection using modified spectral clustering method assisted with FE analysis for distress anticipation in cement-based composites. Sci. Rep. **11**(1), 1–19 (2021)

22. Noh, Y., Koo, D., Kang, Y.M., Park, D., Lee, D.: Automatic crack detection on concrete images using segmentation via fuzzy C-means clustering. In: 2017 International Conference on Applied System Innovation (ICASI), pp. 877–880. IEEE (2017)

23. Westin, C.F., Knutsson, H., Kikinis, R.: Adaptive image filtering. In: Handbook of Medical Imaging Processing and Analysis, pp. 3208–3212. Academic Press (2000)

24. https://in.mathworks.com/help/images/ref/imsharpen.html. Accessed 21 Oct 2021

25. Dhal, K.G., Das, A., Ray, S., Das, S.: A clustering based classification approach based on modified cuckoo search algorithm. Pattern Recogn. Image Anal. **29**(3), 344–359 (2019)

26. Dhal, K.G., Gálvez, J., Ray, S., Das, A., Das, S.: Acute lymphoblastic leukemia image segmentation driven by stochastic fractal search. Multimed. Tools Appl. **79**, 1–29 (2020). https://doi.org/10.1007/s11042-019-08417-z

27. Dhal, K.G., Gálvez, J., Das, S.: Toward the modification of flower pollination algorithm in clustering-based image segmentation. Neural Comput. Appl. **32**(8), 3059–3077 (2019). https://doi.org/10.1007/s00521-019-04585-z

28. Das, A., Dhal, K.G., Ray, S., Gálvez, J.: Histogram-based fast and robust image clustering using stochastic fractal search and morphological reconstruction. Neural Comput. Appl. **34**, 4531–4554 (2021). https://doi.org/10.1007/s00521-021-06610-6

29. Dhal, K.G., Das, A., Ray, S., Sarkar, K., Gálvez, J.: An Analytical Review on Rough Set Based Image Clustering. Arch. Comput. Methods Eng. **29**, 1–30 (2021). https://doi.org/10.1007/s11831-021-09629-z

30. Haralick, R.M., Shapiro, L.G.: Computer and Robot Vision, vol. 1. Addison-Wesley, Boston (1992)

31. https://in.mathworks.com/help/images/ref/bwmorph.html. Accessed 21 Oct 2021

32. Özgenel, Ç.F.: Concrete Crack Segmentation Dataset. Mendeley Data, 1 (2019)

33. Dhal, K.G., Das, A., Ray, S., Gálvez, J.: Randomly Attracted Rough Firefly Algorithm for histogram based fuzzy image clustering. Knowl.-Based Syst. **216**, 106814 (2021). https://doi.org/10.1016/j.knosys.2021.106814

34. Ding, L., Goshtasby, A.: On the Canny edge detector. Pattern Recogn. **34**(3), 721–725 (2001)

35. Ray, S., Das, A., Dhal, K.G., Gálvez, J., Naskar, P.K.: Cauchy with whale optimizer based eagle strategy for multi-level color hematology image segmentation. Neural Comput. Appl. **33**(11), 5917–5949 (2020). https://doi.org/10.1007/s00521-020-05368-7

36. Dhal, K.G., Fister Jr., I., Das, A., Ray, S., Das, S.: Breast histopathology image clustering using cuckoo search algorithm. In: Proceedings of the 5th Student Computer Science Research Conference, pp. 47–54, Slovenia (2018)

37. Deb, M., Dhal, K.G., Mondal, R., Gálvez, J.: Paddy disease classification study: a deep convolutional neural network approach. Opt. Mem. Neural Netw. **30**(4), 338–357 (2021)

Human Gender Classification Based on Hand Images Using Deep Learning

Rajesh Mukherjee[1], Asish Bera[2(✉)], Debotosh Bhattacharjee[3], and Mita Nasipuri[3]

[1] Department of Computer Science and Engineering, Haldia Institute of Technology, Haldia, WB, India
[2] Department of Computer Science and Information Systems, Birla Institute of Technology and Science Pilani, Pilani Campus, Pilani 333 031, Rajasthan, India
`asish.bera@pilani.bits-pilani.ac.in`
[3] Department of Computer Science and Engingeering, Jadavpur University, Kolkata, WB, India

Abstract. Soft biometric traits (*e.g.*, gender, age, etc. can characterize very relevant personal information. The hand-based traits are studied for traditional/hard biometric recognition for diverse applications. However, little attention is focused to tackle soft biometrics using hand images. In this paper, human gender classification is addressed using the frontal and dorsal hand images of a human. A new hand dataset is created at the Jadavpur University, India denoted as JU-HD for experiments. It represents significant posture variations in an uncontrolled laboratory environment. Sample hand images of 57 persons are collected to incorporate more user-flexibility in posing the hands that incur additional challenges to discriminate the person's gender. Five backbone CNNs are used to develop a deep model for gender classification. The method achieves 90.49% accuracy on JU-HD using Inception-v3. Also, improved gender classification accuracy is achieved on 11k hands dataset (Easy-Chair Pre-print: [27].).

Keywords: Convolutional Neural Networks (CNN) · Gender classification · Hand biometrics · Soft biometrics

1 Introduction

Soft biometrics (*e.g.*, gender, age, ethnicity, etc.) are essential for biometric, commercial, surveillance, human-computer interaction, demographic study, and forensics applications [14,15]. These soft biometric based ancillary information, mainly the human face, hand-shape, gait, palmprint, voice, and others are garnered to identify a person [20,30,32]. The human face and hand-based modalities are explored by the biometric researchers, mainly for hard/conventional biometrics, and related applications in the areas of artificial intelligence, machine learning, and pattern recognition. Among several physiological modalities, the fingerprint, hand geometry, dorsal hand-vein, palmprint, etc. have received profound research attention [2,8,26,31]. Hand-shape and palmprint are useful for

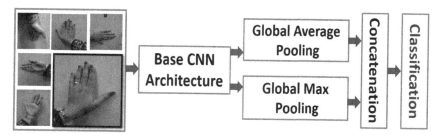

Fig. 1. Proposed gender recognition method. The CNNs compute deep feature maps which are pooled in two paths (global average pooling and global max pooling); and combined them prior to classification. Sufficient pose-variations are considered during sample collection of JU-HD, shown in the left-most grid.

personal authentication for hard and soft biometrics [3,6,7,9,11,21]. Other than traditional biometric authentication (*i.e.*, attendance maintenance), hand images are suitable for gesture recognition [28], gender classification [26], anti-spoofing [11,12], and other relevant areas. These applications are also developed using the face, fingerprint, etc. as a uni-modal and/or their fusion as a multi-biometric system [17,29,33]. Human gender can be classified using the images of face, fingerprint, hand, iris, and other traits [14,18]. However, little interest is focused on the soft biometrics based on non-intrusive features of frontal-dorsal hand images. Thus, our main objective is to recognize the gender of a person from frontal and dorsal hand images which are collected in an unconstrained and contact-less environment considering the posture, illumination, and view variations. The motivation for creating a new dataset is the unavailability of a challenging public hand-image dataset for deep learning [16]. Though, 11k hands [3] is tested for gender recognition, however, the variations and imaging conditions of 11k are limited, shown in Fig. 3. Hence, it may not be sufficient for real-world applications. Some other hand datasets as studied in [3], are created before deep learning era. Those datasets are focused on hard biometrics only, and do not garner ground-truth annotations for gender classification. The hand-breadth and ratio between index- and ring-finger can offer an effective insight for recognizing gender. However, these parameters can vary due to the diversity in populations, geographical, and other constraints [14]. Traditional gender recognition systems follow a common pipeline with subsequent stages [34]. After pre-processing, diverse types of hand-crafted features are computed for classification [5]. Though, these methods offer a good solution, yet, suffer from certain limitations, such as manual supervision during feature extraction and selection. Many methods cannot produce a high performance on a larger dataset. Thus, some recent works have employed convolutional neural networks (CNNs) to improve the accuracy on a large dataset with less manual guidance. The effectiveness of CNNs relies on salient feature extraction from multiple deep layers in an end-to-end pipeline which is used to address computer vision and pattern recognition challenges [23], including biometrics.

The CNNs has been explored for hand shape and palmprint recognition [3, 6,35,36]. However, the application of CNNs for gender recognition is not fully studied. In this work, we propose a simple and effective baseline CNN for gender classification using hand images. For experiments, a new hand dataset is created at our Laboratory at Jadavpur University, India, namely JU-HD. It contains a wider range of variations in hand pose which is novel than other existing datasets, such as 11k hands [3]. Samples of JU-HD illustrating ample posture variations at different environmental conditions are shown in Fig. 2. The main contributions of this work are two-fold:

- A new hand database is created for gender classification, representing the frontal and dorsal hand images at unrestricted and sufficient hand-pose variations.
- A fusion of pooled deep features, extracted from the state-of-the-art base CNN architectures, is applied to assess the performance for gender classification.

The rest of the paper is organized as follows: related work is studied in Sect. 2, the proposed method is described in Sect. 3, and an experimental description is given in Sect. 4. Finally, the conclusion is drawn in Sect. 5.

2   Related Work

Existing works on gender classification use the region and boundary-based feature descriptors such as the Zernike moments, Fourier descriptors, and adapt fusion methods [5]. The geometric features of palm images are tested in [34]. Geometrical measurements of right-hand are used for gender recognition from 50 Iraqis [4]. Few methods are developed for hand biometrics only using hand images of public datasets [10,11]. However, those works have not focused on gender recognition. Recently, few methods have addressed this problem using CNNs, such as 11k hands [3]. It provides a large dataset for both hand biometrics and gender classification using palm and dorsal hand images. The samples are captured in a controlled environment on a contrastive white background (Fig. 3). It has proposed a CNN model considering color images and local binary patterns. It achieves 97.3% and 94.2% accuracy for dorsal and palmar hands, respectively using the pre-trained AlexNet. Global and part-aware network (GPA-Net) evaluates the performance on 11k hands for biometrics [6]. Multiple attribute estimation using multi-CNNs on 11k hand dataset is presented in [25]. Gender and ethnicity classification using palmar images of the NTU-PI-v1 database is presented in [26]. Five CNNs are fine-tuned and tested on the full hand, segmented, and palmprint (RoI) images, and the accuracy for gender classification is 88.13% using DenseNet.

In this direction, other modalities such as the face, palmprint, gait, etc. are studied [13,19,22]. Age and gender classification from unconstrained facial images using CNN is explored in [24]. Gender recognition using pedestrian images is described in [1]. A deep model is proposed using fingerprints in [31]. In this paper, a simple CNN model is tested for gender classification using a new growing hand dataset, JU-HD.

3   Methodology

The proposed method fuses two sets of feature maps, illustrated in Fig. 1. Let, a hand image is $I \in R^{H \times W \times 3}$, where H and W represent the height and width of input-image with 3 color (RGB) channels, respectively. A convolutional neural network $N(\sum_i \omega_i . x_i + b)$ (weight ω_i, input x_i, and bias b at i^{th} layer) is used to extract the deep features $F = N(I) \in R^{h \times w \times c}$ from I, where h, w, and c represent the height, width, and number of channels of convolutional feature maps of the last layer of base CNN, respectively. Next, global average pooling p_{avg} (GAP) and global max pooling p_{max} (GMP) are applied to reduce the spatial dimension by selecting important features via two paths, $f_a = p_{avg}(F)$ and $f_m = p_{max}(F)$. It summarizes the feature maps and maintains the translation invariance. Both pooling schemes are important to emphasize on the most important (max-pooling) as well as mean (average-pooling) value of feature map. Thus, fusing both is an alternative way to adopt their benefits, as followed here. These two feature maps are fused to produce a high-level feature map $f_c = f_a \oplus f_m$, where $\oplus$ is a linear concatenation function. Finally, the *softmax* predicts the probability ($\bar{y}$) to classify the gender from the input image, $\bar{y}[0, 1] = softmax(f_c)$. To solve binary classification problem, '0' is labeled for the 'female' and '1' is assigned as the 'male' class.

$$F = N(I); \quad \text{where } F \in R^{h \times w \times c}; \quad I \in R^{H \times W \times 3}; \quad \text{and } N(\sum_i \omega_i . x_i + b) \quad \text{is a CNN} \quad (1)$$

$$f_a = p_{avg}(F) \text{ and } f_m = p_{max}(F); \quad f_c = [f_a \oplus f_m]; \quad \text{and } \bar{y} = softmax(f_c) \quad (2)$$

Implementation: We have used five backbone CNNs and fine-tuned on the target dataset. The VGG-16, VGG-19, Xception, ResNet-50, and Inception-v3 backbones are used for feature extraction from the last layer of the respective CNN model. Then, we apply the GAP and GMP via two different paths (Fig. 1). Finally, these two paths are concatenated and followed by *softmax* to generate output probabilities. The binary cross-entropy loss function (L) optimizes the training task.

$$L = \frac{1}{k} \sum_{i=1}^{k} -[y_i . log(p_i) + (1 - y_i) . log(1 - p_i)] \quad (3)$$

where, p_i is the probability of female-class, and $(1 - p_i)$ is the probability of male-class, y_i is the true class-label, $\bar{y}_i$ is the predicted class-label, and k is the number of data samples. The stochastic gradient descent (SGD) optimizer is used with a learning rate of 0.01. The model is trained for 100 epochs with 16 mini batch-size. The input image-size is $448 \times 448 \times 3$ and standard data augmentation such as horizontal-flip ± 0.2, and rotation ± 0.2 are applied to enhance data diversity. Pre-trained ImageNet weights are used in base $N(.)$ for quicker learning convergence. The output feature dimension (F) of Xception base is $7 \times 7 \times 2048$, and it varies for other CNNs. The pooling squeezes a feature map of size $w \times h \times c$ to $1 \times 1 \times c$. After applying GAP and GMP, the feature maps becomes $f_a = f_m = 2048$ and the concatenation produces $f_c = 4096$ features. The dropout rate of 0.2 is applied to avoid overfitting problem and it improves the generalization ability.

4 Experiments

We precisely describe JU-HD biometric sample collection from both sides of a hand. Next, experimental analyses on JU-HD and 11k hands using five CNNs are provided.

Table 1. JU-HD summary: frontal, dorsal, and combined both types hand images

Gender	Persons	Frontal		Dorsal		Combined both	
		Training	Testing	Training	Testing	Training	Testing
Female	17	92	50	105	40	197	90
Male	40	220	112	254	82	474	194
Total	57	312	162	359	122	671	284

4.1 Hand Dataset Description (JU-HD)

A new hand dataset is created at the Jadavpur University, India, namely JU-HD. It contains the right- and left- hand frontal and dorsal images of 57 individuals, including UG and PG students, researchers, and professors, most of them are from Computer Science and Engineering Department. During image acquisition, 15–17 hand images are collected from each person with a sufficient posture variations using a Samsung digital camera at 72 dpi. The lighting, hand accessories, and environmental variations are also considered. The image size is 1536×2048 pixels. The age ranges from 18 to 50 years, originating with the Asian ethnicity. We have maintained the ethical issues and privacy of the users during the image collection process. There is no commercial gain involved in this work. These are clearly specified to all participants based on which they have agreed to provide their biometric data. Detailed specification about this dataset is given in Table 1, and samples of JU-HD are shown in Fig. 2. The motivation for creating a new dataset is mainly the unconstrained posture variations and user-flexibility during image acquisition. In this regard, sample images from 11k dataset are shown in Fig. 3. It shows the clear environmental and image acquisition conditions (1200×1600 pixels, 96 dpi), and little posture variations, which might not always be possible in read-world scenarios. Prior to the deep learning era, other hand datasets are created for hand-shape and/or palmprint verification which are not suitable for gender classification due to the absence of ground-truth labels or meta-data for soft biometrics. In contrast, we consider a more challenging image acquisition set-up and incorporate more data variations. Our JU-HD is growing to be a larger dataset.

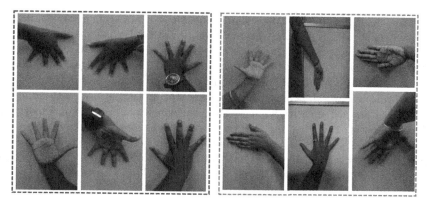

Fig. 2. Sample hands from JU-HD. Left: intra-pose variations (frontal and dorsal) of the same male-person. Right: inter-pose variations (frontal and dorsal) of various female-person, showing different imaging conditions.

Fig. 3. Examples from 11k Hand dataset, showing uniform imaging set-up

4.2   Experiments and Results

The Receiver Operator Characteristic (ROC) curve is used to evaluate binary classification problems. Area Under the Curve (AUC) computes the ability to distinguish between the classes which can be used as a summary of ROC curve. A higher AUC indicates a better performance to distinguish between the female and male classes. The accuracy (%) and AUC (%) metrics are used. The computational complexity of CNN is computed in terms of model parameters in Millions (M).

The experiments are carried out in Google Colaboratory (Colab-Pro). First, the performances using the frontal and dorsal hand images are computed. Then, both categories of hand samples are combined for evaluation. The results are given in Table 2. As the data samples for each type are not sufficient for a deep framework, thus, the models could not learn well to produce good results. As more samples are included in dataset, the model learns to improve the performance. The modern CNNs comprise with less computational parameters and can offer improved performance. Xception (20.9M) and Inception-v3 (21.8M) are lighter models and achieve better accuracy than ResNet and VGG families, evident in Table 2. We have tested and compared the performance on 11k hands [3] with 70:30 train-test ratio, and results are given in Table 3. The accuracy of our method outperforms the classification model using deep features by SVM on

11k with a clear margin. It implies that 11k dataset is not sufficiently challenging compared to JU-HD regarding the performance of CNNs. We have achieved 99% accuracy in almost all the cases on 11k hands, while the accuracy is only 90.5% on JU-HD combining both frontal and dorsal hand images. The training and testing accuracy during the learning process for the combination of both types of samples are shown in Fig. 4. Confusion matrix is useful to conceptualize other standard metrics such as the precision, recall, and specificity. In a confusion matrix, the diagonal values represent the predicted-labels are equal to the true-labels, whereas non-diagonal values represent those which are mislabeled by the classifier. In this test, the best performance (accuracy: 90.49% and AUC: 94.25%) is achieved using Inception-v3. The Xception has produced

Table 2. Gender classification performance of various CNNs using frontal, dorsal, and combined both types of JU-HD images. Model parameters are in given Millions (M)

CNN model	Frontal		Dorsal		Combined both		Model parameters (M)
	Accuracy	AUC	Accuracy	AUC	Accuracy	AUC	
VGG-16	74.10	80.65	80.70	91.92	84.15	87.95	138.4
VGG-19	74.70	80.88	74.59	82.63	82.74	87.33	143.7
ResNet-50	82.53	87.58	90.16	94.42	88.73	92.20	23.6
Xception	**87.35**	**92.79**	92.62	93.70	90.14	93.44	20.9
Inception-v3	84.33	91.26	**92.62**	**94.59**	**90.49**	**94.25**	21.8

Table 3. Gender classification accuracy (%) on frontal, and dorsal 11k Hands

Hand (# Train: #Test)	VGG-16	VGG-19	ResNet-50	Xception	Inception-v3	CNN+SVM [3]
Frontal (3778: 1618)	99.01	99.87	99.75	**99.94**	99.75	94.20
Dorsal (3977: 1703)	98.88	99.65	99.12	99.71	**99.82**	97.30

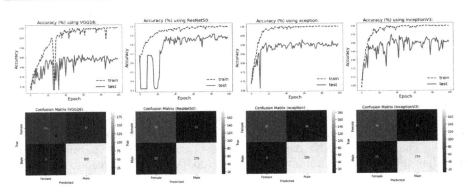

Fig. 4. Gender recognition performance on JU-HD (top: accuracy and bottom: confusion matrix). Left to right (per cols): VGG-16, ResNet-50, Xception, and Inception-v3.

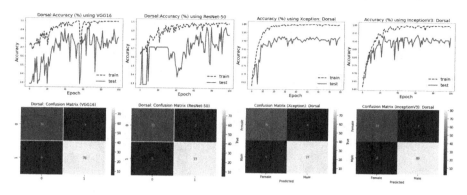

Fig. 5. Gender classification performance on dorsal JU-HD (top: accuracy and bottom: confusion matrix). Left to right (per col): VGG-16, ResNet-50, Xception, and Incep-v3.

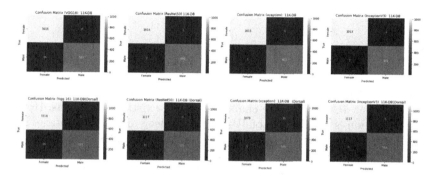

Fig. 6. Gender classification performance (confusion matrix) on 11k hands.

similar results. The VGG family is computationally heavier due to huge model parameters than other CNNs. The Xception, Inception, and ResNet families can outperform VGGs due to their efficient architectures and functional attributes.

Figure 5 depicts few results on JU-HD dorsal hands. Though, promising results are obtained, however, the performance is not directly comparable with existing methods due to dissimilar datasets. The accuracy on frontal and dorsal 11k hands are compared in Table 3. The confusion matrices using various CNNs on 11k are shown in Fig. 6.

Feature Map Visualization: The feature maps from VGG-16 layers are shown in Fig. 7. The low-level feature maps represent hand-shape with finer details at initial layers. Intrinsically, high-level features with less details are represented in deeper level.

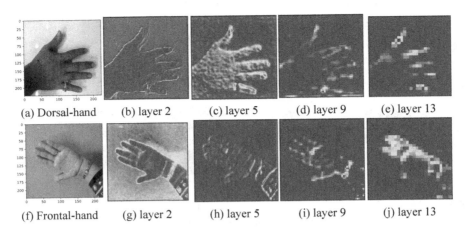

Fig. 7. Visualizations of feature maps from various convolutional layers of VGG-16

5 Conclusion

In this paper, a gender classification method using hand images of JU-HD is studied. The performance is evaluated using five CNNs on 57 persons. The accuracy implies that JU-HD is more challenging than existing 11k hands. However, a major limitation is smaller size of JU-HD. For a deep model, the dataset should be large for learning task. We plan to include hand samples from more people to increase the size and variability of JU-HD. Also, our goal is to develop a new deep model for hard and soft biometrics and a fusion of both for wider applicability of the method.

Acknowledgement. Authors are thankful to the Center for Microprocessor Applications for Training Education and Research (CMATER) Lab, Computer Science and Engineering Department, Jadavpur University, Kolkata-32, India for providing infrastructural resources, and Scholars for dataset preparation and progress during this work.

References

1. Abbas, F., Yasmin, M., Fayyaz, M., Elaziz, M.A., Lu, S., El-Latif, A.A.A.: Gender classification using proposed CNN-based model and ant colony optimization. Mathematics **9**(19), 2499 (2021)
2. Abderrahmane, M.A., Guelzim, I., Abdelouahad, A.A.: Human age prediction based on hand image using multiclass classification. In: 2020 International Conference on Data Analytics for Business and Industry: Way Towards a Sustainable Economy (ICDABI), pp. 1–5. IEEE (2020)
3. Afifi, M.: 11k hands: gender recognition and biometric identification using a large dataset of hand images. Multimed. Tools Appl. **78**(15), 20835–20854 (2019). https://doi.org/10.1007/s11042-019-7424-8

4. Al-Kharaz, A.: Discriminating between genders using hand images of Iraqi adults. In: 2021 IEEE 12th Control and System Graduate Research Colloquium (ICS-GRC), pp. 29–33. IEEE (2021)
5. Amayeh, G., Bebis, G., Nicolescu, M.: Gender classification from hand shape. In: 2008 IEEE Computer Society Conference on Computer Vision and Pattern Recognition Workshops, pp. 1–7. IEEE (2008)
6. Baisa, N.L., et al.: Hand-based person identification using global and part-aware deep feature representation learning. arXiv preprint arXiv:2101.05260 (2021)
7. Bera, A., Bhattacharjee, D.: Human identification using selected features from finger geometric profiles. IEEE Trans. Syst. Man Cybern. Syst. **50**(3), 747–761 (2020)
8. Bera, A., Bhattacharjee, D., Nasipuri, M.: Person recognition using alternative hand geometry. Int. J. Biom. **6**(3), 231–247 (2014)
9. Bera, A., Bhattacharjee, D., Nasipuri, M.: Fusion-based hand geometry recognition using dempster-Shafer theory. Int. J. Pattern Recogn. Artif. Intell. **29**(05), 1556005 (2015)
10. Bera, A., Bhattacharjee, D., Nasipuri, M.: Finger contour profile based hand biometric recognition. Multimed. Tools Appl. **76**(20), 21451–21479 (2017). https://doi.org/10.1007/s11042-016-4075-x
11. Bera, A., Bhattacharjee, D., Shum, H.P.: Two-stage human verification using hand-CAPTCHA and anti-spoofed finger biometrics with feature selection. Expert Syst. Appl. **171**, 114583 (2021)
12. Bera, A., Dey, R., Bhattacharjee, D., Nasipuri, M., Shum, H.P.: Spoofing detection on hand images using quality assessment. Multimed. Tools Appl. **80**, 28603–28626 (2021). https://doi.org/10.1007/s11042-021-10976-z
13. Chai, T., Prasad, S., Wang, S.: Boosting palmprint identification with gender information using DeepNet. Future Gener. Comput. Syst. **99**, 41–53 (2019)
14. Dantcheva, A., Elia, P., Ross, A.: What else does your biometric data reveal? a survey on soft biometrics. IEEE Trans. Inf. Forensics Secur. **11**(3), 441–467 (2015)
15. Dantcheva, A., Velardo, C., D'angelo, A., Dugelay, J.L.: Bag of soft biometrics for person identification. Multimed. Tools Appl. **51**(2), 739–777 (2011). https://doi.org/10.1007/s11042-010-0635-7
16. Duta, N.: A survey of biometric technology based on hand shape. Pattern Recogn. **42**(11), 2797–2806 (2009)
17. Edwards, T., Hossain, M.S.: Effectiveness of deep learning on serial fusion based biometric systems. IEEE Trans. Artif. Intell. **2**, 28–41 (2021)
18. Garain, A., Ray, B., Singh, P.K., Ahmadian, A., Senu, N., Sarkar, R.: GRA_Net: a deep learning model for classification of age and gender from facial images. IEEE Access **9**, 85672–85689 (2021)
19. Greco, A., Saggese, A., Vento, M., Vigilante, V.: A convolutional neural network for gender recognition optimizing the accuracy/speed tradeoff. IEEE Access **8**, 130771–130781 (2020)
20. Hassan, B., Izquierdo, E., Piatrik, T.: Soft biometrics: a survey benchmark analysis, open challenges and recommendations. Multimed. Tools Appl. (2021). https://doi.org/10.1007/s11042-021-10622-8
21. Izadpanahkakhk, M., Razavi, S.M., Taghipour-Gorjikolaie, M., Zahiri, S.H., Uncini, A.: Novel mobile palmprint databases for biometric authentication. Int. J. Grid Util. Comput. **10**(5), 465–474 (2019)
22. Jain, A., Kanhangad, V.: Gender classification in smartphones using gait information. Expert Syst. Appl. **93**, 257–266 (2018)

23. Krizhevsky, A., Sutskever, I., Hinton, G.E.: ImageNet classification with deep convolutional neural networks. In: Advances in Neural Information Processing Systems 25, pp. 1097–1105 (2012)

24. Levi, G., Hassner, T.: Age and gender classification using convolutional neural networks. In: Proceedings of the IEEE Conference on Computer Vision and Pattern Recognition Workshops, pp. 34–42 (2015)

25. Lin, Y.C., Suzuki, Y., Kawai, H., Ito, K., Chen, H.T., Aoki, T.: Attribute estimation using multi-cnns from hand images. In: 2019 Asia-Pacific Signal and Information Processing Association Annual Summit and Conference (APSIPA ASC), pp. 241–244. IEEE (2019)

26. Matkowski, W.M., Kong, A.W.K.: Gender and ethnicity classification based on palmprint and palmar hand images from uncontrolled environment. In: 2020 IEEE International Joint Conference on Biometrics (IJCB), pp. 1–7. IEEE (2020)

27. Mukherjee, R., Bera, A., Bhattacharjee, D., Nasipuri, M.: Human gender classification based on hand images using deep learning. Technical report, EasyChair (2021)

28. Nogales, R.E., Benalcázar, M.E.: Hand gesture recognition using machine learning and infrared information: a systematic literature review. Int. J. Mach. Learn. Cybern. **12**, 2859–2886 (2021). https://doi.org/10.1007/s13042-021-01372-y

29. Nugrahaningsih, N., Porta, M.: Soft biometrics through hand gestures driven by visual stimuli. ICT Express **5**(2), 94–99 (2019)

30. Reid, D.A., Nixon, M.S., Stevenage, S.V.: Soft biometrics; human identification using comparative descriptions. IEEE Trans. Pattern Anal. Mach. Intell. **36**(6), 1216–1228 (2013)

31. Rim, B., Kim, J., Hong, M.: Gender classification from fingerprint-images using deep learning approach. In: Proceedings of the International Conference on Research in Adaptive and Convergent Systems, pp. 7–12 (2020)

32. Tome, P., Fierrez, J., Vera-Rodriguez, R., Nixon, M.S.: Soft biometrics and their application in person recognition at a distance. IEEE Trans. Inf. Forensics Secur. **9**(3), 464–475 (2014)

33. Vasileiadis, M., Stavropoulos, G., Tzovaras, D.: Facial soft biometrics detection on low power devices. In: Proceedings of the IEEE/CVF Conference on Computer Vision and Pattern Recognition Workshops (2019)

34. Wu, M., Yuan, Y.: Gender classification based on geometry features of palm image. Sci. World J. **2014**, 1–7 (2014). http://dx.doi.org/10.1155/2014/734564. Article Id 734564

35. Yuan, Y., Tang, C., Xia, S., Chen, Z., Qi, T.: HandNet: identification based on hand images using deep learning methods. In: Proceedings of the 2020 4th International Conference on Vision, Image and Signal Processing, pp. 1–6 (2020)

36. Zhu, J., Zhong, D., Luo, K.: Boosting unconstrained palmprint recognition with adversarial metric learning. IEEE Trans. Biom. Behav. Identity Sci. **2**(4), 388–398 (2020)

Artificial Intelligence Based Smart Government Enterprise Architecture (AI-SGEA) Framework

Partha Kumar Mukherjee[✉]

The School of Science and Technology, CSE Department, The Neotia University, Jhinger Pole, Diamond Harbour Rd, Sarisha, West Bengal 743368, India
parthakumar.mukherjee@tnu.in, partha.mukh68@rediffmail.com

Abstract. Artificial Intelligence (AI) based Government Enterprise Architecture (GEA) is the inherent AI & Machine Learning (ML) based design and management approach essential across the Government processes coherence leading to alignment, agility, quick decision, effective analysis and efficient assurance. Governments and corporates are collecting an abundant amount of data every day and without an accurate analysis, data is not adequate for actionable insights. Better decision making has the potential to both improve services and save costs. The expanding use of Smart Government Enterprise Architecture (SGEA) framework in government is triggering numerous opportunities for governments worldwide. This framework may also be used by organizations to generate more accurate future prediction and to simulate complex systems that allow experimentation with various policy options. In any Government change management process, the ensuring of interoperability amongst various e-Governance systems, processes and applications across all the Government reference model for analytics is very important. The IT policymakers and the top level decision makers of any country are not concern with how each parameter introduces SGEA deliverables, but concern how national IT strategy is aligned and populated in the form of IT projects, information systems, and other IT assets throughout all references of SGEA. This paper describes the concept framework of Artificial Intelligence driven integrated architecture flow of smart government system. The concept is suitable for the strategic planning and decision making process which may provide possible strategic directions for the organization. This may be able to transform and improve the services for an achievable adaptation efficiency, simplification, cost management, collaboration, and standardization. This may help the organizations to accommodate the rapidly changing digital service usability on digitalization known as "AI driven smart-Government.

Keywords: AI-SGEA · Digital governance · IndEA

1 Introduction

1.1 Overview of the GEA Framework

The digital world is transforming in many areas and contributing to optimize the process where digital divides can be minimized. It is establishing not only a digital culture and a digital mind set, but a paradigm change in the way interactions between humans and between humans and systems. The digital interactions results in exchange of information and transformation of electronic services towards personalization, task-orientation, and intelligence user experiences. The rapid change in the information technology landscape is leading to a quick transformation of legacy and outdated system toeards strategies, architectures and designs of the e-Governance system. Technologies like, the Cloud Computing, Data Science and Internet of things (IoT) have already become mainstream. The technologies like the Artificial Intelligence and Block-chain are strengthening the organizations with the promise of a quantum leap in aligning business services more closely to the user needs and expectations.

In most of the countries, the Government's IT policy and direction aims to make all Government services digitally accessible to citizens through multiple digital channels. To meet this objective, there is a need for an interoperable ecosystem under the framework of GEA, which will make the right information available to the right user at the right time. Under this scenario, it is important to ensure interoperability amongst various e-Governance systems to upgrade the quality and effectiveness of service delivery through proper feedback mechanism model.

Typically, Governments are the largest organizations. They are further characterized by complex federated structures where individual government organizations work in their respective silos. Often this leads to fragmented government business processes and duplicated systems and technologies, creating obstacles in cross agency interoperability. There exists a positive correlation between the desired level of e-government capability and maturity and the required level of architectural maturity of GEA. The major challenges of GEA is the lack of cross-ministry and agency viewpoint and coordination with proper feedback mechanism through the predictive analytic models at enterprise level.

The India Enterprise Architecture (IndEA) reference model [1], based on the "The Open Group Architecture Framework (TOGAF)", establishes best-in-class architectural governance, processes and practices using ICT infrastructure and applications to offer ONE Government experience to the citizens and businesses through cashless, paperless, and faceless services enabled by Boundaryless Information Flow. IndEA includes Performance Reference Model (PRM), Business Reference Model (BRM), Service Component Reference Model (SRM), Data Reference Model (DRM), and Technical Reference Model (TRM). One of the major challenges of most of the GEA model is to satisfy the information needs from government-wide IT policymakers, functional and non-functional information. For example, at the government-wide level, IT policymakers are not concern with how each parameter introduces GEA deliverables, but concern how national IT strategy is aligned and populated in the form of IT projects, information systems, and other IT assets the GEA. That is, GEA artefacts needed to be integrated into one more abstraction towards higher national level. All of the central administrative organizations/departments and local municipalities are subject to the provision of mandatory adoption of GEA. The research paper also aims at proposing a AI based GEA framework for architecture design which addresses smart government non-functional requirements. In order to achieve this, strategies, trends, standards, technologies, and guidelines related to smart government are explored.

1.2   About AI Driven Smart GEA Framework

Over the past few decades, the adoption of AI in the public sector has been slower than in the private sector. As a result, attention paid to AI use in government has been more recent. AI practices and digital transformation strategies from the private sector cannot directly be copied to the public sector because of the public sector's need to maximize public value. Compared to the private sector, there is less knowledge concerning AI challenges specifically associated with the public sector. AI systems are becoming more complex and less predictable, and it is unclear for most governments how this affects public governance. In practice, most governments face limited understanding of the multifaceted implications for public governance brought about by the use of AI in government. Meanwhile, thought-leadership in the areas of governance and AI shrinks compared to the pace with which AI applications are infiltrating government globally. This knowledge gap is a critical developmental barrier as many governments wrangle with the societal, economic, political, and ethical implications of these transformations in AI.

An architecture workflow is proposed to address the supervised and unsupervised data requirements under a smart government ecosystem. This AI driven framework is contextualized by decomposing selected features that served as a basis for understanding the interrelationships between the various components within the framework. This framework may be used as a guide the developers and designers in creating agile enterprise solution architectures. Moreover, additional challenges arise from the lack of transparency of black-box systems, such as unclear responsibility and accountability, when AI is used in decision-making by governments. These realities raise the stakes for governments since failures due to AI use in government may have strong negative implications for governments and society.

Most countries promote their departmental agencies and local governments to introduce GEA, with developing standard principles, frameworks, and reference models. Meanwhile, some other advanced countries have been making an effort to develop national level enterprise architecture which is aimed to provide an integrated view of agencies enterprise architecture. However, there are challenges in the AI-GEA framework to relate the integration and interoperability within and between public agencies. Some researchers find these challenges very hard to overcome.

As for smart government strategy, it is mainly based on people since it is not only about using latest technologies but rather about developing a framework that contributes to productive and innovative citizens. Smart government approach is mainly based on providing efficient systems and processes, consolidated information systems, and communication networks. Governments are faced by many challenges, such as fragmentation and coordination challenges, whereby the lack of standards and integration lead to problems related to work duplication and interoperability, Agility challenges since government should be able to comply with new trends such as mobile and cloud technologies, and cost challenges that may be solved by sharing common business processes. The growth of unstructured data and the ease with which these data can be accessed using different smart devices are changing continuously. Due to the continuous changing of these data types across the various data sources, the data analysis becoming more critical day by day. Thus, the way of interacting of these data with the business stakeholders within the organization are becoming more challenging. To address the issue, the Big Data analytics within the model facilitates faster analysis and better utilization of these resources and optimize the data analysis model at personalization level. Various studies concerning AI use in government exist beyond the highly technical fields of study, there is a scarcity of research on AI governance, policy, and regulatory issues. Furthermore, there is a lack of consensus on how to handle the challenges of AI associated with the public sector in the future state that AI governance and regulation needs to be addressed more comprehensively in public administration research.

2 Conceptual Framework for AI Based Smart Government Analytic Architecture

2.1 Proposed AI Driven Smart GEA Framework

The proposed framework is able to handle the complexity of a various data types in which large amounts of data in various formats and from many business domains are collected, processed, transmitted, and published. At the initial stage it classifies the basic digital service requirements that are essential to understanding the components and interrelationships of SGEA framework. After the identification and analysis of the required data, it integrate the AI based intelligent layer above the GEA framework. One of the salient feature requirement in the AI driven smart government ecosystem is characterized by consideration of various business stakeholders and their different key responsibility areas specific to that business sector within the organization. This model follow the enterprise architecture processes which tries to address the digital services at the personalized level. However, almost none of the previous research papers on GEA, Pallab Saha [1], have investigated this topic more thoroughly in that perspective.

The AI offerings above the SGEA framework described in Fig. 1, can be classified into three categories like, Savings due to operational efficiency through Smart Environmental network of the operational Data Sources, Smart ICT Infrastructure and application services and application reference model personalized digital services and Intelligent Tier framework for data driven decision making where Governments are collecting an abundant amount of data every day. Better decision making has the potential to both improve services and save costs.

For a Smart City operation, Batty et al. [2], describes the GES architecture by focusing on the effective management and sustainability of a city through monitoring and analyzing the relevant data across multiple domains. Al Nuaimi et al. [3], describes how the recent technologies handle high volume and different verities of data to enhance smart city digital services through big data analytics. Thus in GEA framework the smart concept is represented by various data communication protocols within the different layers of network elements. The effective utilization of these heterogeneous types of data is one of the key success factor for the critical data analysis in many service domains within an organization. According to Molinari et al. [4] and Da Silva [5], Burns [6], under a smart GEA, the factors that prevents the investment in smart city are the policy changes, limited capital availability, and the relevant funding structures.

2.2 AI Driven Smart GEA Solution Architecture

The Smart GEA (SGEA) solution architecture provides a list of possible architectural roles at the enterprise level. For the effective and efficient operation of digital data across the social network, the SGEA architecture model required to know what type of data must be collected and are required for the data pre-processing, integration and execution under the various levels.

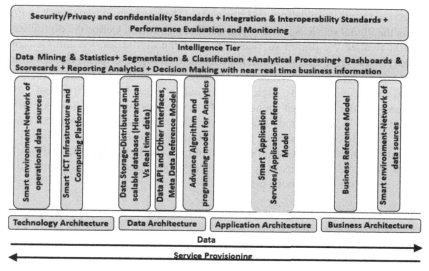

Fig. 1. Conceptual framework for Smart Government Enterprise Architecture model

One of the architectural issue arises under SGEA framework when the stakeholders do not have an adequate level of data operational and execution skills. This issue is mitigated in the context of smart education and awareness programs. It encompasses user participation, collaboration and cooperation of stakeholders as well as measuring their satisfaction of the experience of the digital services provided by the smart system. The AI driven smart system helps the business users about the operational efficiency and the utilization of the organizational data at the personalized level. The conceptual framework is shown in Fig. 1, where the various layers represents the component that is needed to meet the requirements of AI driven smart government analytic architecture. The proposed framework is a combination of four main architectural layers. The four layers of the proposed architecture are the Technology Architecture, the Data Architecture, the Application Architecture and the Business Architecture. It also utilizes and applies all the basic concepts of cloud computing, agile development, Enterprise Architecture Open API-based Micro-Services Architecture, reusable application programming interfaces (API's), and exploratory data analysis.

The data can be retrieved from data repositories by using Application Programming Interface or through suitable extractors. For the data pre-processing and transformation, there should be provided platforms, tools and services for both batch processing and stream processing. The model may be designed in such a manner that the system will be capable enough to perform the smart analytics intelligently. This system can also use scalable machine learning algorithms or other advanced data mining algorithms to provide extraction of patterns from these data and smart application services which represent the communication channel within the organization. With the help of this AI driven system, the business users and the machines can directly interact with each other to make smart decisions intelligently.

The service workflow in the framework in Fig. 2, [1], has been adopted from the digital service standard guidelines and principles. The conceptual framework in Fig. 2, is defining the digital services is into 4-phases. The phases are, Define the digital service framework; Realize the digital services; Measure the digital service and Govern the digital service across the enterprise level. Under the Define phase, the service definition is described which covers the activities like, Description of a digital service; Classification of a digital service; and Prioritization of the digital services. The description of a digital service specifies the benefit of launching of the services which defines its attributes in terms of 'Why', 'What' and 'How'. Under the paradigm of to open government movement, the related processes of participation, collaboration and cooperation must be taken into account when governments set out policies. In this regard, feedback from the various stakeholders is constantly collected and monitored and the system will train itself accordingly on a continuous manner.

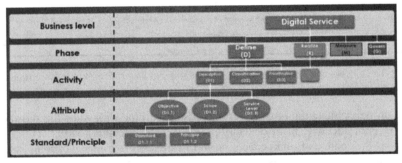

Fig. 2. Digital Service workflow and measurement (Color figure online)

The Digital Service workflow in Fig. 2, is designed at 5 levels, namely, the Business Level, Phase Level, Activity Level, Attribute Level and finally, the Standard/Principle Level. The proposed 5-tier structure will provide support to enables expansibility at any level. Thus the enhancement of the architecture components will occur automatically without impacting the entire framework. The purpose of the Business Level is to track and monitor the progress by the top management. This layer will identify the goals the business would like to pursue, prioritize, and get a feedback on the status of various digital services and the impact they make on the citizens/customers. The Activity Level connotes the different tasks that the concerned teams need to undertake to fulfill the responsibility in each Phase. The Attribute Level will perform the tasks at micro level. It identifies the actual area, topic, theme or component of the digital service life-cycle on which a Standard or Principle has to be specified. The Standard/Principle layer holds all the

Standards, Principles and Guidelines comprising the framework. The Adoption of a color code enables an easy visual comprehension of the framework or any standard/principle comprising the same. The proposed workflow will be capable enough to consistently accept the changes. For the phase wise traceability it adopts the colour codes like, Orange for the Definition Phase, Blue for the Realization Phase, Gold for the Measurement Phase and Green for the Governance Phase.

The various activities across the different layers aim to facilitate the publication, management and sustainability of the open data publication and the data reuse process. The Intelligent tier of the system represents the vital contribution of this work. It is managing and providing intelligence capabilities within Enterprise Architecture Open API-based Micro-Services Architecture-based context including statistical, artificial intelligence, data mining, and other intelligence capabilities added to the organization services. This layer will apply data mining within intelligence layer to empower Smart Government Services. The data security layer is considered to be one of the most serious requirements for data security, application security in across the cyber space. The proposed work recommends that all these components should be based on open standards and open formats, which will increase the interoperability of ICT systems through a low cost solution. The system evaluation and monitoring component must be employed to obtain detailed service feedback. These components support the other components. Finally, the use of The Open Group Architecture. Framework (TOGAF) and its Architecture Development Method (ADM) as a general approach to develop architecture with sufficient details may be recommended.

3   Limitations of the Framework

The conceptualization of AI based Smart Government Ecosystem of any government enterprise architecture can provide easier understanding and interpretation of required components and interrelationships between them. However, there are also several challenges and limitations to this approach. In general, any government organization concerned about the cost and benefits of implementing a smart Government Architecture. There may be many interdisciplinary constraints within organization structures at State and central level, where the same architecture may not apply to at States and central level, mainly because one cannot generalize local, financial, social and environmental restrictions. Another limitation of the system may be there about the classification of the stakeholder's roles and responsibilities that may impact the user collaboration, cooperation and the effort to enable user participation with the organization processes.

4   Conclusions

The potential benefit of this conceptual framework may use in instruction which is yet to be realized in many countries digital governance ecosystem. The major contribution of this AI driven SGEA integrated architecture components is lies in the area of intelligent decision making system in a multidisciplinary environment across the country. The proposed conceptual intelligent framework may enhance the delivery of smart public services to the citizen and the predictive data trends to the policy makers across the country. The system will be intelligent enough to establish the relation between business and applications architecture in the public sector, which may be realized using open smart government processes on real time basis. This AI based framework may be used as a starting point for actual smart government architectures. It should also provide a mechanism to stimulate measurable value generation from analytics in smart cities across enterprises. The business benefits may contribute in instruction include collaboration, cooperation, interaction, active learning, constructive learning, creative learning and social learning, ingredients necessary to help the communication channels like, Government to Citizen (G to C), Government to Government (G to G) and Government to Business (G to B).

References

1. Saha, P.: India Enterprise Architecture framework. In: 21st National Conference in eGovernance, Hyderabad, 26 February 2018 (2018)
2. Batty, M., et al.: Smart cities of the future. Eur. Phys. J. Spec. Top. **214**(1), 481–518 (2012)
3. Al Nuaimi, E., Al Neyadi, H., Mohamed, N., Al-Jaroodi, J.: Applications of big data to smart cities. J. Internet Serv. Appl. **6**(1), 1–15 (2015)
4. Molinari, A., et al.: Big data and open data for a smart city. In: IEEE Smart Cities Inaugural Workshop, December 2014, Trento, Italy, pp. 1–8. IEEE (2014)
5. Da Silva, W.M., et al.: Smart cities software architectures: a survey. In: Proceedings of the 28th Annual ACM Symposium on Applied Computing, pp. 1722–1727. ACM, New York (2013)
6. Burns, P., Neutens, M., Newman, D., Power, T.: Building Value through Enterprise Architecture: A Global Study. Booz & Company Perspective (2009)
7. Liimatainen, K., Hoffman, M., Heikkilä, J.: Overview of Enterprise Architecture work in 15 Countries. Ministry of Finance, Government of Finland, Helsinki (2007)
8. Ziefle, M., Calero Valdez, A.: Decisions about medical data disclosure in the Internet: an age perspective. In: Zhou, J., Salvendy, G. (eds.) ITAP 2018. LNCS, vol. 10927, pp. 186–201. Springer, Cham (2018). https://doi.org/10.1007/978-3-319-92037-5_16
9. Ajer, A.K.S.: Enterprise architecture challenges: a case study of three Norwegian public stores. University of Agder, Kristiansand, Norway
10. Lee, Y.-J., Kwon, Y.-I., Shin, S., Kim, E.-J.: Advancing government-wide enterprise architecture – a meta-model approach. Department of Information Resource Service, NIA (National Information Society Agency), Seoul, Korea
11. Aldrich, J., Bertot, J.C., McClure, C.R.: E-government: initiatives, developments, and issues. Gov. Inf. Q. **19**, 349–355 (2002)
12. Australian Government: Cloud Computing Strategic Direction Paper Version 1.1 (2011)
13. Bakshi, K.: Considerations for cloud data centers: framework, architecture and adoption. In: IEEE Aerospace Conference. IEEE Computer Society. CIO Council (2001)
14. A Practical Guide to Federal Enterprise Architecture, February 2001. Datacenter Dynamics (2011)
15. Mell, P., Grance, T.: The NIST definition of cloud computing (2009). http://www.nist.gov/itl/cloud/upload/cloud-def-v15.pdf
16. Mulholland, A.: Enterprise Cloud Computing. A Strategy Guide for Business and Technology Leaders. Meghan-Kiffer Press, USA (2010)
17. Denzin, N.K., Lincoln, Y.S.: Handbook of Qualitative Research. Sage Publications, London (2000). Gill, A.Q. (2013)

18. Gill, A.Q., Bunker, D.: Towards the development of an adaptive enterprise service system model. In: ACMIS 2013 Proceedings, Chicago, USA. Crowd Sourcing Challenges Assessment Index for Disaster Management, 29 July 2012 (2012)
19. Gill, A.Q., Livingstone, R.: Demanding times. In: AMCIS 2012 Proceedings, Seattle, USA. CIO (2012). Gill, A.Q., Bunker, D. (2011)

Author Index

Printed in the United States
by Baker & Taylor Publisher Services